D1132878

MEDIA
AND THE
AMERICAN
CHILD

MEDIA
AND THE
AMERICAN
CHILD

GEORGE COMSTOCK
and
ERICA SCHARRER

ELSEVIER

AMSTERDAM • BOSTON • HEIDELBERG • LONDON
NEW YORK • OXFORD • PARIS • SAN DIEGO
SAN FRANCISCO • SINGAPORE • SYDNEY • TOKYO

Academic press is an imprint of Elsevier

Academic Press is an imprint of Elsevier
30 Corporate Drive, Suite 400, Burlington, MA 01803, USA
525 B Street, Suite 1900, San Diego, California 92101-4495, USA
84 Theobald's Road, London WCIX 8RR, UK

This book is printed on acid-free paper.

Library of Congress Cataloging-in-Publication Data
Application submitted

British Library Cataloguing-in-Publication Data
A catalogue record for this book is available from the British Library.

ISBN 13: 978-0-12-372542-4
ISBN 10: 0-12-372542-4

For information on all Academic Press publications
visit our Web site at www.books.elsevier.com

Printed in the United States of America
07 08 09 10 9 8 7 6 5 4 3 2 1

■ CONTENTS

CHAPTER II: The Extraordinary Appeal of Screen Media

CHAPTER VI: Television Violence, Aggression, and Other Behavioral Effects

CHAPTER VII: Learning Rules and Norms—Further Evidence of Media Effects   250

CHAPTER VIII: Knowledge for What?   292

■ PREFACE

When we began a revised edition of the first author's *Television and the American Child* (Academic Press, 1991), we had four goals: expand the coverage to include other media; extend the age range to give greater attention to the very young and to teenagers; and emphasize the central role of cognitive stages, particularly in regard to tastes and preferences in media use and responses to advertising, brand names, and products; and, as before, to base interpretations and conclusions on evidence with valid claims to scientific credibility. We leave it to our readers to judge our success.

ACKNOWLEDGMENTS

We owe a major debt to the many dozens of individuals who conducted the studies upon which we have drawn. We hope they will find our treatment of their work of interest.

We are grateful to David Rubin, Dean, S.I. Newhouse School, and Michael Morgan, Chair, University of Massachusetts Amherst Department of Communication, for providing scholarly settings; and to the S.I. Newhouse chair for financial support. We thank Marcia Wisehoon for a painstaking and thoroughly professional preparation of the manuscript. We also thank graduate assistant Jack Powers, whose stalwart mastery of the Internet was invaluable. Finally, the second author thanks her husband, Jody Barker, for being an unwavering source of solace and support.

We found several analyses to be particularly helpful. These key studies include:

Acuff, D. S. (1997). *What kids buy and why: The psychology of marketing to kids.* New York, NY: Free Press.

Anderson, C. A., Berkowitz, L., Donnerstein, E., Huesmann, L. R., Johnson, J. D., Linz, D., Malamuth, N. M. & Wartella, E. (2003). The influence of media violence on youth. *Psychological Science in the Public Interest, 4*(3), 81–110.

The Kaiser Family Foundation-sponsored media use studies:

Rideout, V. J., Foehr, U. G., Roberts, D. F. & Brodie, M. (1999). *Kids & media at the new millennium.* A Kaiser Family Foundation Report. Menlo Park, CA: Henry J. Kaiser Family Foundation. Accessed 6/30/05 at http://www.kff.org/entmedia/loader. cfm?url=/commonspot/security/getfile.cfm&PageID=13265.

Rideout, V. J., Vandewater, E. A. & Wartella, E. (2003). *Zero to six: Electronic media in the lives of infants, toddlers and preschoolers.* A Kaiser Family Foundation Study. Menlo Park, CA: Henry J. Kaiser Family Foundation.

Roberts, D. F. & Foehr, U. G. (2004). *Kids & media in America.* Cambridge, UK: Cambridge University Press.

Roberts, D. F., Foehr, U. G. & Rideout, V. (2005). *Generation M: Media in the lives of 8–18 year-olds. A Kaiser Family Foundation Study.* Menlo Park, CA: Henry J. Kaiser Family Foundation. Accessed 6/30/05 at http://www.kff.org/entmedia/7250.cfm.

McNeal, J. (1999). *The kids market: Myths and realities.* Ithaca, NY: Paramount Market.

Psychological Science in the Public Interest. A Journal of The Association for Psychological Science.

Schor, J. B. (2004). *Born to buy.* New York: Scribner.

Singer, D. G. & Singer, J. L. (2005). *Imagination and play in the electronic age.* Cambridge, MA: Harvard University Press.

U.S. Department of Health & Human Services. (2001). *Youth Violence: A Report of the Surgeon General.* Rockville, MD: U.S. Department of Health and Human Services. Centers for Disease Control and Prevention, National Center for Injury Prevention and Control; Substance Abuse and Mental Health Services Administration, Center for Mental Health Services; and National Institutes of Health, National Institute of Mental Health.

DEMOGRAPHICS AND PREFERENCES IN MEDIA USE, WITH SPECIAL ATTENTION TO THE VERY YOUNG

Childhood and adolescence in the United States (and well beyond) is marked by the centrality of the media. Growing up in the contemporary world means immersion in the sights and sounds supplied by television and computer. Later childhood and adolescence extends these daily experiences to include music accessed through the airwaves, purchased on CD, or acquired through download or streaming audio; a smorgasbord of games to be played on the computer or through high-tech console systems; and, of course, an abundance of glossy magazines that appeal to every whim, hobby, and pursuit. The prominence of media is astonishing—for the degree of gratification they provide, as testified to by the amount of time allocated to them, and the myriad of content-specific uses they serve.

Young people's use of the media raises significant questions. Spending time with media is one of the pleasures afforded by modern life, and analysis of media use patterns constitutes a window into the ways that young people are entertained, informed, persuaded, and educated. Another set of reasons for studying media use is more troubling. There is ample evidence that either the amount of time spent with particular media or the content viewed, read, or heard can have adverse effects (Comstock & Scharrer, 1999). A great deal of research has convincingly linked either

1

amount of media exposure or exposure to particular types of content with a range of important outcomes, including but not limited to performing poorly in school; learning aggression; behaving antisocially; developing unhealthy attitudes and behavior regarding such disparate topics as nutrition, alcohol consumption, cigarette smoking, and sexual behavior; and increasing the odds that a child will be overweight.

We eventually take up all of these troubling (and often controversial) issues, but we begin with a review of media use. We assess preferences within major media categories—genres, programs, and types favored. We focus on aggregates defined by demographics—age, gender, race or ethnicity, and socioeconomic status (usually operationalized by parental education or income)—and orientations toward the media. When possible, we record the uses young people make of media, such as entertainment, information, or communication with others.

We give preference to data that are current and drawn from national, representative samples in order to ensure comprehensive, valid conclusions. We adopt the four-part conceptualization of media offered by Roberts and Foehr (2004):

- Print
- Audio
- Screen
- Interactive media

treating each separately before integrating the data into estimates and characterizations of total media use.

The data on media exposure are striking for their cohesion around two major themes: (1) young people allocate a staggering amount of time to media, and (2) despite the obvious attraction of new media technologies (and with the sole exception of the attention to music that is a hallmark of adolescence), in terms of time use television still reigns supreme.

The most reliable source of data on the media use of young people in the United States comes from a nationally representative sample of just over two thousand (2,032, to be precise) 8- to 18-year-olds, surveyed in 2004 by Roberts, Foehr, and Rideout (2005), under the auspices of the Kaiser Family Foundation. In the dataset, young people of color were over-sampled to allow for comparisons based on race or ethnicity; the respondents were accessed in schools; and questions pertaining to amount of media exposure asked about the number of minutes and hours spent using each form of media on the previous day. The timing of data collection varied, so that each day of the week was represented in "time spent yesterday." Some of the questions posed to the children and teenagers were duplicated from previous data collected in 1999 (Roberts & Foehr, 2004), so that, occasionally, comparisons between 1999 and 2004 are permitted.

A somewhat similar study, also commissioned by the Kaiser Family Foundation, widens the lens to include children younger than 8-years old. These data, collected in 1999, combine in-home responses of parents reporting on behalf of 1,090 very young children (aged 2 to 7) and in-school responses of an additional 2,014 8- to 18-year-olds, employing nationally representative probability samples (Rideout, Foehr, Roberts & Brodie, 1999; Roberts & Foehr, 2004).

Addressing still unanswered questions regarding media use patterns among the youngest of the young, the Kaiser Family Foundation in partnership with the Children's Digital Media Center (CDMC) funded a nationwide study, this time among those six and younger (Rideout, Vandewater & Wartella, 2003). These data were collected in 2003 via a nationally representative telephone survey using random-digit dialing procedures to elicit responses from 1,065 parents of children who ranged from six months to six years old. Finally, the Kaiser Family Foundation sponsored an update to the six-month to six-year-old data, drawing responses from 1,051 nationally representative parents in September through November 2005 (Rideout & Hamel, 2006).

We will also draw from a number of key contributions in the area of young people's use of computer-based media. These include recent data from Robinson and Alvarez (2005) and the U.S. Department of Education (2003).

These sources make possible a comprehensive view of the role of the media in the daily lives of children and adolescents in the United States. For each category of media, we begin with estimates of use. We turn then to differences that demographic variables make. Next, we review content preferences. Finally, we isolate the media use of children seven years of age or younger because of (recent) increased interest in and concern over media use among very young children by parents, caregivers, and academics (child psychologists, pediatricians, teachers, and social researchers). Throughout, we trace media patterns of young people during childhood and adolescence, from six months to eighteen years of age.

I. MEDIA EXPOSURE: PRINT

In many ways, print media—newspapers, magazines, and books—are the granddaddies among the current media choices available to young people. They have been around for so long that one cannot picture a time when they would have been called "new media." Parents and critics alike have expressed concern over the vulnerability of print media to displacement by the newer, flashier, and occasionally even mesmerizing possibilities accessed through screen and interactive media. The fear is that kids will no longer benefit from the imagination-evoking and vocabulary-producing effects of reading.

A. *Use of Print Media*

The data, in fact, document that print media occupy a consistent, albeit modest, presence in the daily lives of young people. Roberts, Foehr, and Rideout (2005) confine themselves to time spent with print media outside of school or work. They place daily leisure-time exposure to all print media at an average of 43 minutes per day for 8- to 18-year-olds. Parents and caregivers may be comforted to know that reading books accounts for the bulk of the print media time, averaging 23 minutes per day. Magazine reading occurs for an average of 14 minutes per day, and newspaper reading for a scant six minutes.

When the sample of respondents is divided by age, estimates of print media use are surprisingly uniform across the board (see Table 1.1). The exception is newspaper reading, an activity engaged in significantly more among the oldest age group (15- to 18-year-olds) compared to the youngest (8- to 10-year-olds)—but even so, the oldest group spent just seven minutes a day with newspapers compared to four minutes for the youngest group.

The Roberts and colleagues (2005) data also show that nearly three-quarters of 8- to 18-year-olds spend at least five minutes with print media on any given day (73%) whereas slightly less than half (47%)

Table 1.1
Average Exposure to Various Media, Ages Six Months to 18 Years

	Age				
	0–3*	4–6*	8–10	11–14	15–18
Screen media	1:47	2:10	4:41	4:25	3:40
TV	1:01	1:10	3:17	3:16	2:36
Audio	1:03	0:49	0:59	1:42	2:24
Print	0:37	0:41	0:44	0:41	0:45
Computers	0:05	0:16	0:37	1:02	1:22
Video games	0:01	0:10	1:05	0:52	0:33

*For these age groups, audio media means listening to music, and print media means reading or being read to. Screen media includes TV, videotapes, DVDs, and movies.

Adapted from Roberts, D. F., Foehr, U. G. & Rideout, V. (2005). *Generation M: Media in the lives of 8–18 year-olds. A Kaiser Family Foundation Study.* Menlo Park, CA: Henry J. Kaiser Family Foundation. Also from Rideout, V. J., Vandewater, E. A. & Wartella, E. (2003). *Zero to six: Electronic media in the lives of infants, toddlers and preschoolers. A Kaiser Family Foundation Study.* Menlo Park, CA: Henry J. Kaiser Family Foundation.

spend 30 minutes or more. Although most young people access print media every day, many tend to spend modest amounts of time with such media. Books, far lengthier than what magazines and newspapers offer (and sometimes more demanding of thought and attention), inspire the dedication of 30 minutes or more a day among just 30 percent of the nation's 8- to 18-year-olds.

Many have expressed concern that young people today are no longer reading newspapers, and there is no doubt that the amount of time adults spend reading newspapers has declined (Comstock & Scharrer, 1999; Robinson & Godbey, 1997). Nevertheless, the data reported by Roberts and colleagues (2005) show about one in every three children and adolescents (34%) takes at least a glance through the paper for five minutes or more on any given day. Roberts and Foehr (2004) point out that although time spent reading newspapers is low for young people in the United States, the proportion of young people accessing newspapers each day has not changed dramatically. Comparing their estimates with those collected in the late 1950s and early 1960s (Schramm, Lyle & Parker, 1961), in the early 1970s (Lyle & Hoffman, 1972a), and in the late 1970s (Newspaper Advertising Bureau, 1978), they find sufficient similarity to conclude, "if 'newspaper reading' is taken to mean at least glancing at some part of the paper for a few minutes, the proportion of U.S. children and adolescents who do so has remained fairly constant over the past 50 years" (Roberts & Foehr, 2004, p. 99). Thus, any increased vulnerability of newspapers to displacement by other media rests not on changes in the use by and familiarity of children and teenagers with newspapers but with attractiveness of other media when decisions about use are made later in life.

B. Demographic Variables That Impact Use of Print Media

Spending leisure time reading books decreases as children grow up (see Table 1.1). In the data of Roberts and colleagues (2005), 63 percent of 8- to 10-year-olds devoted at least five minutes "yesterday" to this activity compared to 44 percent of 11- to 14-year-olds and 34 percent of 15- to 18-year-olds. We concur with the interpretation of the investigators that this shift is likely explained by the increased required reading for schoolwork among those older that would leave less time for reading for pleasure and might make such an activity less appealing.

The youngest kids, although more likely to have spent some time reading a book, were less likely than the two older groups to have spent five minutes or more with a newspaper or a magazine (see Table 1.1). Thus, the desire to keep up with news, sports, and features in the paper as well as an interest in magazines that cover fashion, sports, popular culture, or various hobbies, as we would expect, increases with age.

Additional demographic variables reveal interesting patterns. Roberts and colleagues (2005) found no differences in amount or likelihood of reading print media for children of color compared to White children, or for children from households with varying levels of income (one of two indices of socioeconomic status employed). Gender did not matter much, with one significant exception: girls spent more time with books than boys—28 minutes compared to 19 minutes. However, one particular demographic variable, level of education of the child's parent(s) (the other index of socioeconomic status), had a substantial role. The more educated the parent, the greater the amount of time the child spent with all forms of print media—books, magazines, and newspapers. In total, 8- to 18-year-olds with parents whose education consisted of high school or less spent an average of 32 minutes with all forms of print media, compared to 43 minutes for those with parents with some college education and 50 minutes for those with parents with college diplomas or more. Level of parental education significantly predicted the likelihood that the child spent 30 minutes or more with books or magazines the day before, but not the likelihood that the child spent at least five minutes. Young people with better educated parents read for longer periods of time than those whose parents have less education.

C. Print Preferences among Children and Teenagers

Roberts and Foehr (2004) in 1999 asked the older children and teenagers what they read. The results convey tremendous variability. Looking at newspapers first, the data show the sports section is attended to most often among the 12- to 18-year-olds (52% indicated it), followed by local news (42%), comics (39%), entertainment news (32%), national news (29%), and horoscope or advice sections (28%). Interestingly, fashion was cited by a mere 7 percent.

Book preferences also run the gamut among the teens in the sample. Mysteries (listed by 25%) and adventures (22%) appear to be the most popular, but an additional five genres also garnered double-digit scores including science fiction/fantasy, history/current events, humor, romance, and sports. A smaller number of highly popular magazine genres emerged, the most frequently selected being teen magazines (38%), followed by sports (26%), entertainment/popular culture (21%), and hobby/travel (19%). There was very low interest in health, home, news, and general-interest magazines.

D. Print Use and Preferences of the Very Young

Roberts and Foehr (2004) in their 1999 data extend the analysis of print media use to children below the age of eight. Parents of 2- to 7-year-

olds were asked to estimate the amount of time their child spent reading the day before, as well as the amount of time their child was read
to by an adult. In doing so, the data capture exposure to books, magazines, and newspapers even among children too young to know how to
read.

We can safely conclude that most young children are reading books
or being read to everyday. Eighty-four percent of 2- to 4-year-olds and
74 percent of 5- to 7-year-olds were said by their parents to have spent
at least five minutes with books the day before. Given the brevity of
children's books and the short attention span of the very young, relatively few parents reported 30 minutes or more time spent with books
(just 30% of 2- to 4-year-olds and 15% of 5- to 7-year-olds). Even magazines hold some appeal for these young children. Slightly more than
half (56% of 2- to 4-year-olds and 51% of 5- to 7-year-olds) spent at
least five minutes with a magazine the previous day.

As with the 8- to 18-year-olds, the likelihood of 2- to 7-year-olds
spending time reading is dependent on the education levels of their
parents, although the association is less pronounced at the younger
age. Among the 2- to 7-year-olds, only 6 percent of parents who completed college reported no reading had occurred the day before compared to 18 percent for parents with a high school education or less.
College educated parents also reported that their young children devote
longer periods of time to reading than parents with high school or less.
The difference is largely explained by book reading rather than magazine or newspaper reading. Race or ethnicity had only a small role. No
differences occurred for average amount of time exposed to print media
and only a slight difference emerged for whether any reading at all
occurred the previous day:

- White children, 91%
- Black children, 81%
- Latino children, 80%

Reading to babies and toddlers is common practice. In the Rideout,
Vandewater, and Wartella (2003) data reflecting media use among the
very young, about three-fourths (76%) of zero- to three-year-olds were
read to on a typical day; the figure for zero- to six-year-olds was 79 percent. The most recent data place the figure for zero- to six-year-olds at
83 percent who read or are read to on a "typical" day (Rideout & Hamel,
2006). Daily reading with zero- to three-year-old children occurred in 63
percent of households, and reading several times a week occurred in an
additional 24 percent (Rideout et al., 2003). (Only 12% of parents of
these very young children selected the "several times a month," "less
than several times a month" and "never" categories.) The average

amount of time parents reported reading to or with the six-month-olds to six-year-olds in the sample was 39 minutes per day among all respondents (including those who reported 0 minutes the previous day) and 49 minutes per day among those with some reported use the previous day (see Table 1.1). The typical residence of a very young child in the United States contains quite a few books from which to choose, with 59 percent of parents of children aged six and younger reporting 50 or more books present in the house and 24 percent estimating between 20 and 49 books. Reading with and to the very young is a highly valued activity for which most parents reserve a substantial amount of time every day.

II. MEDIA EXPOSURE: AUDIO

Whether accessed at home or in cars, through the airwaves, on a CD or MP3 player, or by the Internet, audio media occupy an important and even cherished role in childhood and adolescence. *What* is listened to has not changed nearly as dramatically over the years as *how* it is listened to. The means of transmission of audio media for personal use has evolved from records to eight-tracks to cassettes to CDs and now to various forms of digital media that include very small and highly portable devices able to store thousands of songs (like the popular iPod). They still include radio stations whose signals are picked up in the traditional manner but have also expanded to encompass "streaming audio" through the Internet and satellite radio. Regardless of the means of transmission, however, the single most noteworthy aspect of audio media to children and teenagers nationwide is that it provides music. News and sports and other forms of information continue to be available through audio media, but they are not nearly as vitally important to young people as the various types of music for which audio media provide platforms. The result, as noted by Roberts and colleagues (2005), is that one can interpret time spent with audio media as almost synonymous with time spent with music.

A. Use of Audio Media

The most recent data from 8- to 18-year-olds (Roberts et al., 2005) point unequivocally to the large role that audio media play in daily life. The average amount of time these young people spend each day with audio media is 1 hour and 44 minutes, a figure nearly equally divided between the radio (55 minutes a day) and personal media such as CDs, tapes, and MP3 players (49 minutes). The proportion of 8- to 18-year-olds spending at least five minutes with audio media the day before the survey was a very high 85 percent, and almost half (44%) spent an hour or more.

The patterns apparent in the data regarding young people's use of audio media are remarkable for two reasons. First, Roberts and Foehr (2004) observe that audio media—which, again, include both radio and personal music playback devices such as CD, tape, and MP3 players—are the only major media form that increase in frequency of use in a neat, linear fashion between the ages of 8 and 18. Second, audio media have the distinction of being the sole type of media that at any time in the life cycle surpasses television in amount of daily exposure among young people in the United States. In the Roberts and Foehr (2004) data, late adolescence, from age 15 through 18, is the only time in the life of the typical young person in the United States when television is not the medium with which they spend the greatest amount of time. The importance of music in the lives of teenagers allows audio media to surpass television during these years. This rise in the comparative prominence of music in the most recent time use data (Roberts & Foehr, 2004; Roberts et al., 2005) counters earlier findings (Brown, Childers, Bauman & Koch, 1990; Kubey & Csikszentmihalyi, 1990; Larson & Kubey, 1983) and either is attributable to the greater ease of access made possible by new technologies or meticulousness of the more recent collection of data.

B. Demographic Differences in Audio Use

The emerging popularity of rock-and-roll among the nation's teenagers in the 1950s and 1960s is one example of the ability of the tastes and preferences of young people to fuel the billion-dollar music industry. The expression of the many moods of adolescence, from exuberance to angst, seems to find an outlet through immersion in the lyrics and the rhythms of songs and identification with the artists who provide them. The time use data verify the growing importance of music from childhood through adolescence (see Table 1.1). The average amount of time spent with audio media increases linearly from 8 to 10 years of age (59 minutes), to 11 to 14 (1 hour, 42 minutes), to 15 to 18 (2 hours, 24 minutes) (Roberts et al., 2005). The proportion spending at least five minutes the previous day rises from 74 percent of 8- to 10-year-olds to 90 percent of 15- to 18-year-olds, and the proportion spending an hour or more grows from 26 to 60 percent.

The data of Roberts and colleagues (2005) also reveal some interesting gender differences. Girls are both more likely to listen and more likely to listen longer than boys. They spend about a half-hour more per day with audio media. Larger proportions of girls spent both five minutes or longer (80% vs. 69%) and one hour or more the previous day (27% vs. 15%), a difference that is largely attributable to a greater number of girls listening to the radio rather than a greater use of personal playback devices.

C. Audio Preferences of Children and Teenagers

A remarkable array of musical choices is offered by modern media. In the 2005 survey, Roberts, Foehr, and Rideout (2005) provided a list of 17 musical genre options, as well as an eighteenth "Other" category. They asked the seventh through twelfth graders to indicate the genres they listened to through CD, tapes, and MP3s the previous day (because they wanted to focus on actively selected music, they ignored radio listening). Tastes differed somewhat, but a few genres stood out as the most popular. Chief among these was rap/hip hop. About two-thirds (65%) selected rap/hip hop as a genre they listened to the previous day, a figure about double that for the next most popular option. Second was alternative rock, specified by 32 percent. Hard rock/heavy metal was chosen by 27 percent and ska/punk by 23 percent. No other musical genre was cited by 20 percent or more.

Tastes of young people show some variability when taking into account race or ethnicity. Rap/hip hop was universal in its position as the number one choice (by far) of White (non-Latino), African American, and Latino young people, but it was listed significantly more often by African American youth. Eighty-one percent of African Americans cited rap/hip hop compared to 70 percent of Latinos and 60 percent of White, non-Latinos. Rhythm and blues (R&B) music was cited by 33 percent and reggae by 24 percent of the African Americans, and Latin/salsa music had comparable appeal among Latinos, with 33 percent citing that genre. Country/Western was more popular among White, non-Latino youth (26%) compared to African Americans or Latinos, as was classic rock (21%). Race or ethnicity clearly partially shapes musical preferences among the young.

D. Audio Use and Preferences of the Very Young

Music boxes and mobiles above the crib play lullabies to dozing babies. Portable cassette or CD players are carried by toddlers around the house. Music often seems to take center stage. The data that include children from ages two to seven (Roberts & Foehr, 2004) confirm this centrality. Two- to seven-year-olds averaged 46 minutes per day with audio media (see Table 1.1), divided about equally between radio, CDs, and tapes (use of MP3s was not measured in this study). Even among the youngest, the two- to four-year-olds, 75 percent had listened to audio media for at least five minutes the previous day. Recordings created specifically for children—such as stories, nursery rhymes, and children's music—were the most popular choice for those two to seven. The gender differences that appear later in childhood are not present among those seven and under.

In the Rideout, Vandewater, and Wartella (2003) data obtained from parents, 81 percent of zero- to three-year-olds were recorded as listening to music on a typical day. In the more recent data, 88 percent of parents of six-month to one-year-olds reported music use on a "typical" day, as did 84 percent of parents of 2- to 3-year-olds and 78 percent of four- to six-year-olds (Rideout & Hamel, 2006). The average amount of time zero- to three-year-olds spent was just under one hour (54 minutes) (Rideout & Hamel, 2006). Thus, the very young spend a substantial amount of time with music. Rideout and colleagues (2003) describe the array of audio media available to young children and the quickly developed ability to negotiate these devices: "The typical child six or under lives in a home with an average of four to five radios and CD/tape players, and four in ten (42%) even have their own CD or cassette player in their bedroom. One-third of all youngsters this age (36%) know how to use CD or cassette players themselves" (p. 9).

We draw three conclusions: Children are exposed to music virtually from infancy; they develop the skills to play their favorite songs by themselves at an early age; and preschool-aged children enjoy the audio content that is made expressly for their age group.

III. MEDIA EXPOSURE: SCREEN

Even with all of the attractive new options at the fingertips of most American children, television remains the dominant medium. It commands more daily attention with the single exception of audio media for 15- to 18-year-olds. In many ways, new technologies have helped to cement television's position as the leading medium. VCRs and then DVDs, digital video recorders (DVRs) like TiVo, computer links and iPods, flat screens and bigger and better sets with higher definition offering satellite or cable services have served to increase the allure of this already universally appealing medium. Young people as well as adults certainly no longer watch television the way they used to—as a mass audience divided primarily into large segments attending to the broadcasts of ABC, CBS, and NBC. Instead, the "mass" audience is much more divided (primetime shares of the three original networks that once approximated 95% have dwindled to less than 40%), more than three-fourths of households receive their signals from cable or satellite rather than by broadcast, and scheduled signals are extensively supplemented by more selective playback and on-demand sources (Comstock & Scharrer, 1999). The audience now is scattered across dozens of channels, many of which are so specialized that the term "niche" is apt. Other options include a DVD of a favorite show, playback of a recorded program, or renting a movie from a video store, ordering instantaneously through the cable provider, subscribing to a DVD mail service, or accessing a show on an iPod. Yet, in each of these newer scenarios as well as in the conventional sense, watch they do, in numbers that continue to somewhat amaze the social scientist charged with the task of tallying time spent with media.

Our review of time spent with screen media includes television, videotapes, DVDs, and movies, thereby encompassing "all audio-visual systems that deliver content that *does not* depend on *directive* responses from the viewer" (Roberts et al., 2005, p. 23, emphasis in original). The feature that distinguishes screen from interactive media is the content that is not open to alteration by the decisions of the user.

A. Television Exposure

In our earlier work (Comstock & Scharrer, 1999), we estimated children's average amount of TV exposure to be 3 hours and 10 minutes per day and teenagers' exposure to be just under three hours. Data collected by Roberts and colleagues (2005) six years later show that figure to be right on the mark. The 2005 survey records that children aged 8 to 18 in the United States spend an average of 3 hours and 4 minutes per day watching television. This is an enormous amount of time that dwarfs average daily exposure to the other screen media (47 minutes with videos/DVDs, 25 minutes with movies) as well as all of the other media. The estimate of 3 hours and 4 minutes per day not only closely resembles our prior calculation, but also shows negligible change from the Roberts and Foehr (2004) estimate of 3 hours and 5 minutes per day from their 1999 data. With such consensus, we can be abundantly confident in concluding that young people in the United States on average spend just over three hours with television each day.

Eighty-one percent reported that they watched television the day before, 42 percent watched videos/DVDs, and 13 percent watched a movie (Roberts et al., 2005). Daily television use is commonplace. Video/DVD use is decidedly more occasional. Attending movies, always more special than television viewing, could be described as occurring seldomly. A substantial minority of young people are heavy viewers, allocating substantially more time than the average. Indeed, a full one in five (20%) of the young people reported that they watched TV for five hours or longer the previous day.

In light of the continuing diffusion of digital video recording technology—devices that allow for digital time shifting and storing of television programs—comparisons were drawn between time spent with TV shows recorded by oneself and "commercially originated" programs and DVDs (Roberts et al., 2005). The figures show that despite the growing popularity of DVRs and digital time shifting, commercially produced video content is still more popular. Just over one-third (39%) of 8- to 18-year-olds watched a commercially originated program the day before and they spent an average of 32 minutes on them. A decidedly smaller 21 percent watched a self-recorded program and spent a more modest 14 minutes. When looking specifically at the young people who reported owning a DVR (34% of the total sample did), twice as much time was spent with self-recorded content by DVR owners than by nonowners. DVR-owning young people also watch more TV in real time than non-DVR-owning young people, suggesting that this new technology has been adopted in households in which the occupants, including the kids, are particular fans of television (Roberts et al., 2005).

B. Demographic Differences in Television Use

The most recent data confirm a long-standing finding (Comstock & Scharrer, 1999) that television use, after rising during infancy and early childhood, decreases over time during childhood and adolescence (see Table 1.1).

Roberts and colleagues (2005) summarize the specifics of this diminished screen media use with age:

> In general, older kids report less exposure than younger kids. For example, adolescents age 15–18 watch almost 3/4 of an hour less than either of the two younger groups, a difference approaching statistical significance (p < .08 in both cases). Older kids are significantly less likely to watch any TV on a given day, and less likely to spend more than one hour viewing TV. They are also less likely than 8- to 10-year-olds to spend time watching any kind of video recording. When all screen media are combined, the oldest adolescents report an hour less daily exposure than 8- to 10-year-olds and 3/4 of an hour less than 11- to 14-year-olds (both statistically significant differences). (pp. 23–24)

Another persisting demographic pattern—that the race or ethnicity of the child is associated with significant differences in screen media use—is also again confirmed. As we have observed elsewhere (Comstock & Scharrer, 1999; Comstock, 1991), prior analyses have concluded that African American youth tend to spend more time watching television than Latino children who, in turn, tend to watch more than White non-Latino children (Robinson & Godbey, 1997). The data of Roberts and colleagues (2005) not only continue to find this pattern but also extend it to other forms of screen media and rule out parental education or income as the underlying explanation.

African Americans reported spending an average of 4 hours and 5 minutes watching TV compared to 3 hours 23 minutes for Latinos and 2 hours 45 minutes for White non-Latinos, each comparison resulting in a statistically significant difference. Roughly the same pattern holds for the other forms of screen media. Total use was just under six hours daily for African Americans (5:53) compared to about four-and-a-half for Latinos (4:37) and just under four hours for Whites (3:47). The proportion of youth from each racial/ethnic group reporting some screen media use the day before does not differ. Thus, children of color are not more likely to use screen media on any given day but are more apt to spend longer periods of time with screen media. This testifies to the ubiquitous use of screen media by the young as well as to its greater attractiveness to African Americans and Latinos. Roberts and colleagues (2005) conducted additional analyses to ensure that the racial/ethnic differences were not explained by the potentially confounding factor of socioeconomic status. They found, "... at each level of parent education and at each level of income, ... the pattern of African American kids reporting the highest amount of TV exposure, Hispanic kids the second highest, and White kids the least, continued to hold" (p. 24). We conclude, therefore, that cultural norms (or perhaps some unmeasured factor) rather than socioeconomic status explain the tendency for children of color to spend longer periods of time per day watching TV.

In a major surprise, the most recent data of Roberts and colleagues (2005) record absolutely no relationship between either the income of the household or the level of parental education and the amount of time young people spend with television. These findings are quite unexpected. The vast majority of past media use studies have found that higher socioeconomic status—typically measured by income and/ or education—is associated with lower television use, and this has been particularly so for education (Brown et al., 1990; Comstock et al., 1978; Comstock, 1991; Medrich et al., 1982; Roberts & Foehr, 2004; Schramm et al., 1961; Tangney & Feshbach, 1988). Perhaps the time that we predicted (when in a very speculative mode) in our last review of this issue (Comstock & Scharrer, 1999) has arrived—television use has become so ubiquitous as to overshadow any previously distinguishing socioeconomic differences.[1]

---

[1] However, because this outcome conflicts with the survey five years earlier by Roberts and Foehr (2004) as well as many other sets of earlier data, we reserve judgment until we have confirmation from additional samples. It is always possible that this is the kind of statistical anomaly that inevitably sometimes occurs in survey data. We are always skeptical when a long-standing pattern seems to be overturned in new data. We are hesitant to offer a conclusion until we have confirmation (or disconfirmation) from a similar, large, nationally representative sample or from a series of smaller scale endeavors that are in agreement.

The only exception to the lack of association with either income or parental education is a curvilinear relationship that appears between level of parental education and total screen media exposure (but *not* exposure to television). Roberts and colleagues (2005) data demonstrate that young people in households where parents have moderate amounts of education (some college) generally spend less time overall with screen media (3:46) than either those in households with lower (high school; 4:23) or higher (college or more; 4:20) levels of parental education.

C. Viewing Preferences among Children and Teenagers

Lists of television programs drawn from local schedules were employed by Roberts and colleagues (2005) to record preferences among the 8- to 18-year-olds expressed by actual viewing. Programs were categorized by the authors as belonging to one of 18 different genres. The results display the perennial appeal of situation comedies in this age group (Lyle & Hoffman, 1972a). Just over one-third (37%) watched a sitcom on the previous day, a proportion outdistancing the next most popular choice by 12 percentage points. In fact, situation comedies appear to carry appeal across age, gender, race, and socioeconomic status, as it was the only genre listed by a third or more of respondents in every demographic category.

The next most popular genre was children's programming, divided by the authors into educational programming (for which previous day viewing occurred among 25%) and entertainment programming (among a nearly equal 24%). The former included programs with a central educational mission, whereas the latter consisted of cartoons often featuring superheroes or other action-adventure themes. As might be expected, the popularity of these genres declines with age. They were cited by slightly fewer than half of the 8- to 10-year-olds, about 20 percent of the 11- to 14-year-olds, and fewer than 10 percent of the 15- to 18-year-olds.

Next came movies (22%). Remaining genres were cited by fewer than 20 percent. Nonetheless, substantial numbers watched reality shows (17%), entertainment/variety shows (16%), dramas (15%), sports (12%), and documentaries (11%). There were two significant gender differences. Girls were more likely to report watching sitcoms, whereas boys were more likely to report watching sports.

We conclude that tastes for particular program types have changed little over the years from when the first author summarized the research data in 1991 drawing on data from the early 1970s,"... First graders mostly named situation comedies and cartoons. Sixth graders largely replaced the cartoons with action-adventure programs. Tenth graders continued to name many action-adventure programs, but added music and variety ... preferences for cartoons and children's programs declined, while those for adventure-drama and comedy increased with age" between the ages of 5 to 12 (Comstock, 1991, p. 7). Indeed, the recent data (Roberts & Foehr, 2004) also support the conclusion drawn by Comstock (1991) that the shift in childhood from preferring children's programming to adult, mainstream programming occurs at about the age of eight.

D. Television Viewing by the Very Young

When examining screen media use among young children, four distinguishing features are striking. First, television viewing begins extremely early in the lifespan and quickly accounts for substantial amounts of time per day. Second, programming produced especially for children is by far the most popular choice among the very young. Third, programs viewed on videotape or DVD are also exceptionally appealing at this age. Finally, although television use is clearly and uniformly a part of their daily lives, very few spend what could be characterized as an extensive amount of time watching television per day.

The data collected in 1999 puts daily exposure to screen media among children aged two to seven at just over two-and-a-half hours per day (2:33) (Roberts & Foehr, 2004). The lion's share of this figure, as in the older age groups, is explained by time spent with television. A scant two to three minutes are spent daily with videotapes of time-shifted television shows or with movies. Two- to seven-year-olds spend an estimated two hours and two minutes daily watching TV, and 84 percent report some exposure to television on the previous day.

Recently, the American Academy of Pediatrics established guidelines that recommend no television viewing for children less than two years of age. The Rideout, Vandewater, and Wartella (2003) data suggest that following that advice would constitute a pretty dramatic change in the patterns of media use in many families. Their numbers show that 59 percent of all children aged two and under watch TV on any given day, and 43 percent watch everyday. Rideout and Hamel (2006) found 81 percent of 2- to 3-year-olds watch television on a typical day, a much higher percentage than the 56 percent of six-month- to one-year-olds (although the latter is a substantial figure). Nearly three-quarters (72%) of the parents in the sample reported their 2- to 3-year-old watched television every day, compared to 43 percent of the parents reporting on their six-month- to one-year-olds. Accounting not only for television but for all forms of screen media, children two and under spend an estimated two hours and five minutes "in front of a screen" (Rideout et al., 2003, p. 5) a day, 1 hour and 22 minutes of which is time spent watching television. The data lead convincingly to the conclusion that television use becomes integrated into each day very early in a child's life, significant amounts of exposure to television occurs before the age of two, and adherence to the American Academy of Pediatrics counsel would require a near-revolution—or at least a novel display of resolve—in parenting practices in many households..

Programming created expressly for child viewers by far is the most favored television genre. Educational programming, specifically, draws the largest percentage of preschoolers as well as the majority of kindergarten to second graders. For just over three-fourths of all 2- to 4-year-olds (77%) and 60 percent of 5- to 7-year-olds, children's educational programming was named as a preference among television genres (Roberts & Foehr, 2004). Children's entertainment programming was a distant second, selected by one-third of those aged two to four and 43 percent of those aged five to seven. The only other genre drawing substantial amounts of interest from young children was comedy. It was chosen by 19 percent of the 2- to 4-year-olds and 33 percent of the 5- to 7-year-olds. Although a large majority of television viewing time is spent with programs created especially for this age group, the interest in comedy that characterizes later childhood begins early.

A plurality, 48 percent, of the parents of the six-month- to six-year-olds report that their child watches mostly children's shows in approximately equal proportions of educational programs and entertainment programs (Rideout & Hamel, 2006). The next largest percentage, 24 percent, report their young child watches mostly children's educational programs. Smaller percentages report exposure equally divided between children's shows and adult shows or concentrated among kids' shows that are mostly entertainment, 13 percent and 10 percent, respectively. We conclude that television content specifically created for the very young is, indeed, most popular among that group, with educational programming particularly frequently chosen. Yet, the purely educational television diet is relatively rare, even among the youngest of the young.

Many parents have concerns over the suitability of mainstream television programming for very young children. Objections include violence, sexual references, and profanity. For that reason (and others), parents of very young children report substantial use of commercially produced videotapes or DVDs in the home. The typical preschooler in the United States is likely to have ready access to a library of television programs and movies on VHS or DVD that are targeted to child audiences and not recorded by a family member but rather purchased in prerecorded form. DVDs and videotapes containing a number of episodes of educational programs such as *Blue's Clues*, *Dora the Explorer*, or *Sesame Street*, for instance, are likely elements of this library, as are Disney films or other children's movies such as Winnie the Pooh's *Tigger*, *Beauty and the Beast*, or *Toy Story*. The advantages of screen media in this form are that they can be played at the convenience of the parent (to entertain a child while preparing dinner, or as transition to bedtime), repeated viewing of a show is extremely appealing to a child, and the parent is typically both familiar with and comfortable with the content (no surprising violence or unwelcome language).

Roberts and Foehr (2004) place daily exposure to what they call "commercial videos" (the purchased programs and movies) at approximately 30 minutes per day among very young children. Two- to four-year-olds spend an estimated 33 minutes and 5- to 7-year-olds spend 21 minutes with this form of screen media daily. Commercial video use nevertheless is less ingrained into the fabric of daily life than ordinary television viewing. Despite the substantial average amounts of use, Roberts and Foehr record that 54 percent of those aged two to four and 70 percent of those five to seven had no commercial video exposure the previous day—much higher proportions of nonusers than for ordinary television.

Despite the fairly high figure for average exposure to television (2:02) and notwithstanding the fact that most in this age group have not yet entered school and therefore have few demands on their time, only a fraction of 2- to 7-year-olds could be described as very heavy viewers. The latest estimates (Roberts & Foehr, 2004) indicate only 7 percent watched television for five hours or more the previous day. Such a minute proportion for extensive viewing is unique to the very young. The percentage of 8- to 18-year olds reporting five hours or more of television consumption, by contrast, is three times greater (22%). We conclude that parents and caregivers view extensive daily television use as excessive for their very young children, and most avoid it.

IV. MEDIA EXPOSURE: INTERACTIVE MEDIA

Computer-based technologies have significantly changed the media landscape. Interactive media, in which the decisions and actions of the user—the click of the mouse, the turn of the joystick, the operation of the keyboard—change the content of what is seen, have a large and growing presence at school and in the home. The navigation of these media demands active participation on the part of the user and therefore in many ways interactive media differ from more traditional media not only in how they are used but why.

The young are able to embrace such innovations, without the apprehension or indifference that pose obstacles for older adults. Young people are notoriously often more savvy about new technologies than their parents, and many seem to grow up with a mouse in their hand and a seemingly natural ease with computers, video games, and other devices.

Young people's use of the Internet occurs within the context of and is dependent on the level of diffusion of Internet technology across the country. Robinson and Alvarez (2005) provide the most recent thorough account of this diffusion by collating the large-scale surveys of Internet use in the United States. As of August, 2003, the most recent figure available was that approximately 60 percent of the population was online. Despite a trend of fairly steady growth since 1995, the diffusion rate has showed little increase in the year or two preceding this (August 2003) figure. They conclude, contrary to hoopla in the media, that diffusion has occurred more slowly than for VCR technology. The gap between Internet access of males and females present in earlier data has narrowed in recent years, but considerable distance remains between adoption rates associated with race, income, and education. Whites, those with higher incomes, and those with greater degrees of education are more likely to have Internet connections. Robinson, Neustadtl, and Kestnbaum (2002) have also documented a pattern that they have dubbed a "diversity divide." Internet users differ from nonusers not just in terms of demographics but also in their more liberal stances regarding race, gays and lesbians, religion, and women's rights, and these differences were not explained by income or education levels. A readier welcoming of technological innovation apparently is joined by more favorable dispositions toward social innovations. In our present analysis of use of the computer and other interactive media technologies, the changing—and according to the analyses of Robinson and Alvarez, uncertain—status of Internet diffusion must be taken into account. Unlike more established media (such as television, radio, and print) the introductory diffusion process for interactive media has not clearly ended.

A. Use of Interactive Media by Young People

Young people in the United States are spending more and more time with interactive media. Limiting their questions to leisure and excluding school- or work-related tasks, Roberts, Foehr, and Rideout (2005) measured time spent with the computer as well as with video games. They gathered data for six separate computer-based activities: playing games, visiting web sites, spending time in chat rooms, communicating via e-mail, instant messaging (a popular application that allows users to correspond on the computer in real time), and the use of graphics (programs such as Photoshop or PowerPoint). The data of

Roberts and colleagues (2005) set daily leisure time use of the computer among 8- to 18-year-olds at approximately one hour per day (1 hour and 2 minutes, to be precise). Playing games and instant messaging are close competitors for the largest proportion of time at 19 minutes and 17 minutes per day, respectively. Visiting web sites contributes an additional 14 minutes. The remaining activities—graphics programs, chat rooms, and e-mail—account for just four to five minutes of total daily use. Instant messaging, then, is much preferred over e-mail and web sites are frequently visited without the desire to participate in affiliated chats.

Roberts and colleagues (2005) describe the differences that occurred in the five years between the 1999 and 2004 surveys:

> A combination of increased access to computers and the emergence of new, highly popular computer activities has resulted in more than a doubling of the amount of time U.S. kids spent with computers.... (I)n 1999, 73% of 8- to 18-year-olds reported a personal computer in their home; today, 86% report in-home access to a PC.... Five years ago we did not ask about time spent playing games online, about various graphics programs or about time spent instant messaging. Since then, each of these activities has begun to claim substantial computer time from kids. The result is that the average amount of time young people devote to various computer activities has climbed from 0:27 daily to 1:02 daily (the proportion of kids using a computer at all has grown from 47% to 54%, and the proportion using a computer for more than an hour has climbed from 15% to 28%).... (O)nly two computer activities, visiting chat rooms and sending e-mail, have remained fairly constant in terms of the time devoted to them. Time spent using Web sites has doubled (from seven to 14 minutes daily). Time spent with computer games has increased from 0:12 in 1999 to 0:19 in 2004, a change that we believe is at least partly a result of increased availability of online, multiplayer games. And perhaps most striking, a computer activity that did not warrant a question five years ago now claims as much time as visiting chat rooms (working with graphics programs = 0:04), and an activity that barely existed among kids five years ago now ranks as the second most time-consuming computer activity (instant messaging = 0:17). p. 30

The data document that computer use has changed in complexion and in the amount of time it consumes among the nation's youth. In the relatively short span between 1999 and 2004, game playing and Web "surfing" have attracted significantly more daily use, and sending and receiving an instant message (or "IM-ing" as it is frequently referred to) has taken off in jet-propelled fashion. We agree with the conclusion of Roberts and colleagues (2005) that the doubling of overall amount of time spent with computers in the five-year period can be attributed both to more and more families (and young people themselves) owning computers as well as the additional attraction of newer computer applications such as these.

The second major component of interactive media is video games. This category includes video games played on console systems that hook up to the television set such as those created by Nintendo, Sega, PlayStation, or Xbox, and handheld playing systems, such as the Game-Boy, but not games played on the computer, which were categorized as computer use. It is impossible to dispute the popularity of video game consoles and games. The industry is booming, with the financial press prominently charting technical developments, marketing strategies, and the various entrepreneurial maneuvers of the major firms. Systems offer realistic-looking graphics, extensive memory, and an ever-increasing list of titles to choose from with elaborate plots and special effects. Most games cost about $50.

Video games are a popular form of entertainment for the typical American child. Roberts and colleagues (2005) discovered that some 52 percent of 8- to 18-year-olds play a video game on an average day, with 41 percent reporting console use and another 35 percent handheld game play. The average amount of time dedicated to video game use is an impressive 49 minutes per day (32 minutes on the console systems and another 17 using handheld devices). The complexity of the games themselves (as well as their notorious "addictiveness") is likely a factor in the finding that about one in five (22%) play for an hour or longer on any given day.

B. Interactive Media Use and Demographics

Amount of time spent with the computer increases with the age of the child (see Table 1.1). In fact, moving from the 8- to 10-year-old to the 11- to 14-year-old results in a near doubling of daily computer use, from 37 minutes to just over one hour (1:02). The jump is significant from the middle age group to the oldest as well, with 15- to 18-year-olds spending one hour and 22 minutes per day at the keyboard. Instant messaging, examining web sites, and e-mailing all begin to increase substantially in time use at the age of 11. The growth in popularity of two of these computer applications, IM-ing and e-mailing, is most likely attributable to the increase in the desire to keep in touch with friends and acquaintances that marks adolescence. The increased attraction of the third application, visiting web sites, probably represents the emerging interest among preteen and teenagers in sports, musical performers, and other aspects of popular culture.

Although computer use increases with age, video game use decreases (see Table 1.1). The 8- to 10-year-olds are the heaviest users of video game technology, spending an average of one hour and five minutes daily. The estimate declines (but not significantly) to 52 minutes among the 11- to 14-year-olds and then takes a nosedive to 33 minutes per day among the 15- to 18-year-olds. As with television use, perhaps with more demands on the time of older teenagers (including extracurricular activities at school, socializing with friends, and romantic interests), video game playing begins to lose some of its allure.

Gender differences appear. Boys and girls do not differ substantially in the amount of time they spend with computers, but they are distinct in terms of how they allocate that time. Boys spend significantly more time playing games on the computer than girls (22 minutes per day compared to 15). On the other hand, girls spend more time instant messaging (20 minutes per day vs. 14), visiting web sites (16 minutes vs. 12), and e-mailing (6 minutes vs. 4). We concur with the speculation of Roberts and colleagues (2005) that the differences likely stem from gender socialization in which girls learn to be more social and communicative. Boys are more likely to play and to spend longer periods of time with video games. Almost two-thirds (63%) of all of the boys in the Roberts and colleagues (2005) sample were likely to have played video games on any given day, compared to 40 percent of girls. Astonishingly, boys spend three times longer playing video games than girls—one hour and 12 minutes versus 25 minutes. This is the result of the symbiosis between video game marketing and male interests. The video game industry has come to market its product primarily to males (Scharrer, 2004) because video games lend themselves to action, retribution, and violent conflict (Thompson & Haninger, 2001) that are more appealing to males than females.

Computer use is related to race and ethnicity of the child as well as to socioeconomic status. No significant differences emerge in the amount of time spent once on the computer. However, White non-Latino young people are more likely to use a computer each day compared to African Americans or Latinos. There is a 10 to 13 percentage point difference in likelihood of use, with 57 percent of the Whites using the computer on any given day versus 44 percent of African Americans and 47 percent of Latinos. There are also differences in computer applications, with African Americans less likely to play games and to engage in instant messaging. Despite increased adoption of computers in the home, parental education and income continue to predict likelihood of use. On any given day, almost two-thirds (62%) of children whose parents have completed college use the computer, compared to 47 percent of children whose parents have a high school education and 51 percent of children whose parents have some college education. The figures for family income parallel those for parental education. Nearly two-thirds (63%) of those children whose families fall into the high income category used a computer the day before compared to 47 percent of low income and 50 percent of middle income families. A "digital divide" continues to characterize computer access and use in the United States.

Surprisingly, despite the high cost of console systems and games, household income does not predict differences in video game use in the most recent data of Roberts and colleagues (2005). Other demographic variables do. The relationship between video game use and parental education is curvilinear. The middle parental education category records the lowest amount of time; in both the low and the high categories, use is higher. There are also significant differences associated with race or ethnicity. African Americans spend longer periods of time playing either console-based or handheld games than White, non-Latinos (who played for the shortest periods) and Latinos (whose playing time was in between).

C. Preferences in Interactive Media by Children and Teens

With the immense and uncharted domain that constitutes the Internet, it is a daunting task to attempt to ascertain preferences. Similarly, the vast stores of games available to the young consumer make the specifications of preferences difficult. We nevertheless find some answers in the surveys by the Kaiser Family Foundation (Rideout et al., 2003; Roberts et al., 2005; Roberts & Foehr, 2004) as well as in several other sources.

The youngest children spend nearly all their time on the computer playing games. The Roberts and Foehr (2004) figures indicate that for 2- to 7-year-olds this activity is almost wholly made up of "educational games, children's games, or arts and crafts games" (p. 129). Playing games with content that is violent or otherwise arguably inappropriate is very rare among this younger set, with just 6 percent of 5- to 7-year-olds and absolutely no 2- to 4-year-olds exposed to action or combat games.

Action and combat games quickly gain a foothold among preferences of preteens and teenagers. They are favorites of 22 percent of those aged eight to 10, 20 percent of those 11 to 14, and 25 percent of those 15 to 18 (Roberts & Foehr, 2004). Classic or gambling games are popular in the older age groups, too, as are sports games, adventure games, and simulation games.

Computer applications other than gaming also display wide variation in preferences (Roberts & Foehr, 2004). The most popular web sites to visit for the 11- to 18-year-olds include entertainment sites (51% of 11- to 14-year-olds chose this option, as did 62% of 15- to 18-year-olds), sports sites (chosen by 31% and 17%, respectively), and sites chosen for research or to obtain information (13% and 21%, respectively). For the 8- to 10-year-olds, entertainment web sites again were chosen by many (46%), followed by gaming sites (43%), sports sites (18%), and shopping venues (15%). Specific chatrooms included the same topics as the web sites. However, hobbies/groups and relationships/lifestyles also gained adherents, demonstrating the desire of a number of young people to "talk" to others about their hobbies, interests, and relationships.

In the case of video games, gender differences in preferences are striking. In fact, differences between boys and girls are so pronounced that in one study, a national, randomly drawn survey of 1- to 12-year-olds, they occur within all three major racial/ethnic groups (in the authors' categorization, European Americans, African Americans, and Hispanic Americans) (Bickham, Vandewater, Huston, Lee, Caplovitz & Wright, 2003). Thus, we focus on differences between boys and girls.

Boys find games that contain violence more appealing than girls do (Funk & Buchman, 1996). Recent research has not only supported that finding but also offers a number of potential explanations. Sherry and Lucas (2003) and Lucas and Sherry (2004) located important gender differences in reports of uses and gratifications of video game use, including levels of desire for competition, to challenge oneself, to engage in fantasy, and to become aroused through exciting game play, all lower for female respondents compared to males. Lucas and Sherry (2004) similarly found distinct genre preferences for young men compared to young women. Although their sample consists of 593 college-aged respondents, we argue that, because of the stability of gender orientations across age as well as the robustness of their findings, their results are likely to extrapolate to teenagers and quite probably to those somewhat younger. The young women were more likely to prefer traditional games such as those based on cards or dice, "old-fashioned" arcade games like PacMan or Frogger, puzzle games like Tetris, classic board games like Monopoly that had been converted into video games, and trivia games. Conversely, the young men were more likely to like sports games, fighter and shooter games, fantasy/role-playing games, and action adventure games. The authors observe that because games usually are typed as the domain of men and boys, an additional deterrent to girls playing video games is the assumption that to do so requires crossing traditional gender role behavior.

The Roberts and Foehr (2004) data certainly support the extension of the Lucas and Sherry's (2004) results to children and teens. In games played on the computer, they find "boys dominate the action/combat, adventure, sports, and strategic and simulation categories" (p. 130) whereas girls were likely to prefer just one type of game more than boys, the classic and gambling category. This latter category is similar to the cards/dice, and traditional board game groups preferred by girls in the Lucas and Sherry (2004) data. In games played using video game consoles or handheld devices, Roberts and Foehr (2004) found boys again prefer the "action-oriented games," including the action/combat, sports, and simulation/strategic genres. The allure of the fast-paced, often aggressive action gaming genre begins early in middle childhood (around the age of 8) and continues into the early teens.

D. Interactive Media Use by the Very Young

Children are using interactive media at early stages of life. Experience with the computer grows exponentially between the ages of two and four to six. Rideout, Vandewater, and Wartella (2003) found that while only 11 percent of children under the age of two had used a computer, by the time a child enters the 4- to 6-year-old age range, 70 percent had done so. On any given day, just over one-fourth (27%) of all 4- to 6-year-olds used computers, and amount of time spent daily among those who have used the computer averages over one hour (1:04). In the most recent data encompassing six-month to six-year-olds, 16 percent were reported to use a computer on a typical day, for 50 minutes, on average (Rideout & Hamel, 2006). The favorite web sites listed by parents clearly demonstrate the symbiotic relationship between television and computer, and they included Nickelodeon, Nick Jr., Noggin, Disney, PBS Kids, and Sesame Street (Rideout & Hamel, 2006). Computer-related knowledge develops quickly in this age group, as apparent in the Rideout and colleagues (2003) data:

> More than half of all children in this age group (56%) have used a computer by themselves (without sitting in their parent's lap); 64% know how to use a mouse to point and click; 40% can load a CD-ROM by themselves; 37% have turned the computer on by themselves; and 17% have sent e-mail with help from a parent. (p. 5)

By the year 2001, computer and Internet use among children and adolescents was greater than among adults (DeBell & Chapman, 2003). Recent highly reliable figures released by the U.S. Department of Education were gathered using the Current Population Survey conducted in 2003 with an astoundingly large national probability sample of households—29,000 children ranging from nursery-school (preschool) age to twelfth grade. Two-thirds (67%) of preschoolers aged two to five had used a computer before, and 23 percent had used the Internet (see Table 1.2). Kindergartners in the sample, typically five or six years of age, are even more likely to have used both forms of technology (80% for computers, 32% for the Internet). As children progress through the grades, the gap between general computer use and Internet use closes.

Table 1.2
Percentage of Nursery/Preschool Through Twelfth Grade Students Who Use Computers and the Internet at Home, at School, or at Work.

	Computer use	Internet use
TOTAL	91%	59%
Age		
Nursery school	67%	23%
Kindergarten	80	32
1st–5th grade	91	50
6th–8th grade	95	70
9th–12th grade	97	80
Gender		
Female	91%	61%
Male	91	58
Race/ethnicity		
White/Non-Hispanic	93%	67%
Hispanic	85	44
Black/Non-Hispanic	86	47
Asian or Pacific Islander	91	58
American Indian, Aleut or Eskimo	88	50
More than one race	92	65
Parental education		
Less than high school	82%	37%
High school credential	89	54
Some college	93	63
Bachelor's degree	92	67
Some graduate educ.	95	73
Household income		
Under $20,000	85%	41%
$20,000–34,999	87	50
$35,000–49,999	93	62
$50,000–74,999	93	66
$75,000 or more	95	74

Adapted from U.S. Department of Education. (2005). *Rates of computer and internet use by children in nursery school and students in kindergarten through twelfth grade: 2003.* Accessed 6/27/05 at http://nces.ed.gov/pubs2005/2005111.pdf.

By the time they are in high school, 97 percent have used a computer and 80 percent the Internet. These high levels are facilitated by the availability of computers and access to the Internet in schools. The U.S. Department of Education (2003) claims virtually all public schools in the United States have Internet connections and the overall ratio is one computer for every five children.

In contrast, video game use is modest and sporadic among the very young. Thirty percent of the parents of all the six-month to six-year-olds in the Rideout and colleagues (2003) sample reported that their children had played video games sometime in the past. However, only 9 percent reported use on a typical day (spending an average of just five minutes). The comparable figure in the most recent data was 11 percent who reported an average of six minutes spent with video games on a typical day (Rideout & Hamel, 2006). Amount of time spent playing video games varied considerably when analyses were run with non-video game users removed. Among only those that did engage in video game use, the daily exposure time jumped to 55 minutes (Rideout & Hamel, 2006).

As the child grows up, however, video game use increases, presumably as a function of increased ability to manipulate the controls and to maintain attention. Among 4- to 6-year-olds, video game use on any given day occurs among 16 percent and amount of time spent playing swells to just over an hour (1:04) (Rideout et al., 2003). Nonetheless, among very young children levels of daily exposure to video games are dwarfed by exposure to television.

V. PUTTING IT ALL TOGETHER

We turn now to overall amount of media exposure and use (which are not the same thing), simultaneous attention to more than one medium at a time, and the distribution of time across various media. We then address the issue of access to media in the bedrooms of children and teenagers, as well as other indications of the degree of centrality of media in the home. Finally, we invoke the typology of young media users introduced by Roberts and Foehr (2004) to capture particular orientations among children and teens toward the various forms of media.

A. Total Time Spent with Each Type of Media

It is both tempting and informative to simply add up the amount of time spent with each of the media reported by Roberts and colleagues (Roberts & Foehr, 2004; Roberts et al., 2005) to arrive at an estimate of overall exposure. Yet these authors point out that such a technique loses a degree of accuracy in time allocation to media because it does not take into account use of more than one medium at a time. Thus, it neglects a phenomenon that is quite common, attending at least passingly to more than one medium at a time—a teenager watching TV while also communicating with friends on the computer, a child leafing through a magazine or book while a DVD of a favorite program plays in the background. In fact, the ability to "multitask" is commonly thought of as a newly developed skill of today's youngsters who have grown up with a number of sights and sounds continually demanding their attention (Christenson & Roberts, 1998; Lenhart, Rainie & Lewis, 2001).

For this reason, Roberts and colleagues (Roberts & Foehr, 2004; Roberts et al., 2005) employ a two-part strategy. They report both "media exposure," the sum of time spent with each medium, and "media use," the amount of time devoted to media overall after accounting for simultaneous use of two or more media. They provide an instructive example:

> ... imagine a teenager who spends two hours watching just TV, one hour reading and listening to music simultaneously, and another hour playing a video game while streaming music on her computer. Her total media *exposure* would be six hours (TV = 2; music = 2; reading = 1; video gaming = 1). However, her media *use* (i.e., the number of actual hours of the day that she devotes to media) would be four hours (TV = 2; music + print = 1; video games + music = 1). (2005, p. 35, emphasis in original)

Roberts and colleagues (Roberts & Foehr, 2004; Roberts et al., 2005) use diary data collected from a subsample of their total number of respondents to measure media use, adjusting for overlapping media time. Estimates of media use obviously are typically lower than total media exposure estimates, because the former does not "double-count ... overlapping use" (2005, p. 36).

Among all the 8- to 18-year-olds in the latest data collected in 2003 (Roberts et al., 2005), the grand total for overall media *exposure* per day is an extraordinary eight hours and 33 minutes. The grand total for overall media *use* per day is an only slightly less dramatic six hours and 21 minutes. (Remember that these data do not include media exposure in school, and so therefore the "true" total of time spent with media daily has the potential to be even larger.) About one-fourth of all time spent with media thus can be described as multitasking, and that proportion is uniform across most (but not all) subgroups. These figures testify that the daily lives of today's children and teenagers are saturated with media. Young people today are immersed in media for the better part of their waking hours, and will spend more time with media than with any other activity besides sleeping (Comstock & Scharrer, 1999).

Gender differences in total amounts of exposure or use are negligible (see Table 1.3). So, too, are differences associated with parental education. However, two intriguing demographic patterns surface. First, total media exposure is significantly higher among African Americans compared to White non-Latinos and Latinos (see Table 1.3). However, total media use shows only modest differences among the three groups, thereby identifying simultaneous media use as largely responsible for the differences. Indeed, the African American kids in the sample reported 36 percent of their time spent with media is multitasking, whereas the two other racial or ethnic groups reported 21 to 27 percent.

Table 1.3
Total Media Exposure and Total Media Use for 8- to 18-Year-Olds, by Age, Gender, Race, Parent Education, and Income*

	Total exposure	Total use
Overall	8:33	6:21
Age		
8 to 10	8:05	5:52
11 to 14	8:41	6:33
15 to 18	8:44	6:31
Gender		
Boys	8:38	6:21
Girls	8:27	6:19
Race		
White (non-Latino)	7:58	6:15
Black (non-Latino)	10:10	6:30
Latino	8:52	6:30
Parent education		
High school or less	8:30	5:54
Some college	8:02	6:26
College graduate	8:55	6:42
Income		
Under $35,000	8:40	5:02
$35,000–50,000	8:28	6:25
Over $50,000	8:34	6:44

*The only statistically significant differences in the table are for total exposure for Black young people compared to both White and Latino young people, and total exposure for some college education of parents compared to the other two parental education groups. All other differences are not statistically significant.

Adapted from Roberts, D. F., Foehr, U. G. & Rideout, V. (2005). *Generation M: Media in the lives of 8–18 year-olds. A Kaiser Family Foundation Study*. Menlo Park, CA: Henry J. Kaiser Family Foundation. Accessed 6/30/05 at http://www.kff.org/entmedia/7250.cfm.

Roberts and colleagues observe, "... the more than 2 1/2 hour difference between White and Black kids in media exposure is reduced to just 15 minutes when we look at media use" (2005, p. 36). Second, income levels predict proportion of time spent multitasking. Kids from families in the lowest income brackets have the highest levels of exposure but lowest levels of media use (due to their high rate of multitasking, 42 percent of all their media time). The middle and upper income children multitask at a much lower rate of 24 and 22 percent, respectively, and therefore the discrepancies between their media exposure and media use totals are less severe.

Diary data on media exposure and use were also collected in 1999 (Roberts & Foehr, 2004). Exposure to some form of media (television, print, and audio) has remained remarkably stable across the five-year period between 1999 and 2004, and exposure to other screen media (videotapes, DVDs, movies) has seen only a minor increase (see Table 1.4). On the other hand, the "new" media forms of computers and video games have shown significant growth in amount of exposure. (As we previously noted, computer exposure doubled over the five years, and video game use increased from an average of 26 minutes to 49 minutes per day.) Increases in amount of exposure to interactive media thus largely account for an overall increase in media exposure from about seven-and-a-half hours in 1999 to eight-and-a-half hours in 2004. When taking into account simultaneous exposure to more than one

Table 1.4
Comparisons of the Total Media Exposure and Total Media Use Figures for 8- to 18-Year-Olds over a Five-Year Span

Medium	1999	2004
TV	3:05	3:04
Videos/DVDs/movies	0:59	1:11
Print media	0:43	0:43
Audio media	1:48	1:44
Computers	0:27*	1:02*
Video games	0:26*	0:49*
TOTAL EXPOSURE	7:29*	8:33*
TOTAL USE	6:19	6:21

*These are the only statistically significant changes over time.
Adapted from Roberts, D. F., Foehr, U. G. & Rideout, V. (2005). *Generation M: Media in the lives of 8–18 year-olds. A Kaiser Family Foundation Study.* Menlo Park, CA: Henry J. Kaiser Family Foundation. Accessed 6/30/05 at http://www.kff.org/entmedia/7250.cfm.

medium, estimates of use have barely changed at all. Increased amounts of time spent with interactive media occur largely within the parameters of simultaneous media use and have not expanded time allocated to media. With other demands on their time, including such obligatory or valued activities as school, sports, band practice, clubs, hobbies, and, of course, socializing, young people apparently cannot allocate greater amounts of time to media than they do at present.

Roberts and colleagues (2005) speculate that the stability in total media use between 1999 and 2004 (despite substantial increases in media exposure) "may represent a ceiling in the amount of time young people can or will devote to using media" (p. 37).

B. How Time Spent Using Media Is Divided

Roberts and colleagues (Roberts & Foehr, 2004; Roberts et al., 2005) compellingly record that television, perhaps surprisingly to some, continues to dominate time spent by young people with media. Much has been made of the power of interactive media to transform daily life, and interactive media do play an integral and growing part in the daily lives of children and adolescents in the United States. Nonetheless, television unambiguously ranks as Number One. It accounts for 35 percent of all the leisure time young people spend with media. The dominance of screen media in general is also evident in the data. When time spent with television is combined with time spent with other screen media (movies, DVDs, videotapes), the percentage of the total media budget climbs to 48 percent. Thus, nearly half of all time spent with media is dedicated to screen media.

The dominance of television in particular and screen media in general holds across time and across subgroups. There is little reason to believe that the percentage of media time allocated to screen media has eroded dramatically over recent years in the face of continued adoption of interactive media technologies. In the five-year span measured, percentage of time devoted to screen media dropped just three percentage points (a difference well within the range of sampling error), having registered at 51 percent of total media time in 1999 (Roberts & Foehr, 2004; Roberts et al., 2005). There is also no indication that such dominance appears only in some subgroups and not others. Proportion of total media time allotted to television is stable across gender, race, parent education, and income. Only age of the child moderates the size of the television portion of the media budget, with a significant decline occurring in the teenage years, at the same time that the audio portion of the budget increases significantly. Television accounts for approximately 38 percent of total media time at 8 to 10 and 11 to 14 years of age and declines to 28 percent of total media time at 15 to 18 years of age.

With screen media taking up the major share of total time spent with media, smaller shares remain to be divided among other media. Audio media enjoys the largest share, accounting for 22 percent of the overall media budget, followed by print media and computers with each contributing 11 percent (Roberts et al., 2005). Video games earn the smallest proportion of time spent with media at 9 percent. Audio media enjoy ever-increasing amounts of media time throughout childhood and adolescence, growing from only 14 percent of total media time among the 8- to 10-year-olds to 30 percent of the total media time of 15- to 18-year-olds (when it catches up with television). Computer use also increases with age from a low of 7 percent of total media time in the youngest group to 15 percent in the oldest. Conversely, time within the media budget allocated to video game play decreases as the child grows up, from 12 percent of total media time among the youngest to 6 percent among the oldest.

Computer use is the only major medium to have shown a statistically significant change in the five-year period covered by the data. Media time budgeted in favor of computer use increased significantly from a mere 6 percent of overall media time in 1999 to 11 percent in 2004 (Roberts et al., 2005). The rise in percentage of media time spent with the computer was accompanied by a minor decrease in percentage of media time spent with television—TV accounted for 40 percent of total media time in 1999 and 35 percent in 2004—but the change is not statistically significant (again, it is well within the range of sampling error). Furthermore, the dip in percentage of time devoted to television is offset by a slight (nonsignificant) increase in percentage of time devoted to other screen media (from 11% to 13%). At this time, forecasts predicting the abandonment of television and other screen media in favor of the computer among the nation's youth are clearly premature and quite possibly misguided. In fact, although a study by the NPD group garnered news headlines in May, 2006 with claims that desktop computers and video games were more commonly owned than television sets by children under 14, we believe the nature of the methodology—over 3,000 parents were surveyed on the Internet—renders the results less generalizable and the claims more dubious than the data that we have focused on here (NPD, 2006).

C. Prevalence of Media in the Home

With the immense amount of time young people spend with the media, it will be of no surprise to learn that most media are readily available within the typical American household. Today's child grows up in an environment adorned with media. It's a far distance from the single radio receiver, record player, and/or television set often used to enter-tain and inform members of the household both young and old in the increasingly distant past. Typically, several media are available in the home but there is also considerable variation in the media environ-ment of households. One distinguishing feature is the degree of cen-trality of television in the family's daily life (How frequently is the set turned on? Are there any rules or norms limiting its use?)—a factor that has surprising implications for the presence and use of other media within the home.

1. The Media Environment   Most households are equipped with a large number of devices that bring media content to the consumer (Roberts et al., 2005). Nearly every household containing a person aged eight to 18 has a television (99%), a VCR (97%), a radio (97%), and a CD and/or tape player (98%). Only slightly fewer contain a computer (86%), a video game system (83%), and the capacity to go on the Inter-net (74%). More than half (60%) of homes with young people boast instant messaging potential, thereby making possible the substantial amount of time allocated to this form of communication.

In fact, the norm for in-home media availability is not just to have one of each medium but, in many cases, to have more than one. The average number of television sets in households with children and teen-agers is 3.5 (up from 3.1 in 1999), and the average number of VCRs is 2.9 (up from 2.0). Audio media abound, as well, with an average of 3.6 CD/tape players and 3.3 radios in the home. Even video game systems are found in multiples, with an average of 2.1 per household (up from 1.7). The average number of computers in the household has grown from 1.1 in 1999 to 1.5, an increase that is statistically significant. The number of media available to children and teens in the home has led to a change in semantics among those collecting these data, who note that the phrase "media rich" no longer adequately captures the scene (Roberts et al., 2005). They suggest that "media saturation" is now the best descrip-tor, and we would certainly not dispute such a characterization.

The diffusion of technological developments have continually made television more attractive (Roberts et al., 2005). Cable or satellite trans-mission is present in 82 percent of households with children to bring a multitude of channel choices. Just over half (55%) subscribe to pre-mium cable (a popular choice for families with young children, many of whom would like to tune in Disney or Nick Jr. programs at any time of the day). A full one-third of all children in the United States live in a home with a DVR unit that provides enormous flexibility in search-ing out desired programs (digital video recording—the most popular brand is called TiVo but many cable companies are offering these services as well). Flat-screen, plasma, giant size, and high definition television (HDTV) all make viewing more visually pleasurable.

2. Media Use in the Bedroom   Not only are many and varied media located within the homes of children and teenagers, but most have considerable access to media within their own bedrooms. Many media these days are "personal media" for the express use of the young people. In the bedroom, the individual child or teenager usually has control over a television, and often a VCR, CD or DVD player, a video game system, or a computer, without the need to negotiate choices with other members of the family or to respond to the concerns of parents or caregivers regarding violence, sex, or other potentially objectionable content.

The extensiveness of media available to the typical youngster in the United States within their very own personal space, is astonishing (see Table 1.5). In the 2003 Roberts and colleagues (2005) data, there was a television set in the bedroom of 68 percent of 8- to 18-year-olds. Fifty-four percent had a VCR or DVD. Thirty-seven percent of those

Table 1.5
Percent of Children and Teens with Bedrooms Containing Each Type of Media

%	Age			
	0–6	8–10	11–14	15–18
TV	36%	69%	68%	68%
Cable TV	—*	32	38	40
Premium cable	—	16	21	20
DVR	—	8	13	9
VCR/DVD	27	47	56	56
Radio	46	74	85	91
CD/Tape player	42	75	89	92
Computer	7	23	31	37
Internet	3	10	21	27
Video game player	10	52	52	41

*Not measured.

Adapted from Roberts, D. F., Foehr, U. G. & Rideout, V. (2005). *Generation M: Media in the lives of 8–18 year-olds. A Kaiser Family Foundation Study.* Menlo Park, CA: Henry J. Kaiser Family Foundation. Also from Rideout, V. J., Vandewater, E. A. & Wartella, E. (2003). *Zero to six: Electronic media in the lives of infants, toddlers and preschoolers. A Kaiser Family Foundation Study.* Menlo Park, CA: Henry J. Kaiser Family Foundation.

with a TV set had a cable or satellite connection. Just under half (49%) had a video game system in their rooms. Almost one third (30%) had a computer, and 20 percent of the time that computer had an Internet connection.

Several of these personal media showed substantial growth in their presence in the bedrooms of youngsters between the years 1999 and 2004 (Roberts et al., 2005). Televisions, almost universal in 1999, were no more likely to be present, but the accompaniment of a VCR or DVD became more likely, as did the likelihood that the television set receives cable/satellite or premium cable services. The existence of a computer in the bedroom increased 10 percentage points, and the likelihood of a supplemental Internet connection doubled. There is compelling evidence, therefore, that the entertainment and information options personally available to the children or teenagers within the home, already considerable, continue to expand.

Sizeable numbers of children and teenagers in the United States have personal access to a number of additional communication technologies. In the 2004 survey (Roberts et al., 2005), 61 percent of 8- to 18-year-olds had a portable CD or tape player and 55 percent owned a handheld video game player. Forty percent had a telephone in their bedroom, and 39 percent owned a cell phone. Computer-based and digital technologies are becoming more widespread, as well. For example, 18 percent of 8- to 18-year-olds had the ability to engage in instant messaging in their bedrooms and the same number (18%) owned an MP3 player (used to download, store, and playback music digitally). Thirteen percent had a handheld Internet device (such as a cell phone that connects to the Internet), 12 percent a laptop computer of their own, and 11 percent a personal digital assistant such as a Palm Pilot. Today's young person is increasingly wired to the Internet, has the ability to reach friends through a cell phone or instant messenger, and may even have handy, high-tech, portable devices to bring along in the car, at the beach, or elsewhere.

A fair number of even the youngest children have personal media within easy reach in the bedroom (see Table 1.5). Rideout and colleagues (2003) record that 43 percent of 4- to 6-year-olds and 30 percent of six-month to three-year-olds had a television in their bedroom. In addition to the one-third of six-month to six-year-olds that had their own television, 27 percent had their own VCR or DVD player and 10 percent had their own video game playing system in their room. Audio media are frequently present in the rooms of the very young. Forty-six percent had their own radio and 41 percent their own CD or tape player. As would be expected, on the other hand, computers were rare. Just 7 percent of six-month-olds to six-year-olds has a computer in the bedroom. The figures changed very little in the most recent data analyzed by Rideout and Hamel (2006). In the more recent study, the authors asked parents to list their reasons for having a television in their young child's bedroom. The most frequently cited reasons: so that parents and others can watch the shows they like (55%), to keep the child busy so that parents can do chores around the house (39%), to help the child fall asleep (30%), to reward good behavior (26%), and to prevent fights among siblings (23%). Thus, a bedroom TV is seen as a means of family management.

The ownership of media of one's own is an indication that the household in which the child lives is relatively media-centric. In fact, the presence of media in the bedroom of the youngest children, six months to six years old, is associated with significantly more screen media and video game use (Rideout et al., 2003; Rideout & Hamel, 2006). Children in this age group who have a TV set in their bedrooms watch television for an average of 14 more minutes per day than their counterparts without a bedroom TV (Rideout et al., 2003). Those with their own video game console in their room play for 15 minutes longer than those without.

The same pattern holds and is even more marked for those aged 8 to 18 (Roberts et al., 2005). When televisions, video games, and computers are positioned in the bedrooms of these young people, not only does exposure to each of these media go up, but exposure to other media generally rises as well. Young people with a television in their bedrooms watch television almost an hour-and-a-half more per day, play video games for twice as long, and spend about 15 minutes more watching videos or movies compared to young people without a television in their bedroom. They also spend significantly less time reading. The presence of a video game console in the bedroom is, likewise, associated with more television and more videotape and movie exposure (in addition to the somewhat obvious—more video game use). Finally, having a computer in the bedroom of the child or teenager is associated not just with heavier computer use (as would be expected), but also heavier use of all the media forms examined, including television, videos and movies, video games, and time spent listening to music as well as reading. Clearly, having personal media in the bedrooms of young people indicates a strong emphasis within the household toward media in general.

D. Orientations toward Media

The extent to which the television set is on varies across households with young people and, like the presence of personal media, is associated with a strong orientation toward media. In some homes, television is a near-constant presence, turned on and left on for most of the day—even during meals or at times when no one is in the room. In other homes, television is used more sporadically, turned on and off for blocks of time with rules or norms limiting its use. The placement of a household on a continuum from highly oriented toward television use to less so is related to media use in general of the children and teenagers living in the household.

1. Rules and Norms of Media Use in the Home   Rideout and colleagues (2003) in their survey found that they could characterize 36 percent of households containing children six and under as "heavy TV households," in which the TV was reported to be on "always" or "most of the time." The young children in these heavy viewing households were themselves heavier viewers than others their age. They watched television for an average of one hour and 29 minutes per day compared to 51 minutes in households in which the television was on less frequently. Higher percentages of very young children in heavy viewing households were likely to have watched TV the day before compared to those in lighter viewing households—77 percent in the former versus 56 percent in the latter. Finally, the six-month to six-year-olds in heavy television households spent somewhat less time reading or being read to or playing outside compared to children of the same age in lighter television households.

In the data covering the media habits of 8- to 18-year-olds (Roberts et al., 2005), 63 percent reported that the television was usually on during meals, 51 percent reported constant television use, and 53 percent said their household had no rules regarding the use of television. Exactly one-quarter of all respondents belonged to a household meeting all three criteria—television on constantly, including during meals, and no television-relevant rules—and these individuals were categorized into a "high TV-orientation" group. These children and teenagers were notably more likely to have media present in their own bedrooms than the group low in household TV orientation. For example, 85 percent of children in homes with high TV orientation had a TV in their rooms compared to 63 percent of those in homes with low TV orientation. The former group was also significantly more likely than the latter to own a cell phone, and to have a telephone, a VCR or DVD, and a video game system in their room. Personal media ownership in the bedroom (not just of television but of nearly all media) was also negatively related to the imposition of parental rules on TV use.

Rules set by parents regarding television use exist in about half of households; in the 2004 data (Roberts et al., 2005), in 46 percent of households containing 8- to 18-year-olds. The most common type of rule required the completion of homework or chores before television could be viewed (36%), followed by rules about amount of time a child could view (just 14%) and about type of content seen as appropriate (only 13%). As would be expected, rules and restrictions are more likely to be present when the household contains a younger child. There were no significant variations in the presence or absence of rules by gender, race, or parental education or income.

Comparing these numbers with similar figures in past research (Bower, 1985; Comstock, 1991), it appears that the existence of specific rules in the home regarding television use was not markedly more or less likely in 2004 than it was in 1980. In 1980, 50 percent of households containing children had rules (up from 40% in 1960 and 43% in 1970), a figure very similar to the 46 percent found by Roberts and colleagues (2005). The implication of little change between 1980 and 2004 (in fact, the presence of a slight slip downward) implies that the ceiling without a change in circumstances for parental rules and restrictions is about 50 percent. (The presence of rules is more common in households with very young children; 85% of parents of 6-month to 6-year-olds report having rules about what type of content can be viewed and 60% say they have rules about amount of exposure; Rideout & Hamel, 2006).

Our conclusion is that the centrality of media in the household is a major dimension for describing the home environments in which children and teenagers grow up today. The family's disposition toward television—primarily representing the priorities and prerogatives of parents—provides a meaningful index of openness toward media in general. The effectiveness of television as a surrogate for access to and use of other media implies that Americans have come to think of media as technologies that essentially have much in common despite the many concrete, social, and functional differences that distinguish the cell phone, the Internet, the television screen, the iPod, the CD, and the DVD.

2. Typology of Media Behavior among Young People Children and teenagers differ considerably in their use of media, although the frequent use of averages—by age, race, gender, and socioeconomic status—probably as often obscures this fact as emphasizes important differences. Roberts and Foehr (2004) significantly advance the field of media studies by developing a typology of media behavior among young people that provides welcome descriptive variety. Using cluster analysis (a statistical technique that identifies subgroups in a sample making similar responses), Roberts and Foehr found six distinct groups of young people aged eight and older, each different from the other groups in terms of key characteristics. Surprisingly, the groups are similar in size (an aesthetic achievement from the perspective of cluster analysis).

The use of a large, representative sample for the analysis means that these groups can be taken as accurately representing the behavior of American children and teenagers. The groups are exhibited along the two major axes we have used to describe media behavior (see Figure 1.1)—the amount of time spent with media and the degree of access to media.

At polar ends of the two axes are the groups that Roberts and Foehr (2004) call *enthusiasts* and *media lites*. The *media lites*, comprising 18 percent of the sample of 8- to 18-year-olds, have both little access to media at home or in the bedroom and the lowest amounts of exposure of any group. They live in households with rules about television use and low television centrality (not on during meals, not on "constantly") and their media use is fairly traditional in nature, dominated by television, music, and print. Younger children are present in larger than average numbers in this group, and members of the group are slightly more likely to be female and White than to be male or children of color. The *enthusiasts* (19% of the sample) differ in every possible way. They have the highest levels of media exposure and live in environments with the largest number of media available. Nearly every enthusiast has his or her own television in the bedroom, and half have a computer. Television is highly

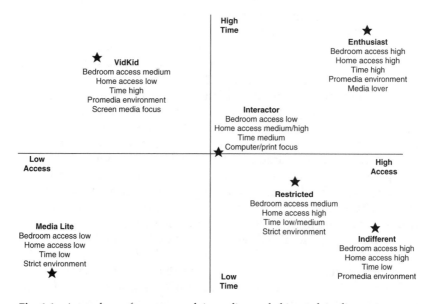

Fig. 1.1 A typology of young people's media use habits and media environments. Reprinted with permission from Roberts, D. F., Foehr, U. G. (2004). *Kids & media in America.* Cambridge University Press.

central in their households and not many report that there are rules to follow about its use. Boys are more common in this group than girls (62% are male) and many are in the middle age group (11 to 14 years old). Black/African American and Latino children also are present in relatively higher numbers in this group and income levels are just below average.

Also in opposing quadrants of the typology (although less dramatically so than the preceding two groups) are the *vidkids* and the *indifferents*. *Vidkids*, comprising 15 percent of the sample, are second only to enthusiasts in amount of media exposure. Their exposure levels are high in each media type except computer use. Few have a computer at home (20%), but most (70%) have a video game console. Most have a TV in the bedroom but few if any other media are present there. Their households are high in television centrality and their parents' education levels are relatively low. Almost half of the children in this group are African American or Latino, and the group contains more girls than boys. The *indifferents* (18% of the sample), on the other hand, have extensive access to media in the home and live in unrestrictive media environments (few rules) but don't seem to care to use media much, spending a full two hours less per day compared to the average (outscoring only the media lites). Household centrality of TV is high in this group and 90 percent have a TV in their bedroom. The vast majority in this group are teenagers (who typically have more social and scholastic demands on their time than those younger), which likely explains their relative indifference to media.

The final two groups are more similar to one another than the pairs described so far, and yet fundamental differences exist between them. The *interactors* (16% of the sample) are distinguished by their high esteem for computers and their high access to computers and the Internet in the home. High in both computer and print media use, they are below average in exposure to TV and live mostly in households relatively low in television centrality. The parents of these children are among the most educated and have high income levels. Finally, the group known as the *restricteds* (15%) spends lower than average amounts of time with media and lives in environments with both the strictest rules and the least likelihood to have the television on at all times. Media in their bedrooms is average whereas media access in their homes in general is high. Again, parental education and household income are high in this group, and the group contains slightly more boys and more 11- to 14-year-olds than the other groups.

The identification of clusters of respondents who have media-related behavioral patterns and household environments in common exemplifies both the considerable variation and substantial uniformities based on amount of use and access. The six groups go well beyond averages in depicting media use among the nation's young. The Roberts and Foehr typology also adds a third dimension—personal preference. For example, the *vidkids* can fairly be characterized as fans of television and the *indifferents* equally fairly can be said to prefer other activities to media use. Thus, access is qualified by taste, and the two together are represented by the amount of time spent with media.

On the whole, daily media exposure is massive, and extraordinarily extensive. The figures become only slightly less astounding by taking into account simultaneous media use. Television continues to occupy the largest portion of the daily media budget by a clear margin for almost every demographic category and each of the six groups making up the media typology. It is rivaled only by audio media during the late teen years in terms of daily allocation of time. Interactive media use is growing and beginning to account for substantial amounts of time in the typical youngster's day, and newer ways to use the Internet (such as instant messaging and, more recently, YouTube and MySpace) are proving to be quite attractive. Video game use is on the rise but claims of immense appeal apply mainly to boys. Print media exposure is by no means dormant. Most young people read for pleasure at least a bit every day. Time spent with books occurs daily for a large majority of toddlers and preschoolers. The typical American household has access to a wide range of media. Substantial numbers of all young people varying in age from six months to 18 years have media in their own bedrooms, and the presence of media of one's own is associated with heavier levels of media use. Households vary according to the centrality of television, and this variation is associated with significant differences in use of other media as well. Thus, media centrality is the more accurate concept at this point in time.

THE EXTRAORDINARY APPEAL OF SCREEN MEDIA

Children and teenagers by a dramatically wide margin allocate more time to television than to any other medium. This is made amply clear by the strong dominance of television within each of the six clusters representing greater or lesser use of different media (see Chapter I). Even those who rank highest in their esteem for other media spend the majority of their time using media with television. This is strong testimony on behalf of the features that make the medium attractive: ease of access, content mostly undemanding in regard to affect or cognitive processing, and great diversity—if within a limited range of popular fare.

The many hours spent each week with television—and other screen media—by most young people can be assigned meaning only with knowledge of the viewing experience. Viewing encompasses every type of response that people make to media—"browse, momentarily ignore, assemble into a mosaic of contrasting bits, passingly follow, attentively consume" (Comstock & Scharrer, 1999, p. 61) and can be defined as "a discontinuous, often interrupted, and frequently nonexclusive activity for which a measure in hours and minutes serves only as the outer boundary of possible attention" to the screen (Comstock, Chaffee, Katzman, McCombs & Roberts, 1978, pp. 146–147).

This description applies to television more than other screen media because of the greater interest, more focused attention, and higher degree of selectivity often associated with the latter. The concept of viewing as a pastiche open to sudden changes is in accord with the normative definition of television viewing exemplified by the readiness of audience members to describe themselves as viewing while confessing that they were not paying full attention (Comstock & Scharrer, 1999; Hopkins & Mullis, 1985), as well as with the empirical documentation of divided attention by time-lapse photography (Allen, 1965) and the videotaping of those viewing (Anderson, Lorch, Field, Collins & Nathan, 1986; Bechtel, Achelpohl & Akers, 1972). We cover five topics: purposes and motives; modes of response; developmental factors; competing activities; and social circumstances of viewing.

I. PURPOSES AND MOTIVES OF TELEVISION VIEWING

We begin with the distinction between ritualistic and instrumental viewing (Rubin, 1983, 1984). We then turn to the three principal gratifications of attending to the screen—escape, social comparison, and awareness (Comstock & Scharrer, 1999).

A. Ritualistic versus Instrumental Viewing

The labels ritualistic and instrumental neatly capture both much of television viewing at any given moment and the behavior typical of individuals among teenagers and adults. They also apply to much of children's viewing, although it is certainly the case that children progress through a number of changes in their disposition toward the medium before their viewing completely matches that of those older.

The distinguishing factor is the degree to which viewing can be attributed to the content of a specific program. The guiding motive of ritualistic viewing is exposure to television. Gratifications are then maximized by choosing the most attractive program among the available options. In contrast, instrumental viewing is driven by content, with gratification derived from attending to a specific program. Thus, programs always have an important role, but are somewhat subordinate in ritualistic viewing. Correlates of regular ritualistic viewing are greater amounts of television use and a preference for content that is affectively and cognitively undemanding. Correlates of regular instrumental viewing on the part of individuals are a preference for programs that strongly arouse the interest of the viewer and lesser overall exposure. Instrumental viewing represents greater selectivity. The majority of viewing is ritualistic; our estimate (Comstock & Scharrer, 1999) is that as much as four-fifths of viewing is ritualistic.

Most of children's viewing is ritualistic. An example is the many hours of passing attention they give to general audience programming, for most of children's viewing is not of programs designed for them.

Displaying some interest in what is on the screen was recorded long ago as beginning as early as six months (Hollenbeck & Slaby, 1979), but this is a matter of attending to imagery and color rather than following a narrative. By the time regular viewing begins between the ages of two and three, an instrumental element enters with exposure to programs designed for very young viewers, such as *Teletubbies*. Content takes on importance. Socialization to use television efficiently—in the sense of varying attention with the degree of narrative interest—has begun.

Children bring a great deal of enthusiasm to their favorite programs and characters, but they are also highly selective in the allocation of this enthusiasm. For example, Argenta, Stoneman, and Brody (1986) observed that among experimental subjects of preschool age the "image of children 'mesmerized' in front of the television set, forsaking social interaction and active involvement with their object environment, held true for only one type of programming, namely cartoons" (p. 370). *Sesame Street* and situation comedies were parsed with comparative nonchalance. The proportion of time that eyes are on the screen is among the highest for children's programs across all programming genres (Bechtel, Achelpohl & Akers, 1972), and thus attending to children's programs by young viewers can be said to be an example of instrumental viewing.

B. Gratifications for Viewing

Viewing at all ages has the same three motives. They are: (a) escape, in the sense of diversion and flight from less pleasant thoughts and experiences; (b) surveying characters, events, and personalities on behalf of social comparison, in order to evaluate personal attributes and, in the case of young viewers, to better fashion a persona; and (c) keeping abreast of the world, which in this instance is represented by the programming on television and the way stories are told and events depicted on the screen as well as by events covered by television news and sports.

Escape is paramount. The data are clear. Among children as well as those older, stress in a variety of guises predicts greater viewing or favorability toward television (Anderson, Collins, Schmitt & Jacobvitz, 1996; Canary & Spitsberg, 1993; Kubey & Csikszentmihalyi, 1990; Maccoby, 1954; Potts & Sanchez, 1994). Our interpretation is that the experience of attending to the screen, however passingly, ameliorates this noxious circumstance. Pleasure and relaxation are also among the reasons for viewing most frequently cited by adults (Albarran & Umphrey, 1993; Bower, 1985). For young and old, viewing is a way of circumventing anxiety and outmaneuvering boredom.

However, social comparison and keeping abreast are not unimportant. The clearest evidence on behalf of social comparison, beyond the particular popularity among young women of talk shows whose guests recount forays of fashion, appearance, and sex (Hamilton, 1998), is the decided tendency for viewers to pay more attention to those on the screen who are in some way like themselves. This holds true for each of the major demographics: race (Comstock, 1991a), age (Harwood, 1997), and gender (Maccoby & Wilson, 1957; Maccoby, Wilson & Burton, 1958; Sprafkin & Liebert, 1978). The evidence on behalf of keeping abreast comes from several sources. There is the obvious attention by some adults and teenagers to the news. In addition, adults frequently cite learning something as a reason for viewing although they are not specifically referring to educational programs, documentaries, or news (Albarran & Umphrey, 1993; Bower, 1985). This is an orientation arguably shared by those younger. Adults also frequently express pleasure over and interest in the quality—style, vividness, compelling narrative, exciting film, interesting personages—of television's depictions (Levy, 1978; Neuman, 1982). This is another orientation arguably shared by those younger.

Typically, viewing by children and teenagers as well as by those older represents low involvement as exemplified by ritualistic viewing. However, as exemplified by programs designed for them, viewing by the young occasionally will represent the instrumental pursuit of pleasures of particular interest and attraction.

Finally, there is the division of motives exemplified by learning about newsworthy events and vicariously participating in the process of news-gathering and reporting—exciting imagery, dangerous circumstances, lurid settings, and favorite newscasters, including the ever-popular weather people (Levy, 1978). This division extends to all of television. Viewers watch to learn about what's going on and about the medium itself. Keeping abreast is an amalgam of news and reporting and trends and people in drama and entertainment.

II. MODES OF RESPONSE

Ritualistic viewing is defined by three modes of response that come to typify viewing as children mature. They are characteristic of teenage and adult viewing, and frequent throughout childhood. They are content indifference where the medium is primary, low involvement, and monitoring. We then introduce the concept of equilibrium to describe the relationship between programming and audience attention at both individual and aggregate or societal levels.

A. Content Indifference

The primacy of the gratifications of the medium rather than the plea-sures of a specific program in attracting viewers is well documented (Comstock & Scharrer, 1999). There are six strands to the evidence.

The first is the predominance of the two-step decision process in choosing programs (Barwise, Ehrenberg & Goodhardt, 1982). Typically, the initial step is deciding whether or not to view television. The sec-ond step is to select the most satisfying program from the available options. The decision to view is less often driven by the programs avail-able than the availability of television.

The second is the similarity uncovered in amount of household tele-vision use in urban areas worldwide despite huge differences in cul-tures, tastes, availability of programming, and the regulatory mecha-nisms governing the medium. This extraordinary phenomenon first emerged in 12-nation UNESCO time-use data from the mid-1960s in which the average amounts of viewing by set owners typically differed from one another by only a few percentage points in cities across the globe—the United States, eastern and western Europe, the former USSR, and Latin America (Comstock, 1991; Robinson, 1972; Robinson & Converse, 1972). Those who owned sets had them turned on for about the same number of minutes each day regardless of the programs. More recently, similar data have been produced on the viewing of chil-dren and teenagers across different societies (Livingstone, 2001; von Feilitzen & Carlsson, 1999).

The third is the powerful role of time available in shaping the view-ing of individuals. Viewing by every demographic segment, including children and teenagers, varies across the day, the week, the season, and a lifetime contingent on the availability of members of a demographic category to become part of the audience (Comstock & Scharrer, 1999; Webster & Phalen, 1997). Thus, the two-step decision process mirrors the predominance of the opportunity to view rather than the search for specific content in the decision to view television. Availability to view is a major determinant of individual viewing regardless of the programs available.

The fourth is the modest figures for repeat viewing—attending to the same program seen the previous day or week. The average is about 40 percent for adults and fewer than 30 percent for those aged two to 11 and 12 to 17 (Barwise, 1986; Barwise, Ehrenberg & Goodhardt, 1982). When viewing at a particular time, young and old alike almost always choose the same option. Thus, low levels of average repeat viewing mean that other activities that are preferable, obligatory, or necessary have supplanted the preferred program.

We do not argue that there are no programs that attract much higher than average levels of repeat viewing. The data indicate that about one out of five programs may attain the status of a favorite that challenges the dominance of time available and other activities. These favored programs will register repeat viewing rates that are 40 to 50 percent higher than the average. However, they are exceptions. Typically, the preferred program at a given time attracts those who already would have been in the audience and does not lead loyal fans to make a special effort not to miss the program.

The fifth is the poor record of predicting viewing from viewer preferences. For example, many years ago Frank and Greenberg (1980) divided a national probability sample of about 2500 persons aged 13 and older into 14 segments based on 18 interests (e.g., "comprehensive news and information," "professional sports," "investments," etc.). The 14 segments differed widely in average age, proportion of male to female, socioeconomic status, and other characteristics. They also differed widely in program preferences. Yet, less than 10 percent of the variation in the viewing of 19 categories of programs was statistically predictable from the data on interests and demographics.

Finally, the surprising—in fact, rather startling—data on the hereditary foundation for some of television viewing also disabuses us of the belief that the content of specific programs fully explains viewing. Using the accepted methodology to distinguish between environmental and inherited bases of behavior, Plomin, Corley, DeFries, and Fulker (1990) found in a sample of 220 three-, four-, and five-year-olds, their siblings, and natural and adoptive parents that there were both significant and substantial contributions by environmental factors and by genetic inheritance to amount of viewing. Our speculation (Comstock & Scharrer, 1999) was that the root cause was inherited differences in susceptibility—the pleasures delivered by—alpha waves, or right brain processing, which generally are acknowledged as representative of the nonverbal, noncritical, and nonanalytic reception typical of much viewing (Krugman, 1971; Rothschild, Thorson, Reeves, Hirsch & Goldstein, 1986). Some (Prescott, Johnson & Mc-Ardle, 1991) have dismissed these Plomin data as a peculiarity without theoretical significance. In contrast, we believe they fit nicely with other data supportive of content indifference, and in particular the multination time-use patterns of similarity in amount of television use across societies vastly different in culture, channel availability, and program content.

The picture depicted by the data is one of primacy for the medium rather than specific programs. At all ages, there nevertheless will be programs that are unusually popular and have much higher than average repeat viewing rates. And the economic health of competing broadcast and cable channels rests on program popularity, which comes to the forefront in the second step of the two-part decision process. At this second juncture, preferences matter both for the industry and the viewer. But the modest role for preferences in predicting viewing means that it is not the programs but the medium and the opportunity to view that create the audience.

B. Low Involvement

Two bodies of data lead to the conclusion that television typically is a medium of low involvement. One consists of surveys of what people have to say about the medium. The other is made up of recordings or reports of the behavior of people while viewing.

Viewers most of the time are only passingly involved in what they are watching. When large national samples have been asked about their viewing the previous night (Bower, 1985; Lo Sciuto, 1972), few mention a specific program, not many thought what they had viewed had been particularly meritorious, few can accurately recall the principal plot elements of programs they say they have watched, and about a third viewed something chosen by someone else in the household.

Studies of behavior while viewing document that attention typically is divided and far from focused. For example, the chronicling of two dozen families found that more than half of adults did not give full attention to programs they considered themselves as viewing (Hopkins & Mullis, 1985), while time lapse photography (Allen, 1965) and the videotaping of viewers (Anderson, Lorch, Field, Collins & Nathan, 1986; Bechtel, Achelpohl & Akers, 1972) record that about 40 percent of the time audience members are not watching the screen and quite often there is no one in the room where a television set is operating.

C. Monitoring less versus Viewing

Viewing is the common term for attending to television, but a more accurate term is *monitoring*. Viewers only pay enough attention to comprehend—to their satisfaction—the unfolding narrative. Depictions, portrayals, events, and exchanges of particular interest are watched, and watching is a function of the cues that signal their worthiness for attention.

The process has been examined only among young children, but the evidence in support of low involvement suggests that monitoring is also an apt term for adult attention to the medium. There are three types of cues that guide attention to the screen (Anderson & Lorch, 1983; Bryant, Zillman & Brown, 1983; Collins, 1981; Huston &

Wright, 1989; Krull, 1983; Lorch, Anderson & Levin, 1979): two are television-based and one is a function of the social milieu that accompanies attending to the set. Audio directs attention to the set when sound and music indicate that something important, interesting, or exciting is about to occur. Visual imagery that promises excitement or the salving of curiosity similarly increases the likelihood of attending to the screen. These television-based responses are mediated partially by the perceptual dependence that occurs when attending to a television screen (Anderson & Lorch, 1983), with attention becoming more likely as length of prior attention increases (see Figure 2.1)—a

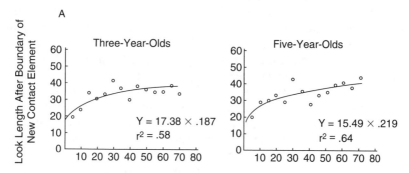

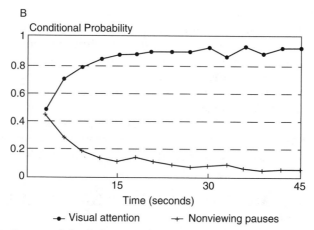

Fig. 2.1 Perceptual dependence at three ages. Adapted from Anderson, D. R. & Lorch, E. P. (1983). Looking at television: Action or reaction. In J. Bryant & D. R. Anderson (Eds.), *Children's understanding of television: Research on attention and comprehension* (pp. 1–34). New York: Academic Press.

phenomenon that occurs not only among the very young (three- and five-year olds) but among young adults (college students). The third cue is the degree to which one or more others in the room are attending to the screen or directing their attention elsewhere. Thus, attention to the screen is guided by audio, visual, and social signals that attest to the value of paying attention.

D. Equilibrium: Understanding versus Inattention

This pattern represents two distinct but related types of equilibrium. At the individual level, the desire to understand what is transpiring on the screen is balanced by the inattention that the redundancy of many television narratives makes possible without loss of comprehension of what is taking place. In fact, episodic programming—news, sports, and commercials—and formulaic storytelling such as soap opera suffer the lowest levels of eye contact (Bechtel, Achelpohl & Akers, 1972), for in none of these instances is expected future satisfaction diminished by past or present inattention. Comprehension drives attention (viewers try to make sense of what is on the screen), whereas the affectively and cognitively undemanding nature of television makes monitoring sufficient to the task (most of the time television doesn't require much effort to achieve comprehension).

At the aggregate or societal level, the affectively and cognitively undemanding programming makes possible the large audiences and many hours per week that many spend with television. The degree of attentiveness that children and teenagers, as well as adults, can give to a television set is limited. Programming that was more demanding would interfere with household tasks (in the case of teenagers and adults) and with the play that accompanies children's television use when the programming is not animated cartoons designed for them. The content maximizes audience size, and the sporadic attention maximizes the time that members of the audience can spend with the medium. The economic success of television that is financed by advertising thus rests on not asking very much of audiences, for the greater the number of hours that viewers spend with the medium the larger and more lucrative the market for the sale of commercials.

III. DEVELOPMENTAL FACTORS THAT INFLUENCE VIEWING

Content indifference, low involvement, and monitoring become typical of most viewing by the age of 12. By then, children essentially have matured into adult viewers in regard to their disposition toward the television set. They will still miss certain subtleties and nuances of some programs and movies aimed at adults because their sophistication in regard to morals and values will still be somewhat undeveloped (Kohlberg, 1984). In effect, they learn to use the medium, and each progressive stage of cognitive development provides greater mastery of the medium and its content. We pursue our theme of cognitive stages for two topics: preferences and reactions to the screen.

A. Viewing Preferences of Children and Teenagers

The program preferences of children and teenagers can be succinctly described as a function of age, sex, socioeconomic status, and ethnicity. The popularity of specific programs is typically transitory; fashion rules as television executives (and producers and writers) mimic new shows with high ratings and shares. Nevertheless, there certainly have been long-running favorites (including the aptly named *Road Runner*) and some characters with a claim to permanent appeal (some of the Disney cast, for example). Conversely, genres are quite stable; the programs that children and teenagers prefer will change because the programming schedule changes, but much the same features will continue to govern their preferences.

When regular viewing begins between the ages of two and three (Hollenbeck & Slaby, 1979), narrative satisfactions are provided only by the increasing but small number of programs and software specifically designed for young children. Nevertheless, Meltzoff (1988) demonstrated experimentally that if what they see on the screen is within their physical capability those as young as 12 and 24 months can imitate what they have seen and will retain this ability for as long as 24 hours after exposure. Thus, even at this early age they can internalize what they have seen, with the unavoidable conclusion that some comprehension of what has been presented on the screen begins quite early.

1. Three-phase Model   The three-phase model proposed by Wolfe and Fiske (1954) in their pretelevision examination of children's enthusiasm for comic books is applicable to the electronic medium. The array of media has changed dramatically, and with it the allocation of time to media. Programs have changed, so what children watch has changed. However, young people have not changed in their core interests and cognitive capabilities as they mature. Thus, broad patterns remain stable while specifics shift continuously. However, if tastes have remained relatively stable, skills employed in using media have changed. Even young children use computers and program a DVR or VCR. Wolfe and

Fiske's description of a "fuzzy animal" period followed by a "super-hero" phase approximates the shift from *Sesame Street* and animal cartoons (which usually appear earlier on Saturday mornings when younger children make up a greater proportion of the audience) to animated action adventure later in the morning (when the proportion of older children has increased). Their final stage of "realistic" content parallels the desertion of the Saturday morning audience by many preteens and teenagers as they become principally consumers of general audience programming.

Wolfe and Fiske asserted that children who became blocked at the superhero phase because of their need to follow a "perfect father figure" and for whom comics became a "religion" or opiate were "maladjusted." Although the language betrays an allegiance to psychoanalytic theory, the conclusion that deep involvement in an easily accessible pictorial medium signals some difficulty in growing up is well-supported. We have already seen, in our rationale for assigning escape the paramount place among motives for viewing, that stress predicts greater consumption of or affinity for television.

Very early in the history of the medium, Maccoby (1954, 1964) concluded from her observation of elementary school children that consumption of atypically large amounts of television often was a symptom of conflicts with parents or peers. Later, Tangney (1988) found, among more than 100 Los Angeles children in the fourth through sixth grades, that heavy viewing of fantasy and animated cartoons was more frequent when parents were low in empathy, sensitivity, and flexibility in expectations about the roles a child might assume. Ekblad (1986) similarly found in Beijing that greater television viewing by children of primary school age was a correlate of estrangement from the family. Morgan, Alexander, Shanahan, and Harris (1990) attributed greater VCR use among several hundred teenagers to chronic conflict with parents. Thus, the link between maladjustment and an easily accessible pictorial medium is robust across time, ages, cultures, and technology.

2. Cognitive Stages and Media Use   This three-phase pattern in media use is consistent with the stages of cognitive development proposed by Piaget (Piaget, 1971; Piaget & Inhelder, 1969) and adapted by Acuff (1997) and John (1999) to describe the changing responses of young people to media, sometimes with minor changes in the age brackets to better fit behavior in regard to the media. These stages direct the enthusiasms and tastes expressed in viewing television, using computer software, and attending to other media. Each stage is essentially a band that represents certain competencies and limitations in the ability of the young person to think about the world, understand human behavior, and solve problems. They are somewhat imprecisely partitioned by age. Individuals differ in their rates of cognitive development. Nevertheless, the stages constitute stable, major steps of increasing proficiency in cognitive ability in the transition from infancy to young adulthood. The stage of cognitive development establishes a framework of possibilities and limitations. Then the availability of options for entertainment and information orchestrates attention as young media users choose among them. Options continually expand, and the rewards and temptations offered by the media grow ever richer, as abandoned choices will remain within the realm of comprehension and can always be reinstated in favor.

The first of these stages has been labelled the *sensorimotor*, between ages zero and about two. The infant resolves a series of fundamental challenges: the imitation of physical movements (which will lead the child to recognize that he or she has something in common with others); the understanding that people and objects are permanent and constant; distinguishing among those in the environment, such as mothers and fathers and siblings; and, by the end of the period, problem solving. Attention is usually sporadic and diffuse, but an object of high interest, such as a puppy, may receive intense, focused attention. There is a high need for nurturing and security, and little interest in television, software, or other media.

The use of the medium of television as a model for behavior nevertheless has begun. Meltzoff (2005) argues that this process of imitation—which draws on media as well as live models, such as a mother or father—is a crucial part of establishing the self, a sense of similarity to others (and with this, the possibility of empathy), as well as the fact of individuation. The infant in the course of imitating discovers that he or she is behaving like someone else. The infant intuits that what he or she is experiencing matches what another is experiencing. This promotes the sense of a common bond and shared experience. The "I" and the "other" become recognizable and meaningful through what they share in this social exchange. The particular role of television in this process at this early stage is trivial, for there is nothing that would not be accomplished by reliance solely on live models. However, it initiates what in later years will make television, movies, and other media important in the means by which individuals establish an identity.

The foundation for an interest in media has been established. The *preoperational* stage between ages of about three and seven embraces regular attention to television, which begins between the ages of two and three. This stage is marked by prelogical thought; intuitive, bipolar decisionmaking; the further imitating of models, including the characters and personages seen on the television screen; self-centered and egotistical behavior and thought; and simple, direct desires. Tastes change sharply and rapidly as increasing cognitive capacity leads to a more differentiated, more extensive, more self-confident perception of the world. Initially, the preoccupation with security leads to a preference for furry animals in television programming, and particularly those without teeth or sharp claws—appendages that might compromise personal well-being. This attraction to animals soon translates into a fascination for those with considerably wider and considerably less benign repertoires—the acerbic and incorrigible "Bugs Bunny," for example. As this stage advances, four aspects of programming govern attention to the screen (Acuff, 1997):

- There is a preoccupation with physical power and the ability to perform extraordinary feats and vanquish enemies; thus, the popularity of superheroes.
- There is also, and primarily among males, an attraction to villains who challenge and mock order and peace; this reflects the impulsivity of this early stage of development.
- There is an attraction to exaggerated animation—boldly drawn monsters, dragons, and out-sized characters—and, again primarily among males, high technology in weapons and transportation; the love of animation is a hallmark of this age group that soon will be abandoned.
- Finally, there is a fascination with transformations, whether from one physical appearance to another or from one function or purpose to another (such as a toy that can be a robot, vehicle, or weapon); this reflects the lack of linear logic during this phase of development that gives these swift and ready changes a certain aura of magic and wizardry as well as a satisfying trumping of physical limits. By the end of the preoperational stage, cartoons remain popular but superheroes have somewhat displaced aggressive animals, situation comedies are becoming popular, and programs aimed at young children have been discarded.

When we turn to data on specific preferences, we must distinguish between favorites and viewing. The former represents affection and approval; the latter, exposure within the constraints of time available and available options. In the present context, favorites are of primary interest because we are concerned with the development of tastes and attraction rather than the recording of programming attended to.

The data of Lyle and Hoffman (1972a, 1972b) who focused on the naming of favorite programs, serve our purpose well. Although collected almost 40 years ago, the data are only out-of-date for specific programs and not for trends in preferences for types of content as children mature. They interviewed about 160 three-, four-, and five-year-old children in a Los Angeles suburb. Almost 90 percent named a favorite, with only about 7 percent not understanding the question. Although one program was named by one out of four children (*The Flintstones*, an animated Hanna-Barbera sitcom set in the Pleistocene era), a wide range of programs falling into eight other categories were named. The sensitivity of popularity to maturational change was dramatically exemplified by the sharp decline in those naming *Sesame Street* (from 30 to 13%) between the ages of three and five. The rise over the same age range in those naming *The Flintstones*, with only 11 percent citing it at age three and 36 percent doing so at age five, again displays the discrimination that marks children's preferences as a function of age and the associated stage of cognitive development.

In contrast, Huston, Wright, Rice, Kerkman and St. Peters (1990) focused on viewing. Thus, tastes and attraction are somewhat compromised by the outcomes representing what the children viewed. They collected data on about 325 Topeka children beginning at ages three and five over a two-year period, resulting in measures of viewing at three ages—three, four, and five, and five, six, and seven. Viewing of *Sesame Street* reached a peak at age four and thereafter declined precipitously. This is consistent with the data of Lyle and Hoffman (1972a), who reported that not enough children to count named *Sesame Street* when they collected favorite program data from first graders. Viewing was greater when encouraged by parents or, among older children, when younger siblings were viewers; thus, social circumstances may play a role in what is viewed. The authors emphasize perceived age appropriateness and time available to view as explanations. We agree that social influences would play a large role, but suspect that a failure to cognitively engage the older children also was a factor. The viewing of situation comedies and animated cartoons rose through age five, then remained at about the same level through age seven.

Thus, selectivity in regard to programs begins very early. By age three, about 80 percent of those interviewed by Lyle and Hoffman understood the concept of "favorite" and had one; by age five, this was almost universal (only 3% at that age said they did not understand the question). There is some individual variation in preferences but bold trends by age are clearly distinguishable among young children.

The *concrete operational* stage between the ages of about eight and 12 marks a crucial boundary. The intuitive, bipolar, egotistical thinking of the preoperational stage is now largely deserted in favor of logical, rational thought and greater discrimination in tastes and preferences. The left brain undergoes substantial development, making linear thinking possible. Toys and other objects were accumulated during the preoperational stage. Now they are often thoughtfully collected. Moral thinking shifts from a rigid sense of right and wrong derived from what parents and, in the media, superheroes say and do toward greater flexibility, and some questioning of authority—although for the most part conformity to the wishes of parents and the behavior of peers is the norm.

Behavior in regard to television undergoes profound changes. Cartoons remain popular at the beginning but by the end of this stage few will hold them in high regard. The enhanced cognitive capacity makes possible the understanding of more complex plots and more involved storytelling and there is a demand for realistic programming instead of the fantasy and cartoons in favor only a few years earlier. This is initially expressed in the increased attractiveness of situation comedies, but later this search for a representative slice of the real world will lead to the greater viewing of dramas, reality shows, the talk shows favored by young women, and general audience programming. By the end of this stage at about age 12, childhood viewing will have been left behind.

Lyle and Hoffman (1972a) employed questionnaires to obtain favorite program data from about 1,600 first-, sixth-, and tenth-grade pupils in the Los Angeles area. First graders mostly named situation comedies and cartoons, with the former favored by about a two-to-one ratio (47 vs. 24%). Sixth graders largely replaced the cartoons with action-adventure and westerns but added music and variety—a category represented today by MTV. First, sixth, and tenth graders all were especially attracted to programs with characters their own age, although during the concrete operational stage there also is a readiness to identify with those slightly older because of their higher status and wider latitude of behavior.

The concepts of similarity and wishful thinking proposed by Feilitzen and Linne (1975) help explain the tides of preference across the preoperational and concrete operational stages. Similarity refers to a preference for characters like oneself. Wishful thinking refers to a preference for characters the viewer would like to resemble. The authors argue that the former is particularly frequent among younger children, whereas the latter increases with age. They suggest that identification with furry, cute animals unequipped with threatening claws or teeth represents similarity because the portrayed animals have a dependent relationship with humans analogous to that of the child with parents or caregivers. They also insightfully suggest that when older children engage in similarity identification, they prefer characters somewhat older than themselves and argue that age eight is the point of transition from a preference for children's programming and characters like themselves to a preference for general audience programming, wishful identification, and similarity identification with those older.

We concur in the broad strokes of this portrait, but not with certain specifics. The data just reviewed makes it clear that similarity identification—at least, that not confined to age—beyond age eight is not limited to those older (although that will often be the case because general audience programming will offer few same-age characters), and a turning toward general audience programming—in particular, situation comedies—occurs somewhat earlier. We would also argue that identification with others who are older in age or different in other characteristics will occur as soon as the child is able to recognize or infer higher status (Comstock, 1991), which presumably was the basis for the shift toward wishful identification proposed by Feilitzen and Linne. Thus, we believe a dual process of similarity and wishful identification is pervasive throughout childhood except during the earliest years when the former would predominate.

We insert at this point a line from a highly unlikely source, Olivier Todd's (2005) biography of Malraux, because of its extraordinary aptness: "I am another, and the others are me" (p. 205). A major preoccupation of this life of the novelist, adventurer, soldier (if among irregular forces), and minister of culture is the dexterity with which he could borrow from the lives of others. Although enacted upon an admittedly grand stage (literature, art, diplomacy, and war), our interest is in the point that a life may be shaped in part by those who can be emulated. In the mundane world of modern everyday existence, the media, and particularly television and films, are major sources of such examples. The imitation that Meltzoff (1988) recorded as occurring as early as the first and second years of life becomes, as young people grow older, a significant means by which individuals adopt successful or at least pleasing strategies for presenting themselves to the world as they wish to be perceived and understood.

The fourth and final stage is the *formal operational*, beginning at about age 13. However, this adolescent period requires a second stage between the ages of about 16 and 19 to fully represent the transition between childhood and adulthood (Kohlberg, 1981). Abstract thought is now possible.

Identity becomes a primary concern. The adherence to group norms becomes a major factor with individuals aligning themselves with in-groups and emphasizing distance from out-groups. Models, including those on television screens, have been imitated since the beginning of infancy, and they have continued to be imitated and emulated throughout the progression of cognitive stages (Bandura, 1986). The subtle change that enters at this point is that this imitation and emulation now serves a motivated formulation of the self. These factors—the increased cognitive capacity and the process of achieving an identity that will provide an entry to adulthood and cast off childhood—lead to a new taste for adult entertainment, much more complicated plots, more extended storylines, and nuances beyond the programs popular during the formal operational stage.

For example, in the Lyle and Hoffman questionnaire data, those in the tenth grade often named the adult format of music and variety while still naming action-adventure and situation comedies (the specific programs presumably would have matched these escalating criteria). As Acuff (1997) points out, these tastes have been nurtured by increasing visual and narrative complexity, MTV, television commercials, and episodic dramas (such as *NYPD Blue*) during the concrete operational stage. Social comparison has always had some role in viewing, and became particularly prominent during the concrete operational stage. Now it moves to the forefront as young viewers seek examples that they use in conceiving of and constructing a satisfying identity. This route branches again into similarity and wishful identification. In the first, there is an increased interest in programs, usually situation comedies, that deal with the problems of teenagers. There are the perennial plot elements: the sought-after friend of the opposite sex; the need to raise money for a special project; the scheme that has gone wrong, with behavior that transgresses a parental rule; the big dance or school election, where everything must go right but nothing at the moment seems to. In the second, there is an increased interest in adults who face various trials and tribulations in achieving their goals, and typically exhibit a variety of admirable traits. In the early part of adolescence, this represents an exchange of the superhero of the past for a more realistic if rather accomplished protagonist.

Later, between the ages of 16 and 19, there is greater interest in subtle, involved, complex and often somewhat ambiguous dramas—in terms of right and wrong. This is what Kohlberg (1981) designated the final *autonomous* stage of moral development (the early stages essentially parallel those of Piaget). Between the ages of 13 and 15, right and wrong became more open to interpretation, the authority embodied by parents, teachers, and other prominent adults became open to some challenge, and the grayness of certain kinds of conduct and speech became apparent. Between the ages of 16 and 19, moral thinking becomes more independent and nuanced. Multiple perspectives on the same issue become recognized. The assumption of a role—rebel, patriot, advocate—cast by the abstract principles of justice and right becomes possible. Tastes and preferences as a consequence become wider. Action-adventure and situation comedies remain among favorites, but there is also an interest in material that is more challenging and now especially pertinent, such as comedies that depict adult romance, its associated perils and the establishing of personal relationships, and material that serves wishful identification focused on acting in authentic adherence to the concept that has developed of oneself.

3. Gender, Race, and Socioeconomic Status   Gender plays an important role. Although one might anticipate a certain unisex quality to preferences in the fuzzy animal stage, in fact gender-related differences appear extremely early. For example, Lyle and Hoffman (1972b) in their interviews with three-, four-, and five-year-olds, found that overall twice as many girls as boys named *The Flintstones* as their favorite (39 versus 19%), and boys were three times as likely to name a violent cartoon (17 versus 5%).

We have observed that viewers give more attention to those on the television screen in some way like themselves. This has been recorded for age, gender, and race. Similarly, Maccoby and Wilson (1957), among seventh graders, and Maccoby, Wilson, and Burton (1958), among college students, found more involvement with movie characters of the same sex, which implies a preference for same-sex portrayals. Two decades later, Sprafkin and Liebert (1978) found that boys and girls chose to view same-sex portrayals in which sex roles were clearly conventional, and more than 80 percent of their sample named same-sex characters as their favorites.

This same-sex preference, apparently exaggerated by the stereotypic, is a phenomenon attributable to the development of convictions about gender identity, stability or constancy, and consistency across modes of behavior and thought. Slaby and Frey (1975) found such convictions predictive of attention to males and females in televised portrayals by boys and girls between the ages of three and about five, and that these convictions develop during this stage in that order—first identity; second, constancy; and third, consistency. By five or six, the triumvirate are in place. The progression derives from the degree of simple ego involvement ("I'm a girl"; "I'll always be a girl"; "I always behave as a girl"), the complexity of the concepts (me; always me; me in all things), and social utility (the expectations of others about behavior that is gender-specific increases with age, and behavior perceived as gender-appropriate increasingly will be rewarded and prove efficacious). The result is that young children who are male prefer activities perceived as male and those who are female prefer those perceived as female, and both shun those perceived as appropriate to the opposite sex. For example, Ruble, Balaban, and Cooper (1981) found among four- to six-year-olds that exposure to a television commercial linking play with gender-neutral toys to one or another of the sexes led to a decided preference for a toy among those of the same sex and avoidance of a toy by those of the opposite sex. Recall similarly is greater for behavior of those of the same sex (Koblinski, Cruse, & Sugawara, 1978). Such gender-based predilections and antipathies are lifelong, although they will become mitigated by experience and advancement to higher stages of cognitive development.

Race and socioeconomic status also make a difference (Comstock & Cobbey, 1979). Lyle and Hoffman (1972a) found Black children among their first, sixth, and tenth graders were particularly attracted to programs with Black characters. Liss (1981) found that third-grade children chose to view programs featuring characters of the same race, and Dates (1980) found that while Black and White teenagers did not differ in viewing selected situation comedies with all-White casts, the Blacks were much more likely to view those with Black characters and to identify, to a greater degree than Whites, with such characters. Surlin and Dominick (1970), in a survey of about 200 high school students, found that programs featuring families were preferred more by teenagers who were Black or who were from lower income households, and that Black teenagers had a much lower preference for variety programs (which at the time would have almost exclusively featured White performers). Maccoby and Wilson (1957) found that identification was more likely with a character who had status to which the viewer aspired than one that approximated the viewer's own.

Several investigations have reported that among older children and teenagers, higher socioeconomic status was directly associated with exposure to more serious forms of entertainment, arts programming, and informational programming (California Assessment Program, 1982; Frank & Greenberg, 1980; Lyle & Hoffman, 1972a). These findings again attest to the major roles of similarity and wishful identification, as well as identifying the milieu established by parents with higher levels of education as a factor in directing young viewers toward more affectively and cognitively demanding programs.

The degree to which expressed preferences are represented in actual viewing is surprisingly modest. The sizable average amount of viewing, content indifference, and the preeminence of time available make program favorites poor predictors of behavior. This remains largely true despite the near-ubiquity of in-home recording and playback devices—VCRs, DVDs, and DVRs—because of the comparative convenience of relying on real-time offerings (Comstock & Scharrer, 1999). When people view substantial amounts of television, favorites and even favorite genres can only occupy a small to moderate place. Because amount of television viewing is inversely associated with socioeconomic strata (Comstock et al., 1978), this becomes increasingly so as one descends the socioeconomic scale. This holds for children and teenagers as well as adults. McLeon, Atkin, and Chaffee (1972a, 1972b), for example, report only a small correlation among their teenage sample between naming violent programs as favorites and overall exposure to violent programming. Similarly, it will be recalled that Frank and Greenberg (1980) in their segmentation of the television audience using a national sample of those 13 and older (and thus including teenagers) could explain less than 10 percent of the variance in the viewing of 19 different genres on the basis of interests and demographics that varied widely and strongly across 14 segments.

4. Perceptual Filters   Children are reputed to be great fans of favored programs and characters, and there is no reason to ignore the testimony of the shelves and stacks in stores of toys, clothing, and paraphernalia representing television characters. These enthusiasms typically shift with changes in cognitive development. However, some characters remain popular across cognitive stages. This is a function of the ability of a character to assume a somewhat different persona at different cognitive stages. Acuff (1997) provides a nice example:

> Characters such as Bugs Bunny and Garfield survive and thrive in the eyes of the 13+ year-olds in large part because of what we call "perceptual filters." If I am five years old I perceive Bugs as a funny bunny with a unique voice and I appreciate his slapstick pie-in-the-face humor, especially his manipulations and outsmartings of Elmer Fudd, his arch nemesis. But most of the *verbal* humor—the sarcasm, puns, innuendo—goes right over my head. If I am nine years old I see a conniving and funny rabbit; I still appreciate a good deal of the more sophisticated humor and sarcasm. By the time I am 13, I am fully equipped neurologically and cognitively to understand just about all of Bugs's humor and still am greatly entertained by his slapstick antics. (p. 112)

B. Reactions to the Screen

We now turn to two distinct responses to television depictions—fright, and changes in attentiveness as children mature.

1. Fright   Media content frequently frightens children and teenagers. Although the percentages reported by Cantor (2001) differ from small sample to small sample, as would be expected, usually a majority of undergraduates report having been at some time seriously disturbed or frightened, usually a majority of children report having been seriously disturbed or frightened, and about 4 out of 10 parents report that their children have been seriously disturbed or frightened. Symptoms include fantasies about imagined dangers, free-floating anxiety, sleeplessness, bad dreams, loss of appetite, and stomach problems.

Cantor adjusts cognitive stages to better fit responses to the media, extending the preoperational by one year (from 3–7 to 3–8). In the preoperational stage, children are highly dependent on visual imagery. Appearance takes precedence over substance, so that harmfulness cloaked in a benign façade will be ignored and a ghastly appearance will be frightening even if the creature or event in fact is harmless (Harrison & Cantor, 1999; Hoffner & Cantor, 1985; Sparks, 1986). Children at this age are not particularly responsive to the advice of parents or others that what is on the screen is unreal or "pretend." They are frightened by events and creatures that are beyond the possible but in appearance are destructive or threatening (Cantor & Wilson, 1984). Cantor (2001) summarizes the fear-inducing experiences in general at this age as including "animals; the dark; supernatural beings such as ghosts, monsters, and witches; and anything that looks strange or moves suddenly" (p. 211). In the concrete operational stage, media-induced fears become more common for the possible but improbable— kidnappings, natural disasters, shark attacks. The general preoccupations at this age cited by Cantor—"personal injury and physical destruction and the injury and death of family members" (p. 211)— form the basis of reactions to the media. The formal operational stage beginning at age 13 sees attention to more abstract concerns and realistic threats attributable to uncontrollable and distant forces—familial unemployment, the environment, terrorism, and the military call-up and thus endangerment of a parent (Cantor, Wilson, & Hoffner, 1986; Cantor, Mares, & Oliver, 1993). The preoccupation of the concrete operational stage with the personal continues, but the emphasis shifts from the symbolic evocation of potential misadventures to concrete circumstances that pose a promise of rupture.

2. Maturity of the Viewer   Television viewing changes in character as children mature (Comstock & Scharrer, 2001). They learn to use the medium, and by the time viewing peaks at age 12 they will be responding to it in the same manner as adults.

Children's devotion to their favorite programs will be abandoned for content indifference and the vicissitudes of time available (see Figure 2.2). Eron and colleagues (1983) intended to measure frequency of viewing, but they used viewing of favorite programs as a proxy. They registered an increase up to grade three and then a precipitous decline. Data from numerous sources indicate that viewing between the first and

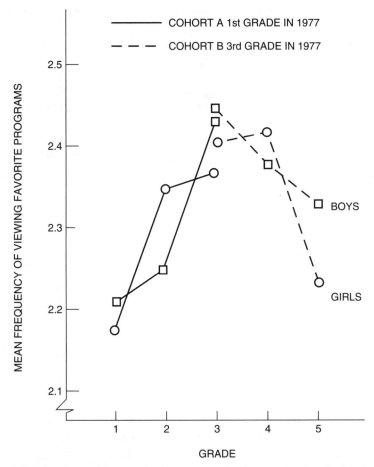

Fig. 2.2 Change in frequency of television viewing from grades 1 to 5—favorite programs. From Eron, L. D., Huesmann, L. R., Brice, P., Fischer, P., & Mermelstein, R. (1983). Age trends in the development of aggression, sex typing, and related television habits. *Developmental Psychology, 19*(1), 71–77.

fifth grades in fact steadily increases (see Chapter I). What they actually measured, then, was the desertion of favorites in the face of other activities and obligations that took priority.

Young children also give particularly close eye attention to the screen when watching programming especially designed for them. This attention is motivated by the desire to understand what is taking place. It increases as demands on comprehension become greater with the viewing of more demanding general audience programming (see Figure 2.3). Then, eye contact declines until it approximates the attention to

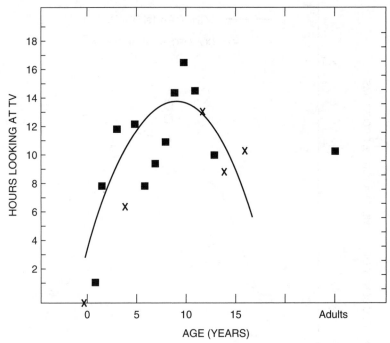

Fig. 2.3   Weekly attention to the screen as a function of age. From Anderson, D. R., Lorch, E. P., Field, D. E., & Sanders, J. (1981). Television viewing at home: Age trends in visual attention and time with TV. *Child Development*, 57, 1024–1033.

the screen extended by adults. The complexities of most television programming have now been mastered, and monitoring becomes the efficient way to view.

These two changes, which in our culture represent maturity in the use of television—content indifference and monitoring—each begin between the ages of about 10 and 12. Ritualistic viewing becomes predominant, although it should be remembered that among the very young, instrumental viewing has been confined to cartoons and educational programs specifically designed for young children.

The adult viewing pattern, with its miserliness of affective and cognitive effort, ironically also will be one of great fondness for and the assignment of substantial priority to the medium. The former is exemplified by the disinclination of people to forego television once experienced; for example, communities that give up television for a period (often, as part of a contest or stunt sponsored by a newspaper) generally do not want to continue their abstinence despite additional financial rewards (Wober, 1988). The latter is documented by the remarkably high proportion of those in the audience who consider viewing to be the primary rather than secondary (or tertiary) activity in which they are engaged. Almost three-fourths of U.S. viewers in the 12-nation UNESCO time-budget study labelled attending to television as the primary rather than the secondary activity. One might well have surmised that, with the passage of time since the data were collected in the mid-1960s (and presumably greater accommodation to the medium), viewing more often would be relegated to a secondary activity. Not so. The recent time-budget data of Robinson and Godbey (1997), with large, national samples, produce approximately the same percentage of those in the vicinity of an operating television set who consider viewing the primary activity. Television viewing is an activity to which people ascribe some importance, although often engaged in jointly with a variety of other activities in a discontinuous and interrupted manner.

IV. THE INFLUENCE OF VIEWING ON OTHER ACTIVITIES

There is no question that children and teenagers allocate a great deal of time to television. Young people eight to 18 spend almost four hours a day using television (including videos, DVDs, and prerecorded shows), and it is by far the most frequently used of all media (Roberts, Foehr, & Rideout, 2005). Robinson and Godbey (1997) call it "the 800-pound gorilla" of time use. A major question has been the influence of television viewing on other activities. The clear evidence that the introduction of the medium changed the way everyone—children, teenagers, and adults—spent time has been widely converted into a conviction that television displaces time that otherwise would be spent on more rewarding or deserving activities. We doubt if this is a very sensible way to think about television at the present time. We review the data on television and other activities from two perspectives: (a) the introduction of the medium and (b) contemporary time use.

A. Introduction of Television

The introduction of television changed the way set owners spent time (Comstock, 1991; Comstock & Scharrer, 1999). The expected displacement occurred for functional equivalents—movie-going, magazine-reading, radio listening, and comic book-reading—that is, for sources of entertainment and information. It also reduced time spent on activities from different realms than entertainment and information—gardening, recreational travel, house cleaning, sleeping, and traditional religious services.

Initially, newspaper reading was unaffected because television did not serve the same interests, but after a few decades, when television had become important as a news medium, there were precipitous declines in the time spent reading newspapers (Robinson & Godbey, 1997).

These data reflect adult behavior, but they are relevant to children and teenagers for two reasons. First, such shifts affect the household milieu in which the young grow up. Second, they exemplify the changes that media and technology can make in time use. The data also indicate that after a few years some of the depressed activities recovered. In general, people returned to abandoned activities to restore variety to their lives while activities that were engaged in to a substantial extent remained depressed to some degree (Belson, 1959; Comstock, 1991).

Nevertheless, there is also considerable data specifically representing children and teenagers, and sometimes their parents. Himmelweit, Oppenheim, and Vince (1958) in Great Britain and Schramm, Lyle, and Parker (1961) in the United States conducted large-scale, multifaceted, landmark examinations of the effects of the introduction of television on children and adolescents. In the case of Himmelweit and colleagues, the basic sample consisted of 1,854 10–11 year olds and 13–14 year olds in four cities. In the case of Schramm and colleagues, the basic sample consisted of 2688 young people from the first six grades and the eighth, tenth, and twelfth grades in San Francisco and 1708 young persons in the first, sixth, and tenth grades in five Rocky Mountain communities. In both cases, data were also obtained from hundreds of parents and teachers, and comparisons could be made between households with and without television. Both also included, in addition to the principal samples, a number of embedded studies with specialized focuses. For example, the basic sample of Schramm and colleagues comprised only three-fourths of the total number of young persons (5991) from whom they obtained data. In both undertakings, one of the topics was leisure and other activities. Their results represent a complementary collage.

In Great Britain, television reduced comic book reading. It also decreased radio listening. It reduced movie going among children but not among teenagers, for whom movie going served important social functions. It reduced participation in clubs and related activities among children but not among teenagers, presumably for the same reason. Book reading initially was decreased, and markedly so among teenagers, but with the passage of time returned to initial levels, presumably because it became clear that television did not readily substitute for books in the satisfactions provided and needs served. Outdoor activities were somewhat decreased, but primarily those of an unorganized or unstructured nature (they give "kicking a ball around" as an example), and the Himmelweit, Oppenheim, and Vince remark that outdoor activities on the whole are too important to children and teenagers for them to be much displaced by television.

In the United States, television markedly reduced movie going, radio listening, and the reading of certain types of magazines (confessions, detective, screen, and pulp adventure) by young people. Sixth and tenth graders with television listened to radio less than half the three hours that were spent on it by those in a community yet to have television; declines for movie going and comic book reading were similar in size. Time devoted to newspapers, books, and quality and general interest magazines was unaffected, and there was some evidence that the reading by the young of general interest magazines actually (and ironically, since such exemplars as *The Saturday Evening Post, Colliers, Life,* and *Look* failed to survive the competition of television) was stimulated somewhat by television. With television, children were recorded as going to bed slightly (about 13 minutes) later, a figure about the same as that obtained for adults in the 12-nation time-use study (Robinson, 1972b; Robinson & Converse, 1972; Szalai, 1972). Among very young children, time spent in play was slightly reduced. Total time spent on the mass media by children and teenagers was markedly increased, with the estimate of about an hour to an hour-and-a-half again similar to that for adults in the 12-nation study. Schramm, Lyle, and Parker conclude that, among young people, the introduction of television "reorganizes leisure time and mass media use in a spectacular manner" (p. 169).

Murray and Kippax (1977, 1978) obtained data from about 100 children and their parents in each of three Australian communities with very different television availability. No television was received in the No-TV town. In the Low-TV town, a single government-owned channel that devoted about a third of its schedule to educational programming for use in the schools had been received for about a year. In the High-TV town, that channel had been received for five years and an additional channel devoted almost exclusively to entertainment, sports, and news had been received for two years. They found only somewhat greater television viewing by children in the High-TV than in the Low-TV town. The frequency of engaging in a number of kinds of leisure activities declined linearly across the three communities. The declines were most prominent for spectator and participant sports and other outdoor activities and for certain media usage (movie going, radio listening, and record playing). Comic book reading was decidedly lower in the towns with television, and total reading time was somewhat less, but the number of books reported as read per week was greater. Among both mothers and fathers, they found declines across the communities in radio listening, movie going, listening to recorded music, theater attendance, and hobbies, and among fathers, in spectator sports, reading, and listening to public addresses. They also found that two-thirds of the children in the High-TV town said they viewed when they were bored, compared with only about 40 percent who said so in the Low-TV town. Presumably, this reflects the gratifications better served by the greater variety and sports and entertainment orientation of the High-TV environment. They too propose "a major restructuring of one's conception of the media and patterns of daily activities" (Murray & Kippax, 1978, p. 42) as a consequence of television availability.

The distinctly different perception of the use of television by children in the Low-TV town almost certainly reflects the extraordinarily high educational emphasis of the only television available. When content is different from what we ordinarily think of as television, the medium is differently perceived, while paradoxically time spent viewing is little if at all affected.

Williams (1986) and colleagues examined the effects of the introduction of a single government-owned Canadian Broadcasting Corporation (CBC) channel in a remote British Columbia community of about 650 that could not receive a signal until late 1973. They collected varied data on both young persons and adults before the advent of television and two years later at this site, which they called Notel, and compared the outcomes with those from two similar communities— one that could receive only the CBC channel (Unitel) and one that could receive a variety of channels (Multitel), including the three major American networks, thereby creating a three-community naturalistic experiment.

They found that the introduction of television decreased participation in the total number of community activities engaged in (see Figure 2.4), and much more so among youths (persons in the seventh through the twelfth grades) than among younger adults (55 years or younger). Television reduced attendance at clubs and meetings, but clearly so only for adults, a finding concordant with the view of Himmelweit, Oppenheim, and Vince (1958) that television does not displace activities socially important to young people. There was some evidence, but it was far less clear, that community involvement in "special days" (defined as weddings, funerals, and elections) and "entertainment" (defined as special movies, parades, and bingo) declined.

The greatest overall decline in participation in activities occurred among older adults, those over the age of 55. The decreases in participation registered for young persons, younger adults, and older adults suggest that one effect of television is to increase segregation by age and to lessen the contact that children and teenagers have with adults,

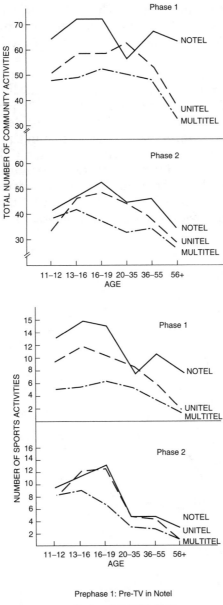

Fig. 2.4 Participation in activities before and after the introduction of television. Adapted from Williams, T.M. (Ed.) (1986). *The impact of television: A natural experiment in three communities.* New York: Academic Press.

and especially with senior adults. Thus, the segregation within the household of adults and the young associated with multiple sets and media in the bedrooms, in fact began with the introduction of the medium.

They found the same rapid adoption of television as had been observed in the United States where, once the medium had become familiar to the public, saturation reached about 70 percent of households within two years after signals became available (see Figure 2.5). Within two years, viewing in Notel equaled that in Unitel, and though viewing was slightly greater in Multitel with its multiple channels, the authors observe that "the differences were less striking than the similarities, especially if hours of availability are considered" (p. 245) (the broadcast day was considerably longer in Multitel than in Unitel or Notel), and conclude that it is the presence or absence of television and

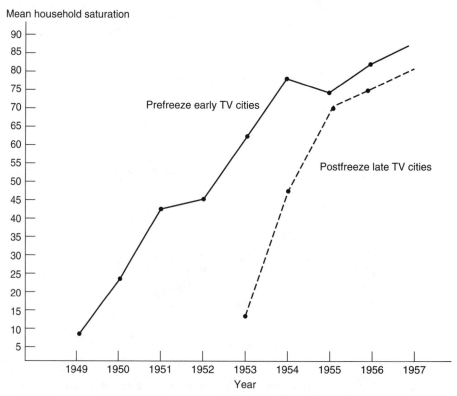

Fig. 2.5   Rate of television adoption. Freeze = no station licenses issued by FCC; prefreeze = stations were licensed in late 1940s; postfreeze = stations were licensed in early 1950s. From Cook, T. D., & Campbell, D.T. (1979). *Quasiexperimentation: Design and analysis issues for field settings.* Chicago: Houghton Mifflin.

not the quantity, character, or variety of programming that has the greater effect on the allocation of time.

Himmelweit, Oppenheim, and Vince (1958) introduce the concepts of functional similarity, transformed activities, and fringe or marginal activities to interpret the findings on the introduction of television. The first leads to the functional displacement hypothesis. It holds that one medium will displace another when it performs the function of the displaced medium in a superior manner, either by being more rewarding at the same cost or convenience, or equally rewarding at less cost or greater convenience. For example, television displaced comic book reading and for younger children, movie going, because it provided similar satisfactions in a superior manner. The second refers to changes within a class of activity, such as the role radio has assumed among young persons. As Schramm, Lyle, and Parker (1961) observe, with the arrival of television, radio ceased to be the primary medium around which the family would gather and became a secondary medium frequently employed by young people to listen to music while doing something else. The third refers to activities largely unaffected and therefore not relevant to the new medium, such as teenage social activities and (in their data) organized outdoor sports. Williams (1986) and colleagues contribute several additional concepts (our italics):

> Television seems especially powerful at displacing other activities. Proponents of the functional equivalence argument contend this is because television is the least specialized medium and therefore able to satisfy the most needs, or to satisfy them best. This may be true, but several other factors strike us as equally if not more important. The first is *time-sharing*. People are likely to spend more time with a medium that can be time-shared with other activities, including other media, than with one which cannot (e.g., ironing can be done while watching TV or listening to radio, but not while reading; reading can be done while watching TV, but listening to records cannot). The second is *perceived ease* of the medium. Salomon (1983) has shown that by comparison with print media, children perceive television to be an easier medium and one at which they are more expert. . . . In addition to ease of time-sharing, *ease of access* undoubtedly is important. For example, we found that television displaced participation in community activities outside the home, but there was little evidence to indicate it displaced private leisure activities, including ones typically conducted inside the home. Participation in organized community activities requires more effort than watching television, whereas some indoor leisure activities can be time-shared with TV. (p. 242)

We reach two major conclusions. The first is that the effects of the introduction of television on the use of time was deep and extensive. The second is that activities that are personally or socially important—as exemplified by teenage movie-going—may be resistant to displacement, with vulnerability depending on the match between gratifications served, the possibility of time-sharing, ease of media use, and readiness of media access. For example, S.B. Neuman (1988) reported that in a sample of 70,000 aged 9, 13, and 17 years there was no association between amount of viewing and engaging in sports or spending time with friends. She also reconfirmed an equally long-standing pattern (Brown, Childers, Bauman, & Koch, 1990; Kubey & Larsen, 1990; Lyle & Hoffman, 1972a) that as young people become older, and especially as they pass from early to late adolescence, television diminishes and music increases in importance, often becoming predominant among media. In neither instance in western culture does television pose much of a threat, and the pervasiveness of this pattern is attested to by Rosengren and Windahl (1989) who report essentially confirmatory findings among Scandinavian youth for both social interaction and leisure and for music.

B. Contemporary Use of Television Viewing

Our reluctance to embrace the concept of suppression as descriptive of the relationship between use of television and other activities at the present time is based on four factors. The first is the realities of time allocation. The second is the pattern of leisure activities among both adults and children for those who view greater and lesser amounts of television. The third is the denotative and connotative inaccuracy of the term "suppression." The fourth is very current data on viewing and engaging in certain other activities by children and teenagers.

1. Realities of Television Viewing   Television was introduced into communities with established, stable agendas of time use. Those agendas then changed, and have been long abandoned. Surely if television—somehow—ceased to be available, both young and old would allocate their time somewhat differently. However, it is unlikely that they would turn to activities that were more demanding affectively and cognitively, even if engaged in at higher levels in a pretelevision era, because they would already have rejected those activities in favor of television. The implication is that any substitute for television would be similar in its demands, such as movies, comic books, and popular magazines.

The governing role of time available then enters the equation. This phenomenon—in which amount of viewing is largely determined by the time available to view—logically implies that any lessening of television use will represent new priorities that circumscribe the time available. Otherwise, it is hard to imagine why amount of viewing would change. For example, in the longitudinal analysis of about 8,000 young persons in South Africa by Mutz, Roberts, and van Vuuren (1993) the displacement by the introduction of television of radio listening, movie going, and reading was not reversed with a decrease in individual viewing. Our interpretation is that these three activities had shown that they could not hold their own against television, but presumably others—either new or reevaluated—could.

2. The Effect of Viewing on Leisure Activities The data on viewing and other activities leads to two conclusions. The first is that for most people there is no relationship over a low-to-high range of one to four hours of viewing daily and engaging in either compatible, time-sharing activities or even some seemingly incompatible activities (Robinson, Keegan, Karth, Triplett & Holland, 1985). There are inverse associations between viewing and interests that are distinctly unserved by television—physical exercise out-of-doors, playing sports, camping, and attending to the arts by way of museum visits, the ballet, opera, classical concerts, jazz performances, and reading fiction. The second is that among children the amount of time spent viewing is unassociated with a myriad of activities—lessons, sports, clubs, hobbies, and play (Medrich, Roisin, Rubin & Buckley, 1982)—whereas there is a clearly negative association between these activities and what we have elsewhere (Comstock & Scharrer, 1999) labelled "household centrality of television," operationalized as the absence of rules about television use, sets that operate constantly, and high levels of viewing by parents. That is, the values and norms associated with television use made a bigger difference than amount of viewing.

3. Suppression of Viewing These varied circumstances lead us to conclude that the concept of *suppression* is unapt and inappropriate. Today's audiences have not had an agenda of time allocation disrupted by what was once the attractive innovation of television. Neither are there powerful negative associations between amount of time spent viewing and a wide variety of activities, including some that would be difficult to combine with television use. People who have interests not served by television do spend fewer hours viewing. The chain of influence, then, more meaningfully travels from the viewer and his or her interests to television use rather than the reverse. This is not to say that there are no effects associated with amount of viewing—only that at the present time the medium should not be held accountable for constraining the amount of time devoted to a wide range of activities. Finally, among children, amount of viewing for the most part is unassociated with engaging in other activities, and the values represented by a central place for television in the household is negatively associated with engaging in such activities. The preeminent factor is not the time spent with the medium but the values and interests of a child and the adults in his or her household. One major exception is reading, where there is a decidedly negative association with amount of time spent viewing (see Chapter IV).

4. Recent Data Regarding Viewing Trends   We have seen that children and teenagers have become progressively adept at multitasking, exemplified by the increasing proportion of time in which they are using more than one medium at once (see Chapter I). The variety of activities in which they engage is striking (see Table 2.1), many of which would have been shared with use of one or more media. As the data from the recent nationally representative, probability sample of more than 2,000 in grades three through twelve (8- to 18-year-olds) collected by Roberts, Foehr, and Rideout (2005) indicate, television consumed the most time, but a larger total was spent on social activities—"hanging out with parents" and "hanging out with friends," by definition social, and "exercise, sports" and "listening to music," which often involve others. There was also an amazing 53 minutes a day spent talking on the telephone among teenagers.

Table 2.1
Time Spent with Media and Selected Non-Media Activities in a Typical Day

Activity	Time
Watching TV	3:04
Hanging out with parents	2:17
Hanging out with friends*	2:16
Listening to music	1:44
Exercising, sports, etc.	1:25
Watching movies/videos	1:11
Using a computer	1:02
Pursuing hobbies, clubs, etc.	1:00
Talking on the telephone*	0:53
Doing homework*	0:50
Playing video games	0:49
Reading	0:43
Working at a job*	0:35
Doing chores*	0:32

*Asked only of 7th- to 12th-graders.

Adapted from Roberts, D. F., Foehr, U. G. & Rideout, V. (2005). *Generation M: Media in the lives of 8–18 year olds. A Kaiser Family Foundation Study.* Menlo Park, CA: Henry J. Kaiser Family Foundation.

When we examine the data of Roberts, Foehr, and Rideout (2005) on media use and other activities, we find no support for the view that media or television among media take time away from other activities (see Table 2.2)—unless we were to take the unbending position that any block of time could be diverted to other uses (the question is not whether time could be otherwise spent but whether greater amounts of time spent in a particular way is associated with less time spent in other activities). As can be seen, greater amounts of time spent with media are associated with greater amounts of time spent with parents, in physical activities, and pursuing hobbies, and greater amounts of time spent with television are associated with greater amounts of time spent with parents and pursuing hobbies. Physical activities and hobbies embrace a fairly wide range of undertakings, although admittedly they do not exhaust all possible activities (visiting museums, for example, ordinarily would not qualify as a hobby). As the authors comment, "The results raise a red flag against too easily concluding that time spent with media is synonymous with time taken from other activities" (p. 51). The results are also strong endorsement of the principle of "more is more" introduced by Robinson and Godbey (1997), which holds that those who engage in one activity are more likely to engage in other activities, and that "activeness" is a trait that generalizes across activities.

Table 2.2
Media Use and Time Spent in Other Activities

	Hours and Minutes Per Day		
Media Use	With Parents	Physical Activity	Pursuing Hobbies
All Media			
Light	1:57[a]	1:21[a]	0:52[a]
Moderate	2:16[b]	1:21[a]	0:56[a]
Heavy	2:35[b]	1:42[b]	1:18[b]
Television			
Light	2:09[a]	1:25	1:03[ab]
Moderate	2:11[a]	1:21	0:54[a]
Heavy	2.42[b]	1:34	1:07[b]

Note: Results in any one column with a different superscript differ significantly. Cut-off points for light, moderate, and heavy usage vary by medium and population, with the goal a reasonable distribution across the spectrum.

Based on Rideout, V., Roberts, D. & Foehr, U. (2005). *Generation M: Media in the lives of 8–18 year-olds: Executive summary*, p. 15. Menlo Park, CA: Henry J. Kaiser Foundation.

V. SOCIAL CIRCUMSTANCES OF TELEVISION VIEWING

The widespread availability of media in American homes, and particularly in the bedrooms of children and teenagers (see Chapter I), has led to dramatic changes in the social circumstances of television viewing. Data from the 1970s and 1980s indicated that (Comstock, 1991):

* Although joint viewing by parents and children was declining with the increase in multiset households, parents reported viewing with their children much of the time.

Table 2.3
TV Rules

	Percentage of children with TV-related rules			
	Rules of any kind	Rules about homework/ chores*	Rules about amount of time*	Rules about type of content*
Total sample	46%	36%	14%	13%
Age				
8- to 10-year-olds	55[a]	NA	NA	NA
11- to 14-year-olds	51[a]	46[a]	18[a]	18[a]
15- to 18-year-olds	31[b]	28[b]	10[b]	8[b]
Gender				
Boys	45	39	15	14
Girls	46	34	12	12
Race/ethnicity				
White	44	35	13	13
African American	43	34	8	7
Hispanic	52	42	19	15
Parent education				
High school	40	33	9	10
Some college	45	39	15	12
College or more	48	37	16	14
Household income				
Under $35,000	47	38	11	14
$35,000–$50,000	47	40	17	13
Over $50,000	42	31	12	12

*Among 7th- to 12th-graders only.
Note: Within each cluster, only those items in each column that do not share a common superscript differ from one another with statistical reliability. Those items without a superscript, or those that share a common superscript, do not differ by a large enough margin to ensure statistical reliability. Adapted from Roberts, D. F., Foehr, U. G. & Rideout, V. (2005). *Generation M: Media in the lives of 8–18 year olds. A Kaiser Family Foundation Study.* Menlo Park, CA: Henry J. Kaiser Family Foundation.

- Although fewer than half of parents had rules about the amount or content that could be watched, sizable minorities did have such rules.
- The imposition of rules of any type was positively associated with higher levels of parental education.

Today, parental participation in media use and parental constraints on how much and what children watch or otherwise make use of media are in retreat. The data of Roberts, Foehr, and Rideout (2005) document that overall, slightly fewer parents now have rules about television viewing and, among teenagers, that the rules in most homes make viewing contingent on the completion of chores and homework but seldom otherwise impose restrictions on time spent viewing or content viewed (see Table 2.3). Significantly, the imposition of rules is no longer strongly associated with higher levels of parent education. In addition, a great deal of viewing is now done alone (see Table 2.4). More than one-third of those 15 to 18 years old in the somewhat earlier nationally representative probability sample of more than 3,100 analyzed by Roberts and Foehr (2004) reported they viewed "mainly alone," and only among younger children did the proportion viewing with

Table 2.4
Who Children View Television with by Day Part and Age (%)[a]

	2–7 years	2–4 years	5–7 years	8–18 years	8–10 years	11–14 years	15–18 years
Proportion viewing mainly alone							
Morning	30	26$_a$	34$_b$	41	33$_a$	42$_b$	54$_c$
Afternoon	25	18$_a$	30$_b$	42	33$_a$	43$_b$	52$_c$
Evening	10	8	11	35	30$_a$	37$_b$	39$_b$
Proportion viewing with parents							
Morning	21	27$_a$	14$_b$	8	13$_a$	8$_b$	4$_c$
Afternoon	15	16	13	13	14$_a$	16$_a$	7$_b$
Evening	30	26$_a$	34$_b$	24	28$_a$	27$_a$	19$_b$
Proportion viewing with siblings or friends							
Morning	25	24	26	19	31$_a$	18$_b$	10$_c$
Afternoon	22	18$_a$	26$_b$	26	34$_a$	29$_a$	15$_b$
Evening	25	19$_a$	30$_b$	32	36$_a$	32$_a$	27$_b$
Proportion of viewing "mainly alone" throughout the day							
Full day's viewing	15	16	14	29	25$_a$	27$_a$	36$_b$

Note: Statistical significance is represented in subscripts that indicate when differences between proportions or means are statistically significant. When numbers share a subscripted letter, they do not differ significantly; numbers with no subscripted letter *in common* differ reliably.

Adapted from Roberts, D. F., & Foehr, U. G. (2004). *Kids and media in America*. New York, NY: Cambridge University Press.

parents at any time outnumber those viewing alone, and then only during prime time. This solitary media use also extends to music listening, VCR and DVD use, and computer use (Roberts & Foehr, 2004; Roberts, Foehr & Rideout, 2005).

Roberts and Foehr propose three possible explanations for the retreat in parental involvement:

- The media are so ubiquitous that they no longer draw much parental attention.
- Many parents may not believe that media messages have any significant influence on children and teenagers.
- Demands on time make monitoring media use too difficult for many parents.

"But whatever the reason," they continue, "it appears that more and more children spend more and more time exposed to media messages absent adult supervision, adult oversight, adult presence, or an adult 'game plan'" (p. 200). Our own misgivings are based on foregone opportunities—the ability of parents by their comments to increase what is learned from television when it has educational value, to increase understanding of whatever has been presented, to temper fear and uneasiness when the medium presents frightening or threatening images and events, and occasionally to guide tastes and preferences in what the media offer.

III THE WORLD AS PORTRAYED BY MEDIA

We examine scientific, systematic content analyses to depict two major aspects of media content—the people that occupy the media and the behavior in which they engage. We will round up the usual suspects—violence, sex, and even profane language—but also will cast a net over less frequently studied elements of content, including (but not limited to) portrayals of people with disabilities, the presence of "prosocial" messages (positive, helpful behavior and interactions), and nutritional content (or lack thereof) in foods advertised to young people.

We place particular emphasis on children's media in order to highlight the unique experiences of the child audience—cartoons, educational shows, video games, and Saturday morning television. Yet, recognizing that children's television programming is watched regularly only by young children, we also review the general audience programming that constitutes the bulk of the media exposure of older children and teens. What results is a view of the sometimes cohesive, sometimes contradictory set of messages delivered each day to today's young people through multiple hours of media exposure.

I. MEDIA CONTENT

Television content created especially for children is favored, by far, by young children (aged 2 to 7), only occasionally retains some of its appeal during middle childhood (aged 8 to 13), then drops off decisively in its attraction in the teenage years (Roberts et al., 2004; see Chapter II). A vast number of television networks, stations, and channels compete to capitalize on the faithful child audience. The original three broadcast networks regularly offered a growing number of children's programs over the first 30-odd years of their existence, but began to curtail such programming when cable channels such as Nickelodeon and The Disney Channel emerged (Pecora, 1998). The Saturday morning time slot nevertheless still has enough offerings to inspire a sizable number of children to tune to the broadcast networks which now, of course, number more than three.

The general audience programming offered at other times of day brings together young and old viewers. The evening hours from 7 to 10 P.M. are the most popular time for children of all except the youngest ages to watch television, but only an estimated 6 percent of the programs that air during those times are made for children (Woodard, 1999). Thus, children watch a great deal of programming created to appeal to a large and heterogeneous audience. Most children's television programs are aired during mornings (50%), followed by afternoons from noon to 6 P.M. (36%). Many more programs are designed for elementary school-aged children (72% of all children's programs) than for preschoolers (21%) or teens (7%) (Woodard, 1999).

Cable quickly became a fierce competitor to the networks' children's programming. Many cable channels had the benefit of the targeting of children as their sole purpose, as opposed to the broadcast networks that have historically reserved isolated pockets of broadcast time for their youngest viewers and devoted other dayparts to other audience segments. Cable channels such as Disney, Nickelodeon, and Nick, Jr. have become big business, obtaining revenue from commercial messages placed either within or between programs as well as from the multitude of merchandise tie-ins—from bedding to clothing and from food products to shampoo—that bear the images of beloved characters (Pecora, 1998).

Woodard's 1999 analysis of a composite week of programming in the Philadelphia market shows that basic cable stations provided 55 percent of all children's programs, followed by PBS at 20 percent, premium cable at 11 percent, and broadcast networks at just 4 percent. Woodard also estimated cable subscribers had access to up to 29 channels offering 279 programs specifically designed for children, comprising the largest number of kids' programs and programming sources ever. Recent cable television shows popular with young audiences include *SpongeBob SquarePants*, *The Fairly OddParents*, and *Hey Arnold!* on Nickelodeon, *Blue's Clues*, *Dora the Explorer*, and *Little Bear* on Nick, Jr. (for young child audiences), and *The Proud Family*, *Lilo and Stitch the Series*, *That's So Raven*, and *Lizzie McGuire* on The Disney Channel.

Public broadcasting has a long history of providing programming designed for the child audience. Much of this programming is educational (*Sesame Street, Mister Rogers' Neighborhood*), and boasts some empirical evidence attesting to some effectiveness in helping preschoolers develop skills that will pave the way for success in school (see Chapter V). Despite the educational focus of these programs, it is increasingly imprudent to assume that public broadcasting is a noncommercial oasis for young people. We (Scharrer & Comstock, 2003) commented earlier:

> The relative ability of PBS to deemphasize market concerns and rely more heavily on funding from the federal government long allowed public television stations to dedicate programming that was concerned, first and foremost, with helping children learn, and only secondarily with entertaining them. More recently, however, decreases in federal funding have necessitated a greater emphasis on revenues generated from underwriting by corporate sponsors as well as by public contributions. Although contemporary PBS programs still have an educational focus, there is frequently a commercial element as well, often through the creation and marketing of videotapes, books, clothing, lunch boxes, backpacks, and other products that bear the images of popular PBS characters. Consequently, recent PBS program lineups have included a litany of programs with multiple product tie-ins, such as *Barney and Friends* and *Lamb Chop's Play-Along* (Pecora, 1998), and the "sponsorship" messages between programs on PBS look increasingly similar to the advertising messages on commercial television. (p. 164)

Although television remains the primary way children and teenagers spend leisure time, it also shares the stage with other media. Therefore, we review content in video and computer games because of their increasing popularity; music television because of the importance assigned to music by teenagers; and advertisements because the commercial structure of the media assures an avalanche of daily exposure.

II. STUDYING THE ATTRIBUTES OF TELEVISION CHARACTERS

Studying the attributes of the people who occupy the television programs, films, and video games popular with children helps us to assemble a demography of the media world that can be compared to the real world in which we live. Such a comparison is important for three reasons. First, it can reveal hidden and not-so-hidden biases present in the process of creating and distributing media for commercial gain that favor some people over others. Second, the issue of representation of social groups—not just the quantity of their presence but the quality of their roles—is a long-standing concern for scholars due to the possibility of audience members learning to stereotype or value or devalue some groups over others based on their media portrayals (or lack thereof). Third, in an ongoing process of learning about the self and one's role in society, the child or adolescent audience member looks to the screens to search for similarities and points of connection between herself or himself and people in the media (Comstock, 1991). When characters or personages who resemble the child are absent or shown in unfavorable or narrow ways, the child's self-concept may be negatively affected. At the same time, identification with a character or personage may serve as the basis for thought, emotion, or behavior.

A. Gender Representation

Gender has been the most frequently studied of all demographics. The evidence points to persisting inequities in the number of female compared to male characters in many forms of media, and continuing gender stereotypes in the settings in which characters appear and the activities in which they engage. Some studies have found evidence for what we have termed "limited and isolated pockets of improvements in portrayals over the years" (Scharrer & Comstock, 2003, p. 165), but the overall pattern favors males in quantity of portrayals and advances rather traditional, narrow interpretations of gender roles in terms of the quality of portrayals.

1. Gender Disparity in Television and Film   Men have long outnumbered women on television and continue to do so (Davis, 1990; Greenberg & Collette, 1997; Lauzen & Dozier, 1999; Signorielli, 1985, 1989, 1993; Signorielli & Bacue, 1999). Signorielli and Bacue, for instance, studied samples of primetime network broadcast television across the decades and found females made up 24 percent of the characters who appeared in 1967 compared to 43 percent in 1996 and 38 percent in 1998. Never have women achieved 50 percent parity, and in the most recent years, women remained underrepresented compared to their actual numbers in the population.

In children's television, specifically, a similarly unequal gender distribution has been observed. Calvert, Stolkin, and Lee (1997) analyzed characters appearing in Saturday morning programs in the 1995–1996 season, and found males outnumbered females by three to one. Conspicuously absent were female cartoon heroes. Commercials aired during child-friendly time slots have also been found to contain more boys and men than girls and women (Browne, 1998; Smith, 1994; Thompson & Zerbinos, 1995). Larson (2001), who coded only child and adolescent characters, found nearly equal numbers of boys and girls overall in commercials during children's programming, but found that among the subset of commercials that featured just one gender, 59 percent featured boys only compared to 41 percent showing just girls. Aubrey and Harrison (2004) investigated gender representation in a list of favorite television programs provided by 190 first and second graders. Five episodes each of the top six vote getters (*Rugrats, Doug, Pokemon, Arthur, Rocko's Modern Life,* and *CatDog*) were examined. Just 29 percent of the lead characters and 35 percent of the minor characters were female. Thus, program and commercial content on television delivered specially to young audiences echoes the uneven gender distribution found in general audience programming.

Music television is a key element of young people's time spent with media. About 80 percent of adolescents watch MTV, for instance, viewing from 25 minutes to almost two hours per day (Brown, Campbell & Fisher, 1986; Kubey & Larson, 1990). Seidman (1993, 1999) conducted two studies of the content of music television, one using data gathered in 1987 and a follow-up using data from 1993. In both, 60 hours of music videos airing on MTV were randomly selected. Videos featuring a musical performance were eliminated, leaving only "concept videos" or videos that tell a story. The first study covered 1,942 characters; the second, 2,348. Males accounted for approximately 63 percent of all people appearing in the videos in both studies. MTV thereby joins children's programming among the worst culprits of underrepresenting women on television.

Many of the roles and activities in which media characters engage are also gender stereotyped. Continuing evidence points to gender roles that largely confine boys and men to activities and settings traditionally viewed as "masculine" and girls and women to those traditionally seen as "feminine."

An analysis of three episodes each of eleven television programs meeting the "social/emotional needs" FCC mandate in children's programming found female characters were portrayed as nurturing and dependent while male characters were presented as active, dominant, and aggressive (Barner, 1999). Commercials airing during Saturday morning and after-school time slots have been more likely to show boys and men outside and girls and women inside the home, and, again, to depict males as more forceful and dominant as well as more authoritative than females (Browne, 1998; Larson, 2001; Smith, 1994; Thompson & Zerbinos, 1995). In one of the most recent studies on the topic, Davis (2003) assessed gender portrayals among 467 characters appearing in the commercials embedded in and between children's cartoons. She found that males were more likely to have major rather than minor roles, to be shown engaging in active movement, and to be depicted in an occupational setting.

Aubrey and Harrison's (2004) study of the favorite programs of a group of first and second graders found some evidence of these and other stereotypes, but also a number of depictions that failed to show gender differences or even ran counter to traditional roles. Female characters were significantly more likely to be seen as attractive or frail compared to male characters but no differences emerged in the dependence or assertiveness of characters. When taking into account the number of seconds that a character appeared on screen, a significantly larger proportion of male characters' time was spent in authoritative, assertive postures—directing others (ordering them or bossing them around), answering questions, displaying ingenuity, achieving a goal, and eating. For a host of additional variables—including expressing opinions, displaying leadership, showing bravery or rescuing another character, exhibiting physical affection, laughing at people, boasting, insulting or threatening other characters, showing anger or physical aggression, giving or receiving comments about physical appearance or displaying concern about one's physical appearance—no significant gender differences appeared. Furthermore, another set of variables showed counter stereotypical gender portrayals. Boys in the sample spent greater proportions of their time expressing affection verbally, following others, obeying others, and crying.

We conclude that, by and large, children's television programs and the commercials contained within often advance gender stereotypes that present boys as active, aggressive, and adventurous and girls as passive, nurturing, and subdued. The content analyses that include large, generalizable samples were consistent in reaching these conclusions. However, such depictions are by no means universal. This is documented by the analysis of favorite programs of the very young by Aubrey and Harrison (2004) using a sample that is not readily generalizable to children's programming as a whole but has validity in representing programs attractive to a group of first and second graders. We believe the fact that five of the six programs examined by Aubrey and Harrison aired on either PBS (*Arthur*) or Nickelodeon (*Rugrats, CatDog, Doug,* and *Rocko's Modern Life*)—both with either a mandate or a concerted effort to provide "prosocial" programming to children—helps explain the less restrictive roles taken on by men and women and boys and girls. Nonetheless, we are heartened that such "progressive" depictions were so popular, and such results remind us that there is in fact considerable variety in children's programming.

In primetime television commercials, household chores and tasks in and around the home often are assigned stereotypically. Female characters do more cooking, cleaning, and child care than males. Recent evidence shows that when males do attempt such tasks they are often shown failing at them, often in a manner meant to be humorous (Bartsch, Burnett, Diller & Rankin-Williams, 2000; Craig, 1992; Kaufman, 1999; Scharrer, Kim, Lin & Liu, 2006). The analysis by Scharrer and colleagues (Scharrer et al., 2006), for example, examined 447 commercials that featured domestic chores airing during one week of primetime programming on all the broadcast networks. Male characters' performance of chores was more likely to be met with a disapproving response from other characters, more likely to be conducted unsatisfactorily (e.g., hastily, not effectually), and more likely to be the subject of humor. The conclusions of this study join prior observations of sitcom fathers of the 1980s and 1990s as largely incompetent and unorthodox in parenting compared to sitcom mothers (Scharrer, 2001). Such portrayals send a message that males are doomed to failure when attempting to engage in activities traditionally thought to be within the purview of females, and thereby reinforce traditional gender roles.

Occupations are one area in which there has been a departure from gender stereotypes. Signorielli's (2001) analysis of primetime television records an increase in the number of professional roles held by women compared to past analyses (e.g., Signorielli, 1984, 1993; Vande Berg & Streckfuss, 1992). In recent years, women are as likely as men to be shown having productive, successful, and even high-powered careers. Nevertheless, Signorielli (2001) found that professional female roles typically are presented as antithetical to family roles—very few models show the challenges and rewards that come with combining, as many women do, family and professional lives.

In music videos, favorites of teenagers, there has been a slight shift away from stereotypes. Seidman (1999) recorded that 90 percent of all occupational roles in a randomly selected sample of MTV videos that would stereotypically be assigned to males (e.g., doctor, mechanic, police officer) were taken on by men, and 100 percent of the roles stereotypically assigned to females (e.g., secretary, nurse) were taken on by females. Occupations that are more gender neutral (e.g., lab technician, singer, office worker) were split 60 to 40 percent in favor of men. Males engaged in both more adventuresome and more violent behavior than females. Females were coded as more nurturing and affectionate. Females were "pursued sexually" more often and were more likely to be wearing skimpy clothing. In fact, one in every three women wore revealing clothing, compared to 7 percent of the males. These estimates were largely unchanged from Seidman's (1992) original study conducted in 1987.

However, some stereotypical behavior was no longer apparent. Males were not more aggressive (a measure that included verbal attacks and comparatively minor physical force rather than "violence"), domineering, or victimized and females were not more dependent, fearful, or engaged in sexual pursuit, as they were in the earlier sample. In the case of music videos, then, we see some abandoning of stereotypes while remaining discrepancies continue to uphold them.

2. Gender Bias in Video and Computer Games   Video games display even more pronounced discrepancies in the number of male compared to female characters. It is rare for a single main character to be female. When an ensemble cast appears in a multiplayer game, or when an individual player selects a character, there are invariably more males than females from which to choose. Males also outnumber females in the ads promoting games. Even educational computer games underrepresent women and girls.

Beasley and Collins Standley (2002) randomly selected 47 Nintendo and PlayStation games and coded each character appearing in the first 20 minutes of play. They found 597 characters. Seventy-two percent were men and 14 percent were women (14.7% were indeterminable). Dietz (1998) studied 33 popular Nintendo and Sega Genesis games and determined that only 15 percent of the games contained female heroes and 30 percent had no female characters at all. Scharrer (2004) studied not video games themselves but rather more than 1,000 ads for video games that appeared in three top circulating video game magazines (popular with older children and teens). In those ads, male characters outnumbered female characters by a ratio of more than 3 to 1. Sheldon (2004) selected for analysis 103 educational software packages listed on Discovery.com as being highly rated and targeting three- to six-year-olds, and found significantly more male characters than females. Thus, in these "new" forms of media, once again, nothing close to gender parity is achieved. Men and boys greatly outnumber women and girls.

Table 3.1 collates data describing a variety of media. Males consistently outnumber females by a substantial margin.

Roles also conform to gender stereotypes. The damsel in distress is estimated in one study to be present in about one out of five popular video games (Dietz, 1998). Male characters are meant to rescue female characters in a number of adventure-style games. In the genre of fantasy video games (popular with kids and presumably more often accepted by parents, due to their less graphic portrayals of violence), female characters are usually peripheral to the action (Gailey, 1993). In addition to traditional roles, this newer medium consistently conveys a message that promotes female passivity and male activity as norms.

Table 3.1
Percentages of Male and Female Characters Appearing in Major Media Forms Popular with Children and Teens*

Media form	% Males	% Females
Video games[1]	72%	14%
Saturday morning TV programs[2]	73	27
Music videos[3]	63	37
Commercials during kids' programs[4]	63	37
Primetime network TV programs[5]	62	38

*Where applicable, estimates of percentages of lead or major characters by gender were averaged together with percentages of minor characters by gender.

[1] The percentages do not add up to 100% due to nonhuman characters. From Beasley, B. & Collins Standley, T. (2002). Shirts vs. skins: Clothing as indicator of gender role stereotyping in video games. *Mass Communication & Society, 5*, 279–293.

[2] Averaged from Aubrey, J.S. & Harrison, K. (2004). The gender-role content of children's favorite television programs and its links to their gender-related perceptions. *Media Psychology, 6*, 111–146. Also from Thompson, T.L. & Zerbinos, E. (1995). Gender roles in animated cartoons: Has the picture changed in 20 years? *Sex Roles, 32*, 651–674.

[3] From Seidman, S.A. (1999). Revisiting sex-role stereotyping in MTV videos. *International Journal of Instructional Media, 26*, 11–13.

[4] From Browne, B.A. (1998). Gender stereotypes in advertising on children's television in the 1990s: A cross-national analysis. *Journal of Advertising, 27*, 83–97.

[5] From Signorielli, N. & Bacue, A. (1999). Recognition and respect: A content analysis of prime-time television characters across three decades. *Sex Roles, 40*, 527–544.

Sheldon's (2004) examination of educational software for young children found that male characters exhibited many traits conceived as "masculine stereotypical," including being active, aggressive, risk-taking, competitive, and adventurous. Occasionally, females showed counter-stereotypical traits but dependence, nurturing, passivity, and cooperation, all "feminine stereotypical" traits, were modeled more frequently by girls than by boys.

A final gender issue in video and computer games in terms of quality of roles is the portrayal of female characters as sex objects. In these games that are so popular with boys, in particular, female characters typically are presented as objects of beauty or sexual desire.

Herrett-Skjellum and Allen (1996), based on their meta-analysis of eight studies of gender representations in general audience television programming, provide a summary of gender and media: Compared to females, "males are seen more often ..., appear more often in major roles, exhibit dominant behaviors and attitudes, and are represented outside the home in jobs of authority" (p. 171). In most of the places that children and teens turn for entertainment and information—primetime television, television programs created for children, commercials, and video and computer games—messages reinforce gender stereotypes.

B. Race and Ethnicity in Media

From television's inception, a large majority of characters have been European American (Head, 1954; Smythe, 1954). New television seasons, studied from 1966 to 1992 by Greenberg and Collette (1997), brought little racial or ethnic variation. Asian Americans, Latinos, and Native Americans have been especially underrepresented on television compared to their population figures (Atkin, 1992). In the 1970s and 1980s, Native Americans and Asian Americans comprised a mere 1 percent of all television characters (Steenland, 1990), and the number of Latino characters was between 1.5 and 3 percent (Gerbner & Signorielli, 1979; Greenberg & Baptista-Fernandez, 1980). More recent data permit no claims of improved status. Mastro and Greenberg (2000), in a one-week sample of primetime programs on ABC, CBS, NBC, and Fox, found 80 percent of all main characters were European American, 16 percent African American, 3 percent Latino, 1 percent Asian American, and none Native American. Mastro and Behm-Morawitz (2005) in a two-week sample of the four largest networks and the WB found very similar figures: 80 percent of characters were White, 14 percent Black or African American, 4 percent Latino, and 1.5 percent Asian.

In children's media, specifically, there is additional evidence of lack of representation. Greenberg and Brand (1993) examined more than 10 hours of programming and over 100 commercials airing in a Saturday morning block on the original three broadcast networks and a weekday morning block on PBS. On the commercial networks, just 3 of 20 programs had a main character from a racial minority group. Each of these very few main characters was male. Past studies have further determined that African American cartoon characters have been rare, as have been interracial interactions (Barcus, 1983; Williams & Condry, 1989). The commercials and the PBS programs in the Greenberg and Brand (1993) data had much more racial and ethnic diversity. As with gender, PBS departs from the norm for the commercial networks.

A study of 724 commercials aired during children's programming on one weekday and one weekend day on all broadcast networks (including Fox, WB, and UPN as well as the original three) and Nickelodeon found 74 percent of characters were White, 19.4 percent African American, 2.4 percent Latino, and 2 percent Asian American (Li-Vollmer,

2002). As other analyses have found, African Americans were slightly overrepresented compared to their population figure, whereas all other racial and ethnic groups were underrepresented (Greenberg & Brand, 1993; Palmer, Smith, & Stawser, 1993).

Video games and the ads that promote them expand the racial and ethnic diversity of the media characters presented to children and teenagers (Scharrer, 2004; Smith, Lachlan, & Tamborini, 2003). In the Scharrer (2004) study, for example, White characters appeared in 86 percent of the ads from popular video game magazines, African American characters in 30 percent, Asian or Asian American characters in 18 percent, Latino characters in 10 percent, and Native American characters in just under 2 percent.

In addition to a dearth of parts for actors of color on television (with the exception of African Americans), there is also evidence that such actors may have difficulty encountering nonstereotyped roles. For example, Mastro and Greenberg (2000) found that over three-quarters of all roles for Latinos were in crime dramas, and the bulk of the roles for African Americans were in either sitcoms or crime dramas. Mastro and Behm-Morawitz (2005) discovered African American characters were more often found in crime dramas (often depicted as officers of the law) and Latino characters in sitcoms (often as family members) than White characters. Female Latino characters enjoyed lower levels of social authority than female White characters and male Latino characters had lower levels of authority on the job than male Whites. Latino characters were also dressed less "appropriately" (e.g., more provocatively, more ill fitting, less formal) than both African American and White characters. Media scholars have noted additional media stereotypes, as well, including the depiction of Asian characters as martial arts experts or "overachievers" (Hamamoto, 1993) and, again, the association of Latinos with crime, either as suspects or police officers (Berg, 1990; Greenberg & Baptista-Fernandez, 1980).

Li-Vollmer's (2002) study of commercials during children's programming also discovered a number of biases. Thirty-six percent of all Asian characters advertised technology-related products. Nearly all (97%) of the Latino characters were in advertisements for restaurants. White characters were much more likely than characters of color to be spokespeople for products, and to have speaking parts when commercials featured multiracial casts. Twice as many African American characters than White characters were shown as athletes. African Americans were also more likely than White characters to be depicted as musicians, singers, or dancers. The author catalogued 15 different roles that ranged from politician/leader to coach to teacher to doctor/dentist. The data (see Table 3.2) led to three observations. First, discrepancies often assign more prestige to White characters. Second, White characters were distributed widely across roles whereas characters of color were relegated to a smaller range. Third, Latinos, Asians or Asian Americans, and Native Americans were underrepresented.

Although some of the estimates of the number of characters of color in video games show representation equal to or even exceeding the size of particular racial or ethnic groups in the U.S. population, the presence of stereotypes sharply curtails the temptation to interpret the estimates as evidence of embracing diversity. Latino characters, for instance, often appear as criminals and/or gang members, and Asian characters are frequently martial arts experts (Scharrer, 2004). The large presence of African American characters is partly explained by sports games,

Table 3.2
Roles of White, African American, and "Other Minority" Characters in Commercials during Children's Television

Role	White		African American		Other Minority	
	%	N	%	N	%	N
Family Role						
Parent or Grandparent	19.5%	97	16.7%	15	25.0%	2
Occupational Role						
Service worker	11.0%	55	16.7%	15	62.5%	5
Professional	8.2	41	5.6	5	0.0	0
Leader or Politician	7.8	39	0.0	0	0.0	0
Teacher	6.4	32	10.0	9	0.0	0
Laborer	4.8	24	28.9	26	0.0	0
Coach	4.8	24	0.0	0	0.0	0
Law enforcement	3.4	17	1.1	1	0.0	0
Royalty	3.2	16	0.0	0	0.0	0
Doctor or Dentist	1.0	5	0.0	0	0.0	0
Scientist or Inventor	0.2	1	0.0	0	0.0	0
Other Role						
Supernatural human	19.5%	97	15.5%	14	12.5%	1
Criminal	7.4%	37	1.1%	1	0.0%	0
Genius	1.8%	9	4.4%	4	0.0%	0
Combination of above roles	1.0%	5	0.0%	0	0.0%	0
Total	100%	499	100%	90	100%	8

Adapted from Li-Vollmer, M. (2002). Race representation in child-targeted television commercials. *Mass Communication & Society*, 5(2), 207–228.

thereby reinforcing a stereotype of Blacks as athletes. Thus, the quantity of the roles for characters of color belies a tendency toward a generally unfavorable hue in the quality of the roles.

Many Latino children in the United States receive Spanish-language television programs in the home. Cartoons, music programs, game shows, and other popular television fare, dubbed into Spanish or created in Mexico and therefore originally in Spanish, provide an opportunity for Latino children to see characters of their own ethnicity on screen (Subervi-Velez & Colsant, 1993). Univision, the leading Spanish-language television network, reached 98 percent of all Hispanic or Latino television households in the United States in 2005, according to its web site (www.univision.net).

We make three well-supported claims about race and ethnicity. First, the growing number of channel options can expand the racial and ethnic diversity of the characters who appear in the media. Second, we acknowledge that palpable progress has been made over the years in terms of the number and, less so, the type of roles for African Americans. Third, we lament that many mainstream media persist in their dismissal of Latinos, Asian Americans, and Native Americans, and continue to advance a number of racial and ethnic stereotypes.

C. Age Distribution in Primetime Programming

Primetime programming has long presented a cast of characters remarkably skewed in age compared to the real world. Gerbner, Gross, Morgan, and Signorielli (1980), for example, examined programming that aired between 8 and 11 P.M. from 1969 to 1978. Most characters were between the ages of 25 and 45, with very few characters either younger or older. Vernon, Williams, Phillips, and Wilson (1991) extended the analysis through the 1980s. Characters 65 years of age or older were dramatically absent from primetime television programs, especially compared to the size of that age group in the U.S. population. In 1990, Robinson and Skill (1995) found characters 65 years and older comprised just 2.8 percent of primetime characters, and Signorielli (2004), based on data spanning the period from 1993 to 2002, similarly set the percentage at less than 3 percent.

The issue of age distribution of primetime characters was revisited recently by Lauzen and Dozier (2005), who studied portrayals in situation comedies and dramas airing during primetime on the six broadcast networks. Examining nearly 1,500 major and minor characters, they compared the presence of males and females of varying ages with U.S. population demographics (see Table 3.3). Teenage boys and men in their 20s were underrepresented. Men in their 30s through

Table 3.3
Age and Gender of Primetime Television Characters Compared to Age and Gender in the U.S. Population

Age	% Males in U.S. pop.	% Males in prime time	Diff.	% Females in U.S. pop.	% Females in prime time	Diff.
13–19	13%	8%	−5	12%	13%	+1
20–29	18	10	−8	16	18	+2
30–39	19	32	+13	18	39	+21
40–49	19	29	+10	18	19	+1
50–59	14	18	+4	14	7	−7
60+	18	4	−14	22	3	−19

Adapted from Lauzen, M.M. & Dozier, D.M. (2005). Recognition and respect revisited: Portrayals of age and gender in prime-time television. *Mass Communication & Society*, 8(3), 241–256.

50s were overrepresented. Men aged 60 and older were severely underrepresented, with population figures exceeding primetime figures by more than four to one. Patterns for females differed slightly. Teenage girls and women in their 20s were slightly overrepresented. There was twice the percentage of women in their 30s on primetime compared to the population. Women in their 40s were only slightly overrepresented, whereas those aged 50 or older were dramatically underrepresented.

These data represent two major themes. First, cultural as well as economic factors explain the large presence of the 30- to 50-year old adult in sitcoms and dramas. Characters both younger and older are decidedly less evident. The commercial imperative of media—to gain revenues from advertising—would seem to justify the strong presence of those in midlife because of their purchasing power. We nevertheless join Lauzen and Dozier (2005) in puzzling over the exclusion of those 60-plus, a population whose ranks are swelling as baby boomers age and whose collective expendable income is impressive. The commercial model fails to adequately explain the age bias, and we suspect that larger cultural norms devaluing the elderly are at play. Second, youth (and the physical attractiveness that is presumed to go along with it) appears to be more of a requirement for girls and women on television than for boys and men. The much more common presence of girls under 20 compared to same-aged boys and the disappearance from the screen of women over 50 both attest that the strong emphasis on youth applies to females more than males.

Female characters consistently have been younger than male characters on primetime television (Davis, 1990; Gerbner et al., 1980; Greenberg, Korzenny & Atkin, 1980; Signorielli, 2004; Signorielli & Bacue, 1999). Female characters over the age of 50 are depicted more negatively than male characters of the same age (Gerbner, Gross, Morgan & Signorielli, 1980; Greenberg, Korzenny & Atkin, 1980; Signorielli, 2004; Signorielli & Bacue, 1999). Thus, the quality of the depiction of older characters on primetime television depends partly on whether the character is male or female, and the data point to a double standard.

Lauzen and Dozier (2005) studied the quality of the roles given to actors of various ages in prime time. Displaying leadership status and exhibiting occupational power were both positively associated with age. No such relationship was found for two other achievement variables—pursuing goals and effectiveness at reaching goals. However, the linearity of the relationship between age and likelihood of displaying leadership and occupational power was disrupted by those in their 60s and older. In each case, the percentage of characters displaying these positive achievements increased neatly by decade from the teens through the 50s, but then collapsed. Furthermore, although the positive association between these role variables and age was largely shared by male and female characters, there were gender differences. Male characters in the middle age groups were more likely than female characters of the same age to be presented in leadership roles, to enjoy occupational power, and to pursue goals.

These data lead to several conclusions. First, the favorable depictions of success and responsibility on the job or elsewhere that generally increase with age stall at age 60. This may represent negative stereotyping of the elderly or a belief that a display of vigor at the border of retirement would be unrealistic to the audience. Second, age and gender interact to reveal sometimes subtle and other times overt biases. Occupational prestige and status are more strongly emphasized for males than for females. This is in accord with the long-held stereotype of men being better suited for careers and women for work within the home. Third, we concur with the observation of Lauzen and Dozier (2005) that the emphasis on a woman's youth extends to the arena of film, in which there is much anecdotal evidence that an actress over the age of 45 finds a dearth of roles available (Angier, 2001). Hollywood fosters a culture in which youth in general is worshiped—witness the billions spent on plastic surgery and the enduring mystique of celebrities who die young. Nevertheless, the Ponce de Leon adulation in the television and film culture is felt more acutely by women for whom youth and beauty appear to be requirements rather than optional attributes.

D. Characters with Disabilities

Data from the early 1980s of primetime and afternoon television estimate the number of characters with disabilities at fewer than one per hour (Turow & Coe, 1985) to about one every four hours (Makas, 1981). There is not a great deal of research regarding the depiction of people with disabilities in the media, perhaps partly because there are so few such portrayals. The disability itself typically has been a central element of the plot, thereby providing little evidence of the full and "normal" lives that people with disabilities can lead (Makas, 1993). Characters with disabilities have usually been White, rather young, unmarried, and male (Zola, 1985). The most commonly depicted disabilities have been physical and involve motor skills and even disfigurement (Cumberbatch & Negrine, 1992). A number of stereotypes of people with disabilities have been evident, including depicting the disabled as dependent and pathetic or, conversely, as heroic and inspirational, or the disfigured as evil (Cumberbatch & Negrine, 1992; Makas, 1993). There is no reason to think that more current data would present a very different picture.

Children's educational television stands out as a stark contrast. PBS' *Sesame Street* has been praised for its inclusion of children and adults with disabilities in a matter-of-fact manner that is meant to draw neither sympathy nor admiration (Makas, 1993). The appeal of such educational programs is confined to young children, and we can conclude that the bulk of the messages that older children and adolescents receive about disabilities through the media correspond more closely to narrow and often unfavorable images.

E. Depiction of Sexual Orientation

The opportunity for young audience members who are gay or lesbian to see characters in the media who share this characteristic is important to their healthy development. Gay youth experience a great deal of harassment, prejudice, depression, and an elevated suicide rate, and from this perspective it is perhaps the most critical attribute to model on television and in other media so that gay youth can find support among media characters and thereby feel accepted and "normal" (Nichols, 1999).

Over the years, the inclusion of a single gay character, often a minor character somewhat peripheral to the narrative, has not been unusual on television. Main characters were, for a long time, invariably heterosexual, thereby establishing heterosexuality as the unquestioned norm. That began to change in 1997 when the character played by Ellen DeGeneres on the ABC sitcom *Ellen* came out to an audience estimated at 42 million (Justin, 1999), becoming the first openly gay lead character on primetime television ("ABC Cancels," 1998). The event captured news headlines, spawned outrage from conservative religious figures, and triggered the withdrawal of commercials from some major advertisers (Hubert, 1999). The show remained on the air for another year, but was then canceled due to low ratings. More recently, Ellen DeGeneres has enjoyed renewed popularity as a successful talk show host.

After *Ellen* paved the way, a number of primetime television programs with main, recurring gay and lesbian characters central to the plot were introduced. Some garnered large audiences and much commercial success (e.g., *Will and Grace, Queer Eye for the Straight Guy*). In 1999–2000, the Gay and Lesbian Alliance Against Defamation (GLAAD) determined that the television season included 27 gay characters, accounting for 2 percent of all television characters, an improvement over past seasons but an underrepresentation compared to U.S. population estimates (Justin, 1999). In scripted programs in the 2005–2006 season on the six broadcast networks, again less than 2 percent of all main characters (16 characters out of over 700) were gay, lesbian, or bisexual (GLAAD, 2005). The trend toward network television's depiction of most gay characters as White males continued (13 of the 16 characters matched both descriptions). Greater numbers of gay and lesbian characters appeared on cable and in unscripted "reality-based" programming.

In terms of the quality of roles, there is much room for improvement. GLAAD, for instance, has advocated that a greater number of lesbians appear on television (the bulk of same-sex relationships on TV typically feature gay males), fewer jokes occur on sitcoms regarding sexual orientation, and, most importantly for our topic of children, teenagers, and media, that there should be a greater number of adolescent gay and lesbian characters to provide role models (Justin, 1999). Some improvement in the latter has been evident, with plot lines featuring teenage characters involved in same-sex relationships on *Desperate Housewives, DeGrassi: The Next Generation*, and *The OC* (GLAAD, 2005). Today's child will grow up in a society in which it is no longer entirely verboten to model same-sex relationships on television and in film.

F. Beauty and Body Images in Media

Thinness is highly valued in U.S. culture (ironic when considering rising obesity rates), and the media uphold this standard. Across virtually all media—television, advertising, video games, magazines—beauty is defined by a symmetrical, flawless face and a very thin body that is paradoxically voluptuous for females and muscular for males. The messages that children and teens receive from the media about body size and shape are highly contradictory—"thin is in" but so are fatty foods low in nutritional value.

The beauty standard for women on television prescribes thinness as a necessity (Fouts & Burggraf, 1999; Harrison, 2000). Fouts and Burggraf, for example, studied 28 sitcoms airing during primetime chosen for their popularity with 10- to 16-year-old females—a group at heightened risk for developing eating disorders. Compared to the U.S. population, females below average in weight were clearly overrepresented. An earlier study (Silverstein, Perdue, Peterson & Kelly, 1986) had determined that just 5 percent of female television characters could be described as "heavy," whereas nearly 70 percent were categorized as "thin."

Verbal interactions among television characters reinforce an aspiration for thinness among women and girls. Signorielli (2001) found that a woman's physical appearance and attractiveness was a common topic in conversations among characters. Fouts and Burggraf (1999) discovered that female characters tended to deride themselves regarding their weight and body shape, and male characters directed a larger number of complimentary comments about appearance toward thin characters than to heavier characters. An example of this verbal corroboration of the thin ideal for women in sitcoms can be found in NBC's now-canceled but long-popular *Friends*. The character of Monica has always been exceptionally thin on the program, but flashbacks to her youth feature actor Courtney Cox Arquette in a "fat suit" and derogatory jokes abound among her "friends" about her weight and ostensibly corresponding lack of attractiveness.

Both music videos and television commercials advance the same message—that it is critically important for women to meet society's highly unrealistic definition of attractiveness. Signorielli, McLeod, and Healy (1994), for instance, found young, very thin female performers to be the norm on music television. Ogletree and colleagues (Ogletree, Williams, Raffeld, Mason & Fricke, 1990) determined that 86 percent of all commercial messages on television concerned with enhancing physical appearance are directed toward young women.

In video games, female characters' bodies are often very thin, yet highly sexualized with large breasts and hips. Clothing on female video game characters can be provocative and intended to emphasize sexuality. Dietz (1998), examining 33 popular Nintendo and Sega Genesis games, found 28 percent of the games depicted women as sex objects. Beasley and Collins Standley (2002) discovered that female video game characters were more scantily clad than male characters, and a full 41 percent of females were coded as "voluptuous" whereas only 2.8 percent were coded as "flat chested." In the Scharrer (2004) analysis of video game ads, female characters were rated as both more attractive and sexier than male characters, and one out of every four females was shown wearing a low-cut shirt or emphasizing cleavage.

We agree with the argument that Gailey (1993) made more than a decade before these recent studies. The characters of women and girls in video games are largely designed to appeal to the sexual fantasies of teenaged and young men, the most ardent fans of the games. The result is an emphasis on the female body and an attendant focus on physical attractiveness that is inescapably apparent, as well as the inclusion of an often highly exaggerated female form that emphasizes curvaceousness and thinness simultaneously (a body type rarely presented by nature).

Although more relentless for women and girls, there is an attractiveness standard for men and boys as well. A muscular ideal has been advanced for males in the media in general (Mishkind, Rodin, Silberstein & Striegel-Moore, 1986) and on music television, in particular (Signorielli et al., 1994). Video games and the ads that promote them also advance a muscular ideal for males. Scharrer (2004), for example, found that the muscularity of males was more pronounced than that of females in the video game ads, tight fitting clothing was donned by one in every four male characters, and 12 percent were shown wearing no shirt.

Media images of women in advertising, video games, and television programming are unwavering in their endorsement of thin beauty as evident in the physical appearance of the characters as well as conversations about body size and shape. A far greater number of male characters are heavy set, out of shape, or overweight, but the media advocates muscularity for boys and men.

III. BEHAVIOR OF MEDIA CHARACTERS

Decades of empirical research support the view that televised portrayals are often given some weight when audience members make behavioral decisions in their own lives (Bandura, 1986; Comstock et al., 1978; Roberts & Foehr, 2003). Children and adolescents, in particular, learn about themselves and the world around them by observing media characters. The young are a group especially likely to model the behavior of media characters as a result of their developing concept of the self and accompanying tendency to "try on" varying thoughts, attitudes, and behaviors to discover which are likely to be suitable in differing circumstances and settings (Comstock, 1991, 1993). Our review encompasses a wider range of portrayals that might affect behavior: violence and aggression, sharing and other prosocial behaviors, alcohol and tobacco use, sexual intimacy and use of profanity, and the consumption of foods and beverages.

A. Violence and Aggression

One of the oldest and most pressing concerns about the media content consumed by children and teenagers has been its emphasis on violence and aggression. Parents, caregivers, teachers, researchers, political action groups, politicians, and pediatricians have registered complaints and voiced apprehension. The use of physical or even verbal aggression to solve a problem or deal with a difficult or frustrating situation is not the life lesson that most adults want young people to learn.

Children and teenagers are exposed to astonishing amounts of violence on television and in other media. With the pervasiveness of cable and satellite television and the growth in popularity of video and computer games, the estimate made by Huston and colleagues more than a decade ago that a child in the United States is likely to have seen 8,000 murders and 100,000 other acts of violence in the media by the time she or he completes elementary school (Huston et al., 1992) is certain to fall short. In one of the great ironies in media studies, children's television programming consistently has contained more acts of violence per hour than adult or general audience television programming. Times during which children in particular are most likely to be present in the television audience—Saturday mornings, early evenings, weekday late afternoons—typically have the greatest number of acts of violence on the screen than any other daypart (Comstock, 1991; Hamilton, 1998), although this violence generally is less graphic than that later in the evening (National Television Violence Study, 1998).

1. Presence of Violence in General Audience Television   There are two authoritative sources of data on the presence of violence and aggression in general audience television—the work begun in the late 1960s and early 1970s by the late George Gerbner and colleagues in the Cultural Indicators Project, and the recent National Television Violence Study (Smith et al., 1998; Wilson et al., 1996, 1997). The former spans decades of primetime content (as well as Saturday morning programming, which we will discuss later in this section) and the latter covers a period of just three years but includes over 10,000 hours of round-the-clock programming from a wide variety of networks and channels. The two essentially concur in their definition of violence as overt instances of physical force that harms another or realistic threats of such force, and they reach many of the same conclusions.

The latest data from the Cultural Indicator perspective (Signorielli, 2003) shows an average between spring 1993 and fall 2001 of 4.5 acts of violence per program in primetime television, with six out of 10 programs containing at least one violent act. About one-third of the violent acts were portrayed as justified, thereby sending the message that violence is acceptable if provoked; over 20 percent were gratuitous to the plot, implying that violence is ordinary and always a possibility; almost two-thirds were depicted without accompanying consequences, thereby glossing over pain, harm, regret, or other penalties that might dissuade an individual from acting aggressively. Although claims have been made that television is becoming more and more violent, Signorielli's (2003) comparison of the latest figures with previous data collected and analyzed by Gerbner and colleagues shows only modest oscillations in number of acts of violence on television over the last 30 or more years. The stability of the presence of violence on the television screen was noted by Scharrer and Comstock (2004):

> The Gerbner data also determine that the rate of violence on television has been quite stable in the long term. Sporadic peaks and valleys in amount of violence on television occur from season to season, explained in part by fluctuations in public and political concern or changing popularity of a violence-saturated genre, but the pattern over decades is one of relative stability. Recent years have represented a "valley," a slight decrease in number of violent acts, presumably due to the political pressure put on the industry to curb violent content . . . However, the longitudinal data suggest such "valleys" are typically short-lived. (p. 174)

How is it that television seems so much more violent today than in the past, when the social scientific data point so convincingly to a pattern of stability in number of acts of violence per hour? The answer, we believe, has to do with *how* violence is shown rather than *how much* violence is shown. There is evidence that violence on television has become more graphic over time, showing increasing amounts of realistic-looking blood and gore rather than more sanitized depictions. Signorielli (2003) found a significant increase in the percentage of primetime television programs containing graphic violence between the years 1993 and 2001. A study conducted by the Parents Television Council (2002) determined that milder violent incidents (e.g., fist fights) during the "family hour" of primetime television (8 P.M. to 9 P.M.) decreased from 44 percent of all violent sequences in 1998 to 32 percent in 2002, whereas violent sequences using guns increased from 29 to 38 percent.

The transformation that occurred in the television industry when cable channels began to create and distribute their own original programming rather than merely transmit programs produced elsewhere also altered how violence is shown. This is attributable to three factors (Hamilton, 1998): the lack of even the modest regulatory oversight that the FCC exercises over broadcast outlets; the public perception of cable as a source invited into the home that people easily could avoid if they wished; and the competitive strategies of the cable channels, and especially the tactic of going beyond what the broadcast outlets can comfortably offer. Cable programs tend to push the envelope toward realistic-looking and often gruesome depictions (e.g., HBO's *The Sopranos*, FX's *The Shield*).

The National Television Violence Study (NTVS, 1998; Smith et al., 1998; Wilson et al., 1997, 1998) went beyond *how much* violence is present on television to consider *in what context* that violence is shown. In year three in the extensive NTVS sample that included programming on cable, broadcast, public, and independent stations in all but the wee hours of the night or early morning, 61 percent of all programs contained at least one violent act. Cable, and especially the movie channels, was found to be more violent than the other types of channels.

There was ample evidence that violence is commonly presented in a context that makes it appear rather harmless or as an acceptable way to solve problems. Only 16 percent of programs with violence portrayed long-term negative consequences. Almost three-quarters of scenes that contained violence (71%) depicted no remorse, regret, or negative sanctions against violence. About half of all violent interactions showed no pain associated with acts that would likely cause considerable physical injury in real life. Another 34 percent included what was characterized as "unrealistically low levels of harm" (p. 171). More than one-fourth (28%) of violent interactions stemmed from circumstances considered justifiable by the characters involved and 39 percent were perpetrated by appealing, attractive characters.

These contextual data have implications for modeling by young audience members (Comstock & Scharrer, 1999; NTVS, 1998; Smith et al., 1998; Wilson et al., 1997, 1998). They are more likely to emulate screen violence when it is perceived as unharmful, trivial, without consequences or serious physical harm, performed by characters with whom they identify (typically the "good guys"), and if the perpetrator has an ostensibly good reason to act out aggressively (which may correspond with the viewer's own "good reason" in life and therefore be especially likely to encourage aggressive behavior). Only 3 percent of the programs containing violence conveyed an anti-violence theme.

We can easily dismiss the argument that violence is used on television primarily to caution viewers against engaging in it.

Music television contains a small but substantial amount of violence, although considerably less than what is found in primetime television. DuRant and colleagues (1997a) examined more than 500 videos from MTV, VH1, BET, and CMT. Violence appeared in 15 percent of the videos at a rate of 6.1 acts per video. MTV, the most popular among adolescents of the cable channels examined, had the highest percentage (22%). Rap and rock were the most violent genres (about 20% of each contained violence). Rich and colleagues (1998), using the same sample as DuRant and colleagues (1997a), determined that although Caucasian males were most frequently perpetrators of violence, African-American males committed violent acts at a disproportionately high rate. Smith and Boyson (2002) used the third year National Television Violence Study sample to examine three music channels, MTV, BET, and VH1. Out of nearly 2,000 videos, 15 percent contained violence. Adult males were overwhelmingly more likely than other groups to be both the perpetrators and victims of violence in the music videos. Across all three channels, there were more Black or African American characters involved in violence (either as perpetrator or victim) than White or European American characters, although this was explained in part by the content of BET. About one-third (32%) was extensive enough to cause serious injury if incurred in the real world, and over half (56%) showed no "injury or incapacitation to the victims of violence" (p. 71). Many of the videos on music television contain no violence (about 85%) but those that do have high concentrations and the portrayals of African Americans have the potential to contribute to racial stereotypes.

Sitcoms, a genre especially appealing to older children and adolescents, regularly employ a form of aggressive behavior—diminishing or hurtful statements (Potter & Vaughan, 1997). Physical injury is largely absent, but such infliction of emotional distress is easily imitated and has for young viewers a wide range of applications.

2. Violence in Commercials   Commercial messages placed within and between media programs have been less frequently studied for aggressive and violent content. Yet, this format may be particularly difficult and irksome for parents and caregivers. There is no telling when a trailer for an upcoming film, a promotional message for another program, or an ad for a product or service that is deemed objectionable may appear on the screen. No program guides exist to preclude accidental or incidental exposure. Such exposure is far from improbable, as a Federal Trade Commission report (2000) found that music, film, and electronic gaming industries have engaged in purposeful advertising to children of products that were rated for adult audiences only.

Anderson (1997) assessed commercials airing during Major League Baseball playoff games. During 15 games, 6.8 percent (104) of the more than 1,500 commercials contained violence. There were 69 instances of violent acts, 90 instances of violent threats, and 27 instances of violent outcomes. Maguire, Sandage, and Weatherby (2000) studied commercials appearing in the day and evening hours on eight channels (ABC, CBS, NBC, FOX, CNN, ESPN, FAM, and MTV), defining violent commercials as those that "depicted humans (or their caricatures) as victims, or potential victims, of legal or illegal physical harm, illegal property damage, and language or behavior that suggested potential or imagined violence" (p. 127). Of the nearly 1,700 commercials in 1996 and 1997 samples, 2.8 percent contained violence, with the figure nearly double in the second year compared to the first. Scharrer and colleagues (Scharrer, Bergstrom, Paradise, & Ren, 2004) found that in one week of primetime programming on the six broadcast networks, a total of 536 commercials (12% of all those aired) featured verbal, physical, or "fortuitous" aggression, with the latter defined as destruction or harm to one character not directly caused by another character (Larson, 2001). Just over half of the commercials presented the aggression as humorous, thereby making light of the harm that aggression can cause. Finally, Oliver and Kalyanaraman (2002) analyzed a sample of 107 movie trailers and found about three-fourths featured violence and slightly less than half contained one or more gun scenes.

Commercials aired during children's television programming have also been shown to contain aggression or violence. Macklin and Kolbe (1984) examined 64 commercials aired on ABC, NBC, and CBS during Saturday morning children's programming and found that eight (12.5%) contained violence (three targeted to males and five gender neutral). Browne's (1998) cross-national content analysis of 298 commercials (148 American and 150 Australian) found that commercials targeting boys were substantially more aggressive (e.g., throwing, hitting, making faces, etc.) than commercials aimed at girls. Most recently, Larson (2001) discovered that of nearly 600 commercials aired in 1997 and 1998 during select children's programming blocks on ABC, CBS, Fox, and Nickelodeon, 219 commercials (37%) featured at least one aggressive act. Physical aggression, object aggression (e.g., hitting or attacking an object), verbal aggression, and fortuitous aggression (e.g., accidents and explosions; aggression with no perpetrator) were coded, with fortuitous the most prevalent (42%).

3. Violence in Children's Television   The stories designed specifically to be told to children via cartoons and live action programs have always been filled with violence and aggression. We attribute this to two factors. First, violence has been conflated with action, and it is a common belief in the media industry that children are drawn to action as a result of their relatively short attention spans and their unique amounts of physical energy. Second, children's books and fairy tales have long included horrible events that climax in a violent confrontation for the supposed purpose of teaching children morals and ethics. The fate of the "bad guys" serves as a lesson to children to be good themselves lest they suffer the same fate. Cartoons and other stories in children's media, therefore, can be interpreted as modern morality tales that underscore the rewards that ultimately accrue to the "good," even in the face of continuing challenges posed by the "evil."

The "violence profiles" drawn from the data analyzed by Gerbner and associates have found between 18 and 32 acts of violence per hour in Saturday morning television, a time slot dominated by cartoons (Gerbner, Morgan, & Signorielli, 1994). The vast majority of the characters that appear in such programs are involved in some way in violence, with an average of 80 percent of all characters being either victims or perpetrators or both. Child characters, in particular, are more often victims of violence rather than perpetrators, with an estimated 13 to 16 child victims for every 10 child perpetrators.

The National Television Violence Study, too, singles out cartoons as having the dubious distinction of containing one of the highest rates of violent acts per hour of any type of programming on television (Smith et al., 1996; Wilson et al., 1997, 1998). In fact, NTVS researchers (Wilson et al., 2002) compared the depiction of violence in television programs targeting children aged 13 and younger to the depiction of violence in general audience television programs (see Table 3.4). In children's television, long-term consequences for violence were more rarely seen, violence was more frequently combined with humor, and unrealistically low amounts of harm were more likely. Overall, then, children's television contains a comparatively large amount of violence, and that violence is frequently shown in a manner that detracts from its gravity and the harm it can cause.

4. Violence in Children's Films   Only a small number of analyses of films popular with children exist. Nevertheless, their content takes on importance in light of the data showing that young children, especially, often adore the films in their libraries, frequently engaging in repeat viewing (Mares, 1998). For their part, parents and caregivers often trust Disney and other producers of children's films to provide content free

Table 3.4
Violence on Children's Television Compared to Violence on General
Audience Television

Audience	Children's	General
Amount or Type of Violence	TV	TV
Amount of Violence		
% of programs with violence	69%	57%
Average number of violent incidents per hour*	14.1	5.6
Average number of violence scenes per hour	6.5	2.7
% of time devoted to violence	11.7	12.3
Type of Violence		
% of all incidents with...		
Attractive perpetrator	36%	42%
Victims that show no pain	63	51
Victims that show no harm	67	43
Unrealistically low levels of harm	66	26
Justification for violence	27	35
% of all scenes with...		
Blood and gore shown	1	21
Violence immediately rewarded	32	21
Violence not immediately punished	81	72
Humor co-occurring with violence	76	24
% of all programs with...		
Bad perpetrators that are never punished	36	34
Good perpetrators that are never punished	68	67
Long-term suffering depicted	3	25
Fantasy-based context	87	9
Animated format	93	3

*To calculate number of incidents, the authors employed the PAT technique. Each time there was a new perpetrator (P), target (T), or type of act (A), a new incident was recorded.

Adapted from Wilson, B. J., Smith, S. L., Potter, W. J., Kunkel, D., Linz, D., Colvin, C. M. & Donnerstein, E. (2002). Violence in children's television programming: Assessing the risks. *Journal of Communication, 52,* 5–35.

from violence, sex, adult language, and other potentially problematic situations and events. The data suggest that such faith may be misplaced.

Yokota and Thompson (2000) studied all G-rated animated feature films available on videotape, released between 1937 and 1999, defining violence as intentional, physical acts with the potential to injure or harm. In a total of 74 films, every one had at least one act of violence. Violent scenes took up an average of 9.5 minutes. Approximately one-third of the films (32%)

contained an explicitly spoken message against violence, whereas 49% seemed to make light of or even celebrate violence through the inclusion of cheering or laughing about violence. Yokota and Thompson detected a significant trend toward increased violence over time in the G-rated films. Finally, just over half of all violent acts (55%) involved the "good" characters fighting against the "bad" characters. We can safely conclude, based on this extensive content analysis of films made expressly for the youngest movie goers (and movie owners and renters), that violence has a clear and consistent presence in even those films with the least restrictive ratings.

5. Violence in Video and Computer Games   Violence also has a starring role in video games. Dietz (1998) discovered that 79 percent of the games in her sample had violence as a central theme. Smith, Lachlan, and Tamborini (2003), in their study of the first 10 minutes of game play in the 20 most widely sold games of 1999, found 68 percent of the games had at least one violent act. Games rated for older audiences (e.g., T for Teen, M for Mature) contained substantially more violence than games with less restrictive ratings. Nevertheless, a full 57 percent of games rated for children or for all audiences contained violence. The games were also determined by Smith and colleagues to show harm unrealistically. The majority, 61 percent, depicted little harm or pain in violent interactions, yet over three-fourths of the violent acts shown would result in moderate to extreme harm in the real world. Nearly all of the games (98%) featured a lack of consequences associated with violence, and 41 percent depicted violence in a humorous context.

Thompson and Haninger (2001) gathered a convenience sample of E-rated games (with E signifying the game is appropriate for "everyone"), coding the ways in which violence was presented during game play. They found that intentionally harming other characters was necessary for progress in 60 percent of the games, and almost half (44%) of the games that contained violence did not carry a "content descriptor" label warning of its presence. In print ads in magazines for video game aficionados, Scharrer (2004) found that just over half (55.8%) contained at least one act of violence, and an average of 2.49 weapons, 1.53 violent acts, 2.17 violent words, and 0.85 verbal threats to commit violence appeared. Although ads for T- and M-rated games contained more violence than E-rated games, the latter still had an average of 0.85 weapons, 0.71 violent acts, 1.01 violent words, and 0.34 threats. The genres of games with the greatest amount of violence were action adventure and fantasy/odyssey games.

Although content analyses of Internet sites are rare (and a discussion of such content extends the boundaries of "video and computer games" to other digital media), Aikat (2004) performed an interesting and relevant study of the amount and types of violence appearing on the web sites for music television—BET.com, Country.com, MTV.com, and VH1.com. Over 900 unique music videos available on the four web sites on a randomly selected weekday and the following weekend day were selected for analysis. Sixteen percent of the videos contained violence. Violent acts occurred at a rate of 1.2 per violent music video (bearing in mind that many of the online videos were shorter snippets of the originals). About three-fourths (76%) of the violent acts employed weapons, with guns the most common (constituting 22% of all weapons). The most frequent types of violence were "property assaults" (28% of all violent acts) and "armed assaults" (22%). Rap/hip hop and hard rock online music videos contained the largest amount of violence, and country music and R&B contained the least. The Internet web sites of music television outlets likely to be accessed by adolescents contain only a modest amount of violence, but the type of violence that does appear is serious in nature, employing guns and other weapons and destroying property or intending bodily harm.

B. Prosocial Behavior in Media

"Prosocial behavior" describes the presence of positive, helpful, ethical, and cooperative behavior among characters and other people in the media. Programming developed for preschoolers, in addition to being educational in terms of teaching children counting, shape sorting, and learning the alphabet, often also attempts to contribute to children's social and emotional skills, modeling getting along with others, having good manners, and engaging in safe and healthy behavior. In programming for older children and teenagers, prosocial content is typically less overt as well as less common, relegated to the "after-school special," public service announcements, or the actions of characters who solve problems and persevere under difficult circumstances.

Potter and Ware (1987) studied a sample of primetime programs on ABC, CBS, and NBC and found antisocial and prosocial acts occur in nearly equal amounts (48% of all acts coded were antisocial, 52% prosocial). The authors defined antisocial to include physical aggression, verbal aggression, and deceit, and prosocial to include altruism, coming to another character's "physical aid," providing information or verbal support, and giving compliments. Woodard (1999) investigated a week of children's programming and found that approximately half of all shows contained at least one "social lesson." Most of this prosocial content, however, occurred in programs for preschoolers rather than older children. PBS offered the greatest number of programs with a social message. Nearly three-fourths (72%) of PBS' children's programs included a social message, significantly larger than the 59% of programs with a social message on either Disney or HBO. The relative dearth of prosocial messages in programs directed toward older children and teens was again apparent in Mares and Woodard's (2001) study of the top 20 programs of two- to 17-year-olds. In that sample, just four programs contained prosocial messages—*Disney's One Saturday Morning, 7th Heaven, Boy Meets World,* and *Hey Arnold!.* Thus, the availability of programs with explicit prosocial content most certainly declines with viewer age.

Numerous educational and prosocial computer games are available to today's child (Subrahmanyam, Kraut, Greenfield & Gross, 2001). Computer software is used to prepare toddlers for school and to engage school-aged children in learning in a wide variety of subjects. Computer games for the very young often underscore the prosocial lessons found in television shows on PBS and elsewhere.

C. Prevalence of Alcohol and Tobacco in Media

Children and teenagers have become familiar with alcohol, cigarettes, and other tobacco products through the media, in which the potential of a negative impact on health is often glossed over or entirely absent. The government forbids some advertising of these products, and the advertising industry itself imposes self-regulation to prohibit the promotion of others, but their use is widely and generally favorably portrayed in programming if not in commercials—at worst, smoking is a sophisticated mannerism and alcohol is a welcome respite—in advertisements. Advertising for cigarettes has been banned from appearing in electronic media by Congress since 1971 and in outdoor advertising within 1,000 feet of playgrounds since 1997 (at the same time that retail outlets were forced to check photo identifications for tobacco sales; Moore, 1999). In 1999, the Distilled Spirits Council of the United States lifted its self-imposed ban of the advertising of hard liquor on radio and television, thereby suspending a voluntary practice that had been in place since 1936 for radio and 1948 for television (Moore, 1999). The four leading commercial networks, ABC, CBS, NBC, and Fox, declined to change their own policies of not accepting hard liquor advertising, but such ads can currently be seen on cable channels and independent or otherwise affiliated stations (Moore, 1999).

Strasburger (1997) estimated that children are exposed to some 1,000 to 2,000 beer and wine commercials—always freely advertised in electronic media—on primetime television each year. Advertising techniques used to peddle these products frequently employ themes and depictions attractive to the young audience, including the use of attractive young models, humor, popular music, and animated or live-action "mascots" such as frogs, dogs, and lizards (Strasburger, 2001). Sports programming on television contains more than twice the number of commercials for alcoholic beverages than primetime programming (Grube, 1995; Madden & Grube, 1994). The typical commercial or print advertisement for beer, malt beverages, and wine shows beautiful and youthful characters engaged in activities that the typical teen may find wistfully appealing—romantic dates, meeting in a bar, frolicking on the beach, snowboarding, or playing touch football.

Television programming itself also models the use of alcohol. One in every four beverages shown during primetime is an alcoholic beverage (Story & Faulkner, 1990); six instances of drinking alcohol are estimated to occur per hour of primetime (Grube, 1993); and one scene featuring alcohol consumption is shown every 22 minutes on television in general, every 14 minutes on MTV, and every 27 minutes during primetime (Gerbner & Ozyegin, 1997). Thus, during time slots that often invite viewing by children and teenagers, messages about alcohol consumption are by no means infrequent.

In the top-grossing films from 1985 to 1995, Everett, Schnuth, and Tribble (1998) found 96 percent contained a scene or interaction that could be coded as "pro-alcohol," including PG and PG-13 films. A series of additional studies has determined that alcohol use is present even in G-rated children's animated movies. Goldstein and colleagues (Goldstein, Sobel & Newman, 1999) found 50 percent of a sample of 50 such films contained alcohol use, with wine being the most commonly consumed alcoholic beverage. "Good" characters were no less likely to be shown consuming alcohol than "bad" or "neutral" characters. Thompson and Yokota (2001) found 47 percent of a sample of G-rated animated films created between 1937 and 2000 showed characters drinking alcohol. Again, wine was the most common type, and there was some indication that such instances had declined slightly over time. Finally, Ryan and Hoerrner (2004) studied 24 Disney films targeted to children that contained an animated human character and found 75 percent had at least one instance of "alcohol exposure," defined as a "continuous display" of an alcoholic product on the screen (p. 266). Such displays ranged from merely picturing the product in the scene to having a character hold or use the product. Beer was most frequently depicted, followed by wine and champagne. We can conclude from the confluence of results that the depiction of alcohol is not uncommon in films, even in those created especially for the youngest audience.

Cigarette use is not promoted in television commercials (due to governmental and self-regulation), but does appear occasionally in television programming and rather frequently in magazine ads, on billboards, and in movies. Hazan and Glantz (1995) estimated that 24 percent of primetime television programs in 1992 contained scenes in which characters were smoking and just 8 percent were determined to have an anti-smoking message. On MTV, DuRant and colleagues (DuRant et al., 1997b) found one-fourth of all music videos showed tobacco use. Gerbner and Ozyegin (1997) catalogued one smoking scene every 57 minutes on primetime television. They also identified movie trailers as a frequent source of favorable messages about smoking. Smoking is up to three times more likely in films compared to smoking in the general population (Hazan, Lipton & Glantz, 1994), and was present in nearly 90 percent of the most popular movie rentals in 1996 and 1997 (Roberts, Henriksen & Christenson, 1999).

Everett and colleagues (1998) found 98 percent of their sample of top-grossing films from 1985 to 1995 contained a "pro-tobacco" instance and only 38 percent included a scene or other event that could be construed as sending an anti-tobacco message. More than half (56%) of the 50 G-rated animated films examined by Goldstein and colleagues (1999) portrayed tobacco use. Among the 81 G-rated animated films studied by Thompson and Yokota (2001), 43 percent showed tobacco use. Finally, within the 24 G-rated animated Disney films analyzed by Ryan and Hoerrner (2004), 75 percent exposed audiences to tobacco products or use. Pipes and cigars were most prevalent. Both the Ryan and Hoerrner (2004) and the Thompson and Yokota (2001) studies that spanned multiple decades agreed that the depiction of tobacco use has decreased over time. As in the case of alcohol, cigarette smoking is fairly frequent in the most popular films and occurs even in G-rated children's films.

Alcohol use is more commonly found on television compared to cigarette use (by a rate of almost three to one, according to Gerbner and Ozyegin, 1997). Yet, both are widely present in the media and we question the ethics of promoting them directly or indirectly in media popular among or intended for children and teenagers when their use of these products is forbidden by law.

The inclusion of alcohol and tobacco use among characters in G-rated films designed for children is particularly problematic. The frequent humorous context implicitly endorses these products. Their use is also often peripheral to the plot, so they could be eliminated easily without affecting the narrative.

D. Influence of Food and Beverages in Media

Frequently reported correlations between amount of television viewing and the likelihood of a young person being overweight (e.g., Comstock

& Scharrer, 1999; Hancox, Milne & Poulton, 2004) have resulted in increased interest in media messages about food and beverages. The nutritional value of many advertised foods and beverages has been questioned, viewing and other media use are usually accompanied by physical inactivity that would promote weight gain, and media use ensures exposure to attractive persuasive appeals on behalf of foods and beverages.

An estimated one-half to two-thirds of all commercials aired during children's television are for food and beverages (Taras & Gage, 1995). A child is exposed to a food commercial every five minutes while watching Saturday morning cartoons (Kotz & Story, 1994). Among the most frequently advertised types are breakfast cereals (often high in sugar, such as Fruity Pebbles or Cap'n Crunch) and "confectionary snacks" such as candy bars and baked goods (Kotz & Story, 1994; Lewis & Hill, 1998). An estimated two-thirds to 80 percent of commercials for foods targeted directly to children are high in fat, oils, sugar, or salt or otherwise lacking in nutritional value (Cotugna, 1988; Kotz & Story, 1994). Food commercials airing during children's television (see Table 3.5) not only are largely for nonhealthy foods but also use a number of

Table 3.5
Types of Food Commercials in Children's Television, N = 564

Variable	% of commercials
Food category	
Fats, oils, and sweets	43.6%
Bread, cereal, rice, and pasta*	37.5
Fast food	11.0
Explicit selling technique employed	
Taste	36.2%
Free toy	16.9
Fun	16.7
Cool/hip	7.3
Healthy/nutritious	2.4
Convenient	1.2
Formal features	
Child actor	84.0%
Partial animation	48.0
Full animation	28.0

*In this category, the largest category of food type was high-sugar cereals.

Adapted from Kotz, K. & Story, M. (1994). Food advertisements during children's Saturday morning television programming: Are they consistent with dietary recommendations? *Journal of the American Dietary Association, 94,* 1296–1300.

persuasive techniques particularly effective with child audiences. These include emphasizing the taste of the food, offering a "free" toy with the product, using child actors, and employing partial or full animation.

The problem is not confined to the United States. In a study of 239 commercials for foods airing during 27 hours of children's television programming in Australia, Hill and Radimer (1997) found that two decidedly nonnutritious categories accounted for almost half of all advertised foods, fast food restaurants (25%) and chocolate (22%). In the United Kingdom, Lewis and Hill (1997) determined that not only do unhealthy foods appear at rates equivalent to those in the United States, but commercials for those foods similarly use animation, humor, and storytelling techniques to appeal to the youthful audience. Hill and Radimer (1997) discovered that just 8 percent of the Australian television commercials showed fruit, 1 percent vegetables, and none meat.

The failure to promote fruits and vegetables also characterizes commercials on children's programming. One reason is that there are no brands for produce that an advertiser can use to sell a product. The consequence is that children are the target of an onslaught of messages attempting to persuade them to eat and drink foods and beverages that are unhealthy.

We see little variation when we shift the focus from children's television to primetime programming. Story and Faulkner (1990) studied messages about food and eating in both programs and commercials, selecting the top-rated sitcoms and dramas for analysis. In the programs themselves, food and beverage references—comments, displays, consumption—occurred at a rate of five times per half hour. The majority, 60 percent, were for beverages low in nutrients (e.g., coffee, alcohol, soft drinks) or foods characterized as sweets. Fruits and vegetables seldom appeared. They were selected by characters as a between-meal snack only 10 percent of the time and depicted as a component of a meal just a few times in the entire sample. In the more than 250 commercials that aired during the programs, just over a third (35%) were for food products. Restaurant fast food was the most common type of food advertised. Only three commercials featured fruits and none featured vegetables.

Not only are fruits and vegetables uncommon, but there is little discussion of nutritious diets in food advertising. Byrd-Bredbenner and Grasso (2000) analyzed approximately 700 commercials that appeared in a sample of primetime programs most frequently viewed by two- to 11-year-olds and found nutritional information was very rare and when present was often misleading.

Finally, in a novel contribution to the literature, Harrison and Marske (2005) studied over 400 food commercials and looked up the nutrition facts on the package labels for 275 of the foods advertised. Convenience foods (such as microwaveable meals), fast foods, and sweets made up a whopping 83 percent of all the advertised foods. Calculations determined that consuming a 2,000-calorie diet of the foods advertised in general audience programs would surpass dietary recommendations for fat, saturated fat, and sodium, and consuming a similar diet of the foods advertised in children's television programs would result in exceeding recommended sodium and sugar intake.

We draw a number of conclusions. The overwhelming majority of commercials seen by children are for salty and sweet snacks, fast food, and sugary cereals. Fruits, vegetables, and meats are exceedingly rare among the foods shown on television commercials or in television programs. The emphasis in food commercials targeted to children is on taste rather than nutrition. Nutritional information, when present, can be ambiguous or even deceptive. If a child's diet incorporated only the foods advertised, it would be too high in both sodium and sugar, and likely too high in fat.

E. Exposure to Sex and Profane Language in Media

A persistent concern of parents has been exposure of their children to "adult content" through television programs, video games, music lyrics, and the Internet. Parents have long registered anxiety about media content that either shows or implies sexual activity, or includes sexual innuendoes or direct talk about sex. Although this concern extends to a variety of media, research regarding some media (the Internet, music lyrics) is so rare that we confine our discussion to television and video games. The recent finding from a sample of 11- to 16-year-olds and their parents in the southeast in which children's reported accidental exposure to negative Internet content such as violence or sex is greater than their parents' perception of such exposure (Cho & Cheon, 2005) suggests additional content studies of the Internet are warranted.

The fracas over the fleeting glimpse of Janet Jackson's breast during the Super Bowl in 2004 set off a storm of criticism from public figures and incurred a sizeable fine for CBS. The now-infamous "wardrobe malfunction" renewed scrutiny of sex and nudity in media content. Although that particular scandal has died down (as all scandals eventually do), research shows that media contain a substantial amount of sexual content, even in general audience programming popular with children and adolescents.

Kunkel, Cope, and Colvin (1996) studied 128 programs airing during the first hour of primetime (8 to 9 P.M., for most areas of the country), and found 61 percent of the programs contained some sort of sexual content, ranging from passionate kisses to implications that intercourse had just occurred or was about to occur. Indeed, the most explicit form of sexual content, depicted or strongly implied intercourse, was present in 12 percent of the programs. Well over half of the programs (59%) featured talk about sex. Just 6 percent of all sexual scenes contained in the programs made mention of risks or responsibilities associated with sex, such as sexually transmitted disease or birth control.

More recently, Kunkel and colleagues (Kunkel, Cope-Farrar, Biely, Farinola & Donnerstein, 2001) employed a much larger sample that encompassed many more time slots and found a similar overall percentage for sexual content. The researchers examined more than 900 programs scheduled between 7 A.M. and 11 P.M. on a large number of channels (the original three networks, Fox, WB, PBS, Lifetime, TNT, USA, and HBO). They found 68 percent of all programs contained sexual content, and such content occurred at a rate of 4.1 scenes per hour. Again, talk about sex was more frequent than depictions of sexual activity.

Fisher and colleagues (Fisher, Hill, Grube & Gruber, 2004) used a three-week composite sample encompassing programs from each of the six broadcast networks as well as BET, Cinemax, HBO, Showtime, and MTV, resulting in the analysis of over 1,200 television program episodes. They found 67 percent of the episodes depicted at least one instance of sexual behavior and 77 percent had at least one instance of talk about sex. Intercourse was implied or depicted in approximately 14 percent of the episodes. Fisher and colleagues found considerable variation in sexual content according to genre. Genres with low amounts of sexual content included children's cartoons (21%), talk shows (28%), and news magazine programs (29%), whereas genres with high amounts included drama/comedy hybrids (100%), made-for-television movies (100%), and feature films (93%). Although not among the top three, sitcoms, perennial favorites with older children and teenagers, had a sizeable presence of sexual content. Ninety-three percent of the sitcoms in the sample contained talk about sex, and 81 percent depicted sexual behavior. When the relationship status of the sexual partners was apparent, 58.7 percent were coded as being in a casual relationship, 23.9 percent were unmarried but in an "established" relationship, and 17.4 percent were married. Finally, once again we see that on television discussions of risk and responsibilities associated with sex were very rare. Just 2.9 percent of programs containing sexual content depicted "sexual patience" and 5.2 percent showed "sexual precautions," with most of the latter category involving a mention of condoms or other form of birth control.

Cope (1998), in an attempt to look not at general audience television content patterns but at patterns evident in television programs favored by teenagers, examined three episodes each of the most frequently viewed programs among 12- to 17-year-olds. She discovered that 67 percent of those shows contained talk about sex, 62 percent featured sexual behavior, and 13 percent depicted or strongly implied sexual intercourse. Once again, discussions about safe sex, protection, or other forms of responsibility were largely absent, apparent in only 9 percent of the favorite program sample.

Pardun, L'Engle, and Brown (2005) extended this approach to a much wider variety of media (see Table 3.6). They obtained via survey an extensive list of media used most frequently by a sample of over 3,000 seventh and eighth graders. From those data, each media "vehicle" used by at least 10 percent of any of four subgroups, Black females, Black males, White females, and White males, was selected for analysis. The process resulted in a sample that included 94 movies; every song on the most recent CD of 67 musical artists; one issue including the ads, photos, and editorial content of 32 magazines; the home pages and ensuing pages obtained using six clicks from the home page of 34 Internet sites; and a two-composite-week sample for each of three newspapers. In order to make reliable comparisons across these six media types, the authors reduced each type to a very small unit of analysis—a continuous shot in television and film; a headline, photograph, or paragraph for newspapers and magazines; a verse in each song for music; and a quarter of a printed page for the Internet sites. Comparing the units containing sexual content to the overall units in each of the six media types, Pardun and colleagues determined that the music in the sample contained the largest proportion of sexual content (40%), followed by the movies (12%), television (11%), magazines (8%), Internet sites (6%), and newspapers (1%).

In music television, an estimated 60 percent of all videos (Baxter, DeReimer, Landini, Leslie & Singletary, 1985) and 76 percent of all concept videos (Sherman & Dominick, 1986)—those that tell a story rather than show the band or artist perform the song—contain sexual content. In soap operas, the average number of sexual instances per hour increased from 3.7 in 1985 to 5.0 in 1994 (Greenberg & Busselle, 1996). If children and teenagers watch R-rated movies, research indicates they may be exposed to an average of 17.5 sexual acts and 9.8 instances of nudity per film (Greenberg, 1994). In advertising, sexual appeals are used to capture and sustain interest, and have also increased in frequency over time (Reichert, 1999). For example, men and women were depicted "in sexually suggestive contact" in 21 percent of magazine ads from 1983 compared to 53 percent from 1993 (Reichert, 1999).

In the arena of video games, a recent controversy has erupted—not capturing quite as many headlines as the Super Bowl hullabaloo—but prominent enough to hit the newsstands nonetheless. The extremely popular *Grand Theft Auto: San Andreas* game was found in July of 2005 to contain hidden, explicit sex scenes accessed using a computer program readily found on the Internet. The game is the latest in a series of *Grand Theft Auto* games that have gained notoriety for their sexual and violent content. (Having sex with a prostitute in the back of a car is an option, as is beating her up or even killing her afterward.) It took several months for the hidden scenes to be publicly revealed, with more than 12 million copies of the game sold since its release in October 2004 (Pham, 2005). Since the revelation of the explicit sexual content, the game has been pulled from the shelves of Wal-Mart and Best Buy, and the ratings board has replaced its prior rating (M for Mature) with an Adults Only designation (Pham, 2005).

Aside from that anomalous instance of explicit sexual intercourse, sexual content in video games is much more likely to be marked by an emphasis on the sexuality of the female characters made apparent through appearance and dialogue (Dietz, 1998). In fact, Thompson and Haninger (2001) concluded that sexual content was rare in games compared to violent content. Just two games from their sample of 55 depicted sex in a graphic, blatant manner. In the Scharrer (2004) sample of over 1,000 magazine ads for video games, only 11 sexual acts appeared in the visuals in the ads. Three ads depicted intimate touching, two disrobing, and one implied sexual violence. Twenty-one of the ads (2% of the entire sample) contained words in the text that were explicitly sexual, and just four more (n = 24, 2.4%) featured sexual innuendoes, defined as more indirect expressions with an implicit sexual connotation, such as "get some action" or, for a billiards game, "nice rack."

We offer several conclusions:

- About two-thirds of all television programs aired around the clock contain some form of sexual content. Similar percentages have been found in specific genres or time slots, including music television, primetime programs popular with young audiences, and the first hour of prime time.
- When shifting the unit of analysis in studies of television content from program to a much smaller unit such as the camera shot (of which there will be many in a single program), as in the Pardun and colleagues study (2005), the percentage of sexual content becomes much smaller.

- Talking or joking about sex is among the most frequent ways sexual activity appears in television content.
- Sexual activity between unmarried characters is much more frequent than sexual activity between married partners.
- Modeling the use of sexual protection or discussing or portraying risks and responsibilities associated with sex is rare.
- There is evidence that the amount of sexual content in many media has risen over time.
- Although most media (except those categorized as pornography) do not contain explicit scenes of sexual intercourse, implying intercourse is not unheard of on television, accounting for over 1 in 10 instances of sexual activity.
- In video games, violence is typically much more frequent than sexual activity or references.

Very rarely has profanity in the media been isolated for formal examination. "Dirty" words, swearing, and derogatory slang certainly seem to have become common. A new study provides rare data to explore this issue.

Kaye and Sapolsky (2004) examined "offensive language" spoken in 151 primetime programs on the 2001 season of the ABC, CBS, Fox, NBC, PAX, UPN, and WB networks. Incorporating such categories as the seven dirty words identified by the FCC (and made famous by George Carlin), sexual words (describing body parts or sex acts), excretory words, "mild—other words," which included irreverent uses of religious words (e.g., "For Christ's sake," "damn," "hell") and "strong—other words" (for which the authors list the examples "bastard, bitch, bullshit," p. 439), the study tabulated over 950 such expressions. They were present in 87 percent of the programs, and occurred at a rate of 7.2 per hour. About two-thirds (63%) of the profanity fell into the "mild—other" category, followed by excretory words (14.6%), sexual words (10.4%), "strong—other" words (7.4%), and the seven dirty words (4.5%). Although the 9 to 10 P.M. time slot contained the largest number of instances of such language overall, the first hour of prime time in which children are most likely to be present outscored the last hour. In fact, from 8 to 9 P.M. alone, Kaye and Sapolsky (2004) found 10 utterances of the seven dirty words, 29 of sexual words, 49 of excretory words, 217 of "mild—other words," and 19 of "strong—other words." Programs rated TV-G contained only a very few instances, yet TV-PG programs contained substantially more profanity than the ostensibly more restricted TV-14 programs. Quite a few instances occurred in programs that did not carry a content-based rating of "L" to warn audiences of coarse language. The authors used previously drawn data from 1990, 1994, and 1997 from the four main broadcast networks to compare to the 2001 data from those same four networks to test for changes over time. Our suspicion (and theirs) of an increase in "adult language" was generally supported. The total number of instances of offensive language rose from 132 in 1990 to 151 in 1994, then dipped to 113 in 1997 and finally shot up to 175 in 2001. We can surmise, therefore, that the late 1990s to early 2000s have featured primetime television programs that contain quite a few instances of profane language; that such instances have been on the rise; and that television programs frequently viewed by children and adolescents (those airing from 8 to 9 P.M. and/or bearing a TV-PG rating) contain moderate levels of profanity.

IV. TWO WORLDS OF CONTENT: FOR THE VERY YOUNG VERSUS THE GENERAL AUDIENCE

We have used these pages to provide a map outlining the contours of media content popular with children and teenagers. We have found much diversity. We have also found clear emphases and specialized niches of content that raise questions about accuracy, value, and usefulness of the impressions about everyday life that young persons may acquire from the media.

We are struck by the realization that there are largely two different worlds of content—the protective, educational, and prosocial bubble provided by media for the very young (infants, preschoolers, and children of early elementary age) and the sometimes harsh and often sensationalized material of media for older children, teenagers, and the general audience (music television, Internet sites, primetime television, video games). The two exist with little buffer, forcing an abrupt change when "children's media" are no longer satisfying.

Exceptions to our two-world dichotomy occur, of course, and the two resemble each other in some ways. Saturday morning cartoons, although created almost entirely for relatively young children, contain large amounts of violence and present a severely circumscribed cast of characters, underrepresenting people of color and women. Disney films and other animated features designed for the very young also feature violence, as well as more than occasional uses and displays of alcohol and tobacco products. Exceptions arise in the other direction, as well, with the majority of music videos that do not contain violence or sex, with the many primetime television programs devoid of profane language, and with the video and computer games that are either educational or otherwise free of violence or female characters targeted for lust or death. Nevertheless, the basic thrust of the observation remains valid.

Young persons have much to learn from observing the people and behavior exhibited in media content. Some lessons are positive and some less so. In the best scenarios, they can learn problem solving, responsibility, conflict resolution, and safety. Young children can learn to sing songs and perform dances, to recognize letters in the alphabet and to count. Young persons can learn about different cultures, different people, and different places around the globe. The media can take young persons outside their own experiences to explore the world around them. In the worst scenarios, however, young persons can learn that aggression and violence are normal parts of everyday life, acceptable ways to address a conflict, unlikely to meet with serious repercussions, and can even be funny. They can learn that their gender, age, race, or ethnicity dictates what is expected of them and the roles they take on, and they can learn to judge others by such qualities, as well. They can learn to think of sexual activity and the use of tobacco and alcohol as largely free of consequence or jeopardy. They can learn to base their food intake on taste alone rather than nutrition, while simultaneously learning that beauty and attractiveness is defined in large part for females by being extremely thin and for men by being muscular.

Despite immense changes in technology and the media landscape that dramatically alter *how* young people receive media—DVDs, TiVo and other digital video recorders, hundreds of channels and stations through cable and satellite, high definition television, the new territory of the Internet, the boom of the video game industry—many aspects of *what* they receive have not changed significantly. Many of the patterns of content in the media used most often by young people have been relatively consistent across media forms and have remained rather stable over time, including depictions of violence, gender, race, ethnicity, and people with disabilities. At this time (and with the sizeable caveat that studies of Internet content are currently very rare), we would argue that new media have done little to displace the usual ways that young people (and those older) are entertained, informed, and persuaded by media. Technology and content, then, also present two worlds, with the one in rapid and continuous change and other stable and largely unchanging.

Table 3.6

Percentage of Types and Characteristics of Sexual Content in Media Used by Seventh and Eighth Graders

	Overall	TV	Movies	Music	Magazines	Internet	Newspapers
Type of sexual content							
Partial or full nudity	41%	63%	46%	5%	30%	35%	12%
Relationships*	25	15	21	52	31	42	35
Sexual innuendo	12	5	11	19	15	8	36
Touch and kiss	14	14	17	8	9	4	6
Sexual intercourse**	7	3	4	15	15	9	10
Pubertal issues	0	0	0	0	1	2	0
Select specific characteristics							
Within relationships							
Sexual activity between non-married characters	25%	21%	25%	31%	26%	37%	29%
Sexual activity between married characters	3	4	3	1	2	0	2
Healthy sexual messages***	6	2	9	6	4	2	4
Unhealthy sexual messages****	2	1	2	4	2	3	2

*Defined as characters involved in a romantic relationship, ranging from dating to marriage.

**Includes references to intercourse as well as depictions of intercourse.

***Includes development, abstaining, masturbating, discussion of STDs, condoms, or contraception, and depiction of "negative emotional consequences" (p. 86).

****Includes lack of protection during sex, rape, and child sex abuse.

Adapted from Pardun, C. J., L'Engle, K. L. & Brown, J. D. (2005). Linking exposure to outcomes: Early adolescents' consumption of sexual content in six media. *Mass Communication & Society, 8*, 75–92.

EFFECTS OF MEDIA ON SCHOLASTIC PERFORMANCE AND THE DEVELOPING INTELLECT

IV

Attending school is the sole activity other than sleep that rivals use of the media in accounting for tremendous amounts of time in the daily lives of children and teenagers. Research has addressed two major questions. What are the implications for scholastic performance and the traits and skills on which it depends of media use? What is the explanation when positive or negative relationships between scholastic performance and media use are observed? We draw on studies from communication, education, psychology, and sociology. We locate considerable agreement regarding the role of the media in some of these outcomes, and unearth substantial disagreement or uncertainty for others.

I. EFFECTS OF TELEVISION VIEWING ON SCHOLASTIC PERFORMANCE

A number of cross-sectional studies have recorded a negative relationship between time spent watching television and grades in school or scores on standardized tests (Anderson, Mead & Sullivan, 1986; CAP, 1980, 1982, 1986; Keith, Reimers, Fehrman, Pottebaum & Aubey, 1986; S. Neuman, 1988; Roberts & Foehr, 2004; Wright et al., 2001). In these data, greater television use is associated with poorer scholastic performance. Other studies have failed to find a negative relationship or have determined that an initial negative relationship disappears under multiple controls (Gaddy, 1986; Gortmaker, Salter, Walker & Dietz, 1990; Roberts, Foehr & Rideout, 2005). Previous reviews have alternately declared television a clear negative influence on scholastic performance (Comstock & Scharrer, 1999) or pointed toward a curvilinear relationship where moderate viewing rather than light or heavy viewing was associated with the strongest academic performance (Razel, 2001; Thompson & Austin, 2003).

Our interpretation of the research record is unambiguous, despite a small number of caveats. There is a negative relationship between amount of television use and academic performance by children and teenagers. Our confidence rests on two types of evidence: the number of studies utilizing very large and generalizable samples of students and a strong research design that have found such a relationship, and the presence of statistical or methodological shortcomings in nearly all of the smaller number of studies that have not. Our caveats pertain to the failure to establish causal direction in many studies (is greater television use causing diminished academic performance, or is diminished academic performance causing greater television use?) and the very recent addition of a study with a large national representative sample that suggests television viewing among high academic achievers has increased in the last few years in large enough degree to call the future of this association between television consumption and academic achievement into question.

A. *The Studies*

As in our previous reviews (Comstock & Scharrer, 1999, 2006), we emphasize the 1980 California Assessment Program (CAP, 1980). We favor these data because of the staggering number of young people represented (282,000 sixth graders and 227,000 twelfth graders), the coverage of two widely separate grades, the measurement of three basic skills, and the inclusion of data on socioeconomic status. Every student present in school that day provided data (99% of those enrolled), and thus the selection of participants for the study is more appropriately characterized as a census rather than a sampling. Television viewing was inversely associated with performance in reading, written expression, and mathematics skills as measured by standardized exams, and the pattern of negative association was very similar for each of the three school subjects and held for both of the grades and across four socioeconomic strata (see Figure 4.1).

There nevertheless were important variations by grade and socioeconomic strata. The slope of the line—which can be interpreted as the strength of the relationship between television viewing and achievement—was steeper for those in the twelfth grade compared to those in the sixth grade. We attribute this to the likelihood that in the twelfth grade, the challenge of performing well is greater and any factor

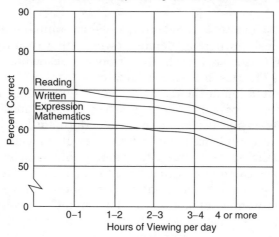

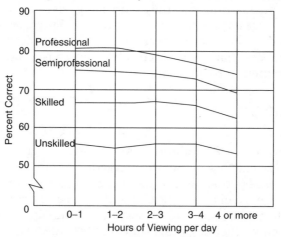

| | Number of students by socioeconomic status | | | | | | | |
| | Hours of television Viewed per day | | | | | | | |
Occupation of head of household	0–1	1–2	2–3	3–4	4 or more	Non-response	Total	Percent
Professional	15,731	11,176	7,022	3,787	4,976	337	43,029	15
Semiprofessional	15,634	12,927	9,449	5,812	9,631	495	53,948	19
Skilled	23,713	21,283	16,966	11,301	21,795	1,189	96,247	34
Unskilled	10,408	9,391	7,591	5,211	11,451	769	44,821	16
Nonresponse	11,505	9,866	7,266	4,627	9,481	1,173	43,918	16
Total	76,991	64,643	48,294	30,738	57,339	3,963	281,968	100
Percent	27	23	17	11	20	2		

Fig. 4.1 Television viewing, achievement, and socioeconomic status: sixth grade. Adapted from "Survey of Sixth Grade Achievement and Television Viewing Habits," California Assessment Program, 1980, California State Department of Education.

exerting a negative influence on performance would be likely to take a greater toll (Comstock & Scharrer, 2006).

The slope was also steeper for higher socioeconomic strata. With each step up in socioeconomic status (in which parental occupation would predict on average higher income and greater education), the negative relationship between viewing and test scores became stronger. We turn to the data of Gaddy (1986). He divided households according to the presence of educational resources such as print media—books, newspapers, and encyclopedias. The data confirm an overall negative association between television viewing and scholastic achievement, measured by reading, vocabulary, and mathematics performance. They also show larger coefficients and therefore stronger relationships in high-resource compared to low-resource households. Households higher in socioeconomic status generally are more likely to have informational print resources in the home (Roberts & Foehr, 2004). Therefore, television viewing among children in high-resource households is likely to supplant more educationally beneficial activities that arise from tapping those resources. Television viewing among children in households with fewer print and educational resources has no such opportunity. We echo our own past summaries (and join others) in concluding that the strength of the role of television viewing in academic achievement depends on the educational and informational quality of the experiences it replaces (Comstock & Scharrer, 1999, 2006; Schramm, Lyle & Parker, 1961; Williams, 1986; Wright et al., 2001).

A number of additional sets of data support our conclusion of a negative relationship between amount of television viewing and scholastic performance. The 1980 California Assessment Program, for instance, was replicated and extended to include performance in science, history, and social science in two follow-up studies (CAP, 1982, 1986). The inverse relationship mostly for reading but sometimes for other subject matter, was also found among a sample of 28,000 twelfth graders in National Center for Educational Statistics (Keith, Reimers, Fehrman, Pottebaum & Aubey, 1986), among 70,000 students in three different grades in the National Assessment of Educational Progress (Anderson, Mead & Sullivan, 1986), and in data pooled from eight statewide tests in California, Connecticut, Maine, Illinois, Michigan, Pennsylvania, Rhode Island, and Texas (Neuman, 1988). The data covering nearly 2,000 eight- to 18-year-olds gathered in 1999 by Roberts and Foehr (2004) similarly found that those reporting the highest level of television exposure also reported earning the lowest grades in school, followed by those with moderate amounts of television exposure who reported similarly mid-range grades, and low television viewers who reported the highest grades. The CAP and these other sets of data are the convincingly large and generalizable studies of which we spoke.

There is evidence that the overall negative relationship between viewing and achievement is occasionally curvilinear rather than linear. In these data, a moderate amount of television viewing is associated with greater achievement than either a higher or lower amount (Fetler, 1984; Neuman, 1988; Potter, 1987; Williams, Haertel, Walberg & Haertel, 1982). Nevertheless, the curvilinearity does not negate the overall inverse association, and also appears to be confined to younger students in earlier grades (Comstock & Scharrer, 1999, 2006).

We also spoke of studies that appear at first glance to fail to support our interpretation. In these two studies, the initial negative relationship is present but disappears when parceling out the influence of additional variables. We contend that the potential for variability in the measurement of achievement in both of these studies is so severely diminished that the possibility of a statistically significant association with television viewing is drastically curtailed. In the case of Gaddy (1986), achievement was measured by the *change* in academic performance between tenth and twelfth grades. The change in grades over this brief period is likely to be so minimal that it would be extremely difficult to predict by any variable, much less earlier viewing. In support of our interpretation, a number of variables that are typically related to scholastic performance failed to have predictive power, including homework time, reading for pleasure, and being in an academic track program. In the case of Gortmaker and colleagues (Gortmaker, Salter, Walker & Dietz, 1990), test scores from the Wechsler Intelligence Scale for Children (WISC) and the Wide Range Achievement Tests in Arithmetic and Reading (WRAT-A and WRAT-R) over the course of four years are used, with prior performance on one or more of the tests entered as a predictor of performance on a subsequent test before the television exposure variable is entered. The association between past and present performance on the tests is so strong that it leaves little room for television (or any other variable, for that matter) to have predictive value.

Longitudinal data, collected not just at one point in time but at multiple points, can assist in the question of causal direction because such data are able to show that one measurement precedes another. Thus, a stronger assertion can be made for causation than would be the case in a cross-sectional study. The longitudinal data on children's television exposure and school performance largely provide additional evidence for an inverse relationship.

In Sweden, for example, watching fictional entertainment programs in preschool was a negative predictor of grades earned in first and sixth grade (Rosengren & Windahl, 1989). Among U.S. preschoolers, exposure to general audience entertainment television predicted poor performance on a letter recognition test at age five, but not on a reading comprehension test administered later (Truglio, Huston & Wright, 1986). Amount of viewing of entertainment television programs (but not informational/educational programs) in a three-year study in the Netherlands was negatively related to subsequent reading comprehension (Koolstra, van der Voort & van der Kamp, 1997). On the other hand, an additional U.S. longitudinal study showed no relationship between viewing cartoons or adult entertainment programs and subsequent vocabulary test performance (Rice, Huston, Truglio & Wright, 1990). With the exception of the Rice and colleagues (1990) study, the longitudinal data allow us to cautiously claim not just that television exposure (particularly exposure to entertainment programs) and academic performance are inversely associated, but that early television exposure can causally affect later achievement.

B. Explanations of Television's Impact on Academic Performance

There are four explanations for how and why television might impact academic performance that have been advanced in the literature (Shin, 2004). Three stem from the assumption of a negative role of television, whereas the fourth envisions a positive role.

The *time displacement hypothesis* holds that television plays a negative role in academic achievement because it supplants time that the child could otherwise dedicate to an activity that may be more intellectually demanding or enriching, such as time spent on homework or studying (Beentjes & van der Voort, 1989; Comstock & Scharrer, 1999; Harrison & Williams, 1986; Valkenburg & van der Voort, 1994).

The *mental effort hypothesis* argues that because many television programs require little cognitive effort on the part of the young audience member, heavy amounts of television exposure can lead to reluctance to expend sustained mental effort at reading challenging material, at school in general, or when engaging in school-related activities (Anderson & Collins, 1988; Armstrong & Greenberg, 1990; Beentjes, 1989; Koolstra & van der Voort, 1996; Salomon, 1984).

The *attention and arousal hypothesis* posits that the fast pace of television (and potentially video and computer games), with many edits, changing camera angles, and quick movements, can spur impulsiveness and difficulty in sustaining attention, thereby posing a threat to academic success (Huesmann & Miller, 1994; Singer, 1980; Singer, Singer, & Rapaczynski, 1984).

The *learning hypothesis* holds that television, particularly educational television, can play a favorable and facilitative role in the scholastic achievement of children (Anderson, Huston, Schmitt, Linebarger & Wright, 2001; Huston et al., 1999; Singer & Singer, 2001; Wright, et al., 2001).

Shin (2004) conducted a clever study to determine which is the most viable. She analyzed data from the Child Development Supplement of the Panel Study of Income Dynamics, a longitudinal survey of a representative population of families undertaken by the Institute for Social Research at the University of Michigan. From the data set, she extracted the 1,203 families with school-aged children between the ages of six and 13 who lived in a household with a working television set. Amount of television viewing, time spent studying and doing homework, and time spent reading were determined from diaries, completed by parents on one weekday and one weekend. School achievement was measured by the reading and math portions of the Woodcock Johnson Revised Test of Achievement, and includes such skills as letter and word knowledge, comprehension of a written passage, calculation, and applied problem solving. A final set of variables measured impulsive behaviors and attentional abilities, with items from the Behavioral Problems Index and the Positive Behavior Scales, which covered such symptoms as having difficulty concentrating, not being able to sit still for long, being overly active or restless, or acting impulsively without thinking.

Shin (2004) found an overall negative association between amount of television viewing and achievement on the math and reading tests (we could add this to our list of studies convincing us of a negative relationship between television exposure and scholastic achievement). As a result, she ruled out the learning hypothesis at least for the kinds of television regularly viewed by these young people, and used structural equation modeling to test the explanations that remained. She reasoned that if the time displacement hypothesis were true, the relationship between television viewing and academic achievement should be mediated by amount of studying and homework. This was, indeed, the case (see Figure 4.2). She also reasoned that if the attention and arousal hypothesis were supported, impulsive behaviors would mediate the relationship. This, too, was evident (see Figure 4.2). Finally, she reasoned that in order to claim support for the mental effort hypothesis, the amount of time the child spent reading should mediate the relationship. This remaining explanation also received support (see Figure 4.2). Each of the three explanations for a negative role of television was statistically supported by the data.

For some of the explanatory variables that Shin (2004) used in her analysis—time and location of homework, time spent reading, and impulsiveness or difficulty sustaining attention—past research supports the ability of television to exert an influence. For others, prior results are decidedly less neat and often less convincing.

1. The Effects of Television on Homework A small, negative association has been found between doing homework while watching television and academic achievement among fifth graders (Fetler, 1984). Quality of homework has also been determined to suffer when it is done in front of the screen (Armstrong & Greenberg, 1990). Achievement in general is positively correlated with amount of time spent on homework (Keith et al., 1986). Yet, in the CAP (1980) data, the heaviest television viewers in high school spent the largest amount of time on homework. Keith and colleagues (1986) also determined that among high school seniors, television viewing and homework do not appear to compete for the same blocks of time. Thus, the previous literature lends some support for time displaced from homework and studying by viewing to help explain the association between amount of television use and diminished academic performance. However, the evidence suggests this particular explanation may be confined to the younger grades (elementary and middle school) that Shin (2004) examined rather than the older children and teenagers investigated in other studies.

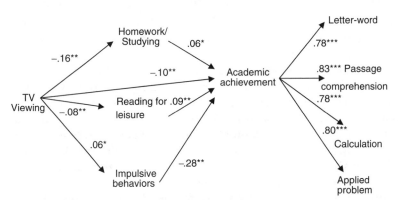

Fig. 4.2 Model of relationships between key variables in scholastic achievement. Coefficients are standardized Beta weights. *p < .05, **p < .01, ***p < .001. Adapted from Shin, N. (2004). "Exploring pathways from television viewing to academic achievement in school age children." *Journal of Genetic Psychology, 165,* 367–382.

2. The Effects of Television on Reading and Mental Effort The literature supports Shin's (2004) finding that the potential for television viewing to supplant reading is an additional culprit. Despite Shin's (2004) use of the label "mental effort" to encompass the role of reading in the relationship between television consumption and academic achievement (and the use of the "displacement" label to cover only time spent on homework and studying), we argue that the time spent reading for pleasure is another instance of displacement.

A number of studies have found that the more television a child watches, the less time she or he spends learning to read or engaging in leisure-time reading (Comstock, 1991; Heyns, 1976; Koolstra & van der Voort, 1986; Medrich et al., 1982; Williams, 1986). For example, time spent viewing cartoons designed for children and general audience programs (but not viewing of educational children's programs) was inversely related to time spent reading and engaging in other educational activities (including art, coloring, puzzles, games, and organized instruction) in a sample of two- and four-year-olds from low- to moderate-income families (Huston, Wright, Marquis & Green, 1999). Among children, therefore, television viewing can and often does displace reading.

Differences appear according to the age of the young person. Among high-school students, the pattern seems to reverse. Over a period of three years of data collection, Morgan (1980) determined that amount of time spent watching television and amount of time spent reading for pleasure were initially negatively correlated, but in later years became positively correlated. Likewise, the CAP (1980) data show positive associations between viewing and time spent reading among high school-aged respondents. Thus, additional studies support the ability of television to exert an influence on academic performance through time spent with reading prior to the teenage years (Comstock & Scharrer, 1999).

Television use has been associated with attitudes toward reading as well as preferences for specific types of reading materials (Comstock & Scharrer, 1999). Both can pose obstacles to academic achievement. Koolstra and van der Voort (1996) found that among second and fourth graders, those who viewed more television expended less mental effort while reading, even under the presence of multiple statistical controls including the mental ability of the child. They also determined that those high in television viewing were more likely to have a negative opinion of reading books as a way to spend leisure time, to think of reading as dull, boring, or otherwise unworthy of their time, and to prefer comic book reading (a comparatively action-packed choice) to other reading choices. Morgan (1980) discovered that heavy television viewing among adolescents is also associated with a preference for reading lighter and less demanding types of print materials. His data led him to conclude that "heavy viewers are significantly more likely than light viewers to prefer stories about love and families, teenage stories, and true stories about stars. Light viewers...choose science fiction, mysteries, and general non-fiction" (p. 164).

Thus, the reading and mental ability explanation for the viewing and achievement relationship is broader, more complex, and possibly more insidious than Shin's (2004) operationalization would suggest. Not only can the influence of television be felt through the devotion of less time to reading, but it can also be felt through a reluctance to expend mental effort at a reading task, the fostering of negative attitudes toward reading, and a preference for nondemanding print media content. These patterns in the research evidence regarding television viewing, reading, and scholastic achievement among children and teenagers have led us to conclude previously that "viewing not only interfers with and displaces scholastic endeavors but also shapes the motives and directs the preferences of the young toward the trivial and the banal" (Comstock & Scharrer, 1999, p. 262).

3. The Effects of Television on Attention and Arousal   There are fewer additional data to support Shin's (2004) claim that television use can lead to deficits in attention and impulse control. A number of studies concur that violent television in particular, can be problematical.

Children's exposure to violent television programming, in particular, is associated with increased impulsiveness (Anderson & McGuire, 1978; Desmond, Singer & Singer, 1990; Salomon, 1979; Singer, Singer, Desmond, Hirsch & Nicol, 1988; Singer, Singer & Rapaczynski, 1984). In the most recent example, Geist and Gibson (2000) examined the effect of network and public television programs on fourth and fifth grade children's ability to attend to a task and time devoted to a task. About 60 children were randomly assigned to watch *Mister Rogers' Neighborhood, The Mighty Morphin Power Rangers*, or no television. No significant differences emerged on the attention variables between the *Mr. Rogers'* group and the no television group. Those watching the *Power Rangers* had more difficulty attending to a task and devoted less time to that task than both of the other groups. Our conclusion is that violent programming can impede a child's ability to devote prolonged time and attention to a task.

The research evidence for television in general (rather than violent television) is less clear, mainly due to a lack of studies designed to test whether overall television exposure can contribute to difficulty in sustaining attention. In a recent study that is an exception, Christakis, Zimmerman, DiGiuseppe, and McCarty (2004) employed the National Longitudinal Survey of Youth to determine whether amount of television viewing among one- and three-year-olds was associated with attentional difficulties as measured by the Hyperactivity subscale of the Behavioral Problems Index. Logistical regression analysis determined that amount of viewing at both earlier ages was a significant predictor of hyperactivity at age seven. The authors estimate a 9 percent increase in risk for attention deficit problems for children for each hour of daily television viewing. However, a Danish study failed to replicate these results in longitudinal data in which viewing at age three-and-a-half was entered as a predictor of attention problems at ages 10 to 11 (Obel et al., 2004). Perhaps age plays a major role (the data of Christakis and colleagues begin two-and-a-half years earlier and end three to four years earlier and are confined to the sensorimotor and preoperational stages). Others have pointed out that the reverse hypothesis—that hyperactive children seek the calming influence of television (or are shepherded toward the television by fatigued parents) and therefore are heavy viewers in early childhood—is also a potential explanation (Pempek & Anderson, 2005). Other studies have found that those already diagnosed with ADHD have difficulty paying attention to educational television when toys or other distracting features in the physical environment are present (Sanchez, Lorch, Milich & Welsh, 1999; Landau, Lorch & Milich, 1992).

In sum, there is some indication that television exposure at a very young age can lead to attentional difficulties that may impair progress later in school. There is convincing evidence that exposure to violent programming on television, specifically, can be associated with an immediately measured inability or reluctance to focus attention on a task—most likely due to the arousing effects of action, suspense, and aggression (Zillmann, 1971). The ability of this type of short-term effect to develop into a trait that would result in a large group of children having trouble at school has not been documented. We weigh Shin's (2004) support for the attention and arousal hypothesis with caution at this time, especially in comparison to the other two explanations.

4. The Learning Hypothesis   We believe that the failure of the learning hypothesis as viable in Shin's (2004) data is attributable to young television viewers' allocation of time to specific types of content. We believe that educational television can assist with the development of skills and knowledge directly and indirectly applicable to performance in school. For all but the youngest children, overall amount of television use is dominated not by educational programming but by entertainment programming that does not purport to have an educational purpose (Roberts & Foehr, 2004; Rideout et al., 2005). In fact, media use studies have shown that time spent with educational television declines between the ages of three and eight, whereas cartoon viewing increases until age five and then levels off (Huston, Wright, Rice, Kerkman & St. Peter's, 1990; Zill, Davies & Daly, 1990).

Our interpretation finds support in a longitudinal study of television viewing among young children in low-income families by Wright and colleagues (2001). In a three-year panel study with 236 two- to four-year-old children sampled from various locations in Kansas, they found that viewing educational programs developed specifically for child audiences at the age of two and three predicted strong performance on standardized tests of reading and number skills, vocabulary, and "school readiness" (which includes colors, shapes, numbers, letters, and size and space relationships among objects) in the subsequent year. The opposite was true for two other types of television, general audience programs (the overwhelming majority of which are entertainment) and animated programs designed for children (which are mainly cartoons). Viewing both general audience programs and animated children's entertainment programs at an early age were associated with performing less well on one or more of the standardized tests. The negative relationship between time spent viewing the general audience programs held for both cohorts of age groups, those who began the study at ages two to three and those who began at ages four to five, whereas the associations between viewing both types of child-specific programs (animated cartoons and educational programs) and performance on the tests were apparent only among the younger cohort.

What is viewed is an important distinction in studies of amount of television use and academic achievement. Educational programs typically are not viewed enough by children school-aged and older to overturn the negative association between overall amount of television viewing and scholastic performance.

C. Caveats and Corollaries

We have presented our case for a negative association between television use and performance in school or on academic-related exams and tasks. However, the relationship is much more complex than an association between two variables. There remain reasons for skepticism, and numerous forces exert an influence on whether and how this relationship is likely to be manifested. We refer to the first set of considerations as caveats and the second as corollaries.

1. Caveats A cautionary axiom repeated often in every research methods class (so frequently as to be a mantra) is important: Correlation is not causation. Most of the studies examining the relationship between amount of television viewing and performance in scholastic-related activities are unable to determine conclusively whether the viewing *causes* the performance. The reverse is also plausible. Children who perform poorly in school or on standardized exams may choose to consume greater amounts of television than those who perform well, perhaps as an escape from the struggles of the classroom or perhaps as a relatively undemanding way to be entertained and pass the time. We believe both causal directions have validity. We have created a mock path analysis illustrating the likely associations between the key variables (see Figure 4.3).

Certainly, young people who view a great deal of television also have attributes that predict lower scholastic performance. Three are lower socioeconomic status, lower mental ability, and stressful circumstances (Comstock & Scharrer, 1999). Each predicts both greater viewing and lower performance. Nevertheless, the data also indicate that viewing may impede effort devoted to reading, discourage book reading, and promote tastes favoring unchallenging entertainment and sources of information. The first assigns responsibility to the viewer; the second assigns responsibility to the medium. Both have a strong claim to validity.

Our argument for a bidirectional relationship also is corroborated by the longitudinal data of Wright and colleagues (2001). In that study, young children's viewing of educational programs predicted strong academic performance and their viewing of general audience programs predicted poor performance. Additionally, strong academic performance at one point in time also predicted greater exposure to informational programs later, whereas poor academic performance predicted greater entertainment program exposure in the future. The analysis of data at multiple points in time provides convincing evidence. The allocation of time either to entertainment or educational television influences later scholastic achievement, and scholastic achievement influences preferences for television programming that have educational value.

A very recent addition to the literature requires comment. The comprehensive investigation of children and teenagers' media use in 2004 by Roberts, Foehr, and Rideout (2005) that was reviewed in detail (see Chapter I) asked respondents to report the grades they typically receive in school, with options ranging from "mostly As," and "mostly As and Bs," to "mostly Ds," and "mostly Ds and Fs." When this question was posed during the 2004 data collection, a full 51 percent of

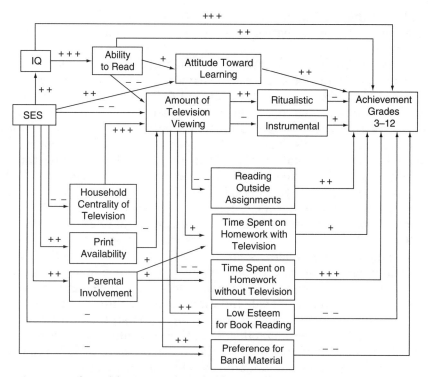

Fig. 4.3 Path model: Viewing, household and individual variables, and scholastic performance. Based on G. Comstock (1991). *Television and the American Child.* San Diego, CA: Academic Press.

the eight- to 18-year-old respondents claimed to receive mostly As and Bs, 35 percent said mostly Bs and Cs, and just 10 percent confessed to receiving Cs or below. Thus, despite assurance from a previous study of a strong correlation between students' reports of grades and actual grades (r = .77; Dornbusch et al., 1987), the tendency for skewing of these reports toward better grades requires that we interpret the subsequent correlations with media use with caution. The authors themselves suggest such a guarded course and acknowledge the potential for social desirability to inflate these grade reports.

The coverage by Roberts and colleagues (2005) of multiple forms of media permits the investigation of the role in academic performance of media other than television. Of the six media for which time estimates were drawn, only two resulted in statistically significant associations with self-reported grades. No differences were found for amount of time spent with television (see Table 4.1). In contrast, the same set of questions posed to respondents of the same age five years earlier in the 1999 data collection (Roberts & Foehr, 2004) *did* find a negative association between amount of television use and self-reported grades.

These are the most up-to-date data on the topic but whether they register an important change in behavior in regard to the media is moot. A comparison of the 1999 and 2004 data pinpoints the highest academic achievers as those who play the instrumental role. No differences are apparent in the overall media exposure (for which television constitutes the lion's share) of those performing fairly or poorly in school in the 1999 data compared to the 2004 data. Among those performing well in school, daily media exposure had increased by 43 minutes over the five-year period. If media exposure levels have risen for high academic achievers, differences that had once been registered for academic performance among low, medium, and heavy television users could be rendered insignificant (statistically and colloquially).

The most recent Roberts & Foehr (2004) data do not yet call for any abandonment of the expected and frequently recorded inverse association between amount of viewing and scholastic achievement. In addition to the possibility of grade inflation, there are three additional reasons why this single sample is unconvincing. First, the difference for high achievers may simply reflect sampling variability—the occasional inevitable bad estimate. Second, the grade measure is less reliable and valid than scores on standardized achievement tests (such as those employed in the CAP data). Third, it is hard to believe that such a

Table 4.1
Exposure to Individual Forms of Media and Self-Reported Grades

	Mostly As & Bs	Mostly Bs & Cs	Cs & Ds and below
Percentage of sample	51%	35%	10%
Medium			
TV	3:06	3:03	3:07
Videos/DVDs/movies	1:05	1:14	1:19
Print media	0:46[a]	0:39[ab]	0:29[b]
Audio media	1:39	1:48	2:08
Computers	1:05	0:58	1:03
Video games	0:48[a]	0:46[a]	1:09[b]
Total media exposure	8:28	8:27	9:15

Within the row, the means that *do not* share a common superscript are statistically different from one another.

Adapted from Roberts, D. F., Foehr, U. G. & Rideout, V. (2005, March). *Generation M: Media in the lives of 8- to 18-year-olds.* Report to the Kaiser Family Foundation.

dramatic change in audience behavior could occur in as few as five years, and even harder to believe that in an industry where annual zigs and zags in ratings become major news stories that it would have been unremarked upon.

The two media for which significant correlations emerge are video games and print media (see Table 4.1). Video games play a negative role. Youngsters reporting mostly Cs, Ds, and of lower standing in their classes also spent significantly greater amounts of time playing video games than youngsters reporting either mostly Bs and Cs or mostly As and Bs. Print media (reading books, newspapers, and magazines for leisure purposes) registered a positive association. Roberts and colleagues (2005) summarize these relationships:

> Grades are positively related to print use. Kids who claim to earn mostly As and Bs report 17 minutes more daily leisure reading time than kids who earn Cs and Ds or lower (with kids reporting mostly Bs and Cs falling between these two groups). Conversely, grades are negatively related to video game exposure. Kids who earn mostly Cs and Ds or below spend about 20 minutes more daily playing video games than A and B or B and C students (the difference between those earning As and Bs and those earning Cs and Ds or below falls just short of statistical significance). Exposure to TV, music, and videos/movies does not significantly differ across the three academic groups. (pp. 47–48)

Video game use and grades were also investigated in an additional, recent study. Gentile, Lynch, Linder, and Walsh (2004) studied 607 teenagers in eighth and ninth grade. Amount of violent video game exposure in particular was negatively associated with grades earned in school. Gentile and colleagues also found that the relationship between exposure and grades was mediated by a measure of the young person's hostility level, suggesting that a negative outlook may account for both the game play and the poor performance.

2. Corollaries   In addition to the caveats that admonish us not to settle for a simplified interpretation of the relationship between media use and academic achievement, a number of studies have also pointed to key third variables.

a. Socioeconomic Status   Searls, Mead, and Ward (1985) found that in low socioeconomic status families, reading achievement was higher for heavy television viewers whereas in high socioeconomic status families, reading achievement was higher for light television viewers.

As we have seen, the CAP (1980) data also found the strength of television's relationship to achievement depended on socioeconomic status, again with the negative influence of television more likely among those high in socioeconomic status. There are likely to be several explanations for these patterns, including the presence of educationally stimulating resources that presumably depend in part on socioeconomic status (Gaddy, 1986), as well as distinctions in media use, with highly educated and high income parents typically encouraging less entertainment television consumption (but not less educational television) and more time reading or being read to (Bianchi & Robinson, 1997; Huston et al., 1990; Timmer, Eccles & O'Brien, 1985).

b. Mental Ability Another potentially mediating variable is the child's mental ability or IQ (Fetler, 1984; Gortmaker, Salter, Walker & Dietz, 1990; Potter, 1987). The strongest variable in predicting grades and performance on standardized tests is the child's intellectual ability. Fetler (1984) has estimated that mental ability accounts for between one-half and three-fourths of the total variance in test scores. Lower mental ability among children has also been associated with greater television viewing, despite some reduction in the size of this association due to greater amounts of television viewing recently among all groupings of children (Gortmaker et al., 1990; Neuman, 1991; Van Evra, 1998). This factor, then, could very well be a crucial third variable operating in many of the analyses of television viewing and scholastic performance.

c. Age and Content We place these two variables together because they are strongly associated with each other. As we have discussed (see Chapters I and II), the viewing of informational programs designed to promote educational goals drops off precipitously as children grow older. Amount of time spent viewing such programs is a positive predictor of academic achievement (Anderson et al., 2001; Huston et al., 1999; Singer & Singer, 2001; Wright et al., 2001). The viewing of general audience programs designed to entertain rather than to educate or inform constitutes the bulk of the television viewing for all but the very youngest of children (Roberts & Foehr, 2004). Entertainment television viewing has been consistently associated with poorer academic performance in the studies we have reviewed. Preferences for lighter, more entertainment-oriented television fare are more likely to occur among heavy television viewing children than among light viewers (CAP, 1982; Fetler, 1984). The role of television consumption in the scholastic achievement of children depends on what type of content is viewed, which in turn depends on the age of the child. The overall negative association persists because educational television is only a small element of what most children and teenagers view.

II. EXPOSURE TO EDUCATIONAL TELEVISION

Exposure to educational television operates much differently than overall television exposure in regard to academic performance. We spoke (see Chapter III) of two different worlds to which young people attend. One is occupied by commercial, entertainment-oriented television and other media. It was shown to be flooded with violence, sexual innuendo or talk about sex, traditional gender roles, and lingering stereotypes regarding race, ethnicity, and sexual orientation. Content is created to attract an audience valuable to advertisers—large, high in consumption, and open to new brands. The other is made up of educational, informational, and prosocial television and other media. It is filled with cooperative and responsible behavior, positive mediation of conflicts, diversity in characters, and themes and lessons that reflect skills that would be nurtured in school—music, art, arithmetic, language, science, reading, and the like. Content is created in a different context—public television, where private enterprise plays a less prominent role; cable television, where advertiser revenue is supplemented by subscription fees; and recently, commercial broadcast outlets under mandate of the FCC.

A. *Setting the Stage*

In recent years, *Blue's Clues*, *Dora the Explorer*, and many others have joined the ranks of stalwarts such as *Sesame Street* in comprising the universe of children's educational television and other media. The research evidence on these types of programs is extensive, and the results are encouraging. Educational programs promote learning, prosocial behavior, and other positive benefits to children.

The face of educational television has changed in recent years with the passing of the "three-hour rule" for broadcasters. As of January, 1997, in order to enjoy an expedited review of their license renewals, commercial, broadcast stations have been required by the FCC to air at least three hours of educational television for children per week. The ruling was widely perceived to have stemmed from the failure of the Children's Television Act of 1990 to result in an increased number of educational shows, despite a provision that required broadcasters to make a "reasonable attempt" to educate children through programming (Children's Television Act, 1990, sect. 303a). The FCC saw the need to stipulate the specific requirement after broadcasters attempted an end-run around the provision by using a very liberal interpretation of "educational" to argue that existing entertainment (like the *Jetsons*) met the criterion, airing a very small number of educational programs, or scheduling such programs in unpopular time slots (Jordan, 1996; Kunkel & Canepa, 1994; Kunkel & Goette, 1996).

The new mandate specified that programs air between 7 and 10 A.M., required at least three hours of programming, and defined "educational and informational television programming" (abbreviated E/I) as "any television programming that furthers the educational and informational needs of children aged 16 of age and under in any respect, including children's intellectual/cognitive or social/emotional needs" (FCC Report and Order, 1996, p. 21). Two types of "educational" programs, therefore, are recognized: those that promote "traditional academic" skills and outcomes (such as science, math, and reading) and those that foster "prosocial" ends (such as sharing, appreciating diversity, valuing family and friendships; Jordan, 2004).

The networks with the largest audiences appear to be emphasizing the more flexible social/emotional aspect of the mandate. Jordan (2004) performed a content analysis of the television programs that broadcasters (ABC, CBS, NBC, Fox, WB, UPN, Pax, Home Shopping Network, and two independent stations) in one large market reported to the FCC in compliance with the three-hour E/I rule. Of all the lessons apparent in a total of 41 programs, 45 percent were prosocial (defined as being about "getting along with others and/or feeling good about oneself," p. 109), 41 percent were traditional academic, 4 percent were about "physical health and well-being" (p. 109), 7 percent combined these types, and the remaining 3 percent had no discernible lesson. The networks with the largest audiences (the original three and Fox) were more likely to offer prosocial lessons compared to academic lessons. Jordan (2004) also conducted interviews with network executives, program producers, and consultants and found that they voiced many concerns and listed many obstacles associated with the three-hour rule, including competition from cable and PBS for this type of programming, disinterest on the part of advertisers in placing commercials during educational shows, and lack of merchandise tie-ins that have made the programs of cable and public television competitors lucrative.

Social science research, for the most part, has yet to examine the effects on children of viewing the programs created and aired by the broadcast networks to adhere to the three-hour rule, possibly because the rule is still rather new. One exception is a recent study by Krcmar (2000) who found that the presence of an E/I rating in the corner of the television screen was related to increased liking of the program for girls aged eight to 11 and decreased liking for boys of the same age. The Krcmar data suggests that for some young audiences, particularly those eight years and older and male, recognizing that a program is educational may backfire. This may be the analogue of the forbidden fruit phenomenon. Not only do some older kids *want* to see what has been deemed "bad" for them (the forbidden fruit), some do *not want* to see what has been determined "good" for them.

The majority of the research focuses on cable programs and programs that air on PBS. *Sesame Street* has inspired the most scholarly inquiry—the reward for being a pioneer, for longevity (it's in its 36th season), and for its popularity. We then turn to the research on other programs before reviewing theoretical mechanisms at play in learning from educational television.

B. Sesame Street—*A Pioneer in Children's Programming*

Sesame Street was revolutionary when first aired in 1969. It was the first children's program created around a curriculum. It was also the first regularly to employ education and child development researchers to team up with television production professionals. The stated mission of the series was "to promote the intellectual and cultural growth of preschoolers, particularly disadvantaged preschoolers" (Cooney, 1968, as quoted in Cook et al., 1975, p. 7). An estimated 1,000 studies—if continuing thematic emphases are ignored—have been conducted on whether that goal and others have been met. *Sesame Street is* "the most heavily researched series in the history of television" (Fisch, Truglio & Cole, 1999, pp. 166–167).

1. Academic Effects of *Sesame Street*   The earliest inquiries into the ability of *Sesame Street* to positively affect preschoolers' development of intellectual and cognitive skills that would correspond directly to what they would later be asked to do in school were conducted by the Educational Testing Service (ETS) (Ball & Bogatz, 1970; Bogatz & Ball, 1971). The researchers concluded that substantial gains were experienced by viewers in such important skills as recognition of numbers and letters and classification and relational processing. Unhappily, these early data obtained by field experiments were tainted by simultaneous home visits designed to promote the program and ensure enough viewers to evaluate effects (complete with the delivery of freebies like balloons, buttons, and magazines endorsing the show). Reanalyses of the data by Cook and colleagues (1975) found some of the effects were diminished in size after accounting for home visits and other effects appeared only among those who had received the promotional home visits.

The conflation of viewing and the home visits was rectified in subsequent research, the majority of which demonstrates clear (if usually very modest) positive effects. It also reaches a large proportion of its target audience (Fisch et al., 1999). An estimated 75 percent of pre-schoolers and 60 percent of kindergarteners watch *Sesame Street* at least once per week, 50 to 60 percent of two- to five-year-olds tune in four or more times per week, and *Sesame Street* viewing accounts for about half of all educational television exposure among preschoolers (Comstock & Scharrer, 1999).

Recent research is consistently supportive of academic benefits accruing from *Sesame Street* viewing. A longitudinal study by Wright and Huston (1995), for example, examined a group of 250 low-income two- and four-year-olds over a period of three years. Those who watched *Sesame Street* when they were preschoolers performed better on tests of recognition of letters and words, math skills, vocabulary, and "school readiness," were rated by teachers as more well-adjusted to school, and were more frequent readers than those who had not watched. Results remained statistically significant even after controlling for a number of variables including education of the parents, days absent at preschool, and language spoken in the home.

Additional support was found by Zill, Davies, and Daly (1994), who examined Department of Education National Household Education survey data, drawn from about 10,000 parents across the country. Viewing *Sesame Street* at preschool-age was associated with stronger reading performance (as measured by the lack of need for remedial instruction and the ability to read storybooks independently) in first and second grades. *Sesame Street* viewing was also correlated with letter recognition aptitude and the capacity to tell a coherent story, even when statistically controlling for parent education, frequency of reading with parents, and school attendance. Importantly for *Sesame Street*'s mission, the associations were strongest for those young people in low income families.

Another example is the "recontact" study of Anderson and colleagues (Anderson, Huston, Wright & Collins, 1998). Over 500 individuals for whom data was collected when they were preschoolers were recontacted when they were in high school. *Sesame Street* viewing in early childhood was positively related to academic performance in high school as represented by grades in math, English, and science. Again, even in the presence of a number of statistical controls (including, but not limited to, early language and cognitive abilities), those who watched *Sesame Street* as preschoolers also read more in high school, had stronger confidence in their academic abilities, and placed greater importance on doing well in school.

We interpret these data with some caution. The correlations, although consistently positive are also consistently small, and we cannot rule out the possibility that they represent the influence of concerned and interested parents on earlier viewing and later scholastic performance. However, the survival of these small, positive correlations after controlling for parental education in our view is a key element. Parental education would be a strong predictor of such behavior, and the data do not permit us to hold parental dispositions as responsible. As a result, we conclude that the most plausible interpretation is a modest causal contribution of viewing *Sesame Street* to later scholastic performance.

Sesame Street has spawned versions of the program that air in numerous countries across the globe, and some have yielded promising analyses of the educational effects of the program. In Mexico, for example, three-, four-, and five-year-olds were randomly assigned to a group that watched *Plazo Sesamo* for six months or one that watched alternative programming (Diaz-Guerrero & Holtzman, 1974). Those who had seen the program performed better than those who had not on number, letter, and word tests as well as on relational and sorting and classification skills. According to Fisch, Truglio, and Cole (1999), the positive effects of *Plazo Sesame* on numerical and literacy-related skills were corroborated in a more recent study (UNICEF, 1996), and have also been found among large samples of children watching *Susam Sokagi* in Turkey (Sahin, 1992), *Rua Sesamo* in Portugal (Brederode-Santos, 1993), and *Ulitsa Sezam* in Russia (Ulitsa Sezam Department of Research and Content, 1998).

2. Prosocial Effects of *Sesame Street* *Sesame Street* since its inception has also had prosocial aspirations represented by such outcomes as cooperation, fairness, and respecting differences (Fisch et al., 1999). Today's *Sesame Street* episodes demonstrate a wide variety of these values, including such issues as caring for pets, dealing with feeling left out or different, embracing racial and ethnic diversity, and encouraging creativity. The research record shows success in facilitating many of these outcomes as well. However, there is evidence that a necessary condition is a close correspondence between the behavior modeled on screen and what the child is asked or given an opportunity to do, and that effects are often short-lived.

In an early study, Paulson (1974) examined the ability of 78 three- and four-year-old inner-city, economically disadvantaged children to cooperate in a series of tasks before and after viewing the third season of *Sesame Street*. Cooperative behavior increased in many of the tasks. However, effects did not extend to free play. The finding that prosocial effects were specific to what was modeled and did not transfer to free play would be replicated in additional studies (Bankart & Anderson, 1979; Leifer, 1975). Another study found that three- to seven-year-olds cooperated with each other *less* in a marble game after exposure to a *Sesame Street* lesson on conflict resolution compared to a control group (Silverman & Sprafkin, 1980) probably because the game did not match the lesson.

Positive prosocial effects on attitudes regarding racial diversity appeared in another study of *Sesame Street*, but were found in a follow-up analysis to fade quickly. Gorn, Goldberg, and Kanungo (1976) assigned just over 200 White children aged three-and-a-half to five-and-a-half to watch a brief segment of *Sesame Street* that either did or did not contain messages regarding tolerance and respect for multiculturalism. The dependent measure consisted of photos of children of differing races and asking who should come to the preschool to play the following day. The control group was twice as likely as the treatment group to choose White children. About 70 percent of those who saw the multicultural messages favored children of color. Triumph, however, was brief. A follow-up study conducted by Goldberg and Gorn (1979) determined that one day after seeing the multicultural messages, children were no longer more likely than control-group members to choose to play with non-White children.

Zielinska and Chambers (1995) found more resounding support for prosocial outcomes in a field experiment with 150 children in eight daycare centers. Research participants saw either a prosocial-only or an academic-only lesson on *Sesame Street*. Some participated in a post-viewing discussion of the lesson of the show, whereas others viewed the program only. More prosocial behavior (including such indicators as helping, turn taking, cooperation, and affection) as well as less aggressive behavior, followed exposure to the prosocial segments, regardless of whether discussion of the lesson accompanied viewing.

The researchers at *Sesame Street* have also conducted inquiries into influence stemming from particular social and personal issues brought up in specific episodes (Fisch et al., 1999). They have found, for instance, that those who had seen the romance depicted between Maria and Luis had more precise definitions of love and marriage and understood that despite an argument members of a couple still love one another (Sesame Street Research, 1988). Those who had seen Maria's pregnancy on *Sesame Street* knew more about carrying a child (Sesame Street Research, 1989) and those who had seen an episode depicting an interracial friendship and playing with multiracial toys were more likely to report they'd like to play with a doll of another race (Sesame Street Research, 1991).

On the whole, the evidence is less decisive for the ability of *Sesame Street* to exert an influence on prosocial outcomes compared to its ability to affect academic outcomes. Short-term, transitory, the necessary condition of a close correspondence between what is modeled and subsequent behavior, a boomerang (probably because that correspondence was absent)—these characterize the data. Nonetheless, evidence warrants the modest claim that *Sesame Street* can have a short-term, positive impact on prosocial attitudes and behavior.

C. Other Educational Television Programs

1. *Mister Rogers' Neighborhood*   The emphasis on *Sesame Street* is on cognitive and academic skills with the prosocial content secondary. The reverse is true for *Mister Rogers' Neighborhood* (Mares & Woodard, 2001). Fred Rogers had a soothing, comforting presence and the program was slow-paced, gentle, and affectionate. Prosocial themes were favored over the presentation of an academic curriculum.

Friedrich and colleagues performed a series of studies in the 1970s on *Mister Rogers' Neighborhood* (*MRN*). In the first, Friedrich and Stein (1973) assigned 93 preschoolers to watch *MRN*, aggressive cartoons such as *Batman* and *Superman*, or neutral programs, 12 times over a span of four weeks. Observations of free play were made before, during, and two weeks after exposure. Children who saw multiple episodes of *MRN* exhibited positive behavioral changes compared to the other groups, including delaying gratification, taking longer to perform tasks, and, for those from households lower in socioeconomic status, more cooperation on the playground. Effects continued, but lessened in magnitude, in the subsequent two weeks. In their second study, Friedrich and Stein (1975) found slightly higher willingness to help (measured by reactions to a classmate's torn artwork as well as in a role-playing exercise) among those kindergarteners who had been assigned to watch four episodes of *MRN*. Among boys, helping was enhanced when program exposure was combined with interpersonal role-playing training using scenes from the show.

Finally, Friedrich-Cofer, Huston-Stein, Kipnis, Susman, and Clewett (1979) compared three treatments: viewing; viewing plus access to books, games, and other resources that advanced the program's messages; and that combination followed by supportive interpersonal activities such as role-playing. No behavioral changes among children in a Head Start program appeared for viewing alone. Viewing and resources stimulated both prosocial and aggressive behavior. In the viewing, resources, and activities group, interactions with other children became more positive and less aggressive. These findings lead to a central axiom: Positive influence of media is more likely when exposure is combined with activities that reinforce the televised message.

2. Blue's Clues *Blue's Clues* was introduced in 1996 and features Blue, an animated dog, interacting with her owner, a young man, as they engage in problem-solving. Blue leaves clues needed to solve a puzzle (e.g., What does Blue want for her birthday?) and the audience members are actively encouraged to "help" her owner find and decipher the clues, by calling out their locations or answering pertinent questions posed by characters speaking directly into the camera. Interactivity on the part of the child is encouraged through both content and formal features. The producers of *Blue's Clues* also pioneered a programming strategy designed exclusively for child audiences. The same episode is aired five days in a row to appeal to young viewers who thrive on repetition as well as to increase a child's sense of having mastered the puzzle, thereby encouraging confidence and self-esteem (Anderson et al., 2000).

Effectiveness of the five-day programming schedule was tested in one of the first studies (Crawley, Anderson, Wilder, Williams & Santomero, 1999). Three- to five-year-olds were shown a single episode once or on five consecutive days. In the multiple exposure group, attention to entertainment content remained consistent, and attention to educational content was slightly higher during the first three episodes. Comprehension scores were significantly greater in the single exposure group compared to a nonviewing control group, but were much greater in the multiple exposure group. Finally, the amount of sought-for participation (e.g., providing answers to questions asked) increased linearly in the multiple exposure group. Somewhat decreased levels of attention but substantially increased participation with repeat viewing also occurs in a subsequent study (Anderson et al., 2000). We conclude (as the authors did) that the programming strategy, although resulting in diminished attention when the content is no longer novel, is generally effective at engaging the participation and increasing the comprehension of preschool audiences.

There is also some indication that *Blue's Clues* can inspire children to view other programs more actively. Crawley and colleagues (Crawley et al., 2002) compared the responses of child viewers who were or were not experienced in viewing *Blue's Clues* to an episode of *Blue's Clues* and an episode of *Big Bag*, a Cartoon Network program that also employs an educational curriculum and encourages participation (see Table 4.2). Attention and comprehension were similar for the two groups, but those with greater familiarity with *Blue's Clues* were more active when viewing *Big Bag*—talking to the screen, answering questions.

Finally, Anderson and colleagues (2000) also present a longitudinal study on the impact of viewing *Blue's Clues*. In a sample of 120 preschoolers, approximately half had access to Nickelodeon on which *Blue's Clues* airs and the other half did not. Parents kept viewing dia-

Table 4.2
Attention to the Screen and Interactions with the Program as a Function of Experience Viewing *Blue's Clues* and *Big Bag*

	Viewing an episode of *Blue's Clues*	
	Experienced *Blue's Clues* viewers	Inexperienced *Blue's Clues* viewers
Percentage looking to the screen*		
Educational content	88.16% (8.81)	96.33% (4.13)
Entertainment content	84.23% (11.24)	93.96% (7.59)
Interactions per minute		
Educational content	0.91 (1.03)	0.67 (0.83)
Entertainment content	0.97 (0.92)	0.60 (1.09)
	Viewing an episode of *Big Bag*	
Percentage looking to the screen	78.83% (16.69)	87.59% (13.02)
Interactions per minute	0.27 (0.28)	0.17 (0.16)

*Calculated by dividing number of frames in the program that the child looked at the screen by the total number of frames in the program and multiplying by 100.

Adapted from Crawley, A. M., Anderson, D. B., Santomero, A., Wilder, A., Williams, M., Evans, M. K., & Bryant, J. (2002). Do children learn how to watch television? The impact of extensive experience with *Blue's Clues* on preschool children's television viewing behavior. *Journal of Communication, 52,* 264–280.

ries, and children were categorized as either experienced or inexperienced viewers. During both of the seasons covered, the experienced group outscored the inexperienced, on both the educational and prosocial lessons of the series. On standardized measures of child development (responses to riddles, perception of patterns and creative thinking, and problem solving) as well as in parent or caregiver reports of problem solving and prosocial interaction with others, the two groups did not differ at the beginning, but after the two seasons the experienced group performed significantly better. This is convincing evidence of the power of *Blue's Clues* to exert a positive impact on its regular viewers.

3. *Barney and Friends* *Barney and Friends* is known for drawing the adoration of preschool viewers and the occasional joke or rolling of the eyes from parents and other adults due to its saccharin-sweet content. The purple dinosaur was first introduced to television audiences in 1993, and the program features song and dance numbers with Barney and a diverse cast of children, as well as lessons both academic and prosocial (e.g., using manners, obeying traffic signals, getting along with others).

Singer and Singer (1998) assigned about 120 preschoolers to a control group, a group that watched *Barney* 10 times over two weeks, a group that watched and participated in follow-up lessons, and a group that participated in the lessons but did not watch the show. Measures assessed knowledge of the messages presented. Results demonstrated consistently that viewing the program in addition to participating in the follow-up lessons triggered the greatest benefits. For example, those in the viewing-and-lessons group averaged 10 correct out of 12 items for one particular dependent measure, knowledge of manners. Those in the viewing-only-group averaged five. Those in the control group had only three correct. Thus, viewing *Barney and Friends* alone can have a positive impact on the learning of manners and other positive messages, but the largest influence (as we concluded earlier) is experienced when viewing is complemented by follow-up activities.

In a second study, Singer and Singer (1998) replicated the experiment using a more racially and economically diverse sample and different episodes of *Barney and Friends*. Again, viewing in addition to receiving the lessons led to evidence of learning. In this case, however, no effects were seen for the viewing only group, and the previous impact on manners did not occur—presumably because it was not emphasized as centrally in the particular episodes viewed. This conforms to the pattern in which strongest prosocial effects occur when messages and measures match.

D. Concepts, Models, and Theory of Television Viewing

Viewing educational television can have many benefits. We turn now to the processes on which these outcomes depend.

1. Attention and Comprehension Attention and comprehension are necessary conditions for both academic and prosocial benefits. Both develop with age. Very young children pay scant attention to the screen. As they mature, they turn their attention more frequently to the screen and to increasingly diverse types of programming (Anderson, Lorch, Collins, Field & Nathan, 1986; Schmitt, Anderson & Collins, 1999). In one estimate, for example, attention to the screen increased linearly from age six months to three years across a variety of types of content (Schmitt, 2001). Anderson and Levin (1976) also found a linear increase in attention paid to *Sesame Street* from one year to four years of age.

Two potentially competing theories have been advanced to explain these looks to the screen. Huston and Wright (1983, 1987) argue that the visual and auditory cues used in television capture very young children's attention. In this perspective, the formal features of television (the sounds, the movement on the screen, etc.) are the primary determinants of attention in the earliest years of childhood. With age, children begin to attend and comprehend television more strategically and purposefully. Anderson and Lorch (1983) assert that a higher order of processing occurs at even the younger ages, with a child's ability to comprehend the content the decisive factor rather than the whistles and bells of formal features.

In recent years, however, the theories have come to seem complementary. Bickham, Wright, and Huston (2001) synthesize the two in the "feature-sampling model." Formal features are salient to very young children and can attract their attention toward television initially. At this point, children determine whether to sustain attention and apply more cognitive effort in processing the information in the program. Bickham and colleagues explain that "salient features and segment transitions may attract attention through their audiovisual properties, but . . . they merely set the occasion for viewers to decide to continue to invest attention if the program matches their current abilities and needs" (p. 108).

Conceived in this way, both the Huston and Wright (1983, 1987) and Anderson and Lorch (1983) models recognize the ability of children to be active audience members with sufficient agency to purposefully control their viewing. Both also acknowledge the potential for television to stimulate considerable cognitive effort rather than a simple attraction to its sights and sounds. Both models can account for the numerous studies in which formal features have proven important in signaling to youngsters that interesting and relevant content is appearing on screen (Comstock & Scharrer, 1999). They also concur in arguing that the subsequent choice of whether to continue attending is due in large part to the content and the child's developmental ability to extract meaning from that content rather than the formal features.

Comprehensibility has proven to be a key determinant of attention to the screen among preschool- and elementary school-age children. For example, Anderson, Lorch, Field, and Sanders (1981) created distorted versions of *Sesame Street* to test the role of comprehensibility among two-, three-and-a-half, and five-year-olds. They reordered scenes, ran the audio track backward, and used foreign languages. They held the formal features constant. Children in all three age groups looked at the screen less when any of these three manipulations were used to decrease comprehensibility.

2. Properties of Attention The models present child viewers as actively involved in quickly-made decisions after glancing at the screen. The issue is whether or not to continue to pay attention. Those decisions are based not merely on attractiveness of formal features but on a reasoned consideration of the suitability and comprehensibility of the content. Conversely, research has also identified properties of attention that are nonstrategically employed (Miron, Bryant & Zillmann, 2001). *Attentional inertia* refers to the tendency for individuals to continue to attend to a stimulus once they have begun, and therefore changes in attention are likely to take place more often in the first seconds of viewing (Anderson, Alwitt, Lorch & Levin, 1979; Anderson, Choi & Lorch, 1987; Anderson & Lorch, 1983). Anderson, Choi, and Lorch have estimated that attentional inertia sets in when a child has attended to television for 15 seconds or more. Bickham and colleagues (2001) explain that "the more time a look has lasted and the more attention one has invested in it, the stronger the forces that sustain its continuance and the weaker the impulse to look away" (p. 111). This is the same phenomenon that advertisers spend billions of dollars hoping to achieve. Somewhat paradoxically, *attentional habituation* can also occur in which the individual becomes so accustomed to the stimulus that something new, novel, surprising, or different is needed to spark further attention (Bickham et al., 2001). Boredom enters, interest suffers.

The *traveling lens model* put forth by Rice, Huston, and Wright (1982) accommodates these various properties of attention. It takes its name from the hypothesized inverted U shape that describes arousal and interest (see Figure 4.4). Maximum efficiency in children's ability to learn from television lies in moderation (the highest levels in the middle of the upside-down U). Program elements that are moderately novel and somewhat familiar, not too complex but not too simple, not entirely incongruous but not overly "wholistic," neither entirely repetitive nor unpredictable, neither too surprising nor expected, result in the highest levels of interest and attention. Too far on one or the other extremes results in either boredom (when the materials are too "easy") or incomprehensibility (when they are too "hard"). Ideally, processing the content is neither too effortless nor too difficult (Bickham et al., 2001). This is similar to Csikszentmihalyi's (1990) concept of flow in which tasks that are challenging but achievable provide the greatest motivation, reward, and pleasure—what sports commentators refer to as "in the zone."

Familiarity thus can have contradictory effects. It can stimulate interest as well as fatigue. Attentional inertia asserts that once a program has captured attention, attention is likely to continue. Familiarity becomes an impediment when the program is too easy to process and plays a facilitative role when content is more difficult and challenging.

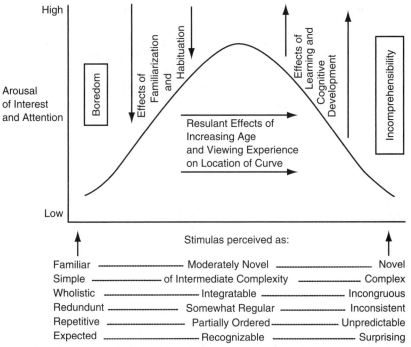

Fig. 4.4 The traveling lens model of children's interest in and attention to television. Adapted from Bickham, D. S., Wright, J. C., and Huston, A. C. (2001). Attention, comprehension and the educational influences of television. In D. G. Singer and J. L. Singer (Eds.), *Handbook of children and the media* (pp. 101–119). Thousand Oaks, CA:sage.

3. Very Young Children and the Impact of Television   In 1999, the American Academy of Pediatrics (AAP) recommended no television viewing for children two years of age and younger. The impetus appeared to be the supposition that children that young are unable to absorb anything of value from television, or at least anything that would be as developmentally stimulating as playing with toys and interacting with others. Little research existed at the time that would either support or refute that supposition. Recent research has begun to address this gap in knowledge, and the findings have implications for theory and models about how children learn from educational television.

Even very young children spend time with television each day (see Chapter I). The popularity of *Teletubbies* and the advent of videos such as *Baby Einstein* targeting very young children appear to have succeeded in extending the ages at which young children attend to the screen (Anderson & Pempek, 2005; Rideout et al., 2005, 2006). Never before had children less than three years of age had programming created expressly for them. High levels of attention, as measured by duration and number of looks to the screen, have been found in the lab for 12- to 15-month-olds for *Baby Einstein* (Barr et al., 2003) and for 18- to 24-month-olds for *Teletubbies* (Frankenfield et al., 2004). In this case, however, looks to the screen do not necessarily stem from comprehension nor signify that learning is taking place.

The role of comprehensibility in whether children this young can learn from educational television is beginning to be evaluated in Anderson and colleagues' ongoing research. Among 18- and 24-month-olds, for example, portions of a *Teletubbies* program that had been manipulated to feature backward dialogue and reordered scenes drew fewer looks than nondoctored *Teletubbies* versions (Frankenfield et al., 2004). This implies that even for these very young children comprehensibility rather than formal features alone draws attention. Also supporting comprehensibility (rather than the attraction of changing sounds and pictures) in spurring very young children's attention to television is a recent study of children ranging in age from six months to nearly five years by Valkenburg and Vroone (2004). The children were all shown six discrete program segments with content differing in complexity. The youngest children paid the greatest amount of attention to the least complex segments, such as *Teletubbies*. The oldest children attended most to more complex children's programming, such as the movie *Lion King II*. For all children, very little attention was paid to adult programming. Valkenburg and Vroone identified the stage at which children move away from focusing on formal features toward being driven by comprehending content as between one-and-a-half and two-and-a-half years.

A very young child's ability to comprehend television content, although it is certainly a necessary condition for learning from television, may not be sufficient to ensure as much learning as might occur from observing a live model (Anderson & Pempek, 2005). A number of experiments have demonstrated decreased readiness to imitate a televised model compared to an in-person model (Barr & Hayne, 1999; Hayne, Herbert & Simcock, 2003), as well as decreased ability to use information provided by a televised model to complete a task (Evans, Crawley & Anderson, 2004; Schmitt & Anderson, 2002; Troseth & DeLoache, 1998). Learning the words used to label objects was also greater in one study when live models were employed compared to models on videotape (Grela, Lin & Krcmar, 2003). The phenomenon of television exposure leading to comparatively lesser learning is referred to as the "video deficit" (Anderson & Pempek, 2005).

These results have led Anderson and Pempek (2005) to conclude:

> . . . the AAP (1999) guideline, adopted without the guidance of almost any relevant research, appears to have been prescient . . . there is very little evidence that children younger than 2 can learn anything useful from television. The evidence indicates that learning from television by very young children is poor and that exposure to television is associated with relatively poor outcomes. (p. 518)

4. The Capacity Model   Fisch (2000) has introduced the *capacity* model to explain how children learn academic and prosocial lessons from television. Drawing on information processing theory (Kahnemann, 1973; Shiffrin & Schneider, 1977), Fisch reasons that television in general requires the processing of both audio and video material and in a circumstance in which the viewer cannot dictate the pace, whereas educational television, in particular, calls for the simultaneous processing of both a narrative (the story, as advanced by the characters) and educational lessons (the presentation of facts or strategies for learning or problem solving). The capacity to learn from educational television, then, depends on the demands of each of the two elements as well as the degree to which they are related or disparate. If the narrative and the educational content are distant from one another, the two elements compete for the same limited cognitive resources and learning is constrained. Conversely, if the narrative and the educational content are closely intertwined, "then the two parallel processes become complementary rather than competitive, and comprehension is likely to be strengthened" (Fisch, 2000, p. 66).

Fisch (2000) catalogues several viewer or program factors that may influence processing. Viewer characteristics include prior knowledge of characters, interest in the subject matter, overall verbal reasoning ability and short-term memory skills, and the existence of mental schemas for how stories tend to unfold or for the formal features used to tell stories on television (such as special effects, camera angles and edits). Program characteristics include the complexity of the story, need for inferences (i.e., whether the information is stated clearly and explicitly or whether it must be inferred), consistency with existing story schema (is the story told in a typical or a novel or unusual way?), temporal organization (whether the story is linear), and advance organizers (such as previews, foreshadowing, or other early hints of developments in the narrative).

The capacity model predicts that when demands for cognitive resources compete between the narrative and the educational elements, the narrative is most likely to win out because television is perceived by children primarily as an entertainment medium (Greenberg, 1974; Roberts & Foehr, 2004), and therefore the individual will devote more cognitive resources to the former rather than the latter. Creators of educational television programs, therefore, would do well to keep the narrative simple so that processing the narrative does not overwhelm the capacity to process the educational messages.

A final corollary of the capacity model is the importance of the viewer's ability to allocate cognitive resources between the two elements of an educational program. If motivation to focus on the educational content is high, a viewer is more likely to favor the processing of this element over the narrative (Salomon & Leigh, 1984). In the presence of facilitative comments made by parents while coviewing, a viewer also becomes more likely to favor the processing of the educational content (Collins, 1983; Collins, Sobol & Westby, 1981; Friedrich & Stein, 1975; Salomon, 1981; Watkins, Calvert, Huston-Stein & Wright, 1980).

Fisch has found support for some aspects of the capacity model in his studies of the television program *Cro* (Fisch et al., 1995). In general, children who had seen the program learned about the science and technology themes (e.g., sound heard through a musical instrument is caused by vibration). Critical differences emerged according to episode. When the narrative and the educational content were closely related, learning was enhanced. When the two elements were more distant, learning was reduced.

An additional study by Fisch, Brown, and Cohen (2001) persuaded Fisch to add "concreteness" of information conveyed to the catalog of factors that influence processing. In an experiment with 135 children aged three to five, Fisch and colleagues tested both the visual concreteness of the content and the use of nonverbal and nonsensical intonational cues involved in the presentation of that content (for example, the noises that the *Teletubbies* make to communicate with each other). In one condition, the educational television stimulus (a segment of the program *Big Bag* featuring Koki, a claymation chicken) sent an educational message about sharing toys that was illustrated visually. In another condition, the educational lesson was about honesty, a concept less readily conveyed visually. Comprehension was higher for the visually concrete message across all ages, although the older children were more able to comprehend the content. No differences emerged according to whether purely nonsensical language was used by the characters ("chicken talk") or whether the occasional interjection of key phrases in English was added (e.g., "my toys!"). Fisch and colleagues contrast this finding with a previous study that showed that children's comprehension of educational television was higher in an

English language soundtrack condition compared to a Greek soundtrack condition (Anderson, Lorch, Field & Sanders, 1981). In the Fisch and colleagues experiment, the preschoolers were able to obtain roughly the same meaning in each of the two language conditions. Using the capacity model, we can infer that the intonations and nonverbal communication used by the characters in this segment did not require additional effort to process, whereas the Greek soundtrack did.

5. Our Interpretation of the Studies   Many factors affect learning from educational television. We agree with Fisch's (2000) capacity model allocation of efficient and effective processing to viewer and program characteristics. We would add that factors within the environment—not only the facilitating parent but also the distracting sibling, the phenomenon of multitasking, and other circumstances— play a significant role. The basic proposition—that two elements of educational television either compete or complement each other, reminds us of the parallel findings for audio and video elements. In educational television (as well as in other types of television content), comprehension and learning are enhanced when the audio and video portions of the message are congruent (Field & Anderson, 1985; Pezdek & Stevens, 1984; van der Molen & van der Voort, 1997, 1998).

Younger children would have an easier time comprehending a message regarding personal and social development when that message was concrete rather than abstract. We nevertheless are by no means ready to abandon the conclusions of Anderson and colleagues (1981) (as well as Huston, Wright, and colleagues) that children use both visual and verbal elements of television programs to infer meaning, despite the finding of Fisch and colleagues (2001) that comprehension did not differ as a function of audio stimuli. We believe that this simply illustrates that when carefully and artfully designed, the nonverbal gestures and intonational utterances of characters in young children's television programs are sufficient to convey meaning. Since children learn very early to make sense of tones conveyed in the expressions of parents and others (Walker-Andrews & Grolnick, 1983; e.g., an angry or cautionary tone compared to a loving tone), this result is not surprising.

Although there are very few studies on which to draw, we believe that it is becoming clear that television, no matter how educational or prosocial, cannot substitute for interaction with parents and other individuals and play with appropriate toys in the cognitive and social development of infants and very young children. The marketing promises of the new child television—exemplified by *Teletubbies*, *Boobah*, and *Baby Einstein*—made to eager parents that very young children will be taught important information and skills are not substantiated.

III. TELEVISION'S INFLUENCE ON THE DEVELOPING INTELLECT OF THE CHILD

Additional research has examined the potential for television and other media to exert an influence on a number of activities pertaining to the developing intellect that are not necessarily captured by (although by no means unrelated to) school achievement. We review the evidence regarding the role of television in general and educational television in particular (as well as, when data allow, other media) in fantasy play and daydreaming, creativity and imagination, and the acquisition of language.

These variables are exceptionally worthy of attention. For the very young, playing is the primary way to learn. For older children, it retains significance in healthy development. Fantasy play, in particular, such as pretending and, generally, enacting a different time, place, or role, is also critical to development and is associated with creativity in adulthood (Dansky, 1980; Fisher, 1992). Valkenburg (2001) defines daydreaming as "mental processes such as musing, mind wandering, internal monologue, and being lost in thought" (p. 122). Daydreaming suggests an active and industrious mind, and is highly compatible with creativity. Creativity is a fundamental expression of individuality and emerges from a curious and flexible psyche. Language acquisition in early childhood is a key indicator of cognitive development. These abilities are critical to a child's developing intellect.

A. Fantasy Play and Daydreaming

1. Fantasy Play Fantasy play and television use have been examined by a wide array of methods. Laboratory experiments (Anderson et al., 1977; Friedrich-Cofer et al., 1979; Greer et al., 1982; Huston-Stein et al., 1981; Noble, 1970, 1973; Potts, Huston & Wright, 1986; Silvern & Williamson, 1987) and quasi-experiments (Gadberry, 1980; Maccoby, 1951; Murray & Kippax, 1978; Schramm et al., 1961) have been conducted. Surveys have provided correlational data (Lyle & Hoffman, 1972a, 1972b; D.G. Singer & Singer, 1981; J.L. Singer & Singer, 1981; J.L. Singer et al., 1984). Qualitative analyses have focused on observations of children (Alexander, Ryan & Munoz, 1984; James & McCain, 1982; Reid & Frazer, 1980) and the memories about play of those growing up in communities with and without television (French & Penna, 1991). Most of the data concerns three- to five-year-olds when play is particularly prominent. Some studies also include five- to seven-year-olds. Play is observable, so inquiry is not dependent on the verbal or cognitive skills of children.

Again, a number of hypotheses have been advanced. Viewing has been predicted to decrease the amount of time children spend in fantasy play by displacing time that could be spent on any other activity. Viewing has also been hypothesized to decrease play for other reasons, such as through television-induced arousal, fatigue, anxiety, and fear. Conversely, television viewing has been hypothesized to increase time spent on fantasy play by providing new ideas. Finally, analogous to daydreaming, the prediction has been made that television use will shape fantasy play by providing examples that can be easily incorporated into such play.

We are persuaded by the assembly of evidence by Valkenburg (2001) that television has reduced time that children spend in play, but we are not convinced that this effect has been significant developmentally. Children between the ages of three and five on average have been recorded as spending over three-and-a-half hours in play on weekdays (and about an hour more on weekends), more than double the amount of time they spend with television (Timmer, Eccles & O'Brien, 1985). Children six to eight spend about an hour a day less on play, but still devote more time to play than to television. This should give ample opportunity for any benefits attributable to play. We also believe that young children, like teenagers, are unlikely to replace activities that are fun and important to them with viewing (Comstock & Scharrer, 1999). We also find no evidence that television viewing increases amount of fantasy play, although playing and viewing can co-occur (Mutz et al., 1993).

Educational programs designed specifically to trigger imaginative activity stand in contrast. Some research evidence has emerged that educational programs can encourage fantasy play (Singer & Singer, 1976), whereas other studies have suggested that effect is confined to either those children already low in such play (Tower, Singer, Singer & Biggs, 1979) or to situations in which the play directly matches what was seen on screen (Friedrich-Cofer et al., 1979).

There is substantial evidence that television viewing can shape how fantasy play is manifested. The second author recalls playing *Charlie's Angels* with her sisters in the late 1970s (and vying strenuously for the role of the glamorous Jaclyn Smith), while French and Penna (1991) found memories of superhero play in childhood more numerous among those in their sample who grew up in households with television.

Finally, the evidence does not show that television viewing in general leads to significant decrease in time spent in fantasy play but many studies do indicate that violent television in particular does so. The explanatory mechanism is unclear, but could stem from the fast pace of such programs (which could render children too fatigued to play), arousal (which could impede play), or anxiety or fear (which would leave them indisposed to play) (Comstock & Scharrer, 1999; Valkenburg, 2001).

2. Daydreaming A full range of methods and a wide array of young people of different ages—from three-year-olds to teenagers—have been employed in studies of television and daydreaming (Feshbach & Singer, 1971; Fraczek, 1986; Hart, 1972; Huesmann & Eron, 1986; McIlwraith, Jacobvitz, Kubey & Alexander, 1991; McIlwraith & Josephson, 1985; McIlwraith & Schallow, 1982–83; Sheehan, 1987; Valkenburg & van der Voort, 1995; Valkenburg, Voojis, van der Voort & Wiegman, 1992; Viemero & Paajanen, 1990). Hypotheses have alternatively predicted that television would decrease daydreaming by substituting for it or to increase daydreaming by providing thoughts to employ. A third hypothesis predicts not a change in quantity of daydreaming, but rather a change in its qualitative features, suggesting that television would shape daydreams by supplying subject matter. Finally, television viewing has been considered not as a cause but as an effect in the hypothesis that unpleasant musings would increase viewing as a means of avoidance or escape.

Free play is a property of childhood. In contrast, teenagers and adults engage in rituals. Daydreaming, on the other hand, is a lifelong pursuit. However, unlike play it cannot be observed and inquiry rests on what young people can tell us. As a result, the research represents those seven and older, including adults.

We find no support for a decrease in daydreaming attributable to viewing. We also find no evidence that television or other media (including movies, books, or recorded music) increase amount of daydreaming. What is clear is that what is seen on television is frequently reflected in daydreams and fantasies. For example, science fiction viewing was associated with thinking about how things work, whereas watching dramas, comedies, and to a lesser degree, music videos, is associated with pleasant thoughts while fantasizing (Comstock & Scharrer, 1999). Qualitative differences in daydreams also appear to depend on the amount of violence in the programming to which the child is exposed. Exposure to violent programs promotes "aggressive-heroic" daydreaming (Valkenburg & van der Voort, 1995; Viemero & Paajanen, 1990). For example, Viemero and Paajanen (1990) determined that eight- and 10-year-old boys and girls who watched a large amount of television violence were more likely than others to fantasize about aggressive behavior and to recount in their minds scenes from violent shows.

One particular study by Valkenburg and van der Voort (1995) allows us to rule out the reverse explanation as wholly satisfying that interest in particular topics surfaces in daydreams and later dictates television program choices. Valkenburg and van der Voort (1995) gathered data from approximately 780 third and fifth graders over a one-year period. Changes in the themes that marked daydreams were linked to the content of programs the children had viewed earlier in the year. This suggests that correlations between what is viewed and what arises in daydreams are not fully explained by previously existing preoccupations.

The hypothesis that unpleasant daydreaming and rumination on disagreeable thoughts leads to increased television exposure as a means to escape those thoughts also receives support. In our earlier account of this body of work (Comstock & Scharrer, 1999), we summarized the evidence: "... fantasies of guilt and failure predict purposeful use of television to dispel negative mood states. ... We interpret these outcomes as representing the search for distraction from the unpleasant state" (p. 240). Anxieties or negative experiences of children (a poor grade at school, getting in trouble, worrying about a family member, etc.) can create a negative mood state, which can, in turn, be strategically regulated through the use of television as a diversion.

B. Television's Effect on Creativity and Imaginative Thinking

A frequently examined hypothesis has been that television use stifles creativity in children. The rationale for this allegation is television's explicit visual imagery, the rigid exposition of a story at a set pace without intervals for reflection, and the conventionality of themes and roles of characters in many television programs (Comstock & Scharrer, 1999)—none of which would encourage inventive thinking. A number of research strategies have been employed, including experimental studies of a child's ability to construct a story (Greenfield & Beagle-Roos, 1988; Greenfield, Farrar & Beagle-Roos, 1986; Kerns, 1981; Meline, 1976; Runco & Pedzek, 1984; Valkenburg & Beentjes, 1997; Vibbert & Meringoff, 1981; Watkins, 1988), surveys in which correlations are calculated between paper-and-pencil measures of creativity and amount of everyday television viewing (Childs, 1979; Peterson, Peterson & Carroll, 1987; J. L. Singer & Rapaczynski, 1984; Zuckerman, Singer & Singer, 1980), and a quasi-experiment that took advantage of a unique opportunity to examine the impact of receiving television for the first time on a remote community (Williams, 1986). The common thread that runs through each is the conceptualization of creativity as a child's ability to generate new ideas, think of things in a novel manner, or elaborate autonomously on a stimulus or suggestion provided (Comstock & Scharrer, 1999).

Two standard tests of creativity were used in the Williams (1986) quasi-experiment. Scores were compared for fourth- and seventh-grade children before and well after a community referred to as Notel began to receive a television signal. Comparisons were also made between Notel and communities that had access to either only one ("Unitel") or multiple ("Multitel") television channels. The tests were Alternative Uses, which probes for different ways to use or apply everyday objects such as a bucket, a button or paperclip, and Pattern Meaning, which asks children to identify shapes in ambiguous drawings. Before television came to Notel, the children in that community scored higher on both tests of creativity than the children in the other two communities. After television arrived in the Notel community, scores on the Alternative Uses test slid precipitously.

The seemingly obvious inference that television reduced creativity nevertheless is unjustified for three reasons (Comstock & Scharrer, 1999). First, the alleged effect occurred for only one of two equally important tests. Second, the data on television and visual skills do not support the convenient explanation that Pattern Meaning responses would have been compensatorily enhanced by the availability of television. That is, there is no convincing evidence that everyday viewing of television programming enhances visual skills (Comstock, 1991)— an outcome that could have explained why pattern meaning, which measures visual adeptness, was exempt from reflecting lowered creativity. Third, amount of television viewing was not associated with scores on either of the tests in Notel after television became part of daily life or in the other two communities—and it is hard to believe that television could suppress creativity without a negative correlation between viewing and creativity. In contrast, Valkenburgh (2001) presents some data in which the amount of everyday viewing is negatively associated with a measure of creativity.

The experiments consistently record that children tend to retell or complete a story seen on television in a less intricate and inventive manner compared to a story they had read or heard. On the other hand, one particular study (Watkins, 1988) found that when a sample of third, fifth, and eighth graders were asked to write a story for television or for real life, the former stories were more elaborate and employed thoughts and emotions more often, and this was especially so for heavy television viewers. These data lead to two conclusions. When television—in comparison to reading or listening—visually conveys a specific concrete tale, the originality and complexity apparent in what the child provides from her or his imagination suffers. In contrast, extensive experience with the medium (as seen in heavy viewers) enhances the ability to construct a tale in a manner that reflects television's narrative conventions.

These experiments provide interesting data. However, they fail to convincingly measure creativity as a personality trait. The ability to complete or tell a story in a contrived setting represents transient performance rather than an enduring, stable trait (Comstock & Scharrer, 1999). Furthermore, the experiments fail to convincingly represent more than the short-term influence of exposure to a television portrayal because both control and treatment groups have had extensive experience with the medium that is ignored and would reverse in creativity scores were they to exchange places. Thus, low scores in this context do not identify a long-term deficit attributable to the medium.

The possibility that educational television can stimulate creativity surprisingly has received little research attention. We are aware of two exceptions. Schmitt and colleagues (Schmitt et al., 1997) presented correlational evidence of significant and positive associations between prior exposure to educational television programming and scores on tests of creative thinking. These data, of course, cannot address the issue of causal direction. A recent experiment that pitted a science curriculum emphasizing creativity and curiosity delivered via television against the same curricular elements presented by illustrated print booklets found no differences in subsequent standardized tests of creative thinking and curiosity about science (Rubinstein, 2000). There thus is no convincing record of achievement for educational television in fostering creative thinking although the record in general suggests it should be possible to design programs to achieve this goal.

The Williams data provides little support for the suppression of creativity on either the quasi-experimental or correlational fronts, and there are only a few instances in which amount of viewing is negatively associated with measures that have a claim to reflecting a stable trait. The experiments do not address the issue of a trait, and the consistent results favoring reading or listening to a story in our view reflect the constraining visual specificity of the medium in which nothing is required of the imagination. Thus, we do not see a strong case for a detrimental influence of television on creative skills—but we would also argue that the issue is unresolved.

Scholars have yet to begin to focus these types of inquiries on newer electronic media rather than television, and we can only speculate about potential patterns. Video and computer games have a similar (and sometimes even more pronounced) emphasis on action and violence, and therefore they may trigger arousal, fatigue, or anxiety that could impede imaginative play (Valkenburg, 2001). On the other hand, the content of such games is much more flexible and dynamic in nature than television's content—users decide what avenues to explore and what actions to engage in and essentially engage in problem-solving—and therefore the possibility that visualization, pacing, and conventionality would make creativity and imaginative play less likely does not seem to apply (Valkenburg, 2001). Interactive (video and computer) game playing has been connected to better spatial visualization skills in young users (Greenfield et al., 1994; Okagaki & Frensch, 1994; Subrahmanyam & Greenfield, 1994), but there is no research to bring to bear on other cognitive outcomes.

C. Television's Effect on Language Acquisition

Naigles and Mayeux (2001) suggest that the ability of children to learn a language from television depends on three factors. First, much depends on whether the focus is grammatical development (rules) or lexical development (words). Second, the type of content plays a critical role, with different findings for educational television versus television in general. Finally, the age of the child is a crucial determinant.

There is little reason to believe that television of any sort (educational or otherwise) can spur grammatical development (Sachs, Bard & Johnson, 1981; Selnow & Bettinghaus, 1982). In the most recent examination of this issue, in fact, television exposure was negatively associated with this index of language acquisition. Mayeux and Naigles (2000, as cited in Naigles & Mayeux, 2001) found in a sample of 60 three- and four-year-olds that amount of television viewing (reported by parents) correlated negatively (albeit modestly) with scores on the grammatical subtest of a standardized language comprehension battery. The negative association appeared regardless of whether educational or entertainment-oriented programming was viewed. The authors infer that viewing displaces opportunities for young children to learn grammatical aspects of language through social interaction. The correlational nature of these data, however, compels us to refrain from indicting television because it is equally likely that children with poorer skills watch more television.

Lexical development, learning the meaning of words, is a different matter. It has been convincingly and consistently associated with educational television viewing. In a series of experiments. Rice and colleagues exposed preschoolers to brief videos of images with matching words that were either very common or highly uncommon (Rice, 1990; Rice, Buhr & Oetting, 1992; Rice, Oetting, Marquis, Bode & Pae, 1994). An example discussed by Naigles and Mayeux (2001) is "gramophone" versus "record player." The words were repeated at least three times and the clips were viewed twice over a one-week period. The dependent measure was changes in correctly identifying a still image that matched the novel words. The children exposed to the uncommon words had significantly greater gains in word and image matching. Five-year-olds in the uncommon-word group acquired an average of 4.8 new words, whereas three-year-olds gained 1.5 words. Naigles and Mayeux (2001) summarize that "these laboratory-based studies demonstrate young children can begin to learn the meanings of words by viewing their referents on video in semi natural contexts while coincidentally hearing the words themselves" (p. 144).

The generalizability of these laboratory-based outcomes to "real world" situations is examined in additional studies. In the longitudinal data of Rice, Huston, Truglio, and Wright (1990), preschoolers' lexical acquisition over a two-and-a-half- year span, as measured by scores on the Peabody Picture Vocabulary Test, was positively related to the amount of time spent viewing *Sesame Street*. This positive correlation remained after a number of control variables were statistically assessed, including parental education and initial scores on the vocabulary test. Viewing *Barney and Friends* has also led to increased knowledge of previously unfamiliar nouns (Singer & Singer, 1998) and verbs (Naigles et al., 1995). Finally, in a recent study by Linebarger and Walker (2005), exposure to particular programs beginning at the age of six months is statistically matched against tests of expressive language ability and vocabulary two years later when the children were 30 months old. Viewing of *Dora the Explorer*, *Blue's Clues*, *Dragon Tales*, *Arthur*, and *Clifford* was associated with stronger language skills. Viewing of *Sesame Street* and *Teletubbies* was associated with poorer language skills. The *Sesame Street* outcome probably is attributable to the design of the program for a much older audience. The *Teletubbies* outcome may reflect the repeated use of nonsense words by the characters. In the Linebarger and Walker data, total hours spent viewing was associated with a reduction in vocabulary—raising again the possibility of displacement of time that might be spent interacting with others—but a slight increase in expressive language. We conclude that everyday viewing of educational television, in which care is taken to present words clearly, consistently, and repeatedly, when age-appropriate, can stimulate the learning of new and novel words among young children.

IV. THE EFFECT OF MEDIA ON COGNITIVE AND SOCIAL DEVELOPMENT

Television viewing by children and adolescents exerts an influence on a wide range of outcomes pertaining to scholastic achievement, social adjustment, and the developing intellect. For decades, viewing has been shown to negatively predict performance in school and on standardized academic tests. There are a number of likely reasons. They include the fact that time spent with television means less time for more educationally enriching activities, and the finding that extensive television use discourages reading and cultivates negative attitudes toward devoting mental exertion to the processing of print materials. It is possible that television use also promotes difficulty sustaining attention among children, which impedes success at school. This is much more clearly true of violent television in particular than programming in general, though television on the whole is quite violent.

It must also be acknowledged that young people who view larger amounts of television have characteristics that predict poorer scholastic performance—lower levels of mental ability, households lower in socioeconomic status, and stress and conflict with others. A very recent national survey has also implicated time spent with video games in a negative relationship with grades earned at school, at least grades as reported by children and teenagers. Intriguingly, that same study fails to find the usual negative relationship with television, an outcome that could be an anomaly, a research artifact, or sign of changing times. Only additional inquiry will tell. Consistently, young people's use of print media is positively related to scholastic achievement.

Educational television performs a vastly different role in the scholastic experiences of children. There is regular and convincing support for the ability of programs such as *Sesame Street*, *Blue's Clues*, and other educational fare to facilitate learning on the part of preschoolers and to smooth their transition into the demands of school. More than one set of data suggest that effects of viewing educational programs as a young child benefits performance in high school. In addition to cognitive and intellectual outcomes, viewing educational series including *Sesame Street*, *Mister Rogers' Neighborhood*, and *Barney & Friends* has also been associated with prosocial effects (including knowledge of manners, positive interactions with others, and tolerance for diversity), although there is some evidence that such effects are short-lived, very limited in range, and do not consistently extend into the day-to-day "free play" of children.

The development of concepts, models, and theories to explain the ways in which children interact with television programs (and particularly young children and educational programs) has aided our understanding. Even the youngest children pay at least passing attention to the screen, and attention paid to television increases as children grow older. Attention is directed more frequently toward content that makes sense than when content has appealing formal features but is incomprehensible. In fact, comprehensibility as a predictor of viewing develops very early in childhood. Sound effects, bright colors, music, changing camera shots and angles, and other formal features can initially spark attention in children. It is nevertheless a more active judgment about the merits of the content that will predict continued interest. Once attention has been captured, the greatest opportunity for learning from television occurs when the educational and entertainment elements of a program are in harmony, when the content is neither too familiar nor too novel, and its cognitive demands are perceived as not too difficult but also not too simple.

We have reviewed the many studies that show television can shape children's imaginative play and daydreams. Ideas and impressions derived from television are often incorporated into play or the mental musings of young persons. The critique that television exposure impedes the healthy development of the imagination is not well supported by the existing evidence. Some authors have suggested such an impact; the data are not so clear. Inference depends in part on whether the research outcome is construed as a personality trait or a transient state of expression. The former receives far less support than the latter. Mixed evidence also has emerged for television's influence on language acquisition in early childhood. Educational television plays a facilitative role in the learning of words and their meanings, and can be effectively designed to do so. Effects on grammatical elements have been much more elusive. Overall, television and other media figure prominently in and can contribute substantially to the cognitive and social development of children.

YOUNG CUSTOMERS— CREATING THE MODERN CONSUMER THROUGH ADVERTISING AND MARKETING

V

There are several interesting and important threads that must be drawn together in regard to marketing to children and teenagers. They include:

- The evolution of advertising to children as an issue, and particularly television advertising (because it is the medium to which they most attend)
- The empirical record of evidence that has been compiled, largely (although not wholly) as a result of the suddenly enhanced prominence of that issue
- The stages of cognitive development that govern both whether children may be said to be exploited by television advertising and their preferences and interests as consumers, and use of those stages in developing products for and promoting them to young people
- A frenzy in the entrepreneurial pursuit of children and teenagers as customers manifest in the direct targeting of children and preteens ("tweens") rather than the more decorous wooing of their parents that was common in decades past.

I. EVOLUTION OF THE ISSUE OF TELEVISION ADVERTISING

Television advertising and its effects on young persons were placed on the public agenda as an issue in the late 1960s and early 1970s. Particularly prominent were the now-disbanded Action for Children's

Television (ACT) and its founder Peggy Charren. During the preceding two decades, television advertising attracted almost no public attention in connection with young viewers. Saturday and Sunday morning programming carried as many as 16 minutes an hour of non-program material, most of which were commercials, compared with an industry code primetime ceiling at the time of 9.5 minutes. This occurred, not because of a belief by broadcasters in the greater forbearance of young audiences, but because these hours were categorized as day segments; advertising ceilings were higher to ensure profitability when audience size was smaller.

A. Public Displeasure of Advertising in Primetime Programming

However, this circumstance invited public displeasure once displeasure had some advocates. As L. Brown recounts in *The New York Times Encyclopedia of Television* (1977):

> Although children helped to build circulation for stations, and good will for the new television medium, they were not initially perceived as a major marketing group for products. Television was considered too high-priced for child-oriented products in the 50s and early 60s when the single or dual sponsorship of programs was the rule. Prime time programs were particularly expensive, considering that they reached a large proportion of adults who were not targets of the advertisers. But a number of factors converged around 1965 to make children's programs a major profit center of networks: first, the proliferation of multi-set households, which broke up family viewing... second, the drift to participation advertising as opposed to full sponsorships, which encouraged more advertisers to use the medium; and third, the discovery that a relatively "pure" audience of children could be corralled on Saturday mornings (and to a lesser extent on Sundays) where air time was cheaper, advertising quotas were wide open and children could be reached by the devices used years before by comic books.
>
> By the late 60s television programming aimed at children was confined, with few exceptions, to Saturday mornings in the form of animated cartoons. Moreover, the animation studios developed a form of limited animation for the undiscriminating youngsters, involving fewer movements per second, which was cheaper than standard animation. Recognizing that children enjoy the familiar, the networks played each episode of a series six times

over two years, substantially reducing costs. And while prime time programs, under the Television Code, permitted 9.5 commercial minutes per hour, Saturday morning children's shows carried as many as 16 commercial minutes per hour. Citizens groups did not become aroused, however, until the networks began to deal excessively—in their competitive zeal—with monsters, grotesque superheroes and gratuitous violence to win the attention of youngsters. Advertisers by then were making the most of the gullibility of children by pitching sugar-coated cereals, candy-coated vitamins and expensive toys. (pp. 82–83)

(C)ommercials directed specifically at children... became a highly controversial aspect of television, raising questions on the morality of subjecting children to sophisticated advertising techniques. In the 70s consumer groups began protesting the differing commercial standards for children and adults, as well as other allegedly abusive practices, among them promoting nutritionally inadequate foods, using program hosts as salesmen, tempting purchases by offering premiums, and advertising expensive toys in a deceptive manner. (pp. 81–82)

ACT emphasized the clutter, the quantity, the ostensibly dubious practices and techniques, and the alleged inherent unfairness or deceptiveness of advertising directed at children. It argued that many members of the audience were too young to understand the self-interested motives behind commercials, and therefore could not properly evaluate them. Through appearances before congressional committees, petitions to the Federal Communications Commission (FCC) and the Federal Trade Commission (FTC), complaints to broadcasters and advertisers, and coverage by the press, ACT and others created an atmosphere in which some conciliatory response by broadcasters and advertisers, fearful of government interference or public hostility, was almost inevitable.

The most immediate effect was a substantial increase in research concerned with television advertising and children and teenagers. Eventually, these studies would figure importantly in hearings by the FTC in conjunction with the FCC on the possibility of new rules and regulations.

B. NSF and FTC

The National Science Foundation (NSF) in the mid-1970s took the unusual step of commissioning a review of this growing body of evidence to serve as the basis for possible rule-making by the FCC and the

FTC. *The Effects of Television Advertising on Children* (Adler, Lesser, Meringoff, Robertson, Rossiter & Ward, 1980) was a landmark in the literature on television advertising and children. Its major conclusions:

1. Young children do not understand the persuasive vested interest of commercials.
2. Commercials are often successful in persuading children to desire products, and this is particularly so for foods.
3. Purchase requests to parents are common, parental yielding is typical, and parent-child disputes over purchases are not rare.

In response to the report, the FTC in 1978 (a U.S. Government Printing Office version appeared in 1977, three years before commercial publication, and of course drafts were available to the FTC and FCC earlier) proposed to ban or limit advertising to children (FTC, 1978). This raised three interesting questions. Would children's television entertainment disappear if it were not supported by advertising? Would the FCC be willing to place a "children's tax" on broadcasters by requiring such programming without supportive advertising? If limits— rather than an outright ban—were imposed, what would be the parameters? Despite extensive hearings, economic power and political influence triumphed. Kunkel (2001) tells the story:

> The painstaking level of detail the FTC pursued in marshaling its supporting evidence contrasted sharply with a serious miscalculation about the extent of the political opposition to its proposal (Kunkel & Watkins, 1987). The broadcasting and advertising industries were joined by many of America's largest corporate conglomerates in opposing the ban. These businesses owned subsidiaries producing toys, sugared cereals, and numerous other types of child-oriented merchandise. Fearing adverse impacts on their profits, these industries initiated campaigns to influence the public to oppose the ban. A key element of their strategy was the claim of First Amendment protection for the right to provide "information" about products to America's budding consumers.
>
> The FTC's formal rule-making process for implementing the proposed ban moved forward. Open hearings were held. Elaborate briefs assessing the research evidence regarding children's comprehension of advertising were submitted by all sides. On this front, the forces seeking regulation fared reasonably well. Although some inevitable qualifications were lodged, a consensus emerged among researchers that young children were indeed uniquely vulnerable to television's commercial claims and appeals.

At the same time, however, a much different outcome was occurring on other fronts of the political battle. Using their influence with elected officials, the FTC's corporate opponents succeeded in derailing the agency's proposal, employing an innovative strategy. Responding to corporate pressure, Congress rescinded the agency's authority to restrict advertising deemed unfair by enacting legislation ironically titled the FTC Improvements Act of 1980. Besides removing this aspect of the FTC's jurisdiction, the act specifically prohibited any further action to adopt the proposed children's advertising rules. The agency soon issued a final ruling on the case formally implementing the congressional mandate (FTC, 1981), and since then there has been no further effort to resurrect this initiative. (pp. 387–388)

II. THE EVIDENTIARY RECORD

We begin with the five principal points of contention. We then turn to the empirical evidence on each.

A. *Points of Contention*

1. Recognition and Comprehension of Advertising   Critics have argued that commercials directed at children are inherently deceptive and unfair because before reaching a critical age, children may not be able to distinguish between commercials and program content, may not perceive commercials as persuasive rather than informative, and may not recognize that the statements made by brand representatives are in the self-interest of the advertiser. They have also argued that the audiovisual techniques employed may mislead young viewers about product attributes, and that premium offers distract them from product attributes, which ostensibly are the correct basis for choosing among products. The reply of those favorable toward directing commercials at children (mostly those in the businesses of advertising or broadcasting, or representing companies that market products to the young) has been that early in their years of viewing, children perceive commercials as differing from program content even if they cannot define what advertising is; children cannot be damaged, even if unaware of persuasive intent and self-interest, because they lack the disposable income to act on desires created by commercials; and, that a premium in fact is a product attribute that merits consideration.

2. Harmfulness of Advertising to Young Viewers   Critics have argued that acceptance of some or all of a commercial message may result in psychological or physical harm to a young person. The former include the inducement of feelings of inferiority, lack of self-esteem, and relative deprivation either through the attractiveness and skills of those portrayed or the failure to have use of an advertised product. The latter include the consumption of heavily sugared and fast foods, to the detriment of nutrition and the benefit of obesity. The rejoinder has been that puffery—placing the product in the best light through the use of superlative language and boastful claims—and the use of attractive characters are inherent in advertising and that nutrition is unaffected because advertising does not influence basic preferences but only choices among brands.

3. The Effect of Advertising on Parent–Child Relations   Critics have argued that television advertising directed at children often initiates a secondary persuasive process in which children seek the compliance of parents. Parental refusal may lead to conflict. Avoiding conflict constitutes an incentive for parents to accede, although giving in may be counter to their best judgment. The reply has been that any conflict is not substantial enough to merit remedy, and requests can be used to teach children the bases for rational choice (Do we need it? Is it affordable? How does it compare in attributes and price with competing products?).

4. Should Advertising Drive Programming?   Critics have argued that reliance on advertising to support programming for children subverts program quality and value. Popularity across a wide age range becomes the goal, because revenues increase with size of audience. Animation, swift scene changes, loud music, violence, and other narrative techniques to hold attention predominate. Educational affective and cognitive benefits and programming for particular ages are assigned a minor if any role at all. This is in addition to the time taken up by commercials, which could be used for other purposes, such as public service announcements (PSAs) aimed at children. The reply has been that the popularity among children of the television entertainment designed for them documents that it is what they want, and that without advertising there would be no television entertainment for children because the FCC is unlikely to mandate programming on such a scale.

5. Does Advertising Take Advantage of Program Content?   Critics pointed out that the 1980s saw the emergence of numerous series either designed to portray existing toy lines or concocted in conjunction with the development of new toys, with the result a program-length commercial. The critics saw this as an escalation in the type of practice that earlier restrictions on the use of television characters and personalities in commercials on programs in which they appeared were supposed to restrain. The reply was that the practice of marketing toys in conjunction with television characters and personalities has a long history including such notables as Mickey Mouse and Donald Duck, and the programs contain no persuasive messages on behalf of purchase. The FCC essentially concurred by ruling in the late 1980s that programs featuring characters, devices, and personalities sold as toys do not, by that fact, constitute commercials on behalf of those products.

The contentions have been many, and the industry response, defensive. Yet, social science research evidence allows for some rather definitive conclusions.

B. Evidence of the Effects of Television Advertising

Two excellent analyses of the effects of television advertising on young persons are the early review by Adler and colleagues (1980) that figured in the FTC hearings and a comparatively recent review by John (1999). The former was confined to children aged two to 11. The latter includes teenagers. We will begin with children, because many issues and controversies pertain specifically to them. We will turn to teenagers in connection with the role of cognitive development in consumer behavior and present-day marketing strategies.

1. Recognizing, Comprehending, and Evaluating Commercials We cover four topics: distinguishing commercials from programs; understanding the persuasive intent of advertising; the effectiveness of certain audiovisual alternatives in commercial comprehension; and the role of premiums in product choice.

a. *Commercials versus Programs* Adler and colleagues concluded that the mental capability to distinguish commercials from programs and to understand the persuasive intent of advertising increases with age, as one would expect, but that a "substantial proportion of children, particularly those below age seven or eight, do not draw upon the concept of selling intent in defining commercials, in distinguishing them from programs, or in explaining their purpose, suggesting little comprehension and/or low salience of persuasive intent as a criterial feature of advertising" (p. 214). We believe it is crucial to distinguish between:

- Identifying commercials as different from programs, versus
- Understanding their persuasive intent, or identifying commercials by function.

The data unambiguously document that children below the ages of seven or eight recognize commercials as different in some way from programs. Zuckerman and Gianinno (1981) showed photographs of animated characters from either commercials or programs to 64 four-, seven-, and 10-year-olds, asked questions about the photos, and asked them to define a commercial. The younger children could not define a commercial, but most could identify who the characters appearing in commercials were and could match them with the products they vended; in fact, in testimony to their inability to comprehend the concept of "commercial," more could make such matches than were correct when asked which characters were "in a commercial." Macklin (1987) found among 120 children of preschool age that only a minority correctly selected, from an assortment of 10 different scenes, a picture of a boy and girl with a woman making purchases at a supermarket checkout counter as indicating what the commercials they had just seen *wanted* them to do. The rate for four-year-olds was about 8 percent; for five-year-olds, 20 percent.

In a follow-up study, 45 such children, after viewing commercials, were asked to choose a play environment that satisfied the same query. The correct choice was a play store. About 13 percent chose the store, although the figure was 40 percent for five-year-olds and zero for three-year-olds. Similarly, Butter, Popovich, Stackhouse, and Garner (1981) found that although a majority of 80 preschoolers could recognize commercials as different from the *Captain Kangaroo* sequence in which they were embedded, even larger majorities could not define commercials or say why there were on television. In a complementary vein, Ward and colleagues (Blatt, Spencer & Ward, 1972; Ward, Reale & Levinson, 1972; Ward & Wackman, 1973) found that, among those aged five to 12 years, the younger children distinguished commercials from programs on affective (they were funnier) or coincidental (they were shorter) grounds, whereas only the older children often introduced the criterion of purpose (they sell).

b. *Persuasive Intent* The distinction between recognition and comprehension of intent is made clear by the research of Blosser and Roberts (1985), who exposed 90 children varying in age from preschool to fourth grade to a variety of television messages, such as excerpts from the news, commercials, and instructional PSAs (see Table 5.1). When the criterion of comprehension was recognition that a commercial presented something that *could* be purchased, more than half before the age of seven could recognize a commercial. However, when the criterion was perceiving the message as persuasive in intent, it was not until age eight that a majority could be said to recognize a commercial. News was identified earliest, commercials were next,

Table 5.1
Age and Comprehension of Message Intent

	Age (years)					
Message type	0–5 (*N* = 10)	5+–6 (*N* = 24)	6+–7 (*N* = 19)	7+–8 (*N* = 14)	8+–10 (*N* = 13)	10+ (*N* = 10)
Percentage comprehending message content						
News	30	21	53	50	77	90
Child commercial	80	83	95	93	100	100
Adult commercial	40	67	84	86	92	100
Educational	100	83	90	93	100	90
PSA	60	92	95	100	100	100
Percentage correctly labeling each message type						
News	60	88	95	100	92	100
Child commercial	10	62	53	71	85	100
Adult commercial	10	58	63	79	92	100
Educational	0	0	0	7	23	30
PSA	0	0	0	7	23	20
Percentage articulating correct message content						
News	0	38	63	86	100	100
Child commercial	0	0	16	36	77	60
Adult commercial	0	13	11	21	61	60
Educational	0	8	11	36	62	40
PSA	0	8	5	29	39	60

Adapted from Blosser, B. J. & Roberts, D. F. (1985). Age differences in children's perceptions of message intent: Responses to TV news, commercials, educational spots, and public service advertisements. *Communication Research, 12*(4), 455–484.

and PSAs came last; this exemplifies the problematic nature of commercials for children's comprehension, because they without doubt exceed news in prior experience and yet become fully understood only at a later age.

We also draw on the experiment by Gentner (1975) in which she examined the acquisition of the verbs "have," "give," "take," "sell," "buy," and "spend." Two Muppet dolls from *Sesame Street*, Bert and Ernie, were seated behind tables on which there were money and objects. Children ranging in age from three-and-a-half to eight-and-a-half years were asked to make the dolls engage in these activities. A typical instruction was, "Make Ernie sell a truck to Bert." Even those in the youngest of the five yearly age brackets (between three-and-a-half and four-and-a-half) understood give and take, with the former almost universally grasped and the latter comprehended by four out of five. However, at this young age there was little sign of comprehension of buy and sell.

Comprehension of these two concepts increased with each advancing age bracket, until for the oldest (between seven-and-a-half and eight-and-a-half), it reached 95 percent for buy and 65 percent for sell. Except for those in the second bracket (four-and-a-half to five-and-a-half), when comprehension of the two was about equally modest (25–30%), sell consistently and sizably lagged behind buy.

Buy and sell involve more complex transactions than give and take. In addition to prior or future possession, they call for the exchange of money on the condition that there is an exchange of object. Sell probably lags behind buy because it is less familiar to children and possibly (as proposed by Geis, 1982) because it is associated with an ego gratification that children have yet to experience; conversely, they have far more frequently experienced the pleasures of buying a wanted product at the supermarket checkout. The interpretation that the inability to role-play the transaction symbolically represented by a commercial signals less than full comprehension of advertising is further supported by the finding of Faber, Perloff, and Hawkins (1982) that, among 65 first and third graders, comprehension and the ability to role-play were positively associated.

In this context, the importance of children being able to distinguish commercials from program content takes on a reduced significance. If children cannot recognize the persuasive intent of commercials, their ability to distinguish commercials as different from the program is irrelevant. If we hold for children the same standards we hold for adults, then television advertising directed at them is deceptive for many children under the age of eight, and the proportion for whom it is deceptive increases markedly with decreasing age. Adults are conventionally protected from being deceived by advertising that might be mistaken for legitimate news reports by disclaimers. The rationale is that accurate evaluation rests on the understanding of motive. If children do not recognize persuasive intent, deception by the standards held for adults is inevitable.

Recognition and comprehension are not synonyms. We would not take choosing a picture of a child in a supermarket (from one or more alternatives) as the goal of a commercial as evidence of comprehension among very young children as Donohue, Henke, and Donohue (1980) or Macklin (1985) have. However, we do not doubt that in each of these two instances the correct selection was frequent, increased with age, and an increase in the options decreased the number of correct responses, as they report. Instead, we would consider these and similar outcomes as more evidence that very young children associate characters and elements of commercials with marketed products.

   c. *Audiovisual Techniques* Commercials obviously employ as many recognized means of attracting and holding attention as possible. In the case of young persons and especially children, this means high levels of action, pace, scene shifts, and visual change; familiar or highly appealing characters or personalities; and verbalizations that are catchy and invite imitation. These techniques are demonstratively effective. For example, Ross and colleagues (1984) found, among more than 400 boys between the ages of 8 and 14, that the use of live auto-racing footage in a commercial for a toy race car led to overestimates of its size, speed, and complexity.

   Here, we become specifically concerned with the use of techniques ostensibly employed to improve the recognition of a commercial or the comprehension of product attributes. The first has been represented by the use of so-called bumpers or separators to demarcate commercials from program content. The second is exemplified in the use of disclaimers, usually verbal appendages at the bottom of the screen. Both have been adopted by advertisers and broadcasters in response to their critics. Neither seems to have the support of empirical evidence.

   Palmer and McDowell (1979) found that the then-common separator of animated characters with a voice-over announcing "'_____' will be right back after these messages" did not increase the recognizability of commercials among young children. Stutts, Vance, and Hudleson (1981) found, in a sample of 108 three-, five-, and seven-year-olds, that separators visually distinct from the preceding program and subsequent commercials were ineffective at ages five and younger; they were helpful for the seven-year-olds, but these children are approaching an age at which help is not necessary. Similarly, Liebert, Sprafkin, Liebert, and Rubenstein (1977) found that the then-standard disclaimer "Assembly required" was understood by few children, whereas most understood the more colloquial "You have to put it together." Stutts and Hunnicutt (1987) provide supportive data from children of preschool age for the phrases "Each sold separately" and "Batteries not included." Meanwhile, Ballard-Campbell (1983), while giving further support to Palmer and McDowell (1979) in their finding of null efficacy for regularly employed separators, found that a more intense colloquial version that presented a symbol of termination was far more effective among boys aged four, six, and eight years. The voice-over declared, "O.K., kids, get ready, here comes a commercial" while the visual accompaniment was a red stop sign. Paget, Kritt, and Bergemann (1984), in a sample of 84 ranging in age from preschool to young adults, found (as we would expect) that the ability to place oneself in the role of others, including advertisers, was comparatively quite low at the earlier ages and increased with age; of particular pertinence, they found that the persuasive intent of a commercial was recognized at a much earlier age when an unadorned spiel is directed at the viewer, rather than the common television format of a visual anecdote featuring the product.

We are not at all surprised to find that separators and disclaimers are not effective. It is in the interest of whatever channel is being viewed not to disrupt ongoing monitoring and risk channel shopping; disclaimers are not information an advertiser wishes to convey, but serve as a legitimization of the message. Similarly, it is hardly surprising that various conventions of commercial design discourage the recognition of a persuasive attempt and encourage exaggeration of the positive attributes of the product; both, again, are in the interests of the communicator.

d. *Premiums* Premiums have been said to distort the product choices of young persons by drawing attention away from product attributes. Adler and colleagues assert that the "inclusion of a premium in a commercial does not seem to distract children from other product attributes (as measured by recall of the content of the commercial), nor does the premium appear to increase children's evaluation of the product" (1980, p. 216). Our reading of the evidence leads us to conclusions that differ from those of both Adler and colleagues and the critics of advertising.

For example, Ward (1980) reports that Rubin (1972) and Shimp, Dyer, and Divita (1976) found premium offers effectively competed with product attributes in responses to cereal commercials. The former found that among first-, third-, and sixth-graders, premiums at every age were better recalled than product attributes; decidedly few at every grade level perceived the cereal as what the commercial was supposed to make them want; and more first graders perceived the premium than the product as what the commercial was supposed to make them want. The latter found a modest association between brand choice and liking for the premium. Atkin (1975b, 1975c, 1978a) found that more than three-fourths of mothers of children from preschool to fifth grade reported that their child cited a premium in asking that a cereal be purchased, and almost 10 percent of children's requests unobtrusively recorded in a supermarket included mention of a premium. A national survey by a marketing research company is described in which, among about 900 children ranging in age from six to 14, those younger consistently cited the premium as more important in choosing a cereal than such factors as "nutritious," "natural," or "enriched or fortified." We interpret the evidence as suggesting that:

- Premiums figure importantly in the response of young persons to advertised products
- Among younger children, recall of product attributes is lower than among those older, and recall of premiums is superior to that of product attributes
- Younger children perceive premiums to be more important than product attributes in choosing among products
- Premiums are cited frequently by children when they ask a parent to purchase a product (the almost 10% supermarket figure is certainly an underestimate of premium-based requests, because one would not expect many children spontaneously to recall, in the bustle of a store, an offer seen hours or days earlier on television)

Premiums in our view are undeniably often the basis of product choices, and especially among those younger. However, with products as fungible as those marketed to children (who would wish to assert that one or another cereal differs enormously from the rest in nutritional value?), a premium often is as rational a basis as any for a decision.

2. Accepting the Message of a Commercial   We cover five topics: endorsements, threats to self-esteem, use of proprietary and illegal substances and use of alcohol, food choices and nutrition, and the role of amount and frequency of exposure to commercials.

a. *Endorsements*   A popular tactic of advertising is the endorsement, in which a person, often a celebrity, recommends a product or course of action. Adler and colleagues reach a firm conclusion: "A number of studies have demonstrated that the mere appearance of a character with a product can significantly alter children's evaluation of the product, with the evaluation shifting positively or negatively, depending on children's evaluation of the endorser" (p. 215). For example, Ross and colleagues (1984), in addition to the exaggerated perceptions among boys aged from eight to 14 about a toy race car produced by live footage of a race car, found that the appearance of a famous race driver increased preference for the toy; that commercials with celebrities were better liked, led to higher product ratings, and that the celebrities were perceived as more competent than noncelebrities; and that these effects were attributable principally to teenagers, who would be much better able than those younger to recognize celebrities or recognize a resemblance between those portrayed and celebrities.

Kunkel (1988b) provides evidence both on behalf of the effectiveness of endorsements and a policy against host-selling in which a character on a program also vends a product. He found, among about 160 children aged from four to five or seven to eight, that commercials within episodes of the *Flintstones* and *Smurfs* featuring characters from each program were more effective among the older children in creating favorability and intent to ask a parent to purchase the advertised cereal, and at both ages such commercials were less frequently recognized as such than when they appeared embedded in a different program. Hoy, Young, and Mowen (1986) in contrast did not find any greater difficulty of recognition among about 80 children from three to seven in age when a host-selling commercial was embedded in its program, but did find lowered recognition when the commercial followed the program and lesser recognition of selling intent—which in general was very low because of the ages of the children—for host-selling than nonhost commercials.

The evidence on behalf of the influence of endorsements essentially documents the persuasive effectiveness of programs whose characters and paraphernalia are sold as toys or logos. Their characters implicitly self-endorse by bestowing by their presence approval upon each other and the weapons, vehicles, and equipment they employ and the costumes they wear. This identifies these vehicles as commercials if not by label at least certainly in function.

b. *Threats to Self-Esteem*   We concur with Adler and colleagues that the evidence demonstrates that both explicit and implicit endorsements affect product evaluations by young viewers. We are less in accord with their conclusion that there is no evidence of effects on self-esteem.

The three major means by which commercials might adversely affect self-esteem are by portraying achievements, whether social, physical, or mental, of which the young viewer is incapable; by portraying others in some way, socially, physically, or materially, as better off than the young viewer; or by portraying persons like the young viewer in roles socially inferior to those of other young persons. It is true that in the review by Rossiter (1980a) only one experiment is discussed that bears directly on the first, but we think that Atkin (1975a) demonstrates the potential for such outcomes. He showed one group of children a commercial in which a child builds an immense and complex, intricate tower with building blocks, and showed another group a commercial in which the tower is architecturally much more modest. Those in the first condition displayed somewhat more anger and frustration when subsequently playing with the blocks.

In regard to the second, we think the evidence on behalf of the well-known contrast effect in which comparisons with attractive persons lower attractiveness ratings for self and others (Comstock, 1991) is sufficiently strong to indict commercials. In regard to the third, the data on gender-based responses to portrayals makes a *prima facie* case for such effects. The evidence is clear (Comstock, 1991; Comstock & Scharrer, 2005) that portrayals of nontraditional roles can increase the acceptability of such activities among both sexes, portrayals of females in traditional or nontraditional roles can shift the thought and behavior of females toward accordance with the portrayals, and the linking of an activity with a gender in a portrayal decreases the likelihood that those of the opposite gender and increases the likelihood that those of the same gender will engage in it.

The content of commercials with regard to gender remains largely traditional, although they are decidedly less so than two or three decades ago (Comstock & Scharrer, 2005; Scharrer & Comstock, 2003; see Chapter III). The implication is that they encourage acceptance of a role of lower status. In sum, portrayals in each of the three categories that would lower self-esteem are common in television commercials.

When commercials portray achievements at which the young viewer is competent as valued, persons like the viewer as better off, or roles engaged in by the viewer as superior, as desirable, socially approved, or powerful, the obverse occurs. Self-esteem is enhanced. However, given the present makeup of commercials (see Chapter III), such effects would not be particularly common, and would be far more common for males than for females.

c. Drugs and Alcohol   A special case arises when advertising aimed at adults may influence young viewers. Two such product categories—drugs and alcohol—have been the focus of both considerable controversy and empirical inquiry.

Contrary to some popular misgivings and a petition in the mid-1970s by 14 state attorneys general to the FCC to ban all drug advertising between 6 A.M. and 9 P.M. (Bellotti, 1975), teenage drug abuse does not seem to be encouraged by exposure to commercials for proprietary over-the-counter drugs. The argument was that such commercials portray drugs as a handy means of relief—thus, they would promote illicit as well as licit drug use.

Milavsky, Pekowsky, and Stipp (1975–1976), however, did not find among 300 males aged 13 to 15 years, from whom data was obtained six times over a three-and-a-half-year period, any association between cumulative exposure to drug commercials and illicit drug use, or between such exposure and an attitude favorable to taking drugs, although such an attitude was positively associated with use of both licit and illicit drugs. In short, the necessary link between attitude and behavior was present but not the necessary link between exposure and attitude. On the other hand, they did find that cumulative exposure was positively if modestly associated with the use of proprietary drugs. This pattern is in accord with the interviews with almost 700 third-, fifth-, and seventh-grade boys and girls by Robertson, Rossiter, and Gleason (1979), with questionnaires from an almost equal number in the same grades obtained by Rossiter and Robertson (1980), and the questionnaires from about 260 boys and girls obtained by Atkin (1978b). As described in the review by Robertson (1980a):

- "Beliefs, attitudes, and requests for medicines" on the part of young persons are positively but modestly associated with exposure to television commercials for proprietary drugs.
- Young persons highly anxious about illness are a "vulnerable subgroup." They are more favorably inclined toward proprietary drugs, they are exposed to more commercials on their behalf, and among these young persons there is a decidedly positive association between such exposure and the holding of favorable beliefs about these drugs. Nevertheless, the correlation between exposure and use, although positive, is small.
- Various differences in other subgroups (those younger, from households of lower socioeconomic status, and those more often ill) in favorability, exposure, use or their interrelationships, provide no evidence that exposure has any effects.
- Parents do not typically discuss drugs and illness with their offspring very often, but such mediation is associated with more favorable beliefs and attitudes on the part of young persons toward drugs. This suggests that it occurs mostly as a means of getting children to take medicines.

Both Milavsky, Pekowsky, and Stipp (1975) and Robertson, Rossiter, and Gleason (1979) measured exposure by meticulously counting the frequency of drug commercials in programs reported as viewed, so their measures provide an accurate index of relative amount of exposure (it is only necessary to differentiate between those who had seen greater and fewer commercials regardless of the rate of inattention for all commercials). Thus, both give credible evidence on behalf of the view that proprietary drug advertising, although not aimed at young viewers, has some influence on them. However, the influence is confined to favorability toward and, at older ages, use of proprietary drugs. This is in agreement with the more recent finding of Thornton and Voigt (1984) that, in a sample of 3500 between ages of 11 and 17, amount of viewing was unassociated with illegal drug use.

We concur with Adler and colleagues that the available data are inconsistent with the facilitation of illegal drug use by exposure to commercials for proprietary over-the-counter drugs. The very modest positive correlations on behalf of over-the-counter drugs hardly give cause for alarm because they are available by that means precisely because the risks they impose are slight.

Unfortunately for analytic tranquility, these conclusions cannot simply be applied to alcohol consumption and abuse, because the two product categories vary in important ways. Unlike proprietary drugs, alcohol in our society has a symbolic role in the transition from child to young adult, with access a privilege of the latter. Alcohol is physiologically and psychologically rewarding to a degree unmatched by most over-the-counter remedies. Alcohol often figures importantly in conflicts with parents. Alcohol has prominent social functions in interacting with peers of both the same and opposite sexes. Alcohol also is frequently consumed by characters in television daytime and primetime drama. Illegal drugs, of course, share these properties to some extent except for the frequent and usually favorable portrayal of alcohol in television drama (see Chapter III). However, liquor is legal except for the important (in this case) age restrictions. Social taboos for liquor are far less forceful than for illegal drugs, and the persuasive threshold that advertising would have to cross is far lower. Thus, the triangulation between product, society, and individual requires independent treatment.

The television advertising for alcohol certainly differs from that for over-the-counter drugs. Drug ads emphasize chemical efficacy. Alcohol ads emphasize social interaction, having a good time, and partying. There is also a dichotomy between what is advertised and what is portrayed in programs. Mostly lighter alcoholic beverages are widely advertised on television (beer, ale, wine, and wine coolers), although earlier self-regulatory restrictions on commercials for hard liquor have largely been cast aside in the pursuit of profits. In contrast, hard liquor frequently is consumed by characters in programs. Finally, in a bow to critics the advertisements typically do not show people drinking, but only beverages of the advertised brand being served.

The experimental literature makes only a very modest case for effects of either portrayals in programs or commercials. However, it is always possible that effects might be stronger with more powerfully designed depictions than those that were employed. The survey literature records in some cases very small positive correlations between exposure to advertisements in various media and alcohol consumption and abuse, but the sole large national sample (and thus, the most credible body of data)—with one singular exception—produces no positive correlations between exposure to television and its commercials for alcohol and consumption.

Kotch, Coulter, and Lipsitz (1986) found, among about 40 boys aged 10 to 12 years, that those who saw a montage of drinking scenes assigned somewhat more importance to the good than the bad effects of alcohol. Among those aged eight to 10 years who saw a segment of *M.A.S.H.* with three scenes with martinis, Rychtarik, Fairbank, Allen, Foy, and Drabmon (1983) found that more subsequently chose whiskey instead of water as appropriate to serve adults than those who saw the same sequence without the martini scenes or those who saw no *M.A.S.H.* segment. Alcohol consumption in programming would be especially likely to prime the young male viewer (that is, make drinking more salient and desirable) because most of it is done by high-status males who are favorably portrayed (Breed & DeFoe, 1981).

Although commercials for alcoholic beverages obviously never portray teenagers or children, they often employ famous athletes, and endorsements, implied or direct, have proven very effective with young viewers. In two experiments (Kohn & Smart, 1984, 1987), there was some evidence of an effect for both males and females of commercials on consumption. In one, college-age males saw varying quantities of beer advertisements embedded in a video of a soccer match in a comfortable group setting in a lounge. Exposure to the commercials was associated with ordering beers sooner, but not with quantity consumed. In another, college-age females similarly saw varying quantities of wine commercials in a similarly lengthy television program in the same setting. Exposure to the commercials was associated with somewhat greater consumption of wine.

Several surveys record positive associations between television viewing (which implies greater exposure to alcohol commercials) or specifically between exposure to television or other alcohol advertising and alcohol consumption. Tucker (1985) found, among about 400 high school males, that heavy viewers consumed significantly more alcohol than light viewers, consumption was linearly associated with viewing, and the imposition of statistical controls for demographic variables led to a strengthened association between viewing and consumption. Strickland (1983) found a very small positive association ($r = +.12$) between exposure to television alcohol commercials and consumption when controlling for demographics and total television viewing among about 775 teenagers in the seventh, ninth, and eleventh grades. The association was much stronger with having friends who were heavy drinkers and among those who identified with those portrayed in commercials or said they viewed commercials to learn about new products and modes of behavior. Atkin, Hocking, and Block (1984) found, among 665 young persons aged 12 to 17 years, that exposure to print and television alcohol advertising was associated positively if modestly with consumption of beer but not wine, even after a myriad of variables were controlled including, in addition to demographics, church attendance, social influences (such as parent and peer drinking), and exposure to other media (such as PSAs about alcohol or drinking in television entertainment). Those high in exposure were also more likely to have tried advertised brands.

Atkin, Neuendorf, and McDermott (1983) pooled the data from Atkin, Hocking, and Block (1984) with data from about the same number of young adults to examine abuse. They found a very small positive association between total media alcohol advertising exposure and excessive drinking when controlling for other variables, and a similar small positive association between such exposure and drinking while driving or otherwise in an automobile. Strickland (1983) reported a small, direct positive association between exposure to television alcohol advertising and only one of five misuse measures (such as drinking alone or rapidly)—belligerence. However, overall consumption was very modestly associated with the misuse measures, which means that advertising could make a minute indirect contribution to misuse if it encouraged consumption.

Chirco (1990) analyzed data from about 2,000 teenagers collected by the federally financed Monitoring the Future study. She found heavy drinking associated with having friends who drink and whose attitudes are favorable toward drinking, and with opportunities to drink defined as unsupervised time away from home. No association was found with television exposure, except among a subset of young females who consumed excessive quantities of wine. The pattern for marijuana use was similar. Friends, attitudes, and opportunity produced positive correlations; television use did not. This parallelism departs from what one would expect if commercials played a role in alcohol consumption, because alcohol is an advertised legal substance, and marijuana is not.

The case for some influence of television on alcohol consumption is weaker, in our view, than that for drug commercials on over-the-counter drug use (because of the consistent, positive correlations in sizable samples in the latter case), but it is stronger than that for the influence of drug commercials on illegal drug use (because of a lack of correlation in the most credible sample). This is somewhat surprising given the many factors (physiological, psychological, and social) not present for proprietary drugs that would favor experimenting with or consuming alcohol.

We agree with Atkin (1988a, 1988b) that, on the whole, there is some evidence of a small contribution by advertising. However, we conclude that the contribution of television commercials or programming appears to be minor if present at all. If television does have any influence beyond brand choices, it is probably, as Atkin argues, at the period when young persons decide whether or not to begin drinking between the ages of 10 and 14. This is the period when the male models, the promised camaraderie, and the entry into the adult world would be most attractive.

d. *Food Choices*   About one-third of the estimated $23 billion spent by children 7 to 11 years old annually in the late 1990s went for food and beverages (McNeal, 1999). This is in addition to parental purchases influenced by children. Adler and colleagues (1980), based on the substantial empirical evidence presented in the review by Meringoff (1980), reach a firm conclusion:

> Empirical evidence attests to the general effectiveness of food advertising to children. Children have been found to learn the information provided in food commercials, believe the product claims made about advertised foods, draw inferences about product benefits, and influence the purchase of the foods advertised to them. In the short-term, exposure to specific food commercials has produced significant increases in children's expressed preferences for the products promoted. (p. 217)

For example, Goldberg, Gorn, and Gibson (1978) manipulated the exposure of 80 first-grade children to commercials for sugared foods or PSAs for highly nutritional snacks, with both embedded in a television program. Those who saw the commercials chose more sugared foods; those who saw the PSAs chose more nutritional snacks. Goldberg and Gorn (1978) found that exposure of 8- to 10-year-old boys to a commercial for an unfamiliar brand of ice cream led to learning of the flavors offered and a preference for this brand, with the preference increasing with exposure to three different commercials instead of a single commercial on its behalf.

In a convincing demonstration, Gorn and Goldberg (1982) found among 288 children aged from five to eight years, that the regular viewing of commercials made a decided difference in their choice of snacks immediately afterward. The children viewed Saturday morning programs with fruit and fruit juice commercials, candy and Kool-Aid commercials, pronutritional PSAs, or no commercials for 14 days. Those who saw orange juice commercials chose that juice far more often than did those who saw Kool-Aid commercials, and the candy commercials resulted in more candy than fruit being chosen. This experiment is particularly credible because of the natural circumstances of viewing regular programming in groups, the modest repetition of commercials that mirrors television scheduling, the free choice of snacks, and the fact that the groups did not differ in a postexperimental measurement of what they said they thought the experimenters wanted them to do.

Bolton (1983) provides evidence on long-term effects. Among about 260 children between the ages of 2 and 11, she found only small effects attributable to exposure to television food advertising compared to other factors, such as parents, but such exposure did increase, to a small degree, snacking and caloric intake, and overall slightly decreased quality of nutrition.

Nutritional behavior, however, cannot be said to be easily influenced to a substantial degree by video presentations when the sought-for behavior is counter to what young viewers think is tasty. Peterson, Jeffrey, Bridgwater, and Dawson (1984) examined recall, information, preference, and behavioral choice by about 100 nursery school children after exposure daily for 10 class days to a 20-minute video promoting consumption of nutritional foods both by program content and PSAs. They found only recall and information affected. By implication, this challenges the effectiveness of brief disclaimers recommending product use as "part of a balanced breakfast." Galst (1980) found, among three- to six-year-olds, that pronutritional commercials did not affect food choices unless followed by supportive recommendations by a live adult, while invariably the majority of choices were of low-nutritional sugared snacks. Stoneman and Brody (1981a) found among 120 children in the fourth grade that preferences for a salty snack could be increased by a commercial on its behalf, and then further increased or decreased depending on whether a live peer pointed to a slide screen illustration of the snack or a nonsalty food item. On the whole, these findings lead to little optimism over altering the generic choices of children by television-based interventions, for pronutritional messages always will be overwhelmed in number by commercials for sugared and salted foods that children find highly palatable.

Amount of television viewing by young persons has been recorded as positively associated with obesity, negative mood states, loneliness, conflict with others, and diminished physical, mental, and social well-being (Anderson et al., 1996, 1998; Canary & Spitzberg, 1993; Potts & Sanchez, 1994; Sidney et al., 1998; Tucker, 1986, 1987). We do not burden these correlations with the interpretation that television is a cause of these states. Instead, we believe they are evidence on behalf of escape from daily stress as a principal motive for television viewing (Comstock & Scharrer, 1999). However, they do suggest strongly that these young people would be particularly vulnerable to appeals for heavily sugared or highly salted unnutritious snacks and foods and highly sugared beverages, which also offer a form of easy gratification and whose flavors would offer another path of escape. We thus see a cost of the advertising of such products on television measured by the lessening of the well-being of some young persons.

e. *Amount and Frequency of Exposure*   The data present contrasting impressions for (a) concentrated campaigns and (b) the typical product commercial in regard to amount and frequency of exposure. In the former, the repetitive exposure that occurs during intensive campaigns appears to be very effective in persuading young persons about the desirability of products. In the latter case, repetition is a modest factor although it is clear that a variety of commercials on behalf of a product is more effective than a single commercial even when that commercial is viewed several times.

The Christmas toy campaigns that begin on television five or six weeks before the holiday include a number of factors that precipitate the making of choices within the parameters of the campaigns. The product class is extraordinarily salient, the advertising is concentrated and repetitive, and there is a date for decisions after which both commercials and desires become comparatively irrelevant. These circumstances constitute conditions in which greater amount and frequency of exposure translate into more powerful persuasion. Rossiter and Robertson's (1974) examination of the toy and game preferences of about 290 first-, third-, and fifth-grade children during the pre-Christmas advertising season provides convincing evidence. In early November, they found that children with superior affective and cognitive defenses—they disliked (an affective defense) and distrusted (a cognitive defense) advertising more—selected fewer advertised toys. By mid-December, defenses ceased to predict choice and those with initially strong defenses chose more advertised toys and games. The "big build-up" had worked.

In regard to the typical commercial that is encountered regularly throughout the year, the role of amount and frequency of exposure is much diminished (Adler et al., 1980; Comstock & Scharrer, 1999; Rossiter, 1980a):

• Repeated exposure to a commercial by young persons ordinarily does not increase persuasiveness, and once a commercial is understood repeat exposure only reestablishes the beliefs and attitudes about product attributes and the commercial elicited by prior exposure.

- However, sometimes more than an initial exposure is required for the message of a commercial to be understood. This applies to both adults and young persons but is particularly so for children with their more limited cognitive processing skills.
- Multiple exposure to different commercials on behalf of a product, as we have seen in the case of ice cream (Goldberg & Gorn, 1978), will increase persuasiveness.

Repetition is nevertheless a formidable strategy. This is not because persuasiveness of a specific commercial is progressively increased by repetition but bacause the principal mission of television commercials is to establish and maintain the salience of brands among consumer options (Comstock & Scharrer, 1999). Repetition achieves this goal. This mission of salience conservation explains the fierce opposition of prominent national advertisers and marketers to restrictions on television advertising directed at children. They are afraid of losing market share, for there is no other medium by which they could reach the young as effectively and television in effect provides for the financially well-endowed a means of purchasing market share and thwarting less well- endowed or regional brands.

3. Exchanges between Parent and Child   We cover three topics: purchase requests, parental yielding, and conflicts between parent and child. These are topics for which empirical data provide only useful impressions. There are two reasons. First, no measure—interviews and questionnaires directed at children or parents, in-store observation—can produce more than a rough estimate. Second, there is no agreed upon criterion that signals that some degree of concern is merited.

a. *Purchase Requests*   Atkin (1975c) divided his sample of about 740 ranging in age from preschool to fifth grade into light and heavy viewers. Among about 440 light viewers "a lot" was chosen to describe the frequency of their requests by 16 percent for toys and 24 percent for cereals, and 64 percent and 50 percent chose "sometimes" over "never." This totals between 75 and 80 percent at least occasionally making requests. Among about 300 identified as heavy viewers, "a lot" was chosen by 40 percent for both toys and cereals. Isler, Popper, and Ward (1987) found from diaries completed over four weeks by about 260 mothers of children between the ages of three and eleven that about one-sixth of all purchase requests were attributed to television advertising. Requests decreased by age, with the average for those three to four about 25, and for those nine to eleven about 10; attribution of the request to television similarly declined, with figures of about 26 and 9.

Rossiter and Robertson (1974) in their Christmas advertising study found television the most frequent source of toy choices among their several hundred first through fifth graders. Data such as these lead to the conclusion that young persons typically ask with some regularity for products advertised on television.

Source of request varies by product (Isler, Popper & Ward, 1987). Television is preeminent for products heavily promoted in the medium. Friends, siblings, and experiences in stores are more important for less promoted items, with friends and siblings particularly important where norms matter, such as clothing.

b. Yielding   The evidence on parental yielding is similarly imprecise. If mothers are asked how often they yield, we have only a crude parental estimate of the outcome of an interaction that may range in frequency for a particular family from hardly ever to several times daily (Ward & Wackman, 1972). If we choose to observe parents and children in the supermarket or elsewhere, we have only a sampling of time and space that surely underestimates the number of requests and possibly the frequency of yielding (Atkin, 1975b; Galst & White, 1976; Wells & LoSciuto, 1966). Even if the metric were accurate, yielding would be an imperfect measure of the influence of children on parental purchases because it excludes what Wells (1965) long ago called "passive dictation"—the establishment by the child of a purchase agenda to which parents conform without further requests from the child.

Yielding is a function of product category (Robertson, 1980b). Yielding is greatest for products that will be consumed by children and where matching their tastes is a prerequisite for satisfaction. Thus, cereals, snack foods, and games and toys typically rank high in the data. For example, one survey (Ward & Wackman, 1972) found that 87 percent of mothers said they yielded to cereal requests, and only 7 percent said they yielded to requests for pet food.

Atkin (1978) ingeniously contrived to record the conversations of parents and children by stationing observers in the cereal aisle of a supermarket (see Figure 5.1). Although these data of course cannot be said to represent any particular population, there is no reason not to take them as a typical and informative slice of market life. Most proposed purchases were initiated by children, and many more were phrased as a demand than a request. Parents yielded to both demands and requests most of the time. Parents were less successful. When they specified a particular purchase ("directs selection"), a majority of the time the child rejected the choice. At least for products they consume such as cereals, children are opinionated and forceful customers.

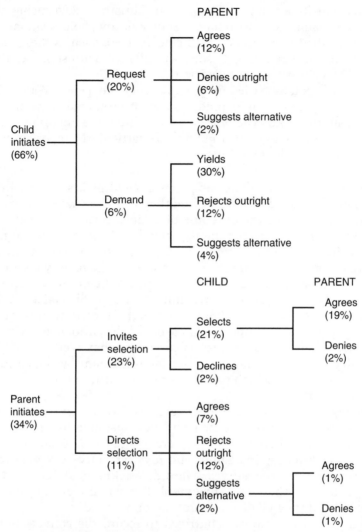

Fig. 5.1   Parent-child supermarket aisle interaction over breakfast cereal. Adapted from Atkin, C.K. (1978). Observations of parent-child interaction in supermarket decisionmaking. *Journal of Marketing, 42*, 41–45.

c. *Conflict*   The degree of conflict and disappointment that occurs when requests are denied also is difficult to gauge precisely, but the evidence is clear enough that it occurs more than rarely and probably somewhat more than warrants the term occasionally. Shiekh and Molesti (1977) and Goldberg and Gorn (1979) make a *prima facie* case for a fair amount of conflict. The former presented 72 boys and 72 girls in the first, third, and fifth grades with a story about a child who watched a television program, saw a toy commercial, and asked that the toy be purchased. They asked the children what the child would do if the parents refused. About a third said the child would feel bad, about a fourth said the child would accept the decision, about a fourth said the child would become aggressive, and about one out of six said the child would persist. The latter manipulated exposure to a toy commercial among about 160 four- and five-year-olds. Those who saw the commercial were more likely to believe that a child for whom the toy was not purchased by the father would not want to play with the father and would be unhappy.

Two studies by Atkin provide some figures. In one (Atkin, 1975b), one-fifth of a sample of children said they became angry "a lot" when a toy request was denied, and one-sixth said they argued "a lot" in the same circumstance. The comparable figures for "sometimes" were two-fifths and one-third, which sum to half or more becoming angry or arguing over toy denials. Similar but slightly lower figures were recorded for cereal requests. In the other (Atkins, 1975c), the observations of parents and children in supermarkets led to about two-thirds of denials recorded as evoking anger from the child and one half as inducing disappointment. Isler and colleagues (1987), relying on diary data from mothers, offer lower but not minute figures—a refusal was said to be met by disappointment about one-fourth of the time, by brief arguing in an additional one-sixth, and by extensive arguing in about one out of 20 instances.

III. THE BUYING MACHINE

Children and teenagers are exposed to an enormous quantity of television advertising. The average child 2 to 11 in age sees almost 40,000 commercials a year. About 12,500 are for products in which a child might take an interest. For children's programming, cereals and candies top the list, followed by toys and fast foods. In general audience programming, these are joined by soft drinks, shoes, and clothing. Teenagers watch less television but are likely to find more product commercials of interest—about 16,000 of the approximately 27,000 they will see. However, these measures understate the role of children and teenagers in marketing on three grounds—other media, their latent role as future customers, and what has become ingloriously called the "nag factor."

A. *The Influence of Other Media*

Although very young children are reached primarily by advertisers through television, soon other vehicles begin to have a role (Acuff, 1997; McNeal, 1999; Siegel, Coffey & Livingston, 2004). Billboards and in-store displays reach even the very young. Soon, window displays in

malls and on city streets become attractive. Older children and especially tweens will be reached by print media and radio. Special events,
clubs, and promotions, often with gifts and souvenirs, will be used by
marketers. Computers, the Internet, and personal communication
devices increasingly can be turned toward marketing goals—the tie-in
between a product, a television character, and a web site is a prominent
example of a current application.

B. The Latent Role of Children as Consumers

James U. McNeal, whose 1987 book *Children as Consumers: Insights
and Implications* is credited with establishing young people as a
lucrative but specialized market, argues in his recent *The Kids Market: Myths and Realities* (1999) that the young market has three
dimensions:

Primary Market—young people as the customer from whom the purchase is sought. Among those younger, this is the candy, cereals, toys,
fast food, soft drinks, shoes and clothing of television advertising.
Among those older, the catalogue expands to include sports equipment, media, music, and entertainment. Based on McNeal's data
(1999), we estimate (extrapolating to the present) spending by this
primary market at about $40 billion annually.

Influence Market—the young person is not the customer but an
influence on spending by parents, and often for products that represent
household or family consumption as well as for products that the
young person will consume. Parents take into account the tastes and
preferences of young persons in purchasing beverages, cereals, snacks,
and other edibles without consulting the young consumer. The same
influence operates in regard to toys, shoes, apparel. This influence market, however, extends the role of the young person well beyond the
products he or she will directly consume. Parents often give some
weight to the preferences of children in regard to such household items
as furniture and automobiles and such family ventures as vacations,
television sets, and weekend recreation. Based again on McNeal's data,
we estimate expenditures (again extrapolating) at about $400 billion
annually—10 times greater than the primary market.

Future Market—the young person is courted for patronage at a later
stage of life. This has two dimensions. On the one hand, favorable
experiences when young may lead a parent to introduce children to
the same brand or store. In particular, this would affect sporting
goods, clothing and shoes, and supermarkets. In addition, young people may be directly persuaded to favor specific stores and certain
brands in the future. This has a wide array of applications, including

clothing, shoe, and sporting goods outlets and a vast array of products, including cosmetics and toiletries, proprietary drugs, computers, jewelry and watches, automobiles and auto accessories (such as batteries), airlines and hotels, and clothing, shoes, and sporting goods. There are only two sources of new customers for a company—the competition and newcomers entering a market as they mature. From the perspective of marketers, this is an area of great potential.

The expenditures on advertising to the young are comparatively modest. McNeal (1999) offered an estimate of about 3 percent of television advertising and about 1 percent of advertising in general for children 4 to 12. Marketers nevertheless believe that the young are a segment that has great potential and will see considerable growth. The reason is not the primary market they constitute, but the influence market and the future market. The first of these two is already 10 times greater than the primary market, and its potential lies in the possibility of expanding the types of products over which young people have influence. In the past, influence increased with the likelihood that the young person in the household would consume the product (Comstock & Scharrer, 1999; McNeal, 1999; Siegel, Coffey & Livingston, 2004). However, the same data shows that influence is often far from nil for products for which the young person will not be the principal consumer. Examples include vacations, hotels, and furnishings. Thus, there is the potential for increasing the range of purchases influenced by the young. The second, the future market, is largely untapped but offers many opportunities—travel, furnishings, alcoholic beverages, department stores, mass retailers, supermarkets.

C. The Nag Factor

Almost certainly, many advertisers long have expected (and hoped) that young viewers would respond to the commercials on Saturday morning television by asking their parents to purchase the products. However, until recently this phenomenon at least officially was looked upon by those in advertising as an externality—an inevitable happenstance of directing commercials at children rather than the intended outcome. The target, ostensibly, was the parent. On the one hand, this was a gesture to ethical behavior by denying an attempt to manipulate children at the expense (literally as well as figuratively) of parents. On the other, marketers hoped to persuade a parent (usually the mother, who would more often buy things for children) of the desirability of the product, with the expectation that parental persuasiveness would have some permanence.

Advertising industry codes discouraged appeals that would incite children to pressure parents for products (Comstock, 1991). This began to change in the late 1990s with the appearance of data from commercial research firms that established requests—often called nagging when repeated—as a crucial element in eventual purchase (McNeal, 1999; Schor, 2004; Siegel, Coffey & Livingston, 2004). Child requests repeatedly increased the likelihood of purchase for a wide range of products. About a third of parents indicated they would not have made a purchase in the absence of nagging for quick-service restaurants, movie-going, apparel, videos, CD-Roms, and food; higher figures were registered for cereals, snacks, and toys. This initiated a major change in retailing, and a greater focus on children as the principal targets of marketers.

The consequence is that marketing is now often unambiguously directed at children, and parents are seen as secondary. Marketers seek the acquiescence of parents, but often are no longer shy about attempting to persuade children to ask their parents to purchase advertised items.

The nag factor, in our view, is a predicable extension of the new importance as a market that children and teenagers took on at the end of the last millennium. A volatile market (in terms of tastes and the popularity of particular products) expanding in importance presents a quite different landscape from a stable market with widely agreed upon ways of operating. There is enormously greater promise, and the consequent temptation to violate norms, experiment, and cross boundaries.

McNeal (1999) assigns the late 1980s the role of turning point. The size of the population of young people had increased only slightly, but they suddenly seemed much more important as consumers, and particularly as an influence market. They were, in effect, newly enriched and empowered by several converging long-term trends. As a result, young people became newly recognized as a population of customers:

- A reduction in the number of children per family, which meant that more could be spent on each (McNeal cites a decline from about 3.5 in 1960 to about 2.0 in 2000)
- Delayed child-rearing, which meant that parents were better established in their careers and had more to spend on their children
- Fractured families, which meant multiple parents and grandparents who would bestow gifts and money, and otherwise would cater to the desires of the young
- The increase in single-parent households, where children become consumers on their own earlier and for a wider range of products

The corollary to an expanded market, of course, is the need for greater information about the motives, interests, and preferences of its members. In the case of young persons, this leads to a sharp multitiered segmentation of the market because of the many changes young people go through, mentally, socially, and physically, as they mature. The most useful and widely employed framework for advertisers and marketers is cognitive development (Acuff, 1997; Siegel, Coffey & Livingston, 2004) because it governs responses to advertising and marketing campaigns as well as the social relations of young people, and is the filter that gives practical meaning and marketing significance to the physical changes. It is not simply that young persons will need bigger shoes and larger clothes as they grow older; it is that they will come to choose these items for different reasons and in response to different factors, and these shifts in motive and influence will affect all their product consumption.

IV. CONSIDERATION OF COGNITIVE DEVELOPMENT IN ADVERTISING

The role of cognitive stage is central to any understanding of the responses of children and teenagers to advertising and marketing, and from all perspectives. For those concerned with ethics and regulation, whether self-imposed or governmental, cognitive stages establish the boundary between deceptive exploitation and the full comprehension by young children of the nature of advertising. Those interested in marketing to children and teenagers find mercantile uses for the same data. On the one hand, they segment the young population into three tiers in order to better characterize those to whom they wish to advertise and market. On the other, they divide these tiers into more narrowly defined strata to devise products and campaigns that will appeal to the changing interests, limitations, and aspirations of the young as they mature. Meanwhile, those with academic and scholarly motives—psychologists, child development specialists, and communication researchers—find cognitive stages an indispensable means to describe what transpires between the age of innocence and ignorance (the sensorimotor), and the strategic use by individuals of brands and logos (which will not be in full display until the formal operational).

A. The Boundary of Comprehension

The very young child has only a scant concept of advertising as a particular kind of communication with goals that are specific and proprietary to its sponsor. The television commercial targeted to the very young is simply a visual and aural presentation of a product that stands apart from the accompanying program by being funny or brief (Ward & Wackman, 1973). By the preschool age of four, a majority recognize commercials as distinct from programs, but only a small minority recognize that a commercial is intended to prompt a purchase (Levin, Petros & Petrella, 1982; Macklin, 1987). They can, however, match characters in commercials with the products they sell (Zuckerman & Gianinno, 1981), testifying to the efficacy of commercials in drawing the attention of children to specific products. At this age, it is the rare child who can define a commercial—as self-interested, as intended to lead to a purchase, as motivated by the desire of the advertiser to receive money in exchange for a product.

As would be expected, much has been made by those in advertising and marketing of the ability of quite young children to distinguish between commercials and the programs they accompany and to recognize commercials and their characters as associated with products. Their argument is that such perception betrays a fundamental understanding of commercials that eludes verbalization because the necessary concepts and vocabulary are not yet at the command of the child. This is analogous to arguing that if a person can tell the difference between red, black, and green they subconsciously recognize the symbolic and psychological uses to which they might be put by designers or the role they might play in different cultures. It is not enough that difference is recognized. What is required is that the basis and not merely the appearance of the difference be understood.

The research of Blosser and Roberts (1985) and Gentner (1975) neatly establish the boundary of comprehension at about age eight. The former, as will be recalled, confirmed that children below the age of five comprehend the message of a commercial in regard to promoting a product but they usually cannot yet apply the label "commercial." In contrast, a majority of those older than five will correctly use the label. However, it was not until after the age of eight that a majority could correctly define the self-interested nature of a commercial. Gentner asked children of varying ages to role play various exchanges, such as give, buy, and sell using *Sesame Street* characters. Sell lagged behind buy in comprehension, and it was not until between the ages of seven-and-a-half and eight-and-a-half that sell was understood by a majority. In sharp contrast, give was understood by almost everyone between the ages of three-and-a-half and four-and-a-half.

The message is unambiguously clear. Below the age of eight a majority of children do not fully understand what a commercial is as measured either by their ability to articulate the features of a commercial or by their ability to act in accord with motives of those who sponsor commercials. In this context, their ability to recognize commercials at a younger age by distinguishing them from programs or by identifying them as making appeals on behalf of products become measures of advertising effectiveness rather than evidence of a fundamental if inarticulatable comprehension of the nature of advertising.

We argue that by the standards that are applied to adults in regard to print media in the United States, children under the age of eight are exploited by advertising aimed at them. Print material that might be mistaken for editorial content (an advertisement in the form of a news story, a special section on a destination in a travel magazine, an announcement promoting the advisability of a prescription drug) typically are accompanied by disclaimers, such as "Paid Announcement," "Special Advertising Section," or "Paid Advertising." The rationale is that readers would be disadvantaged in assessing the claims of these messages were they to think they had been advanced by the editorial staff rather than by advertisers with a vested interest. It is analogous to the principle recognized—although not very effectively implemented—by the FCC's ban on host selling in a commercial accompanying a program in which the character appears (more effective would be a ban on appearances in commercials by characters from television programs at any time). Most of the advertising to which young children are exposed, of course, is television commercials, where the exploitation and deception inherent in their lack of understanding of the self-interested nature of advertising is exacerbated by the fluid flow of images and language that elude careful and accurate processing by children—and, for that matter, by adults.

B. The Child and Teenage Marketplace

The changes in cognitive skills, along with the shifts in motives, interests, and preferences that accompany them, have led marketers to construe the child and teenage marketplace as having three broad tiers (McNeal, 1999; Siegel, Coffey & Livingston, 2004):

- Children: Ages 4 to 7
- Tweens: Ages 8 to 12
- Teenagers: Ages 13 to 18

However, marketers have also concluded that these seemingly plausible, disparate groupings are insufficiently precise. McNeal (1999) argues that much earlier than the age of four children express an interest in products, and this is confirmed by his data on shopping experiences. The median age for the first in-store request for a product was 24 months, with the earliest request occurring at seven months. Even the first physical selection—that is, grasping hold—of a product in-store occurred at a median age of 42 months, with the earliest recorded at 24 months. The first tier, then, should begin at age two. McNeal and Siegel, Coffey, and Livingstone (2004) both argue that these groupings mask significant changes in motives, interests, and preferences. There are differences between those younger and older within each of the three tiers. Three tiers, then, are not adequately descriptive.

The strata that result from the ensuing segmentation are used by marketers to develop products that will appeal to young persons. Narrow segments are required because of the many striking changes that occur within a comparatively few years as young people mature from infancy to adulthood. These products and their designers attempt to maximize marketing success by taking into account three factors that govern the motives, interests, and preferences of young persons:

- *Cognitive stage*, which establishes the framework of skills for attending to and processing the appearance and character of products, advertising claims, and marketing strategies employed on their behalf.
- *Norms*, which may mitigate or reinforce gender differences, and which derive from cultural, regional, and social class distinctions and specify what is appropriate.
- *Desertion of childhood*, in which young persons as they grow older insistently distance themselves from those younger by rejecting toys, apparel, food and beverages, and entertainment associated with them.

We believe six strata realistically and effectively satisfy the interests of marketers. Each is large and broad enough to serve as a target group in the design and advertising of products, and they differ sufficiently, with the borders demarcating young persons who are distinct in important ways, to justify product differentiation. We base our descriptions on cognitive theory and its application to marketing to young persons, and include product categories and occasionally specific products that provide examples of a fit between strata and products (Acuff, 1997; McNeal, 1999; Piaget & Inhelder, 1969; Roberts & Foehr, 2004; Schor, 2005; Siegel, Coffey & Livingston, 2004). We emphasize motives and dispositions because they provide an unchanging framework against which future and imagined products as well as the successes (and if recalled, the failures) of the past can be measured. We give no attention to the underlying neurological changes (although we recommend Acuff (1997) for a clear and concise treatment) because we are solely interested in the implications of cognitive stages for the design and marketing of products.

Our strata:

Age   Motives, Interests, and Preferences

2–3   Very young children. Seek security, affection, recognition, pleasure. Toys should be without a trace of threat (no big teeth). Dolls, fuzzy animals as playthings. Play is a central activity, consuming between three to four hours a day. Play is typically solitary and ego-centered, even when another child is present. TV viewing begins.

First product chosen in-store—usually a cereal in a colorful box at the supermarket. Food, snacks and beverages are product choices and the supermarket is the usual venue.

4–7   Young children. Prelogical, bipolar thinking. Perception dominates. Focus on obvious physical characteristics and appearances. Fixate on product features. Enjoy feelings of nurturing and authority. Two historic marketing successes: Cabbage Patch Kids and Power Rangers. Kids trafficked on small size, distinctive appearance, personalized names, and the adoption process. The child became a caregiver. Rangers more straightforwardly represented power and achievement. Their transformation into superheroes with a specialized vehicle had a fascination that would vanish when thought processes became more logical and abstract. At this age, boys often imitate monsters and villains to prove their mettle. Toys become predominant among product choices—replacing food, snacks, and beverages as ego-satisfaction emerges as the goal of consumption and store experience widens to include mass retailers and malls. Barbie popular among girls. Play remains important—early, it clearly overrides TV viewing and by the end of the period still leads TV by a small margin in time use. Early in this period, most play is nonsocial; when another child is present, play is usually parallel rather than interactive.

8–10   Early preteens. Seek acceptance and success. Abstract thought possible. New skills at classification and seriation. As a result, there is pleasure in collecting toys, athletic cards, and other objects rather than accumulating them as was the case earlier. Respond to abstract symbols, and brands take on meaning and significance. For the first time, brands have social implications (what kind of person would use this product?) as well as a key to status (what do they think of me?). There is more interaction in play, and friendships become newly important. However, play itself dwindles to between an hour and an hour-and-a-half a day. Sports very popular with both boys and girls. Athletic equipment (balls, Frisbees) popular products. Enjoy competition, complexity, and challenge. Read preteen magazines—*Nickelodeon*, *National Geographic for Kids*, *Disney Adventures* (more girls than boys), *Sports Illustrated for Kids* (many more boys than girls). Make most of own purchases—clothes, shoes, snacks, soft drinks, music and entertainment. Boys in particular continue to play video games. Barbie retains interest for some as a collectible, and particularly because of the many costumes and accessories available. This begins a period of great physical change—about a 20 percent increase in height and about a 50 percent increase in weight between the ages of 8 and 12. Conformity is very important, especially with clothes, shoes, and appearance.

11–12   Transitional preteens. Seek popularity, proof of worth and talent, superiority, and amusement. Play falls to about a half hour a day. Clothes, shoes, appearance very important. Conformity with peers remains a priority. A "billboard"—a term used by one observer (Acuff, 1997) to describe a public display of apparel or other product better fitted to someone younger—is avoided. Music becomes important, especially among girls.

13–15   Early teenagers. Abstract, symbolic reasoning possible. Turn to adult media. Face independence. Largely consume adult products—cosmetics, toiletries, apparel. Begin reading newspapers. Childhood essentially over.

16–18   Late teens. Adult concerns—job, career, romantic involvement, college. Gender differences remain but are much more muted than among those younger. Sports remain a major interest of both males and females. Products such as autos and services such as banks become of interest. Puberty is complete.

There are several rather dramatic changes. As consumers, children shift from an indifference to brands to their strategic use as codes for labeling (and by implication, reaching an understanding of) others and for the social advancement of the self. What has transpired in this particular case is a transformation in the means of satisfying the ego. In childhood, the ego was served through possession of an object. In the late teenage years, ego-satisfaction derives from the knowledgeable manipulation of symbols to achieve personal ends. From the point of view of the marketer and advertiser, the role of advertising has remained the same. From the perspective of the consumer, it has changed significantly—from a display of something to be desired to a means of relating to the world at large. This change in mental landscape is accompanied by the inevitable increase in independent consumer behavior. The striking datum is how early this independence begins. A third factor is that the population in question differs so much from one stratum to another. The autos and banks that hold some interest for the 16- to 18-year-olds are of scant concern to either of the tween strata, and the physical stature of the early tween stratum, despite the large role of independent purchasing in their consumer behavior, renders some shopping venues somewhat alien and uncomfortable on physical grounds, because the merchandise displays are sized for adults, and on social grounds because the milieu created by music, colors, and interior design is decidedly parental.

C. The Scholarly View of the Influence of Advertising

For a further examination of the rise to prominence of symbolic manipulation in the responses of young persons to advertising, we turn to the comprehensive and insightful review by John (1999). She artfully charts the cognitive changes that take place, using a Piagetian schema (see Table 5.2). There are three broad stages:

- In the first stage, when perception dominates responses for those 3 to 7, possession but not brands is important, commercials are recognized as different from programs but their persuasive intent is largely unrecognized, and the major strategy for acquisition is the direct request.
- In the second stage, between the ages of 8 and 11, persuasive intent becomes understood, brands become important in choosing products, and there is a much wider range of acquisition strategies, including persuasion and bargaining.
- In the third stage, between the ages of 12 and 16, there is skepticism of bias or deception, products and brands are evaluated as symbols as well as for concrete qualities, and the value placed on products derives from scarcity and social significance.

The shift is from the product as a desired object to the product as representative of social meaning and a means to a desired end. This is attributable primarily to the increase in abstract and logical thought that occurs with cognitive development. The boundary again is age eight, and for the obvious reason that the same new-found ability to think abstractly serves not only the recognition of the persuasive intent of commercials but also the symbolic uses of products and brands. Among those aged three to seven, products have little social meaning. Among those 8 to 11, products become recognized as representative of more than their concrete properties. This symbolic use of advertising and brands then reaches its fullest expression among those 12 to 16 who have reached maturity in cognitive development. They become useful to the young person in cataloguing and understanding others, and in the presentation to others of the esteemed and desired self.

Table 5.2
Responses to Advertising by Cognitive Stage

Topic	SUMMARY OF FINDINGS BY CONSUMER SOCIALIZATION STAGE		
	Perceptual stage, 3–7 years	Analytical stage, 7–11 years	Reflective stage, 11–16 years
Advertising knowledge	• Can distinguish ads from programs based on perceptual features • Believe ads are truthful, funny, and interesting • Positive attitudes toward ads	• Can distinguish ads from programs based on persuasive intent • Believe ads lie and contain bias and deception—but do not use these "cognitive defenses" • Negative attitudes toward ads	• Understand persuasive intent of ads as well as specific ad tactics and appeals • Believe ads lie and know how to spot specific instances of bias or deception in ads • Skeptical attitudes toward ads
Transaction knowledge: Product and brand knowledge	• Can recognize brand names and beginning to associate them with product categories • Perceptual cues used to identify product categories • Beginning to understand symbolic aspects of consumption based on perceptual features • Egocentric view of retail stores as a source of desired items	• Increasing brand awareness, especially for child-relevant product categories • Underlying or functional cues used to define product categories • Increased understanding of symbolic aspects of consumption • Understand retail stores are owned to sell goods and make a profit	• Substantial brand awareness for adult-oriented as well as child-relevant product categories • Underlying or functional cues used to define product categories • Sophisticated understanding of consumption symbolism for product categories and brand names • Understanding and enthusiasm for retail stores

Shopping knowledge and skills	• Understand sequence of events in the basic shopping script • Value of products and prices based on perceptual features	• Shopping scripts more complex, abstract, and with contingencies • Prices based on theories of value	• Complex and contingent shopping scripts • Prices based on abstract reasoning, such as input variations and buyer preferences
Decision-making skills and abilities: Information search	• Limited awareness of information sources • Focus on perceptual attributes • Emerging ability to adapt to cost-benefit trade-offs	• Increased awareness of personal and mass media sources • Gather information on functional as well as perceptual attributes • Able to adapt to cost-benefit trade-offs	• Contingent use of different information sources depending on product or situation • Gather information on functional, perceptual, and social aspects • Able to adapt to cost-benefit trade-offs
Product evaluation	• Use of perceptually salient attribute information • Use of single attributes	• Focus on important attribute information—functional and perceptual attributes • Use two or more attributes	• Focus on important attribute information—functional, perceptual, and social aspects • Use multiple attributes
Decision strategies	• Limited repertoire of strategies • Emerging ability to adapt strategies to tasks—usually need cues to adapt	• Increased repertoire of strategies, especially noncompensatory ones • Capable of adapting strategies to tasks	• Full repertoire of strategies • Capable of adapting strategies to tasks in adult-like manner

(Continued)

Table 5.2
(Continued)

Topic	SUMMARY OF FINDINGS BY CONSUMER SOCIALIZATION STAGE		
	Perceptual stage, 3–7 years	Analytical stage, 7–11 years	Reflective stage, 11–16 years
Purchase influence and negotiation strategies	• Use direct requests and emotional appeals • Limited ability to adapt strategy to person or situation	• Expanded repertoire of strategies, with bargaining and persuasion emerging • Developing abilities to adapt strategy to persons and situations	• Full repertoire of strategies, with bargaining and persuasion as favorites • Capable of adapting strategies based on perceived effectiveness for persons or situations
Consumption motives and values: Materialism	• Value of possessions based on surface features, such as "having more" of something	• Emerging understanding of value based on social meaning and significance	• Fully developed understanding of value based on social meaning, significance, and scarcity

Adapted from John, D.R. (1999). Consumer socialization of children: A retrospective look at twenty-five years of research. *Journal of Consumer Research, 26,* 183–213.

TELEVISION VIOLENCE, AGGRESSION, AND OTHER BEHAVIORAL EFFECTS

VI

Certainly the most persistent and one of the most controversial of all qustions regarding screen media and young viewers has concerned aggressive and antisocial behavior and their link, if any, with violent entertainment. Our analysis focuses on such behavioral effects but is more wide-ranging.

Among the issues and topics we address are:

- The pioneering laboratory-type experiments that have served as a paradigm for so much subsequent research
- The meta-analyses that so robustly record quantitatively a positive association between violence viewing and aggression and antisocial behavior
- The three most prominent theories that explain the positive association and their integration in what its originators term the General Aggression Model (GAM)
- Surprising but compelling evidence on the role of cognitive dispositions—attitudes, beliefs, and values—in any link between violence viewing and behavior
- The role of such mediating factors as predispositions, age, gender, and severity of behavior

- The strength of the so-called "reverse" hypothesis
- The corollaries for violent videogames and the emerging empirical evidence in their behalf
- Three other hypothesized effects of violent screen entertainment: fear, desensitization, and cultivation
- Our broad (but confident) interpretation of the evidence in regard to violence viewing as establishing principles of media influence that apply to a broad range of behavior as well as a wide range of ages

I. EVIDENCE OF INCREASED AGGRESSIVENESS CAUSED BY TELEVISION VIOLENCE

The first two experiments demonstrating that exposure to violent portrayals can increase aggressiveness were published in 1963 in the *Journal of Abnormal and Social Psychology* (Bandura, Ross & Ross, 1963a; Berkowitz & Rawlings, 1963). Since then, an enormous and methodologically varied literature has developed. It gives no comfort to those who assert that the findings are evenly divided between positive and negative outcomes that ecologically or methodologically inferior studies are responsible for any association between exposure and behavior, or that there are not circumstances in which portrayals influence behavior. Nevertheless, different issues arise and differing qualifications and emphases are required, depending on method, the seriousness of the aggressive or antisocial behavior, and the age of the population in question.

A. Experiments with Young Children

In one pioneer 1963 experiment, Bandura, Ross, and Ross (1963a) observed the behavior of nursery schoolchildren in a playroom with a Bobo doll and other toys, after they had seen either (a) no behavior involving a Bobo doll; or the Bobo doll attacked verbally and physically by (b) a live model in ordinary attire, (c) the same model in a film sequence, or (d) a female in a film sequence attired in a cat costume such as might appear in children's entertainment. To heighten the likelihood of aggressive behavior, the children were first mildly frustrated by being taken away from a room full of attractive toys. Children in all three treatment groups (b, c, and d) displayed more aggressive behavior than those in the control condition. Nonimitative as well as imitative aggressive behavior was affected, although the effect was most prominent for imitative acts. The children exposed to the Cat Lady exhibited decidedly less aggression than those seeing the live model, but definitely more than those in the control condition.

In their next experiment, Bandura, Ross, and Ross (1963b) manipulated the exposure of children of nursery school age to film sequences involving young adults identified as Rocky and Johnny. In one version, Rocky successfully takes Johnny's toys away and is rewarded with cookies and a beverage. In the other, Johnny successfully defends himself against Rocky, and Rocky, in effect, is punished. The first increased imitation of Rocky's play with the toys, and led to derogatory comments about Johnny as well as criticism of Rocky.

In the initial experiment, behavior is a function of observation; in the second, of perceived efficacy. They are typical of the several dozen subsequent experiments, by Bandura and others, testing propositions derived from social learning theory in regard to the influence of violent television and film portrayals on the aggressiveness of young children. This formulation—expanded and revised as social cognition (Bandura, 1986)—holds that observation of the behavior of others will enhance or introduce the capability to act in a like manner; ways of behaving may be acquired by observation. Observation also will affect the appropriateness and efficacy attributed to a particular way of behaving.

These experiments have a strong claim to external validity for the behavior of young children. That is, the results can be generalized to everyday life. This is because they approximate childhood experience—adults in charge, mild frustration involving toys, a little television, and an opportunity to act aggressively with little or no likelihood of punishment. They also cannot be ascribed to the perceived demands of the setting because subjects at this age do not understand the concept of experimentation and thus could not practice guile or otherwise role play. Furthermore, the circumstances are realistic for play is the context of most childhood aggressiveness.

External validity for those of about the same age also is enhanced by three other sources:

1. Experiments that introduce more naturalistic or ecologically valid elements but continue to produce positive findings. Steuer, Applefield, and Smith (1971) and Josephson (1987) provide perhaps the two most dramatic examples. In the former, a small group of children who viewed violent children's programs during nursery school recesses became more aggressive in everyday playground interaction than a small group comparable in pretreatment playground aggressiveness who viewed nonviolent programs (see Figure 6.1). In the latter, several hundred boys in grades two and three watched either a violent or nonviolent television sequence in groups of six. Those who watched the violent program who also earlier scored higher in aggressiveness subsequently

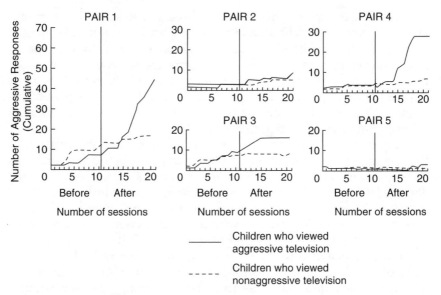

Fig. 6.1 Aggression during play as a function of exposure to violent children's programs. Adapted from Steuer, F.B., Applefield, J.M., & Smith, R. (1971). Televised aggression and interpersonal aggression of preschool children. *Journal of Experimental Child Psychology, 11*, 442–447.

displayed greater aggression while playing floor hockey, and the effect was heightened by exposure to a cue—in this case a "walkie-talkie"— that was displayed in the violent sequence.

2. The three-community British Columbia quasi-experiment by T.M. Williams (1986) and colleagues in which the playground aggressiveness of children increased between the first and fourth grades in the community where television was introduced, but not in the two communities where television was already present (see Figure 6.2).

3. A series of studies by the Singers and their colleagues (D.G. Singer & J.L. Singer, 1980; J.L. Singer & D.G. Singer, 1980, 1981, 1987; Singer et al., 1984; Singer et al., 1988; Desmond et al., 1985) in which the everyday aggression of young children—for the most part, of preschool age—was positively associated with the everyday viewing of violent television entertainment, with no evidence from the many variables measured that this association was wholly attributable to something other than the influence of television on behavior.

These three sets of data have a common strength—the viewing of violent programs in an ordinary way, coupled with the measurement of aggressive behavior within a paradigm that either permits causal inference

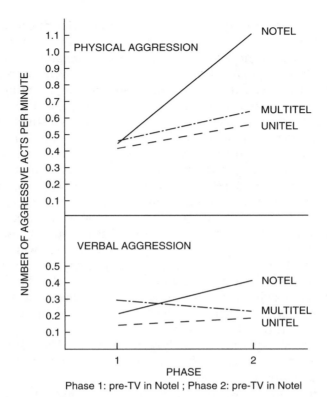

Fig. 6.2 Introduction of television and playground aggression. Adapted from Williams, T.M. (Ed.). (1986). *The impact of television: A natural experiment in three communities.* New York: Academic Press.

(Steuer et al., 1971; Williams, 1986) or would lead to the falsification of such a hypothesized relationship were another measured variable responsible (the series by the Singers and colleagues). This use of data obtained by different means to assess the generalizability of the findings of experiments in laboratory settings presages the model that will be applied to experiments using teenagers and young adults as subjects. In that case, we will draw on surveys representing viewing and behavior in everyday circumstances.

The issue of the external validity of experiments whose subjects were young children reminds us of an axiom: When real life approximates the circumstances of an experiment (however rarely), the challenge of external validity is vanquished.

B. Experiments with Teenagers and Young Adults

In the pioneer experiment by Berkowitz and Rawlings (1963), which was designed to challenge the interpretation of catharsis theory (Feshbach, 1961) that reductions in hostility subsequent to viewing a violent portrayal were attributable to the purging or release of aggressive drive, college-age subjects saw the prize fight sequence from the film *Champion* in which Kirk Douglas is brutally beaten. Before viewing, subjects were given justification for hostility toward the experimental assistant by his insulting remarks while they took a bogus I.Q. test. The crucial comparison was between those who were led to perceive the portrayed beating as justified and those who were led to perceive it as unjustified. Subjects were thus alike in provocation, vicarious experience of violence, and opportunity to express hostility. Catharsis would predict no difference in expressed hostility, since both groups experienced the same vicarious violence. Berkowitz and Rawlings, however, predicted greater expressed hostility in the justified violence condition on the grounds that the perception of justification would lower inhibitions over retributive aggression. The measure of hostility was the rating of the competency of the experimental assistant, which the subjects presumably would have seen as potentially hurtful because they were told the ratings would affect future employment. Results supported Berkowitz and Rawlings. As a consequence, inhibition instead of catharsis became the accepted explanation when media portrayals appear to reduce aggressive or antisocial behavior.

In subsequent experiments, Berkowitz and Geen (1966, 1967) manipulated the degree to which the experimental assistant was linked to the film by identifying him as either "Bob" or "Kirk," the name of the actor in the film. Anger was encouraged by the assistant giving the subjects the maximal number of possible electric shocks as feedback in solving a problem. Aggression was measured by the number of electric shocks delivered to the assistant by the subject when roles were reversed. Aggression was greater when the assistant and the victim in the portrayal were linked by name.

Berkowitz and Alioto (1973) and Geen and Stonner (1972) in later experiments employing the same paradigm manipulated the motives ascribed to those engaged in the portrayed behavior. In two instances, boxers were described as engaged either in a professional encounter or in a grudge match in which their goal was injury; in another, football teams were so distinguished. Subjects told that the behavior was motivated by an intent to injure engaged in higher levels of aggressiveness.

These findings exemplify the dimensions of normativeness and pertinence. Normativeness of aggressive and hostile behavior is strongly implied when portrayed events are described as merited retribution or the motive attributed to participants is injury to one another. Pertinence represents the degree to which a portrayal is linked by a viewer to real life, in this instance achieved by the commonality of cues in the portrayal and real life: the name of the target.

Susceptibility—the vulnerability of subjects to influence—was heightened, of course, by the induced anger as it was by the toy deprivation in the Cat Lady experiment. That there sometimes may be subtle links between the factors involved is apparent from Geen and Stonner's (1972) finding that the relationship between vengeful motive and greater aggressiveness occurred only among angered subjects; among nonangered subjects, the "professional" condition evoked greater aggression. Anger apparently was necessary for the normativeness imputed to vengeful violence by the portrayal to be meaningful. In the absence of anger, such behavior might have been dismissed as irrelevant.

The role of excitation transfer or arousal is demonstrated in an experiment by Zillmann (1971). Using the same paradigm employed by Berkowitz and colleagues (provocation followed by the manipulation), college students were shown either a violent sequence, an erotic sequence, or a bland sequence with neither element. Electric shock delivery was greatest in the erotic condition, followed by the violent condition. Later, Zillmann, Johnson, and Hanrahan (1973) demonstrated that subsequent aggressiveness was greater when a violent sequence was unresolved than when it was resolved by a happy ending. In these instances, behavioral effects are attributable to the transfer of excitation induced by the portrayals to subsequent behavior.

Effects on teenagers and young adults occur repeatedly in the laboratory setting. Since a numerous and decisive majority of experiments (Andison, 1977; Comstock & Scharrer, 1999) demonstrate that a variety of types of violent portrayals increase aggressive or antisocial behavior, the inhibitory capability of media violence is far from invariably, or arguably even very regularly, exercised.

The challenges to external validity are nevertheless serious. The experimental setting for teenagers and young adults departs from the everyday in the perceptions of the subjects, in the brevity of the television exposure, in the absence of the possibility of retaliation, in the exclusion of competing and countervailing communications, and in the criterion of immediacy as the measure of effects. Experiments are especially sensitive to detecting effects and may register outcomes that would not occur in everyday life; thus, there is some risk of a false impression of frequency, degree, seriousness, or even occurrence of an effect.

The solution is to collect data that represents behavior outside the laboratory in everyday settings. The seemingly most plausible tactic is the field experiment, which contrives to produce in naturalistic surroundings the factors on which causal inference in experimentation depend. These factors are comparability among groups and the valid manipulation of experience. If groups are comparable, subsequent differences between them can be attributed to differences in the experience imposed by the experimenter.

Unfortunately, comparability and the valid manipulation of experience are not easily achieved outside the laboratory. Random assignment is often impossible. Frequently, intact groups—classes, schools, clubs—must be used and the necessary comparability of control and treatment groups is uncertain. Experience also may be difficult to control or manipulate, and imposing or denying access to certain programs may lead to anger or frustration. For example, in one instance the experimenters (Feshbach & Singer, 1971) had to dilute their nonviolent condition by the addition of a violent favorite, and it is possible an added consequence was increased aggression in this condition in response to the fact of manipulation rather than the content of the treatment. There also may be unusually large attrition of subjects as the institutions within which these intact groups reside may not be able to guarantee the participation of individuals, and this would be especially so for designs that require measurement at two or more points in time. The consequence is that the price of increased naturalism often is decreased confidence in causal inference.

Several field experiments involving teenagers or young adults (Feshbach & Singer, 1971; Leyens & Camino, 1974; Leyens, Camino, Parke & Berkowitz, 1975; Loye, Garney & Steele, 1977; Milgram & Shotland, 1973; Wells, 1973) are mixed in outcome, and the ambiguities courted by the method do not encourage attempting to discriminate between the more and less convincing. We agree with Cook, Kendzierski, and Thomas (1983) that as a body of evidence, they are difficult to interpret. In our view, it is an analytic error to combine the results of field experiments with those of surveys—in effect, to subjectively average them—as measures of real-world outcomes as occasionally has been done (Freedman, 1984), because the first are vulnerable to methodological weaknesses to which the latter are not subject.

C. Using Surveys for Causal Inference

The remaining recourse is to seek evidence that reflects everyday events from a source other than field experiments. Such evidence is available from a series of surveys that began to influence conclusions about the effects of television and film violence when the first of the genre were published as part of the research sponsored by the Surgeon General's 1972 inquiry (Chaffee, 1972; Comstock et al., 1978). They divide into eight groups based on sample, date, and method of data collection (see Table 6.1).

Table 6.1
Surveying Violent Entertainment and Aggression

Sample	Principal Findings
1. Surgeon General's inquiry (McIntyre & Teevan, 1972; Robinson & Bachman, 1972), with the former made up of about 2,300 males and females from 13 high schools, and the latter a probability sample of about 1,560 19-year-old males drawn from 87 high schools scattered across the country	1. The Maryland (McIntyre & Teevan, 1972) and national (Robinson & Bachman, 1972) samples measured violence exposure by the content of four named favorites. The former found positive associations between violence-viewing scores for both boys and girls and both serious delinquency and less serious misbehavior. The latter found positive associations among the young adult males between violence viewing scores and both interpersonal aggression (but only among those earlier recorded as high in that respect) and serious delinquency (property damage and hurtful aggression).
2. The Wisconsin sample of about 600 high school boys and girls in the Surgeon General's inquiry (McLeon et al., 1972a, 1972b), whose data parallel a portion of that for the Maryland survey to make up a pooled Wisconsin-Maryland sample	2. The Wisconsin-Maryland sample (McLeon et al., 1972a, 1972b) documented a modest positive association for both boys and girls (the typical $r = .30$) between viewing violent programs and behaving aggressively. Exposure was measured by weighting frequency of self-reported viewing by a program violence score obtained from a viewer panel. Aggression was measured by ratings for interpersonal conflicts—righting, name-calling, and the like—obtained from classmates. The data also indicated that, first, the relationship was not attributable to those more aggressive preferring violent entertainment because the correlation between preferences and behavior was much smaller than that between viewing and behavior. Second, a third variable such as poor school performance that might be associated with both greater viewing and greater aggressiveness was not responsible. Third, a causal, developmental sequence was a distinct possibility because of a correlation with much earlier viewing that was as large as that with contemporary viewing. (Decay of reliability of measurement as a consequence of the lengthier time span should result in a smaller correlation unless the association with earlier viewing in fact is larger.)

(Continued)

Table 6.1
(*Continued*)

Sample	Principal Findings
3. Panel surveys in which data were obtained from the same samples at times as distant from one another as a decade (Lefkowitz, Eron, Walder & Huesmann, 1977), as well as over briefer spans (Huesmann, Lagerspetz & Eron, 1984), with the former, part of the Surgeon General's inquiry, involving several hundred upstate New York boys and girls who were in the third grade at the first measurement and in their late teens at the second measurement	3. In their 10-year panel data Lefkowitz and colleagues (1977) found that earlier exposure of boys to television violence was more strongly associated with later teenage antisocial behavior than with concurrent antisocial behavior (although the latter correlation also was positive). These data increase the plausibility of a developmental sequence by the over-time association. They also increase the likelihood of a causal role for television by the resilience of the longitudinal association to the statistical elimination of any contribution by a major determinant of future antisocial behavior (Baron & Richardson, 1994)—prior aggression.
4. Samples of about 3,500 males and females in the third through the twelfth grade in a large southern metropolitan area (Thornton & Voigt, 1984) and of about 750 young persons ranging in age from preadolescence (about 11) to early adulthood (early 20s) in Manhattan (McCarthy, Langer, Gersten, Eisenberg & Orzeck, 1975)	4. Thornton and Voigt (1984) drew probability samples from three large high schools, measuring antisocial behavior by a 27-item delinquency scale and exposure by the violence among four favorite programs and amount of television viewed. They recorded modest but statistically significant positive associations between the stated program preference measure and delinquency that were somewhat larger for the two most serious forms of delinquency—criminal damage to property and hurtful aggression using weapons. The two less serious categories of delinquency for which the significant positive correlations were somewhat smaller were minor theft and rebelliousness, exemplified by running away. Delinquency was negatively associated with amount of weekday viewing and unrelated to amount of weekend viewing, and there was no association between any of the television measures and drug- or alcohol-related delinquency. These two outcomes eliminate the possibility that the correlations are artifacts of the mode of measurement of either viewing or delinquency. They place the onus on the type of content viewed and its links with specific forms of delinquency—those representing antisocial behavior and not substance abuse. This pattern occurred after the control of 10 major variables, including demographics (age, sex, and socioeconomic status) and

various "social control" variables, such as attachment to school and parents, engaging in constructive activities, commitment to conventional goals, and belief in the legal system. All of these social control variables were strongly and negatively associated with the four types of delinquency correlated with the television violence exposure measure. For two other social control variables, there were strong relationships for all the types of delinquency, including drug- and alcohol-related: delinquency of companions, positively related, and parental control over whereabouts, negatively related.

McCarthy and colleagues (1975) examined the 5-year follow-up of a larger probability sample of about 1,050 young people ages 6–18 living between Houston and 125th Streets, with television violence exposure measured by the violence of four favorite programs weighted by total amount of viewing. Data were obtained from interviews with mothers. Two types of antisocial behavior, fighting and delinquency, were positively associated with the violence exposure measure. In contrast, scores for "desirable life experience" (which would go up with the making of a new friend, an improvement in the feelings of parents, or getting along well with a teacher) and overall mental health were negatively associated with the television measure.

5. A survey of about 1,600 London male teenagers [Belson, 1978]

5. The Belson (1978) sample of about 1,600 males 12 to 17 in age is not only large but remarkably is statistically representative of London boys of that age. Exposure and behavior data were collected in clinical interviews. Judges were employed not only to score viewed programs for violence, but also to score acts for seriousness. Scales include behavior that is unambiguously criminal and seriously harmful, such as attempted rape, attacking someone with a tire iron, and falsely reporting bomb plantings to the police. By sample and method, it is the most substantial survey to date.

- Male teenagers who had viewed a substantially greater quantity of violent television programs than those otherwise like them in measured attributes committed a markedly greater proportion—about 50%—of seriously harmful antisocial and criminal acts. As with the Maryland and Wisconsin data, there was no justification for attributing this association entirely to the seeking out of violent entertainment by those rating high in antisocial behavior.

(Continued)

Table 6.1
(Continued)

Sample	Principal Findings
	• Less serious categories of antisocial behavior also were positively correlated with violence viewing. However, the reverse hypothesis that this represents the media behavior of those who engage in such acts could not be dismissed with as much confidence.
	• Behavioral and cognitive variables were not symmetrical. There were no associations between violence viewing and beliefs and dispositions (that is, norms and values) favorable to aggression—attributing violence to human nature, willingness to engage in violence, thinking of violence as a way to solve problems, or being preoccupied with violence.
6. A panel survey spanning 3½ years in the lives of more than 2,000 boys and girls and several hundred male teenagers in two American cities (Milavsky, Kessler, Stip & Rubens, 1982a, 1982b)	6. The panel survey by Milavsky et al. (1982a, 1982b) collected data in Fort Worth and Minneapolis from about 2,400 boys and girls in the second through sixth grades and about 800 male teenagers. Over 3½ years, measures of television exposure and antisocial behavior were obtained repeatedly, resulting in 15 instances ("wave pairs") in which earlier viewing could be matched with later behavior. Attrition resulted in the number from whom data were collected at two times decreasing markedly as span of time increased; for example, among elementary school males with 3 months between measurements, n = 497; at 9 months, n = 356; at 2 years, n = 211; and at 3 years, n = 112. The major findings were as follows:
	• At each point in time there were small positive statistically significant correlations between exposure to television violence and interpersonal aggression for both elementary school boys and girls and the teenage males.
	• There was a pattern of positive correlations between earlier viewing and later behavior and especially so for the elementary school boys. In that case, all were positive and noticeably larger in size for the 5 of the 15 pairings representing the longest time spans (two years or more).

- Among 95 subgroups of elementary school boys formed on the basis of 43 social and personal attributes, a large majority of these wave-to-wave associations were positive, and 9% achieved statistical significance ($p < .05$); similar but less pronounced results occurred for the girls.

7. The six-country data roughly parallel the similar, earlier U.S. surveys by Lefkowitz and colleagues. Some group and cultural distinctions appear; not all investigators are in accord in interpretation. As we observed earlier, the relationship between violence viewing and antisocial or aggressive behavior apparently is robust enough to occur under a variety of social and cultural conditions.

8. Huesmann and colleagues (2003) found violence viewing between the ages of 6–10 predicted aggression 15 years later after controlling for aggression and other possibly contaminating variables at the earlier age. Johnson and colleagues (2002) found young adult aggression predicted by amount of adolescent television viewing, again after control for possibly contaminating variables.

7. A set of panel surveys conducted in roughly parallel fashion spanning 3 years in the lives of boys and girls in six different countries: Australia, Finland, Israel, the Netherlands, Poland, and the United States (Huesmann et al., 1984; Huesmann & Eron, 1986; Wiegman, Kuttschreuter & Baards, 1986).

8. Two longitudinal studies, one spanning 15 years beginning in 1977 with a sample of Chicago-area first graders (Huesmann, Moise-Titus, Podolski & Eron, 2003), and the other covering 14 years in the lives of an upstate New York sample of more than 700 (Johnson, Cohen, Smailes, Kasen, & Brook, 2002).

Based on Comstock, G. & Scharrer, E. (1999). *Television: What's on, who's watching, and what it means*, 278–287. San Diego, CA: Academic Press.

The surveys of course vary individually by sample, measures, and ages. Each has its own particular features and strengths and weaknesses. Our approach is to treat them as a vast archive on which we can draw to address several concerns that have been paramount in the research on violence viewing and behavior:

1. *Relationship.* The surveys early established that there are positive correlations between various measures of violence viewing and various measures of aggressive and antisocial behavior.

2. *Content.* The surveys quickly began to produce data favoring the influence of violent content rather than television viewing in general, and data supportive of an influence of viewing on behavior.

3. *Longitudinal influence.* Data soon began to indicate that viewing as a child could influence behavior many years later, although the strongest long-term effects came from continued violence viewing from childhood through the teenage years.

4. *Seriously harmful behavior.* The bulk of data represent interpersonal aggression, which only occasionally borders on the seriously harmful ("fighting," "hitting"), but later surveys produce clear-cut positive correlations between violence viewing and seriously harmful behavior.

5. *Causation.* Although the data are limited (unlike experiments) in their amenability to causal inference, statistical analyses produce much evidence consistent with a causal interpretation, and this is particularly so for the failure to produce any other variable or variables that wholly explain the consistent and persistent positive correlations between violence viewing and aggressive and antisocial behavior.

The three and a half year panel data of Milavsky and colleagues (1982b) require extensive review because of two secondary analyses that importantly strengthen interpretation. Cook and his coauthors (1983) identify patterns that make a strong case for an effect of viewing on behavior. Kang (1990) performed statistical manipulations that produced significant additional positive associations.

Cook and colleagues (1983) arrayed the data by time span, with three important outcomes. First, the increasing degree of association with lengthening of span appears to hold generally for both boys and girls, except for spans of middling length. Second, the possibility that the strongest pattern, the positive associations for elementary school males, is an artifact of socioeconomic status (an interpretation proffered by Milavsky and colleagues) is eliminated by the outcomes for middle class girls (about 70% of the entire female sample), which display the same trend as do the males. Third, they isolated what they judged to be the data of highest quality for the teenage male sample and found (a) for personal aggression, nonnegative coefficients that increase with the span of time between waves; (b) for teacher aggression, nonnegative coefficients unrelated in size to the time spanned; (c) for property aggression, inconsistent results; and (d) for delinquency aggression, nonnegative coefficients that increase with the span of time between waves. Thus, in three of four instances there were nonnegative (if not significant) associations and in two of the four the same pattern of increasing size with time span.

Kang (1990) first applied a banal correction for heteroscedasticity (uneven clustering of the data). The frequency of significant positive associations among the elementary school males increased from two to five (out of a possible 15). He then employed exploratory data analysis (Tukey, 1977) to examine the influence of outliers. When a very few extreme cases were eliminated (an average of six per wave pairing) the number of significant, positive associations increased to eight.

This second outcome identifies an important substantive phenomenon: the real-life relationship between violence viewing and antisocial behavior in any large sample may be somewhat disguised by what McGuire (1986) has called "wimps," who watch a lot of television but engage in no antisocial behavior, and "street fighting men," who are so occupied with antisocial behavior they have little time for television.

Kang also found that with the additional coefficients the pattern of increasing size with longer time lags became pronounced. Five of the eight significant coefficients represented the longest time lags. In contrast, a test of the reverse hypothesis (that greater aggressiveness predicts higher levels of violence viewing) produced only four significant coefficients with three clustered among the shortest time spans. The Kang analysis, then, points to an increasing effect of television violence on aggressiveness as children grow up, and primarily short-term effects of aggression on violence viewing—so that the aggressiveness of viewers is not a convincing explanation for long-term associations between the two.

Kang discovered that most of his newly uncovered significant associations involved a single cohort. This raises the possibility of an important, unidentified necessary condition or conditions. However, it does not call into question our reliance on the Kang analyses because we would expect these same circumstances to apply to numerous other groups of young persons.

D. Meta-analyses

We began with the experiments and the surveys in some detail because they represent the core of the evidence on violent entertainment and aggression and antisocial behavior. Nevertheless, the easiest and quickest summary of the evidence comes from quantitative aggregations of their findings, most of which follow the meta-analytic paradigm introduced by Eugene Glass (1976).

The strength of quantitative aggregations is that they rest upon the pooling of data from many sources, thereby increasing through the enlarged number of cases the accuracy and reliability of the estimated relationship between two variables (Hunt, 1997). However, they are no substitute for knowledge, interpretation, or judgment. Experiments and surveys still must be weighed for their testimony on behalf of everyday causation, and particular studies sometimes will provide important findings that escape the larger net of a quantitative aggregation.

There are seven quantitative aggregations, and they not only document that the relationship between violence viewing and aggressive or antisocial behavior is positive but that it is remarkably robust across methods, measures, and types of portrayal (see Table 6.2). Andison (1977), the pioneer, categorized the outcomes of 67 experiments and surveys as to the direction and size of the relationship. Hearold (1986) was the first to apply the meta-analytic practice of using the statistical measure of variance, the standard deviation, as a criterion of effect size to media and behavior. A student of Glass at the University of Colorado (credited with developing meta-analysis in the 1970s in an attempt to quantitatively discredit H.J. Eysenck's claims that psychotherapy was ineffective), she examined more than 1,000 relationships drawn from 168 studies between exposure to antisocial and prosocial portrayals and antisocial and prosocial behavior. In contrast, Wood, Wong, and Chachere (1991) focused narrowly on spontaneous antisocial behavior in designs that permitted causal inference, examining 23 experiments in which the dependent variable was "unconstrained interpersonal aggression" among children and teenagers. Allen, D'Alessio, and Brezgel (1995) aggregated the data from 30 laboratory-type experiments in which the independent variable was exposure to video or film erotica and the dependent variable was aggression. Hogben (1998), a sociologist, assessed only studies measuring everyday viewing (thereby excluding laboratory experiments) but included a wide variety of outcomes, including aggressive behavior, hostile attitudes, personality variables, and in one instance (Cairns, Hunter & Herring, 1980) the inventing by children of imagined news stories. Bushman and Anderson (2001) plotted a time series representing the correlations between exposure to violent portrayals and aggressive behavior by five-year intervals over 25 years. Paik and Comstock (1994), in a comprehensive updating of Hearold's assessment of the relationship between exposure to television violence and aggressive and antisocial behavior, included 82 new studies for a total of 217 that produced 1,142 coefficients between the independent and dependent variables.

Table 6.2
Selected Effect Sizes from Seven Meta-Analyses of Media Violence and Aggression

Author	Independent variable	Dependent variable	N[*]	Effect Size (r)
Andison, 1977	Television violence	Aggressive behavior	67	.28[**]
Hearold, 1986	Antisocial portrayals	Antisocial behavior	528	.30
Wood, Wong, and Cachere, 1991	Aggressive portrayals	Unconstrained interpersonal aggression	23	.20
Allen, D'Alessio, and Brezel, 1995	Pornography	Aggressive behavior	33	.13
Hogben, 1998	Violent programming	Aggression-related responses	56	.11
Bushman and Anderson, 2001	Television violence	Aggressive behavior	202	.15[**]
Paik and Comstock, 1994	Television violence	Aggressive behavior	1142	.31

[*]Number of coefficients represented by effect size.
[**]Calculated from the distribution of coefficients by size of effect.
Note: In some cases, Cohen's d converted to r by Table 2.3 (Rosenthal, Rosnow & Rubin, 2000, p. 16). All r's are statistically significant; for example, the Paik and Comstock p is less than .0000.
Based on Comstock, G. & Scharrer, E. Meta-analyzing the controversy over television violence and aggression. In D.A. Gentile (2003). *Media violence and children: A complete guide for parents and professionals*, 208. Westport, CT: Praeger.

The implications of these analyses are threefold:

1. There are positive effect sizes for both experiments and survey designs, and this holds for the analyses that include both as well as for those that focused on one or the other.

2. The violence exposure effect is extraordinarily robust across the circumstances not only of design but of type of violence. Each of the seven analyses produces a positive, statistically significant coefficient between the independent variable (exposure to television or film violence) and the dependent variable (aggressive or antisocial behavior).

3. Taken in conjunction with the absence of any set of data—much less a consistent pattern—in which another measured variable wholly explained this association (the most prominent candidate, the "reverse" hypothesis is, as we shall see, a loser), these analyses constitute a strong argument for a contribution by television (and film) to everyday aggressive and antisocial behavior. This argument rests on:

- The causation demonstrated within the framework of the experiments, where such an inference is the very purpose of this type of design.
- The confirmation by the surveys that the necessary circumstances occur in everyday life to permit generalizing from the experiments, positive correlations and the lack of an alternative convincing explanation.

E. The Role of Mediating Factors

We begin by reemphasizing the evidence on behalf of a developmental pattern. We then turn to aggressive predisposition. Finally, we examine the role of gender, the seriousness of affected behavior, and the size of effects.

1. Developmental Pattern   Four sets of data provide significant evidence of a developmental sequence. Two are the 10-year panel by Lefkowitz and colleagues (1977) and the three-and-a-half-year panel by Milavsky and colleagues (1982b). Both strongly support a developmental sequence by the robustness and size of their positive associations over long periods of time. In the first instance, the decade-long overtime correlation for boys exceeds that for aggression at the time of first measurement, and remains as strong when prior aggression is statistically eliminated as an influence—*prima facie* suggestive of causal influence. In the second, the five largest of the eight coefficients significant after the adjustments of Kang (1990) occupy the longest time spans of two to three years.

The contribution of television to the development of the trait of aggressiveness is further strongly supported by the data of Huesmann, Eron, Lefkowitz, and Walder (1984) and Huesmann, Eron, Dubow, and Seebauer (summarized in Eron and Huesmann, 1987), which spectacularly add one and two decades, respectively, to the original 10-year panel of Lefkowitz and colleagues. Twenty and 30 as well as 10 years after the third-grade period of initial measurement, those higher earlier in the viewing of violence scored as more aggressive. Eron and Huesmann (1987) attempt to place these findings in perspective:

> It is not claimed that the specific programs these adults watched when they were 8 years old still had a direct effect on their behavior. However, the continued viewing of these programs probably contributed to the development of certain attitudes and norms of behavior and taught these youngsters ways of solving interpersonal problems which remained with them over the years. (p. 196)

As we have explained (Comstock & Scharrer, 1999), the Belson data support a different underlying mechanism. Dispositions, a cognitive route, is not a necessary condition. Instead, the mechanism supported by the Belson data is availability or access in the behavioral repertoire (Comstock, 2004; Comstock & Scharrer, 2003).

The Milavsky data pinpoint the developmental effect as primarily occurring before the teenage years because the increases in magnitude of association over the three and a half years were greater for the elementary school sample than for the teenage male sample. The Milavsky data also encourage the view that early plus continuing high exposure is a factor because the associations for the longer time spans are considerably larger when there is no control for earlier exposure to television violence (see Tables 6.1 and 6.2, pp. 126–127; Tables 8.14 and 8.15, pp. 239–240).

2. Predisposition to Aggressive or Violent Behavior   Predisposition asks whether some are more susceptible to the influence of violent television entertainment as a consequence of being more aggressive or antisocial in behavior or inclination. There is in fact ample evidence that predisposition, represented either by attributes that are correlates of or actual higher levels of initial antisocial behavior, identifies those who are very likely to be affected by violent portrayals.

For example, the male teenagers who scored higher in viewing violence in the Belson (1978) sample were statistically matched in other characteristics with those scoring lower and a penchant for delinquency was apparant in the performance by these lower scores of such acts at a substantial although lower rate (see Table 12.4, p. 374); thus, predisposition was decidedly present. Robinson and Bachman (1972) found in their national sample of 19-year-old males that interpersonal aggression was correlated with violence viewing only among those earlier scoring higher in interpersonal aggression. Josephson (1987) found that only those high in initial aggressiveness increased their aggressive behavior as a consequence of exposure to a violent portrayal in a naturalistic experiment with 400 second- and third-grade boys playing floor hockey. Celozzi, Kazelskis, and Gutsch (1981) found that measures of hostility were greater after exposure to a violent 10-minute hockey film among those scoring higher for the trait of aggressiveness. Paik (1991) in her meta-analysis found that effects of television violence were greater among those scoring higher on one or another measure of aggressive predisposition.

Certainly, the portrayal of successful violence administered to a disliked recipient whose punishment can be ethically justified would be particularly likely to influence those who are highly aggressive. Such stimuli not only will evoke aggressive thoughts and identify a target whose punishment will provide satisfaction, but also such a viewer will possess a superior repertoire of aggressive acts. However, lower inhibitions and greater aggressive skills often will be associated with diminished media influence because these very individuals may be as aggressive as prudence or self-preservation will permit. The disinhibition of internal restraints and the linking of aggression with environmentally present cues will affect those both higher and lower in initial aggression and the enhancement of aggressive skills will be greatest for persons comparatively lacking in them—those lower in initial aggressiveness. Finally, the high rate of positive outcomes for experiments implies that predisposition is not essential for effects unless the concept is stripped of any meaningful distinctiveness. Our conclusion is that predisposition is an important predictor but not a necessary condition.

3. Does Gender Play a Role? The early experimental literature appeared to indicate that males were more susceptible to influence than females (Comstock et al., 1978) and two of the most prominent surveys (Lefkowitz et al., 1977; Milavsky et al., 1982b) record somewhat stronger patterns of association among males than among females. However, the meta-analysis of Paik and Comstock (1994) makes it clear that measured effects are quite similar, with the best measure of actual effects, the survey, almost identical for male and female outcomes (see Table 2, p. 528). Our conclusion is that males and females are affected about equally with the similarity in scores on the same scales particularly convincing given the inclination of males and females to differ in the expression of aggression, with the former typically more direct and the latter typically more indirect (Bjorkqvist, 1994).

Theory developed from experimentation in fact supports such an expectation. Gender of model and viewer interact (Bandura, 1965, 1973; Bandura et al., 1963a, 1963b; Berkowitz & Rawlings, 1963). Among boys, males are more effective as models. Among girls, males and females are about equally effective. The least effective pairing is the female model and the male subject. Status, which would favor the male, and appropriateness of behavior, which in the case of aggression would also favor the male (behavior perceived as inappropriate is likely to lower regard for the perpetrator, and thus decrease the likelihood of emulation by an observer), take precedence over the demonstrated effectiveness of similarity between model and viewer. Male models, plentiful in entertainment as violence perpetrators, are thus not without influence on females. The influence of violent entertainment on females would also be enhanced by social changes: the increasing number of aggressive female models in entertainment and the increasing degree to which behavior once considered the province of males is perceived as unisexual.

4. Seriousness of Aggressive or Violent Acts   The interpersonal aggression that has been measured most often represents behavior that would be unpleasant, unwelcome, and often painful and sometimes injurious to victims and sometimes painful and injurious to perpetrators. That is clearly denoted by the "fighting," "hitting," and "name-calling" that are part of the typical interpersonal aggression scale.

In the Belson (1978) data, the most convincing outcome was among delinquents for seriously harmful and criminal acts. These included, "I twisted a boy's arm until he yelled with pain," "I broke into a house and smashed everything I could find," and "I threw the cat into the fire." None qualifies as benign.

The meta-analysis of Paik and Comstock (1994) recorded similar effect sizes for simulated and interpersonal aggression and smaller effect sizes that progressively declined with the seriousness of illegal and seriously harmful activities. However, the three instances of data of good quality that permit direct comparisons among acts varying in seriousness—the data of Thornton and Voigt (1984), Milavsky and colleagues (1982a, 1982b), and Belson (1978)—do not encourage a conclusion of sharply declining television influence as seriousness increases. Thornton and Voigt (1984) found slightly stronger relationships with more serious forms of delinquency, even when other variables were controlled. Within the teenage sample of Milavsky and colleagues (1982a, 1982b), the size of the association for interpersonal aggression was only somewhat greater than for the more serious teacher and delinquency measures. Belson (1978), of course, found the largest proportional and inferentially most convincing difference for the most serious offenses.

Finally, the Surgeon General's report on youth violence cites violence viewing between the ages of six and 11 as an early risk factor for committing seriously harmful, felony-level criminal acts between the ages of 15 and 18 (U.S. Department of Health and Human Services, 2001). This is a singular and important judgment in regard to seriousness, because the Surgeon General ignored the data on aggressive and antisocial behavior at a lower level, such as interpersonal aggression or playground hitting, fighting, and verbal abuse, and confined the analysis to evidence on behalf of serious crimes. He also accepted only outcomes that were supported by more than one set of data, in this case drawing on the meta-analysis of Paik and Comstock (1994). The coefficient would rank as small by Cohen's (1988) well-known criteria (+.13). However, of the more than 20 risk factors identified, about three-fourths are of about the same magnitude, including such topics of "obvious" concern as poor relations with parents, psychological deviance, antisocial behavior, a broken home, and low mental ability.

Thus, this conclusion of a federal agency stands as a strong endorsement of the view that effects extend to the seriously harmful and criminal.

Our wary interpretation is that some categories of illegal and seriously harmful acts are affected to a degree not much different than is interpersonal aggression but that probably the most harmful acts are affected to a smaller degree. We base the former on the within-study comparisons and the inclusion in interpersonal aggression of acts that are or could escalate into illegal or seriously harmful behavior. We base the latter on the small effect size in the meta-analysis for violence against persons and our belief that in those instances social taboos and possible sanctions would constrain media effects.

5. Effect Size   Estimating the magnitude of the influence on aggression and antisocial behavior of violent television and film entertainment requires data that represent everyday viewing and behavior. Experiments discriminate among treatments, ages, and other attributes of subjects, but do not provide an estimate of everyday effects. There are three possibilities. We can turn to a singular study that clearly meets the criteria of everyday viewing and criminal behavior, we can draw on the meta-analyses for their aggregation of outcomes, or we can collate the outcomes of surveys of everyday behavior.

A group led by the methodologist Thomas Cook (Hennigan et al., 1982) offers a dramatic documentation of the effect of the introduction of television on larceny theft (see Figure 6.3). The design, an interrupted time series with switching replications (Cook & Campbell, 1979), has the strength of testing the relationship at two points in time, and this replication in this instance occurs twice over with separate sets of data for cities and states. This fourfold replication makes a powerful case for an effect on criminal behavior, and the midpoint of estimated magnitude is 10.3 percent (Comstock & Scharrer, 1999).

Hearold (1986) and Paik and Comstock (1994) offer similar overall estimates of effect size in their meta-analyses, which Bushman and Anderson (2001) compare favorably in magnitude with other deleterious effect sizes (see Figure 6.4). We do not mean to argue that these coefficients are strictly comparable, and that media violence poses a higher risk than most other threats that have been examined. Meta-analytic, like all coefficients, will vary in validity as a function of the mode of measurement. What we do argue is that by the criteria established by the practice of meta-analysis the violence coefficients are not trivial or tiny, and that unreliability in the measures for viewing and behavior—which are likely to be much higher than for clinical diagnosis of disease and illness—suggest these coefficients are underestimates.

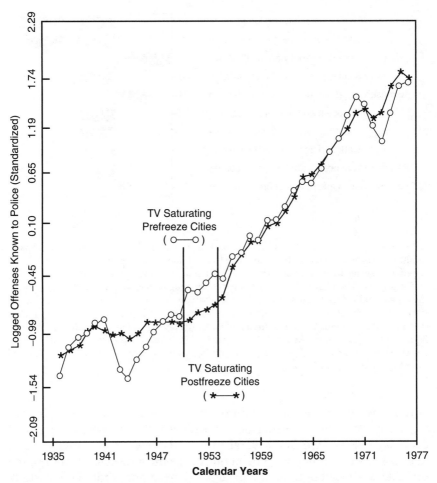

Fig. 6.3 Larceny theft rates and introduction of television. Adapted from "Impact of the Introduction of Television on Crime in the United States: Empirical Findings and Theoretical Implications," by K.M. Hennigan, L.Heath, J.D. Wharton, M.L. Del Rosario, T.D. Cook, and B.J. Calder, 1982. *Journal of Personality and Social Psychology, 42*(3), pp. 461–467.

The Hearold and Paik and Comstock overall coefficients are of medium size by Cohen's (1988) well-known criteria. However, narrow sets of selected data grouping different independent and dependent variables produce estimates ranging from small to large. Nevertheless, whatever the focus, the meta-analyses produce the most reliable and valid estimates because they derive from pools of several or more studies (over 200 in the case of Paik & Comstock) rather than a single study with its particular weaknesses (Hunter & Schmidt, 2004).

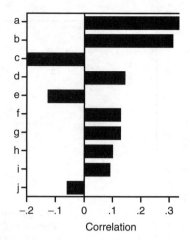

Fig. 6.4   Effect Size for Media Violence and Aggression and Selected other Effect Sizes.
Note: A correlation coefficient can range from −1 (a perfect negative liner relation) to +1 (a perfect positive liner relation), with 0 indicating no linear relation.

Sources: (a) The effect of smoking tobacco on lung cancer was estimated by pooling the data from Figures 1 and 3 in Wynder and Graham's (1950) classic article. The remaining effects were estimated from meta-analyses; (b) Paik and Comstock (1994); (c) Weller (1993); (d) Wells (1980); (e) Needleman and Gatsonis (1990); (f) Fiore, Smith, Jorenby, and Baker (1994); (g) Welten, Kemper, Post, and van Staveren (1995); (h) Cooper (1989); (i) Smith, Handley, and Wood (1990); (j) Hill, White, Jolley, and Mapperson (1988). Adapted from Bushman and Anderson (2001).

When we examine the variation across about 25 separate estimates from surveys—the preferred design because of the representation of everyday events—we find several in the 10 percent range but some as low as 4 percent. When we look at one of the most discussed studies, the multidecade panel of Eron & colleagues (Huesmann, Eron, Lefkowitz & Walder, 1984; Eron & Huesmann, 1987), we return to the 10 percent figure. The estimate of Belson (1978) of 50 percent undoubtedly holds for the small subset of his sample comparing those with characteristics predictive of delinquency who were high and low in exposure to violent entertainment, but when taken as a proportion of the whole sample certainly would regress to our 4 to 10 percent estimate. Similarly, the data of the two recent longitudinal surveys each covering about a decade-and-a-half of Huesmann and colleagues (2003) and Johnson and colleagues (2002) also are consistent with this estimate of 4 to 10 percent.

Our conclusion is that the range of 4 to 10 percent of the variance is most consistent with the empirical evidence. This range fits well with all three of our sources—the single dramatic study, the meta-analyses, and the survey of surveys.

II. REVERSE HYPOTHESIS: DO AGGRESSIVE PERSONALITIES SEEK OUT VIOLENT ENTERTAINMENT?

The obvious challenge to our interpretation is the reverse hypothesis—that the associations represent the preferences for violent entertainment of those who behave in an aggressive or antisocial manner. There is no doubt that some sets of data record a positive association between aggression and the viewing of violent entertainment (Atkin, Greenberg, Korzenny & McDermott, 1979; Bryant, 1989; Bryant, Comiskey & Zillmann, 1981; Huesmann, 1982; Huesmann & Eron, 1986). However, the data on the whole do not give strong support to this alternative view.

Kang found only one instance (out of a possible 15, the total number of wave pairs) of mutual prediction, the criterion for reciprocity (Granger, 1969). There were only four instances in which aggression predicted later viewing of violence, whereas there were eight in which violence viewing predicted later aggression. Furthermore, the fewer associations for behavior-to-viewing were concentrated among the shorter time spans of nine months whereas five of the eight for viewing-to-behavior occupied the longest time spans of two years or more. These data are wholly inconsistent with a strong explanatory role for aggressive behavior, give little support to reciprocity, document that any contribution by behavior is confined to the short term, and make it clear that for longer time spans behavior-to-viewing does not constitute an alternative explanation. They are particularly convincing because they not only validly represent viewing and behavior but also incorporate an important foundation for causal inference that is missing from much of the survey data—time order, with the predictor variable preceding the dependent variable. That is, these linkages do not represent associations at a point in time but rather predictions of a later state by a circumstance occurring earlier.

Belson (1978) similarly concluded, after a painstaking analysis, that among his sample of delinquents high in violence viewing who committed the most serious offenses, the data were not consistent with a behavior-to-viewing hypothesis. McCarthy and colleagues (1975) in their Manhattan sample found no correlation between fighting and delinquency and a stated preference for violent programs. Menzies in two separate studies (1971, 1973) found no relationship between the violence committed by the criminally incarcerated and the choosing of violent entertainment. Chaffee (1972) in his analysis of data from the surveys sponsored by the Surgeon General's inquiry concluded that any contribution to viewing by behavior was minor compared to the contribution to behavior by viewing (primarily because the correlation in the same sample between actual viewing and behavior was much greater than between four favorites and behavior).

Our conclusion is that there may be some contribution to viewing by behavior. However, that it is less certain or strong than a contribution to behavior by viewing, and does not fully explain the positive associations between viewing and behavior.

III. EXPLANATION OF THE INFLUENCE OF VIOLENCE IN TELEVISION AND FILM

There are three major theories that have been formulated to explain this influence of violent television and film entertainment:

- *Social cognition* (Bandura, 1986), formerly known as social learning theory
- *Neoassociationism* (Berkowitz, 1984, 1990), previously known as cue and disinhibition theory
- *Excitation transfer* (Zillmann, 1971, 1982), sometimes referred to as arousal theory

A. Social Cognition

Social cognition assigns a central role to the observation of others as the means by which behavior is shaped. However, it is not strictly a theory of imitation although it encompasses the imitation of what is observed. Rather, it is a theory of modeling in which mental processing is directed toward the goals of success and avoidance of discomfort and failure. The two principal processes are acquisition of behavior and the estimation of the desirability of performing the behavior. People learn how to behave in a particular way by seeing others perform the same task. Observation thus leads to or enhances the ability to behave in a certain way. In the simplest case, a child learns a dance step. In a more complex sequence, an adult learns how to make a quesadilla. Meaning also is applied to what is observed, and observed behavior, in addition to being added to the repertoire of the individual, is evaluated in regard to its likely effectiveness, normativeness, and pertinence. This trio serves the two motives of success and avoiding unpleasantness—the ability of the behavior to achieve a desired end, the social acceptability and approval of the particular behavior, and the extent to which it is perceived as appropriate for the individual and his or her circumstances.

Social cognition also anticipates more complex, covert modeling in which the individual will rehearse and reformulate behavior to fit the expected circumstances. Thus, it is a theory of constructive coping that applies to all behavior. It would predict that reinforcement of an act in some way would increase the likelihood of its repetition, but it would not require reinforcement for the acquisition of an act because of the role of observation. However, it would predict a more prominent place in the behavioral repertoire of acts observed as reinforced because that would signal effectiveness.

Social cognition asserts that observation may occur in real life or though the mass media, which in this case includes depictions by any means—print, audio, interactive, or screen. Nevertheless, among the media a particularly strong role is proposed for screen media because of the visual portrayal of lifelike models. In the case of television and film violence, it would predict the facilitation of aggressive and antisocial behavior by two routes—the increased knowledge and capability to perform such acts and the enhanced esteem in which such acts are held as a consequence of their frequent portrayal as effective, normative, and pertinent.

B. Neoassociationism and Neural Circuitry

Neoassociationism holds that behavior is importantly guided by semantic linkages in the neural circuitry of the brain. These semantic linkages are brought into play by stimuli that autonomically call them forth. The linkages themselves consist of thoughts, images, and memories that are supportive of one another and are drawn from the same universe. This universe might encompass any of the possible domains that could occupy the mind—philanthropy, hostility and retribution, childcare. The stimuli function as cues that prime these particular linkages because the linkages have become associated with them. The basis of these associations are prior joint occurrences. Neural circuitry thus produces a web of connections that make behaving one way or another more or less likely. With repetition, the association between stimuli and semantic links becomes more strongly forged.

Here, as in social cognition, observation has a central role. When behavior on the part of someone is observed, there will be several cues or symbols associated with it—a cell phone, a red jacket, a police baton. When these cues or symbols are encountered, the likelihood of recalling the act becomes enhanced, and so too, does the retrieval of supportive linkages—thoughts, images, and memories called forth by the stimuli. The consequence is that behavior in accord with the linkages becomes more likely. In addition, if these acts are recalled in ways that assign them effectiveness, normativeness, or pertinence, there may be a disinhibiting effect in regard to performing them. Conversely, if behavior is recalled as lacking in these qualities the outcome may be enhanced inhibition—the behavior becomes less likely to be performed. Thus two key elements are cues that lead to the retrieval of thoughts, images, and memories and the disinhibition or inhibition of behavior by the qualities attributed to it. As with social cognition, the mass media enter because they are a source for experiencing, although vicariously, the behavior of other persons, and television and film are especially prominent because of the visual, lifelike models portrayed.

Neoassociationism puts less emphasis than social cognition on the acquisition of behavior, but the clear implication is that observed behavior will be acquired and may be performed depending on the way it has been portrayed. It also holds that the linkages within the brain are in flux, becoming stronger, weaker, or more or less elaborated, depending on the experience of the individual. The more aggression, violence, and retribution experienced, the greater the number of cues that will elicit such thoughts, images, and memories. In the case of television and film violence, it would predict the facilitation of aggressive and antisocial behavior by three routes—the development of cues that will bring such acts and thoughts to mind, the establishment of firmer and more elaborate links among aggressive and antisocial thoughts and acts in the mind, and the casting of those thoughts and acts as effective, normative, and pertinent.

C. Excitation Transfer

Excitation transfer posits simply that the physiological arousal experienced as the result of an exciting event often will increase the intensity or likelihood of subsequent behavior. Violent television and film portrayals would sometimes be physiologically arousing, as would some depictions in the news, sports, and other forms of entertainment. In case of aggressive and antisocial behavior, media portrayals would increase their intensity or likelihood when they were either the behavior engaged in or the behavior most likely to be performed after experiencing a physically arousing event or depiction. A key concept here is threshold. The behavior in question can be thought of as at a certain threshold and the transfer of excitation moves it beyond that threshold.

D. General Aggression Model

Anderson, Bushman, and Huesmann (Anderson & Bushman, 2002; Anderson & Huesmann, 2003) have proposed a synthesis of these three theories labelled the General Aggression Model (GAM). It specifies three major routes to aggression—arousal, affect, and cognition. In this schema, arousal refers to the physiological excitation that would make an aggressive act more likely, affect embraces the evaluative component of favorability or unfavorability toward an act, and cognition represents the concrete thoughts about the act's execution and consequences. Media portrayals of violence would operate through these three routes, activating and enlarging or diminishing the likelihood of an aggressive or antisocial response.

In identifying the conditions on which effects are contingent the primary source is experiments, because one of their principal functions is to permit causal inference about the relationship between variables. In this case, we have a catalogue of 16 contingent conditions (see Table 6.3).

Table 6.3
Experimentally Documented Conditions on which Behavioral Effects are Contingent

Condition	Source
1. Reward or lack of punishment for the portrayed perpetrator	Bandura, 1965; Bandura et al., 1963b; Rosenkrans & Hartup, 1967
2. Portrayal of violence as justified	Berkowitz & Rawlings, 1963; Meyer, 1973
3. Cues in the portrayal likely to be encountered in real life, such as a name, attribute, or object	Berkowitz & Geen, 1966, 1967; Donnerstein & Berkowitz, 1981; Geen & Berkowitz, 1967
4. Portrayal of the perpetrator as similar to the viewer	Rosenkrans, 1967
5. Involvement with the portrayed aggressor, such as imagining oneself in his or her place	Turner & Berkowitz, 1972
6. Depiction of behavior ambiguous as to intent—such as violent sports—as motivated by the desire to inflict harm or injury	Berkowitz & Alioto, 1973; Geen & Stonner, 1972
7. Violence portrayed so that its consequences are not disturbing, such as violence without pain or suffering on the part of the victim, sorrow among friends and lovers, or remorse by the perpetrator	Berkowitz & Rawlings, 1963
8. Violence that is presented realistically or ostensibly represents real events	Atkin, 1983; Bandura et al., 1963a; Feshbach, 1972; Geen & Rakosky, 1973; Hapkiewicz & Stone, 1974
9. The portrayal of hypermasculinity on the part of those who commit violence, and especially among viewers scoring high in hypermasculinity themselves	Scharrer, 1998
10. Portrayed violence that is not the subject of critical or disparaging commentary	Lefcourt, Barnes, Parke & Schwartz, 1966
11. Portrayals of violence whose commission pleases the viewer	Ekman et al., 1972; Slife & Rychiak, 1982
12. Portrayals in which the violence is not interrupted by humor	Lieberman Research, 1975
13. Portrayed abuse that includes physical aggression instead of or in addition to verbal abuse	Lieberman Research, 1975
14. Portrayals, violent or otherwise, that leave the viewer in a state of unresolved excitement	Zillmann, 1971; Zillmann et al., 1973
15. Viewers who are in a state of anger or provocation before seeing a violent portrayal	Berkowitz & Geen, 1966; Caprara et al., 1987; Donnerstein & Berkowitz, 1981; Geen, 1968; Thomas, 1982

(Continued)

Table 6.3
(*Continued*)

Condition	Source
16. Viewers who are in a state of frustration after viewing a violent portrayal, whether from an extraneous source or as a consequence of viewing the portrayal	Geen, 1968; Geen & Berkowitz, 1967; Worchel, Hardy & Hurley, 1976

Adapted from Comstock G. & Scharrer E. (1999). *Television: What's on, who's watching, and what it means*, 300–301. San Diego, CA: Academic Press.

These can be more economically summarized as representing four dimensions:

1. *Efficacy*—the degree to which a particular way of acting is portrayed as likely to achieve a reward or gain a desired outcome.

2. *Normativeness*—the degree to which a particular way of behaving is portrayed as ordinary, normal, expected, and likely to have social approval or acceptance.

3. *Pertinence*—the degree to which portrayals seem especially relevant to the viewer by rough matches between the viewer and the portrayal in age, ethnicity, gender, and setting and circumstance.

4. *Susceptibility*—the degree to which the viewer is in a state of arousal, frustration, or anger, or otherwise motivated to engage in an act of aggression or antisocial behavior.

Such economy has two purposes. First, it makes these conditions more accessible by suppressing the details of each experimental variant. Second, by creating general principles from specific findings it encourages their creative application on a much wider basis to uninvestigated or future events.

The first three are obviously dependent on the perceptions of the viewer. Most of the time for most viewers the perception will be an obvious product of the portrayal. A reward denotes efficacy. Disguised aggression in sports implies normativeness. Characters of the same age usually ensure pertinence. Typically, they can be thought of as properties of the stimulus. However, it is also important to recognize that occasionally these contingencies will not be obvious from a portrayal. An insult may represent efficacy when delivered to a disliked rival. Normativeness may be inferred from the cachet within a small band of deviants rather than the approval of the society in general. An alienated, angry individual may perceive an alienated unattractive figure as a pertinent model.

In our adaptation of the GAM (see Figure 6.5), we have retained the three routes and the choice paradigm where outcomes are either impulsive (and risky and possibly hurtful) or carefully thought out (usually less risky, but meticulously planned; vicious retribution cannot be ruled out). Both impulsive and carefully thought out options could lead to flight, aggression, or some combination of the two. The difference lies in the underlying mental processing—greater affect and more reliance on heuristic shortcuts in the case of impulsive behavior and much more thorough weighing of costs and benefits in the case of carefully thought out behavior. The former seizes on a tactic; the latter hopes to implement a strategy. We have then added our contingent conditions, using our four dimensions for their economy, accessibility, and creative applicability.

It is important to recognize that a cognitive route in which dispositions—attitudes, norms, and values—play a major role is not a necessary condition. Our four dimensions may well operate frequently through making one or another mode of behavior or act more prominent in the behavioral repertoire of individuals. In this interpretation, these dimensions function as gatekeepers. Portrayals that do not promote efficacy, normativeness, or pertinence, and viewers who are not in a state of susceptibility, lead to the discard of behavior in the dustbin of inhibition.

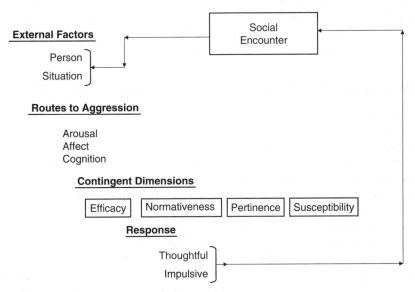

Fig. 6.5 Modified general aggression model.
Based on Carnagey, N. L. & Anderson, C. A. Theory in the study of media violence. In A. Gentile (2003). *Media violence and children* 97–100. Westport, CT: Praeger.

The data of Belson (1978) are particularly persuasive on this point. His survey of about 1,600 London teenage males is one of the largest samples in the television violence literature, and the only one that is a true probability sample (meaning that generalizations can be made to the city's male teenage population). The interviewing was meticulous, lasting several hours for each respondent. Aggressive acts were sorted into categories of seriousness based on the opinions of adult judges, thereby establishing the societal validity of the rankings. His major and strongest finding was an association between violence viewing and seriously harmful aggression that statistical analysis identified as probably attributable to the influence of violence viewing on behavior. There were also associations with less serious aggression, but statistical analysis indicated that they were far more open to the interpretation that aggressive youth had sought out violent entertainment. Among his measures were four representing attitudes, norms, and values. These were 10-item, highly reliable scales representing antisocial attitudes, approval of violence, hostile personality traits, and willingness to commit violence. In addition, there was a measure of social contagion (the committing of antisocial acts in the company of others)—which has a dispositional aspect because it should at least in part be a function of the attitudes, norms, and values of companions. If dispositions are the key link, then there should have been positive associations between violence viewing and these measures (as well as between these measures and aggressive and antisocial behavior). In fact, in none of the five measures did Belson record the necessary positive association between viewing and dispositions.

IV. THE EFFECTS OF VIOLENCE IN VIDEO GAMES

The paradigm—by which we mean the hypotheses, analyses, and findings—that we have developed for violent television and film entertainment applies to violent video games, but with several major qualifications. These qualifications concern the amount or reliability of the evidence, the changing character of games that challenges the relevance of much early research, and the particular features of video games that may enhance their influence compared to television and film.

Our paradigm has consisted of experiments that demonstrate outcomes of heightened aggressiveness subsequent to exposure to violent television and film entertainment, various conditions on which these outcomes are contingent, and surveys that document that children and young adults who have viewed greater amounts of such entertainment in fact engage in everyday life to a greater degree in aggressive or antisocial behavior. The experimental designs permitted causal inference;

the survey data confirmed that media consumption and aggressive and antisocial behavior were positively associated, and failed to identify alternative variables as responsible. We also presented several meta-analyses that document that these relationships occur across numerous studies at levels achieving statistical significance and demonstrate remarkable robustness as the seven analyses we discuss each has a different focus. The positive association holds up for a wide variety of independent and dependent variables as well as different methods. For example, effect sizes (the term in meta-analytic jargon for the magnitude of a relationship) are positive for violent erotica, experiments in naturalistic settings, viewing in everyday circumstances, limited exposure in a laboratory setting, and depictions of interpersonal aggression—as well as other variants in independent and dependent measure and design.

We find a similar pattern for video games. Experiments demonstrate causation within their constrained circumstances (Kirsh, 1998; Kirsh, Olczak & Mounts, 2005; Anderson & Murphy, 2003; Bartholow & Anderson, 2001; Ballard & Lineberger, 1999). Surveys record positive associations between violent video game play and aggressive or antisocial behavior (Bartholow, Sestir & Davis, 2005; Anderson & Dill, 2000; Gentile, Lynch, Linder & Walsh, 2004). There is some variety in the independent variables, with different games represented, and in the dependent variables, where presumed antecedents of aggressive and antisocial behavior as well as such behavior itself are represented. There are also two instances of meta-analysis (Anderson, 2004; Anderson & Bushman, 2001; Sherry, 2001), and though both recorded positive and statistically significant effect sizes, it is particularly noteworthy that the outcome was stronger in the most recent of the two because it is the most up-to-date and representative of current video games.

However, the evidence on the contribution of violent video games to aggression and antisocial behavior is much less plentiful than that for violent television and film entertainment. The inferential problem is that the quantity of consistent data is a small proportion of that for television and film. This is essentially an issue of reliability. We cannot have the same confidence that the results so far validly represent the possible universe of outcomes.

There are also the intriguing changes in the very character of violent video games. As Gentile and Anderson (2003) point out, the games divide into three distinct eras in which the display of violence and aggression vary dramatically. The Atari era, from 1977 to 1985, had games of token violence reminiscent of the perils of a board game played in front of a television set. Resemblances to the living among targets were confined to stick figures. The vanquished typically simply disappeared. Games were often won by a singular victory over a sole adversary. As Kirsch (2006) observes, the introduction of multiple assailants was considered a large step toward greater violence.

In the Nintendo era, from 1985 to 1995, violent games became much more realistic. Human characters killed and were killed. Kirsch describes "crimson blood spurting," a "torso... ripped in half" as well as "a spine... torn from the body" (p. 229). The third era, in which we still reside, was introduced by the Sony PlayStation, which quickly became the top-selling console. Games now began to feature violence that was far more graphic, explicit, realistic, and comprehensive, although the realism would vary with departures from symbols of real life for fantasy environments and characters. Targets and settings exploit male fantasies of retributive mastery, with sexually provocative females and uniformed officers of the law joining dragons and aliens as targets. These trends in visual elements have been accompanied by sound effects that reproduce the scream of artillery shells, the pummeling of the ejaculations of automatic weaponry, and the screech of rapidly moving vehicles and projectiles. The consequence is that the data from video games in the initial era of their evolution may misrepresent the effects of the violent games that children and adolescents play today. Thus, the stronger outcome posted by the most recent meta-analysis takes on particular importance in suggesting that research on earlier games underestimates the influence of current games on aggressive and antisocial behavior.

Major questions surround the degree of involvement in the narrative of the game by players. The Surgeon General's 2001 (U.S. Department of Health & Human Services) report on youth violence, which concluded television violence viewing at an earlier age was a risk factor for felony-level violence at ages 15 to 18, speculated that video games and other interactive media might have more powerful effects than television or film depictions because of the active role of the user. Video games are participatory. The player actively pursues a target or defends against attack. Rewards are earned through the accumulation of points or by victory over competing players. The 40 percent rate of indifference, embodied in the percentage of time that there is no eye contact with the screen, is replaced by constant attentiveness and decisionmaking. Thus, the observation of a violent narrative and the apprehending of violent acts, sometimes truly vicious (we have no doubt that the examples we would offer will have been surpassed by more recent offerings at the local Cineplex and convenient premium channel), in the case of video games is exchanged for participation in the imposition of violence for which the player is responsible, rewarded, and presumably enjoys, with attendant heightened levels of arousal and interest. These are largely circumstances that would seemingly amplify any influence of exposure to a violent narrative—in fact, the term "vicarious" so often applied to television and film violence (Bandura, 1988) would no longer apply.

Similar issues are raised by the varying perspectives assumed by the player. Although there are many variants, Kirsch (2006) identifies three main types. In first-person shooter games with a complex environment, the player sees events from the perspective of the character but in a varied and changing environment. Kirsch is apt:"... the game is played as though you were looking down the barrel of a gun" (p. 231). In contrast, first-person shooter games with a "rail" grid abandon the open environment for a series of staged encounters in which the point is to destroy any threat as quickly as possible. In contrast, third-person games place the player above or adjacent to the character. There is the involvement of attack and defense, but the game is played out at a comparative remove. A question yet to be addressed by research is whether these genres differ in their influence on arousal, hostile or aggressive thoughts, and imagery that might serve as antecedents of aggressive or antisocial behavior.

Video games furthermore are susceptible to differences by gender and age. We have seen that video game play is markedly more frequent among males than females (see Chapter I), which accounts for their emphases on violence and physical mastery. In turn, this raises questions about the types of games preferred by young females (most research points to puzzle-and-solution games) and the relationships that exist for young females who do play violent games in regard to motive, interest, gratifications, and effects. Age also raises intriguing questions. Young people typically go through three stages: growing interest (between about six and nine), high involvement (between about 10 and 14), and declining interest (beginning at age 15). Adult video game devotees are rare. This contrasts with television viewing where the life cycle rises throughout childhood, declines during high school (and, for some, college and graduate school) and rises to its childhood levels when young adults leave school and enter the workforce. This leads to the plausible speculation that video games effects may peak among young males in pre- and early adolescence, while for television and film violence the largest effect sizes have been recorded in the research literature for very young children and for those of college age (Paik & Comstock, 1994; Comstock & Scharrer, 1999, pp. 287–297).

These circumstances lead us to render a qualified verdict. We conclude that the evidence at present identifies violent video game play as increasing aggressive and antisocial behavior among children and adolescents. We also conclude that violent video game play fits well within the explanatory framework of the General Aggression Model (GAM) (Anderson & Dill, 2000; Anderson, Gentile & Buckley, 2007). We believe that the processes involved in the contribution of violent television and film entertainment to aggressive and antisocial behavior operate similarly in the case of violent video games. Finally, we conclude that effects are greatest among males 10 to 14 in age.

V. OTHER HYPOTHESES REGARDING MEDIA INFLUENCE

The hypothesis that exposure to violent television or film entertainment increases aggressive or antisocial behavior by far has received the most attention of any possible effect of media violence. Frequently, this hypothesis has been extended to include presumed antecedents or correlates of such behavior—for example, hostile thoughts, aggressive personality traits, or attitudes and values favorable to causing others discomfort, inconvenience, or pain. Additional hypotheses, however, have focused on mental states and their consequences, and in each case there is evidence of media influence.

Three hypotheses have received considerable attention:

1. *Fear*—the expectation that the depiction of some events by the media will incite reactions of fear or anxiety (Cantor, 2001).
2. *Desensitization*—the expectation that violent depictions in television entertainment and news will result in lower levels of excitation in response to violent events (Drabman & Thomas, 1974).
3. *Cultivation*—the expectation that the emphases of television will influence beliefs and impressions about the world at large (Gerbner, Gross, Morgan, Signorielli & Shanahan, 2002).

A. Fear

Fright responses to television and film depictions by children and teenagers have been investigated by Cantor (1998a, 2001) and colleagues (Cantor & Hoffner, 1990; Cantor & Nathanson, 1996; Cantor & Reilly, 1982). As we recorded earlier (see Chapter II), symptoms include imagined danger, free-floating anxiety, sleeplessness, bad dreams, loss of appetite, and stomach problems.

What frightens children and teenagers is dependent on stage of cognitive development. Young children are perceptually dependent. A friendly demeanor and pleasant appearance of a character will be encoded as good, whatever the secret intention or malevolent motive. A grisly, deformed creature will be encoded as threatening. Visual manifestations of conflict, risk, and endangerment override other considerations. Monsters and physical transformation—human being to monster or insect—are disturbing because the child thinks largely in terms of black-and-white and takes appearance as synonymous with character. The child viewer is unlikely to forecast that the nanny in the film is from hell, although the child characters in the film usually catch on very quickly. Perceptual dependence thus leads these young children into fright at depictions of the impossible while ignoring more realistic but subtler threats. In contrast, older children typically are less frightened by the impossible but visually compelling, and become more likely to be frightened by the improbable than the impossible. Examples are kidnappings, auto accidents, physical abuse, threats from those older or stronger, and harm to pets or parents. Cataclysms—war, earthquakes, hurricanes—are not of much significance to very young children unless depicted with graphic intensity. Older children find such events frightening because they are better able to imagine the great harm that such an event can deliver. As children grow older, perceptual dependence becomes subordinate to a wider range of expectations and inferences about people and events.

As a result, in preadolescence and the teenage years, forebodings that are bereft of visual properties but combine harm with some degree of plausibility become frightening, and visually provocative portrayals are consigned to the contemptible category of things that scare kids. Examples of such abstract threats are parental unemployment, food shortages, plagues, and the death of a parent.

However, television and film portrayals that combine stunning visual depictions with a plot that has a certain plausibility and a readily understood storyline often will be frightening to young people regardless of stage of cognitive development. A much cited and clearcut example was the movie *Jaws*. The menace of the predatory and seemingly invincible shark was clear enough to those who relied on what they observed; no subtle motives here. Nevertheless, we would expect older children and teenagers to be particularly affected because they would more often go into the water alone and would be more likely to venture into deeper waters. It is not surprising that many young people reported that this film made them anxious about visiting a beach—an effect probably repeated often for those older children and teenagers who pay attention to the news where shark attacks often become prominent.

B. Desensitization

Exposure to violent media portrayals consistently has been shown to be associated with subsequent reduced responsiveness to violent stimuli on the part of children and young college students (who would be at the end of their teenage years). Drabman and Thomas (1974) and Thomas, Horton, Lippencott, and Drabman (1977), for example, had third- and fourth-grade children view a violent or nonviolent film episode. The children were then asked to check up on the play of children elsewhere in the building by video monitor. If anything went amiss, they were to signal an adult by pressing a button. When the play of the children on the monitor became violent and they began destroying furniture, the children who had seen the violent episode were slower to press the button. Cline, Croft, and Courrier (1973) sorted children between the ages of five and 12 into two groups—those with histories of heavy and light television viewing. When shown a violent television depiction (in this case, a boxing match), those with histories of heavy viewing were less emotionally aroused as measured by physiological reactions. The authors argue plausibly that amount of viewing would serve as a proxy for exposure to greater or lesser amounts of violent entertainment.

Donnerstein, Linz, and Penrod (1987) and Linz, Donnerstein, and Adams (1989) arranged for circumstances in which college students voluntarily saw repeated but varied film depictions of violent erotica in which males imposed their sexual wills on females. The continuous exposure to violent erotica had two consequences: (a) the students became less likely to label new depictions of a similar sort as violent or pornographic, and (b) the students became more likely to assign responsibility to the female victim of a rape.

We do not argue that the evidence supports desensitization by exposure to media depictions to bloody violence witnessed in real life—such as the shooting of a colleague in the office next door. The studies we have described largely used media as the stimuli to which responsiveness was lowered by prior exposure to a violent depiction. The children in the experiments by Drabman and colleagues were asked to watch a video monitor of other children at play. Cline and colleagues physiologically measured responses to a video sequence of a boxing match. One of the effects reported by Donnerstein and colleagues was reduced labeling of violent erotica as "violent" or "pornographic." In the case of the rape victim, the students did not see the rape but were responding to what was described in trial testimony. Thus, the evidence supports desensitization to depictions and not real-life violence.

However, this distinction does not render such effects trivial. Media portrayals are the major means by which children and teenagers, as well as adults, learn about the larger world. Our pictures of reality in many cases are primarily constructions based on media depictions (Comstock & Scharrer, 2005). The events depicted often include destruction and suffering, and raise questions of justice. The role of the media in desensitizing readers and viewers to such events has been well understood by nations, which typically employ media to justify the retribution exacted on an enemy. We acknowledge stepping far beyond the boundaries of desensitization to an array of similar stimuli. Our point is that desensitization to media depictions can have important consequences for judgments about the world in which we live. Bandura (1986) has referred to this as the process of dehumanization—the substitution for attributes that might arouse sympathy of those that justify indifference. Thus, one implication of the evidence on desensitization is that the media may render readers and viewers—young and old—less sensitive to human suffering and may curtail the extension of empathy.

C. Cultivation

"Cultivation theory" has become the accepted label for a formulation developed by the late George Gerbner and colleagues (Gerbner, Gross, Morgan & Signorielli, 1980; Gerbner, Gross, Morgan, Signorielli & Shanahan, 2002; Hawkins & Pingree, 1990) in which television's primary influence is the shaping of beliefs and perceptions. Television is purposely said to "cultivate" impressions rather than change or create them to emphasize the small scale of such effects; the connotation of its synonym, "effects," is specifically avoided.

There are two fundamental assumptions. One is that television programming is quite homogeneous in its make-up—exemplified by ubiquitous violence and crime; preeminence of the white male in news, sports, and entertainment; and an overrepresentation of the middle and upper-middle classes. The corollary is that the cultivation effect will be a function of amount viewed.

Television is unique among media in this version of cultivation because of its ubiquity, reach, and large amounts of time spent viewing in many households. Other media—newspapers and magazines with comparatively narrow demographics based on age, gender, and ethnicity—may similarly shape impressions but they would do so on a much more limited basis. Thus, cultivation fundamentally is a theory of the influence of technology, for it is the technology of television that makes possible the wide and pervasive dissemination of its messages (Gerbner, 1990).

The major hypothesis advanced by cultivation theory is that the emphases of television programming will be reflected in the beliefs and perceptions of viewers as a function of amount of viewing. A typical cultivation comparison would match light and heavy viewers in regard to a belief or perception relevant to the content of programming. Morgan (1989) has catalogued a substantial number of such analyses that are consistent with the cultivation hypothesis— those classified as heavy viewers hold views that are more in accord with the emphases of programming than do those classified as light viewers. For example, heavier viewers are more likely to perceive the world occupationally and racially as resembling television casts—they overestimate those in law enforcement and health, and underestimate those who are nonwhite.

Two propositions that have been advanced in regard to violent depictions are:

- Heavier viewers will be more likely to perceive the world as risky and dangerous (often called the "mean world syndrome").
- Heavier viewers will be more likely to be fearful of becoming the victim of a crime or assault.

There is considerable empirical support for the first corollary. In surveys with large and nationally representative samples (Hughes, 1980), as well as in smaller-scale endeavors (Shanahan & Morgan, 1999), positive correlations between such pessimistic views of the social environment and amount of viewing appear consistently. Importantly, these positive correlations persist after variables are taken into account that are predictors of both viewing and such pessimistic views and thus might conflate the viewing-pessimism correlations (for example, lower socioeconomic status, senior citizen status, being black, or being female—each of which predicts greater viewing and greater pessimism).

The second has not fared as well (Hughes, 1980; Tyler, 1980, 1984). Television viewing in general (as contrasted with the occasional exposure to terrifying or frightening depictions, which has consequences specific to the content of the depictions) has proved to be unrelated to fearfulness when other, possibly conflating variables are taken into account. Hughes (1980) presents critical evidence from a large, nationally representative sample of about 2,000. The data permit the comparison of mean world and fearfulness responses with possibly contributory variables taken into account (such as socioeconomic status, age, ethnicity, and gender). Three out of four mean world items remained positively correlated with amount of viewing (and were statistically significant). In contrast, the single fearfulness item reversed direction after the entry of such variables. Scores now became smaller as amount of viewing became greater. This is the opposite of what cultivation theory predicted.

The two initial assumptions thus have held up well in regard to the mean world syndrome. Data collected and analyzed in accord with them have supported the theory. However, they do not convey the whole story. The logic behind the first assumption—television's homogeneity of content—implies that exposure to any homogeneous media content would affect beliefs and perceptions. Those who concentrate their viewing on a particular genre—action-adventure, crime, news, soap operas—by analogous reasoning would be affected by its particular emphases. This has proven to be the case (Hawkins & Pingree, 1980, 1982)—which follows logically from the initial assumptions because the effects on which cultivation focuses surely would become more intense as the emphases of the programming became sharper and the measured exposure to those emphases became more precise.

This distinction between genre-specific content and the overall homogeneity of television programming does not really challenge the initial formulation of cultivation theory. As Gerbner (1990) has pointed out, the theory concerns the ultimate impact on beliefs and perceptions of the technology of television. The evidence on specific genres simply give further support to the major hypothesis that the emphases of programming cultivate impressions.

The cultivation data so far mostly has represented adults. However, in the few instances where children or teenagers have been the population studied the same patterns have appeared (Hawkins & Pingree, 1982; Hawkins, Pingree & Adler, 1987; Pingree & Hawkins, 1981). Other data also support the view that young people are particularly likely to rely on the media when firsthand knowledge or experience are absent. For example, DeFleur and DeFleur (1967) found that children's impressions of occupations that they did not regularly encounter in everyday life were strongly influenced by television depictions of those occupations, Wrobleski and Huston (1987) found that knowledge of occupations not regularly encountered was equal to knowledge to those regularly encountered when those occupations were portrayed on television, and Ryan, Bales, and Hughes (1988) found that among teenagers from households low in socioeconomic status amount of television viewing was associated with higher expectations about obtaining a high status job (which, it will be recalled, in the lexicon of cultivation theory is one of the homogeneous emphases of television programming). These additional findings thus support the applicability of the cultivation perspective to children and teenagers.

D. Sexual Activity

There has long been speculation that media influence sexual activity among the young. Media are certainly filled with depictions of sexual behavior, talk about sex, sexual innuendoes, and narratives that deal with sexual relations—movies, television programs, music (see Chapter III). These are all media highly popular with the young, and music in particular becomes increasingly popular at the age when sex becomes a matter of interest to the young. Positive correlations between exposure to sex-related media content and sexual behavior have been reported (Brown & Newcomer, 1991; Peterson, Moore & Furstenberg, 1991), but the cross-sectional nature of the data have precluded any bravery in causal attribution. New data, however, take a large step toward three goals:

- Establishing a causal contribution to sexual behavior by exposure to the sex-related content of specific media
- Identifying specific aspects of sex-related content in specific media that influence sexual behavior
- Extending the findings for specific content and media to a wider range of media

The new data are the work of a group of researchers at the Rand Corporation. Three analyses they have presented have several strengths in common. In one, they obtained measures of the viewing of sex-related television content and sexual behavior among a sample of 1,792 adolescents 12 to 17 years of age at two points in time a year apart (Collins et al., 2004). In another, they extend their inquiry to include the influence of perceived safety in sexual practices on sexual behavior among a sample of 1,292 12- to 17-year-olds (Martino et al., 2005). In a third, they examine the influence on sexual behavior of exposure to "degrading" music lyrics among a sample of 12- to 17-year-olds from whom data were obtained at two points in time two years apart (Martino et al., 2006).

These undertakings share several assets that make them valuable as sources of information. They have very large samples that are fairly representative of the national population of the same ages. The statistical analyses are very sophisticated, and the very large number of variables whose influence is controlled for (18 in one instance) means that any surviving statistically significant link is likely to reflect the influence of one on the other. The designs encompass time order, which makes in possible to treat one variable as a cause of a change in another variable. Measurement of variables was strong for both the media and the behavior and attributes of respondents (within the limits of telephone interviews, which were employed in all three cases).

Of course, designs of this kind can never completely eliminate the possibility that some unmeasured variable is responsible for an association between two variables that is seemingly causal, because in principle the number of such variables is infinite. However, in practical terms these three analyses render such a circumstance highly unlikely. The samples and quality of measurement ensure the reliability and validity of the data, while two aspects of these designs lay a strong foundation for causal inference—the numerous control variables and the clear demarcation of time order.

These three analyses lead to an important set of findings:

1. Those who were exposed to greater amounts of sex-related content on television were more likely to engage for the first time in intercourse within the ensuing year (Collins et al., 2004).

2. Those who were exposed to greater amounts of sex-related content on television were more likely during the ensuing year to advance in noncoital activity, as measured by a scale that began with kissing and ended with oral sex (Collins et al., 2004).

3. Exposure to portrayals of sexual behavior and depictions that included sexual talk were similarly associated positively with initiation of intercourse and advancing on the scale of noncoital activity (Collins et al., 2004).

4. The positive association between exposure to sex-related television content and the initiation of intercourse was mediated by greater perceived self-efficacy in being able to engage in coitus safely (Martino et al., 2005).

5. Although the authors are certainly correct in arguing that their data do not "confirm" either perceived norms about sexual conduct or expectations of negative outcomes for sexual activity as mediating sexual activity, we endorse their view that the role of these two variables remains open (Martino et al., 2005)—because neither possibility was strongly measured.

6. Extensive exposure to music with lyrics emphasizing whores, rape, sexual acrobatics and sexual proficiency, and male sexual dominance ("degrading lyrics," as contrasted with nondegrading lyrics referencing sex and romance) was associated positively with the initiation of intercourse and advancing on the scale of noncoital behavior during the subsequent two years (Martino et al., 2006).

These outcomes reinforce three conclusions. Sexual behavior among the young is influenced by media. Media influence extends to a wide range of behavior. A variety of media can influence behavior, although context (as exemplified by degrading vs. nondegrading lyrics) remains crucial.

VI. GENERALIZABILITY FROM EXPERIMENTAL DESIGNS

We conclude that exposure to violent television and film entertainment increases the likelihood of aggressive or antisocial behavior based on the confirmation by the survey data that the everyday associations between viewing and exposure favor generalizing from the experimental designs—which permit unambiguous causal inference within their limited settings—to everyday life. We are thoroughly in accord with the recent conclusion of the eight authors (Anderson, Berkowitz, Donnerstein, Huesmann, Johnson, Linz, Malamuth & Wartella, 2003) in *Psychological Science in the Public Interest*, a journal assigned the duty of acting as an arbiter of controversial social and behavioral science, that television and film violence contributes to real-life aggressive and antisocial behavior. The evidentiary pattern we present is strengthened by the seven meta-analyses, which document that:

- The associations between viewing and behavior achieve statistical significance across a variety of studies.
- Fail safe numbers—the quantity of studies with null results that would be necessary to reduce the recorded associations to null—are generally large and often huge.
- Positive statistically significant associations have been recorded for both experimental and survey designs.
- The associations are not trivial in size, and although many are small, some are medium or even large in magnitude and they generally are as large as or larger than meta-analytic effect sizes that have been recorded for other harmful influences.
- The pattern holds for simulated aggression (questionnaires about hypothetical circumstances), interpersonal aggression (such as name-calling and fighting), and seriously harmful antisocial behavior (use of weapons, felony violence), although the meta-analytic effect sizes for the latter are smaller than for the first two.
- The association between viewing and behavior is extraordinarily robust, for it occurs as statistically significant levels in each of the seven meta-analyses despite wide variations in the operationalization of the independent and dependent variables (viewing varies from the brief exposure of experimental designs to the extended exposure of everyday television use and from violent entertainment to violent erotica; behavior varies from verbal and physical aggression to personality traits and hostile thoughts).

We believe the three theories of social cognition, neoassociationism, and excitation transfer explain these outcomes, but they are most usefully synthesized in the General Aggression Model (GAM) through three principal routes to aggressive and antisocial behavior:

- Arousal
- Affect
- Cognition

In everyday life, of course, these often combine. For example, retribution against a long-standing antagonist would be fueled by excitement over the coming conflict, dislike and possibly loathing, and explicit memories of past mistreatment.

In our adaptation of the GAM, we give a prominent place to the dimensions that summarize the many specific factors on which behavior in response to the media has been recorded as contingent:

* Efficacy
* Normativeness
* Pertinence
* Susceptibility

Whatever promotes these four circumstances—whether through direct experience, observation in real life, or experience conveyed by television, film or other media—will increase the likelihood of behavioral influence. Conversely, absence of these factors will make an effect less likely.

These principles developed to explain the effects of exposure to television and film violence on aggressive and antisocial behavior in our judgment in fact apply widely to other types of behavior. This is empirically demonstrated in the meta-analysis of Hearold (1986). When she examined the relationships between exposure to prosocial and antisocial portrayals and prosocial and antisocial behavior, she found a stunning symmetry for the studies highest in ecological validity and scientific quality:

* Exposure to prosocial portrayals was associated with higher levels of prosocial behavior and lower levels of antisocial behavior.
* Exposure to antisocial portrayals was associated with higher levels of antisocial behavior and lower levels of prosocial behavior.

Prosocial behavior included a wide range, such as generosity, empathy, and play with children of another race. Antisocial behavior was similarly wide ranging but mostly represented a display of aggression. The symmetry of outcomes thus makes a strong case for applying the principles to media in general rather than confining them to violent media.

The parallel patterns for violent portrayals, prosocial portrayals, sexual portrayals, and the robustness of the violence-and-behavior link across meta-analyses are very strong evidence for the generalizability we propose. This circumstance leads us to propose the transformation of the GAM (see Figure 6.5) into a General Behavior Model (GBM). The GBM would extend the GAM to behavior other than aggression, providing the same economy of conceptualization as the GAM with its synthesis of several lines of investigation but on a much wider front, and would encourage recognition of the commonalities that underlie many—perhaps most—modes of behaving.

Further support for generalizability comes from two sources. One is social cognition, which has been developed into a general theory of socialization and individual coping within a social framework by Bandura (1986). The other is the health belief model (Becker, 1974; Becker & Maiman, 1975), which bases a theory for changing individual health practices using the media and other interventions on these same principles. In each of these two cases, there is a theory of behavior with a good, empirically confirmed record of predicting media influence on a range of behavior. Thus, they enhance our confidence that the evidence on the behavioral effects of television and film violence applies to other types of behavior in addition to aggressive and antisocial behavior. However, the Hearold data has the advantage of demonstrating concretely and concisely that behavioral effects of television and film media are similar across vastly different genres of content. Indeed, a recent extension of Hearold's work, in the form of a meta-analysis conducted by Mares and Woodard (2005), demonstrated positive behavioral effects of consumption of prosocial television on stereotype reduction, aggression diminishment, display of altruism, and participation in peaceful, cooperative play among children. The analysis of 34 experiments and surveys found effects were strongest for televised depictions of altruism, which is likely explained by the more explicit modeling of this type of behavior in children's programming, thereby once again demonstrating the concepts of the GBM. Finally, in accord with Hearold, Mares and Woodard found self-selected exposure to prosocial content was just as likely to produce a positive effect on children as self-selected exposure to antisocial content was to produce a negative effect. They conclude, "the results suggest that television is no more prone to fostering violence than it is to fostering prosocial behavior" (p. 316).

Video games when violent have been recorded as having effects similar to those of violent television and film entertainment. However, questions remain about the possibility that effects are stronger or more powerful—that is, larger, more widespread among users, and conceivably more serious in outcome—because of three factors that apply particularly to video games: (a) the actual participation in violent events, (b) the greater psychological and physical involvement, and (c) the higher degree of graphic, hurtful violence and bodily harm. All three would seemingly facilitate aggression-related arousal, affect, and cognition. There is also a possibility that effects may differ with game genre, which vary in the degree that the player participates, is involved, and executes graphic bodily harm.

Three other hypotheses have also received empirical support:

- Children and teenagers are sometimes seriously frightened by television and film portrayals, and these reactions sometimes have unpleasant symptoms and sometimes are long lasting. What frightens young people depends on cognitive stage; as children grow older visual elements that sometimes involve the impossible become subordinate to more realistic and sometimes abstract threats.
- Desensitization by the media affects responsiveness to future depictions. The implication for news coverage of human suffering is a constraint on sympathy and empathy, and general indifference.
- The emphases of television programming cultivate beliefs and perceptions, and these lead to distorted impressions of the world. One consequence is the mean world syndrome; another is taking the demographics of television shows as representative of the general population.

We return to our theme of generalizability. The empirical evidence in regard to aggressive and antisocial behavior largely has reflected the effects of violent entertainment. Sports has made only a rare appearance. The outcomes in regard to fear, desensitization, and cultivation, however, also encompass news. Our view is that the principles developed apply to media in general—entertainment, sports, and news. Differences in effect should not be thought of as a property of a genre of content or a medium. Effects should be construed as the consequences of the attributes of the portrayal (which obviously may vary systematically with genre and medium)—efficacy, normativeness, and pertinence, and the degree to which the depiction exploits the susceptibility or motives of the reader or viewer.

LEARNING RULES AND NORMS—FURTHER VII EVIDENCE OF MEDIA EFFECTS

The people appearing on television and in other media demonstrate the ways of the world to children and teenagers. They do so by the ways they dress, speak, behave, express attitudes and emotions, and interact with others. The implicit subject matter is the norms, values, and expectations of our society. These impressions, costumed as entertainment, sports, information, and news, will guide the performance and affect the success of viewers and readers.

Children and adolescents are uniquely vulnerable to the media as agents of socialization. Ideas about social roles and cultural norms are in flux. So, too, is identity—the sense of personal positioning within those roles and norms. Firsthand knowledge is circumscribed by age and limited experience. The media inevitably become an important source of information and understanding about circumstances beyond the boundary of the life lived by the individual.

The media obviously are not the sole socializing influence experienced by children and adolescents. Parents and caregivers, teachers and other prominent adults, siblings and peers, and clubs and organizations—including the religious, social service, and leisure-oriented— also provide young people with cues they may use to navigate the social world. This socialization can be direct, such as when a parent endorses gender expectations by admonishing his or her son, "Boys don't cry." It can also be indirect, through the mere modeling of ways of behaving. This is exemplified by friends and classmates demonstrating the "right" way to dress in junior high. Agents of socialization of course also intersect in their shaping of the conceptualizations and

250

orientations of the child (Klapper, 1978). Nonetheless, we focus on the contributions of television and other media. Following is a rationale for our media-centric approach (Comstock & Scharrer, 2004):

> We believe that the media are powerful agents of socialization for many for three major and interrelated reasons. First, the media have an unparalleled ability to disseminate information about the culture, and especially information that can be expressed in the narratives of news, sports, and storytelling. Second, individuals typically spend a considerable amount of time attending to the narratives of the media. Third, there is discernible homogeneity in many of the media's stories, which results in a degree of consistency in what individual audience members can learn about the social environment. Just as direct learning can occur from media exposure—for example, preschoolers can learn the alphabet by watching *Sesame Street* and adults can learn names of world leaders from watching the news—media audience members can also be taught more indirectly about cultural values and social roles. (p. 243)

Many scholars have construed television's role in socialization as experienced by the individual as subtle, not easily articulated, and often occurring at an essentially unconscious level. Yet, there is evidence that children and adolescents are cognizant of the presence of values and norms in television programming (Tan, Nelson, Dong & Tan, 1997; Thompson & Zerbinos, 1997). For example, Tan and colleagues (1997) found in a sample of over 400 15- to 18-year-olds that recognition of values conveyed on television was associated with acceptance of many of those values, and particularly so if the values were deemed instrumental to success.

I. ROLES AND NORMS AS INFLUENCED BY MEDIA

As we have seen in other chapters of this book, consumer, scholastic, and aggressive behaviors are learned in large part through media consumption. We now extend this argument to a broader canvas, examining the media's role in socializing children and teens in the topics of citizenship and politics, gender roles, career expectations and desires, fashion brands, and physical presence.

A. Politics

Studies have found that many young people adopt the political party affiliation of their parents, and particularly so if politics are important to parents and adolescents accurately perceive their parents' dispositions (Hess & Torney, 1967; Hyman, 1959; Tedin, 1974). Becoming a Democrat, Republican or Independent in large part because of one's family's allegiance remains a common experience (Calavita, 2004; Comstock & Scharrer, 2005). Yet, the influence of parents and family members on political socialization does not preclude media influence. When examining the party affiliation and political opinions and dispositions of young persons, media join such factors as parent-child interaction and civic education as contributing forces (Atkin, 1981; Comstock & Scharrer, 2005; McLeod, Eveland & Horowitz, 1998; Smith & Ferguson, 1990). Moreover, a number of studies have found that media use makes conversations between and among family members about politics more likely, so that media are a means for the exercise as well as occasionally a modifier of family influence (Atkin & Gantz, 1978; Chaffee & Yang, 1990; Hawkins, Pingree & Roberts, 1975; Jackson-Beeck, 1979).

As it does in adults, media use has long been found to contribute to political knowledge in children and teens, as evidenced in samples of young people that vary in age from 9 to 17 (Atkin, 1978; Chaffee, Ward & Tipton, 1973; Drew & Reese, 1984; Drew & Reeves, 1980; Garramone, 1983; Rubin, 1978). Thus, young people learn about political figures, issues, and elections by attending to media. That knowledge then facilitates political and civic engagement and participation.

Eveland, McLeod, and Horowitz (1998) examined the role of age in acquisition of political knowledge. Their expectation was that cognitive changes experienced as children mature would lead to progressively more fruitful conversations with parents, teachers, and others about politics as well as an increased ability to integrate new information with past political knowledge. Nearly 300 children in the fifth through the twelfth grade and their parents in San Jose, California provided the data. Four of six mass and interpersonal communication variables interacted with age to predict political knowledge. Political discussions, newspaper reading, attention to campaign news, and reflection on campaign information increased political knowledge more strongly for older respondents than younger.

In a more recent study, Pasek and colleagues (Pasek, Kenski, Romer & Hall Jamieson, 2006) find not just news media but entertainment media are associated with participation in extracurricular activities and community service in a nationally representative sample of over 1,500 14- to 22-year-olds. Going to the movies, watching television programs, reading books, and reading magazines joined using the Internet to obtain information, watching television news, and listening to the news on the radio in significant, positive correlations with such participation. Heavy viewers of television, however—particularly those watching more than eight hours per day—operated as outliers, reporting less frequent participation in extracurricular and civic activity than light viewers. Entertainment media consumption was largely a negative predictor of political awareness, however, with movie going and television viewing associated with scoring poorly on a test of key figures and functions of government (e.g., "What office does Dick Cheney hold?"). Information media consumption, on the other hand, was a positive predictor of such awareness. We conclude that news media use among young people certainly facilitates civic participation and political awareness, whereas entertainment media (except for very heavy television consumption) can stimulate the former and not the latter.

1. Autonomy in the Development of Political Dispositions   Lest we consider socialization a purely passive process, there is recent evidence of considerable autonomy in the development of political dispositions among young people in that adolescents are actively engaged in developing their political identities (Kiousis, McDevitt & Wu, 2005; McDevitt & Chaffee, 2002; Niemi & Hepburn, 1995). McDevitt and Chaffee (2002), on the basis of data from those taking civics classes, conclude that once interest in politics is sparked adolescents can act as socialization agents themselves, bringing their newly defined views back to the family dinner table. Political scientists have noted that the civics curriculum in high schools has changed over the years, giving greater emphasis to civic responsibilities and participation, and contemporary research should take the potential influence of participation in that curriculum into account (Niemi & Hepburn, 1995; Sigel, 1995). Thus, civics instruction becomes newly legitimate for research on the sources of political involvement.

Evidence for a substantial degree of autonomy includes the lack of consistently large correlations between the political views of parents and children, the growing parental perception that adolescents possess expertise on some public issues, the increasingly nonfixed and shifting nature of the political views of many adults, and the complexity of influence apparent when the research focus is the family rather than the individual (McDevitt & Chaffee, 2002). During adolescence, changes in young people's political knowledge and attitudes generally outpace changes in their parents' political knowledge and attitudes (Niemi & Hepburn, 1995), supporting the view that the young person is not always simply on the receiving end of parental perspectives. If political socialization is expanded to encompass not just the development of knowledge, skills, and attitudes toward electoral politics, but also attitudes and knowledge about issues of social justice, public policy, and civic responsibility, the partial autonomy and agency of the adolescent becomes clear (Flanagan & Gallay, 1995).

2. School   The relationship between a school-based intervention and media influence on adolescents' partisan and ideological development has been examined in regard to the in-school curriculum, "Kids Voting." McDevitt and Chaffee (2000) found the intervention, run by a nonpartisan organization to promote civic engagement, led to greater newspaper and television news use among students in San Jose, California. In a subsequent study, Kiousis, McDevitt, and Wu (2005) determined that participation in the intervention triggered both news media use and discussion with parents and peers among eleventh and twelfth grade students in three communities: Maricopa County, Arizona; El Paso County, Colorado; and Broward/Palm Beach counties, Florida. The analysis by Kiousis and colleagues also found support for an agenda setting function (McCombs & Shaw, 1972) in political socialization. News media use by the students increased issue salience, which, in turn, was associated with greater strength of political opinions. The authors found further that:

> . . . though news media attention is important for predicting issue salience and opinion strength, it does not have a bearing on political ideology, directly, but has indirect influence. Discussion with parents, on the other hand, does directly shape both political ideology and partisanship, but peer discussion does not. (p. 771)

We draw attention to the path analysis of Kiousis and colleagues (see Figure 7.1). Numerous factors have a role. The socializing influence of the parent is acutely felt in the formation of party allegiance; peers have no persistent influence; and, media influence in this case is indirect. We conclude that the adolescent exercises considerable autonomy in his or her political development, both mass and interpersonal communication play a part, and school-based civics curricula can serve as an instrumental triggering mechanism.

3. Participation in the Political Process   Compared to their predecessors, today's young people nevertheless express lower levels of social trust (Brehm & Rahn, 1997; Putnam, 1995) and higher levels of cynicism about politics (Lau & Erber, 1985), and also display lower tendencies to vote (Delli Carpini, 1986; Miller, 1991), and more modest stores of political knowledge (Delli Carpini & Keeter, 1996). One potential culprit is negative political advertising, which has become increasingly common in recent campaigns (Comstock & Scharrer, 1999, 2005; Finkel & Geer, 1998), and has been accused of nurturing alienation (Capella & Jamieson, 1997). The argument is that the negativity and corresponding perceptions of backstabbing and corruption in modern politics have turned off the nation's younger citizens. Some empirical support comes from an experiment by Rahn and Hirshorn (1999). Children exposed to negative political advertising were more likely to report sad thoughts (rather than happy) when asked to think about America; in addition, among those low in self-efficacy, declared interest in voting was lowered.

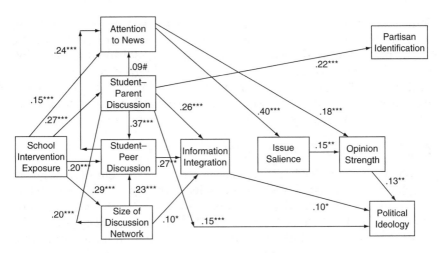

Fig. 7.1 Path model of school, media, and interpersonal influences on the political socialization of adolescents. Adapted from Kiousis, S., McDevitt, M., & Wu, X. (2005). The genesis of civic awareness: Agenda setting in political socialization. *Journal of Communication, 55*(4), 756–774.

Austin and Pinkleton (2001) enlarged the focus to parents as a means of promoting negative dispositions. The path from parental skepticism about media to discussions about politics with children traveled through news media use. They surveyed a randomly drawn sample of parents of children aged two to 17 in Washington state to examine the relationships between parents' media use, parents' levels of skepticism about advertising (in general, not just political advertising), parents' positive or negative mediation of the news media (again, in general), and their discussion with children about politics. Positive mediation entailed discussion that affirmed the media message; in negative mediation, the media message was challenged, questioned, or critiqued by the coviewing parent. Parents' skepticism about media predicted the frequency with which they engage in negative mediation. Conversely, lack of skepticism predicted positive mediation. Negative mediation predicted frequency of political discussion. None of the other key variables had a direct impact on political discussion—skepticism, television news exposure, coviewing, or positive mediation.

Whether critical discussion about politics facilitates or impedes participation centers on whether skepticism or cynicism results. Cynicism, characterized as distrust or lack of confidence that results in dampening one's desire to seek out additional information or discussion, impedes political participation (Capella & Jamieson, 1997). Skepticism, on the other hand, can include "genuine concerns regarding public affairs processes" and encourages a "search for additional information to validate or invalidate information already received" (Austin & Pinkleton, 2001, p. 225) thereby facilitating participation. The data of Austin and Pinkleton (2001) suggest a positive utility for parental skepticism in promoting discussions with young people about politics.

B. The Impact of Gender Differences

At about the age at which they enter kindergarten, children begin to develop gender constancy, or the knowledge that gender is not based on transitory or circumstantial factors such as dress or hair length (Kohlberg, 1966; Ruble, Balaban & Cooper, 1981). When the concept of gender constancy is new, children become very interested in information that is relevant to the rules and norms that govern the establishment of "appropriate" behaviors for members of their gender (Calvert, 2000; Slaby & Frey, 1975). Like other socializing forces, the role of television in individuals' learning about gender thus varies as a function of age. At the beginning of the stage of gender constancy, children are particularly vulnerable to effects of gender stereotypes on television (Bigler & Liben, 1992; Ruble et al., 1981). Such effects dissipate but do not disappear as the child matures and increasingly is able to engage in complex and flexible thought (Bigler & Liben, 1992; Ruble et al., 1981).

Parents, peers, school, and media exert overlapping and important influence on the development of gender identity and gender-related attitudes and perceptions in children. Witt (2000) summarizes those major spheres of influence on the child:

> Parents have an impact on their children's gender-role identity in many ways. Through day-to-day interactions, by acting as role models, by reinforcing the larger messages of society, and by offering approval or disapproval of the child's actions and behaviors, parents express their own values and thus exert much influence on how children view the roles of males and females. The impact of the media on children has been much discussed in recent years. From thousands of hours of viewing television, watching movies, and reading print, children receive messages about gender roles from yet another influential source. As children enter school, the input of teachers and the school curriculum regarding gender roles cannot be overlooked. Finally, as children develop friendships with both same-sex and opposite-sex peers, they continue to develop new ideas and receive reinforcement of previously learned ideas. (p. 1)

We give most of our attention to television because its ubiquity bestows an unparalleled ability as a socializing agent. Unsurprisingly, the majority of media research on socialization has focused on its role. We also divide our treatment into three distinct areas: politics, roles, and occupations.

1. Gender Differences in Politics   Girls and young women typically show reluctance compared to boys and men to exhibit and act upon political knowledge (Huston, 1985; Niemi & Junn, 1998; Owen & Dennis, 1988). Smith-Lovin and Robinson (1992) have explained the phenomenon as occurring because "socialization and peer group interaction lead boys and girls to develop gender identities with rather different values on status, power, and expressivity" (p. 133).

The tension between normative gender roles for girls and leadership behavior contributes to the discouragement of girls and women to participate in politics (Jennings & Niemi, 1974). The present political system appears to reward traits and roles more often taught to boys and men than girls and women. These include an aggressive and controlling leadership style above a collaborative and consensus-oriented approach (Eagly & Johnson, 1990; Kathlene, 1995; Rosenthal, 1998). An analysis of a common opportunity for adolescents to participate in a political process, the Model UN, has found female participants contribute with much less frequency and are considerably more dissatisfied with the experience compared to male participants (Rosenthal, Rosenthal & Jones, 2001). Thus, girls often receive a message early on that politics tends to be dominated both by males and by traits and ways of interacting associated with males. As a result, they may feel disinclined to participate, or become disenchanted when they do.

In addition to the potential of gender role socialization to curtail young women's interest and participation in politics, there is also evidence that it can direct their interest and participation toward one particular political party. There has been, beginning in the 1980s, an increased identification on the part of women with the Democratic Party (Roper Center, 1996; Trevor, 1999). This pattern exemplifies the imperfect transmission of political party identification from parent to offspring.

Trevor (1999) argues that gender role socialization combines with political socialization to help explain women's greater affinity for the Democratic Party. Girls are taught to be compassionate and to work collaboratively to help others in need. These ideals typically are espoused more strongly by Democrats than Republicans. The Democratic Party places stronger emphasis on issues directly impacting women, such as abortion rights. Furthermore, there is the possibility that girls are more likely to adhere to the party allegiance of parents because they are given less latitude to question parental authority and assert independence than boys and because they are likely to spend more time in the vicinity of parents during early and middle adolescence (Gilligan, 1982). This socialization differential would slightly favor the Democratic Party because of the higher Democratic voter registration.

We agree with Trevor that the processes of political and gender socialization complement each other. We would add media as a factor that exemplifies the intersection. The gender-role depictions of entertainment media for the most part promote conceptualizations of girls and women as nurturing, peace loving, cooperative, and conflict avoiding. Each has implications for political party affiliation and manner of political participation. We would also suggest that media depictions of politics in entertainment and news often depict politics as largely the domain of men—a depiction that certainly reflects but also contributes to the continued preeminence of males in American electoral politics. Recent exceptions both real (e.g., news coverage of high-powered women such as Condoleezza Rice) and fictional (e.g., Geena Davis as president in the television program, *Commander in Chief*) are in contrast to the overall pattern.

2. Gender-biased Roles We begin with the earliest scholarly inquiries into the effects of television on young people's conceptualizations of gender, highlighting the contributions of early experiments and surveys. The experiments establish the ability of short-term exposure to shape or evoke attitudes and conceptions that correspond to the gender-related messages of the television content. The surveys attempt to examine the influence of long-term, cumulative exposure in contributing to gender role conceptualizations. We next address two key areas: children's selections of particular content and the role of those selections in media effects, and the ability of parents to mitigate the effects of stereotypical content by taking a critical stance.

a. Early Research Beginning in the mid-1970s, researchers began to explore the potential of television to contribute to conceptions of "proper" and "improper" roles, traits, and activities assumed by males and females. Early experiments found television can teach both stereotypical and counter-stereotypical attitudes (Davidson, Yasuna & Tower, 1979; Eisenstock, 1984; McArthur & Eisen, 1976; Pingree, 1978). Counter-stereotypes are those that depict women or men engaging in behavior, occupations, or the display of traits or other roles that are contrary to expectation. Examples would include female characters portrayed as physically aggressive, male characters depicted as emotionally sensitive, or either gender presented in a career that has traditionally been primarily occupied by members of the opposite sex. These early studies quickly and convincingly established that exposure to a televised depiction that runs counter to traditional gender role expectations can encourage more flexible gender-role orientations on the part of children (Atkin & Miller, 1975; Eisenstock, 1984; McArthur & Eisen, 1976).

The ability of television exposure to influence not just gender-related attitudes but also gender-related behavior was also confirmed more that two decades ago. Cobb, Stevens-Long, and Goldstein (1982), for example, found that four- to six-year-olds who had been shown videotapes in which the characters' words and actions assigned masculinity, femininity, or gender-neutrality to a set of neutral toys were more likely to choose toys that had been described as appropriate for their gender during free play. McArthur and Eisen (1976) found that the tendency of young audience members to model characters of the same sex was so robust among a sample of preschoolers it overrode preconceptions. Both boys and girls were more likely to imitate behavior they had seen performed by characters of their same gender during free play regardless of whether they were traditionally "masculine" or "feminine."

The early studies remind us that perceptions of gender and gender identity are typically rather strong guiding forces in early and middle childhood, and many youngsters behave in rather strict allegiance to what they perceive as normative gender roles. The direction of the television influence toward or away from gender stereotypes, however, depends on the presence of same-sex characters and their modeling of particular attitudes and behavior. Depictions featuring gender stereotypes can have a narrowing effect; those featuring portrayals that defy stereotypes can have a liberating effect. A key governing principle is the tendency for both boys and girls to look toward television characters of their same gender for guidance. Young audience members both male and female identify more strongly with a television character of their same gender; this has been a long-standing and consistent research finding (Comstock, 1991; Comstock & Scharrer, 1999).

Yet, because so much of television content, and especially children's television content, is narrow and even stereotypical in terms of gender portrayals (see Chapter III), surveys that measure overall amount of time spent with television have long found television use to be positively correlated with traditional views of males and females (Freuh & McGhee, 1975; Gross & Jeffries-Fox, 1978; Morgan, 1982; Rothschild, 1984). Morgan (1982), for example, found prior television viewing was positively related to higher scores on sexism measures two years later among girls (but not boys) in the sixth through eighth grade. Those measures included whether mothers or fathers should be employed full time, whether men have the most drive and ambition, whether women are happiest at home with children or are interested in jobs outside the home, and whether society discriminates against women. The reverse explanation (that higher sexism scores led to greater television use) was ruled out in the longitudinal data for the girls, but found support among the boys. Katz and Boswell (1986) compared the strength of influence from parents, peers, and media on the gender-role dispositions of kindergartners and third graders (measuring toy preference, current activities, tolerance for nontraditional behavior in others, and plans for future careers), and found peers and media exerted a stronger impact than parents. The media's influence was felt most intensely when respondents were asked about their intended occupations.

Thus, early and continuing research in this topic area established that television has the potential to reinforce or challenge traditional views of gender roles depending on its content. Most often it achieves the former, since content is skewed toward traditional and stereotypical roles. Although counter-stereotypical portrayals have been shown often to have a liberalizing effect some studies indicate that these portrayals may be misconstrued by the viewer or quickly forgotten (Bigler & Liben, 1990; Calvert & Huston, 1987; Drabman et al., 1981). Drabman and colleagues (1981), for example, found that a substantial proportion of children (in preschool, first, and fourth grade) who were shown a portrayal featuring a man as a nurse and a woman as a doctor later recalled that they had seen the reverse (male doctor and female nurse). The implication is that gender stereotypes are so pervasive and compelling that children are often ill-equipped to process portrayals that fly in the face of convention.

b. Mediation   The ability of teachers, parents, caregivers, or other adults to mediate the effects of television on children has also been examined in the literature. Mediation refers to comments by parents or caregivers while coviewing television with one or more children. Often it has been used to refer to criticism or evaluative comments. However, the parental reactions to what's on the screen can also reinforce portrayals by expressing approval or displaying great interest (Comstock, 1991). Multiple television sets—which have become the norm with more than three-fourths of households having two or more sets (see Chapter I)—decrease family viewing and increase independent viewing by age cohorts. The comparable figure for 1970 would have been less than half that.

The resulting decline in coviewing by young persons and adults has implications for the effects of television (Austin, Roberts & Nass, 1990; Buerkel-Rothfuss, Greenberg, Atkin & Nuendorf, 1982; Desmond, Hirsch,

Singer & Singer, 1987; Desmond, Singer, Singer, Calam & Colimore, 1985; Messaris, 1983; Messaris & Sarett, 1981; Stoneman & Brody, 1983a). What parents or other older persons say and do about what has been viewed can affect how a young person responds cognitively and affectively. One particular early study found conversations during and about viewing were frequent, with one-half of a national sample of adults reporting that half of the exchanges during viewing were about television, and one-fifth saying that they talked about television after viewing (LoSciuto, 1972). If the content of conversations paralleled that of thoughts occurring during viewing, the majority concerned television as a medium in some way (Neuman, 1982)—the quality of the programs, the plots, and the actors. These conversations are not entirely trivial for the young viewer, because they constitute informal education in regard to taste and judgment in the arts, entertainment, news, and sports.

However, conversations of two kinds have a special claim to importance: those that deal with the reality of what is portrayed, and those that deal with the rightness or wrongness of the portrayed behavior. In these cases, adult viewers may set limits on, mitigate, eliminate, or give direction to any influence that television may have. This mediation arguably extends beyond the cognitive and affective to the behavioral. It also seems to vary somewhat by type of program, with children interacting with each other and with parents least during cartoons; parents concerned about particular specimens thus will have to exert themselves.

The evidence has long suggested that parental mediation—when it employs critical discussions and interpretations of what is depicted and sets some guidelines on television use—can increase the understanding of television, improve judgments about reality and fantasy, and reduce total viewing. Desmond, Singer, and Singer (1990), based on a two-year study of 91 children who at the beginning were in kindergarten or the first grade, and a third-grade follow-up of the 29 who were the heaviest viewers, reach precisely these conclusions. As Buerkel-Rothfuss and colleagues (1982) said about their inquiry into the influence of television and parental mediation on the beliefs about families of about 650 fourth-, sixth-, and eighth-grade children:

> In particular, it appears that parents' positive intervention, such as their guiding their children toward family shows, viewing with them, commenting on show content, and maintaining control over the amount of viewing, can enhance what children learn about affiliative behavior from viewing family television shows.... Given the influential nature of parental comments, parents who discuss the reality and utility of such programs with their children could additionally influence the amount and kind of their children's learning from television. (p. 200)

Coviewing with one or more parents is not by itself the answer, because Dorr, Kovaric, and Doubleday (1989) found, among almost 400 second, sixth, and tenth graders, that such practice mostly reflected common habits and preferences and only modestly predicted any kind of parental mediation or conversational involvement. Parental mediation also is not invariably beneficial. As Desmond, Singer, and Singer (1990) point out, parents can also draw attention to, give implicit or explicit approval to, and in general endorse antisocial and violent portrayals, unwise or dangerous behavior, or commercials questionable in merit.

Decades ago, Corder-Bolz (1980) found that active mediation led to heightened effects of counter-stereotypical content on children, enabling children to become more accepting of reverse-stereotypical roles compared to children who had seen the same program but not received the mediation.

Nathanson, Wilson, McGee, and Sebastian (2002) found that among 83 children in kindergarten through sixth grade, a mediation that involved providing information that contradicted the gender stereotype advanced in a television program led to less favorable judgments of stereotyped characters, more negative evaluations of the program among those without close monitoring of viewing at home, and less acceptance of stereotyped attitudes. We conclude that concerned parents and caregivers can speak up while coviewing with children and can use narrow portrayals to exert an influence that defies stereotypes.

c. Media Preferences   One way that contemporary research has advanced what we know is by taking into account children's media preferences. The hypothesis has been that individual differences lead children to select particular types of content that, in turn, will be associated with gender-related attitudes and behavior. We draw attention to three recent studies.

Aubrey and Harrison (2004) used content analysis to identify stereotypical, counter-stereotypical, or neutral messages about gender roles in the favorite programs of children. Among boys (but not girls) in first and second grade, preference for programs that stereotype males predicted assigning greater value to two of four traditionally male-oriented traits—the importance of being good at telling jokes and of working hard. Preference among boys for programs that depict females counter-stereotypically was associated with the same two dispositions—but negatively with joke telling and positively with working hard. Preference among boys for programs that run counter to male stereotypes negatively predicted the value of being hard working. Among the girls, no program preferences of any type predicted importance assigned to any of the eight traits examined (four "masculine" and four "feminine"). However, such preferences did predict attraction to the characters in the programs. Preference for female counter-stereotypical and gender-neutral programs was a positive predictor of affinity for female characters among the girls.

We conclude that among young children, the gender-related associations with television preferences (as measured by the value assigned to particular traits) were considerably stronger for boys than girls. Among the boys, the direction of the association depended on the stereotypical or counter-stereotypical thrust of the program. Girls, in contrast, did not exhibit the gender-related associations in regard to traits but did demonstrate an appreciation for portrayals counter to gender stereotypes.

We would not conclude that survey data of this sort documents a causal connection between preferred programs and gender-related dispositions. It is equally plausible that those with particular dispositions find certain programs especially attractive. However, these data do document that preferences align with predispositions, and the result may be reinforcement of stereotypic attitudes.

Calvert and colleagues (Calvert, Kotler, Zehnder & Shockey, 2003) invited more than 300 children in second through sixth grade to report on educational and informational programs that they had seen. They sought evidence of gender stereotyping in characters discussed, pronouns employed, and traits and actions emphasized. The children discussed more male characters and used more male pronouns than female. Boys and girls did not differ in the number of male characters they mentioned or male pronouns they employed, but girls mentioned more female characters and used more female pronouns than boys. Male characters were perceived as primarily engaged in traditionally masculine behavior, whereas female characters were seen as performing both traditionally masculine and traditionally feminine behavior.

The data of Calvert and colleagues (2003) joins earlier research in concluding that although both boys and girls prefer programs with characters of their own gender, girls tend to be less closely tied to same-gender portrayals and often demonstrate more flexibility in gender role conceptions (Beal, 1994; Goldstein, 1994; Luecke-Aleksa, Anderson, Collins & Schmitt, 1995; Ruble & Martin, 1998; Singer & Singer, 1990; Turner, Gervai & Hinde, 1993). In both the Aubrey and Harrison (2004) and Calvert and colleagues (2003) data, boys were more likely to experience a traditional gender role reinforcing association with television than girls. Finally, the Calvert and colleagues (2003) data demonstrate that even those programs designated as educational and informational are processed through a gendered interpretation by many children.

Knobloch and colleagues (Knobloch, Callison, Chen, Fritzsche & Zillmann, 2005) conducted a cross-cultural study to examine the role of children's selective exposure in "self-socializing" aggressive and other gender-typed roles. Four- to six-year-olds in the United States, China, and Germany were given videos from which to choose, and the videos' covers differed according to sex of the protagonist and whether aggressiveness or peacefulness and nurturing were emphasized. Across each of the three countries, boys exhibited a preference for aggressive themes, and girls for peaceful and nurturing themes. However (as we would now anticipate given their greater flexibility and lower rigidity), the preference of the girls toward gender typical content was less strong than for the boys (see Figure 7.2, top). Also across the three settings, both boys and girls expressed a preference for protagonists of their own sex, a tendency that increased with the age of the child, which suggests the impact of gender socialization increases over time (see Figure 7.2, bottom). Contrary to expectations based on previous work in which boys tended to be governed by gender preferences more so than girls, the girls in this study from China and the United States (but not from Germany) exhibited a stronger same-sex protagonist preference than

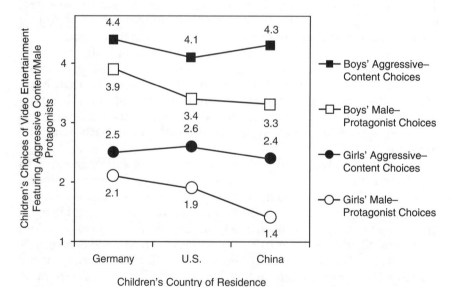

Fig. 7.2   Preference for video depicting aggressive content vs. peaceful content and choice of a male protagonist as well as preference for video featuring a protagonist of the same sex as the respondent, by gender and country. Adapted from Knobloch, S., Callison, C., Chen, L., Fritzsche, A., & Zillmann, D. (2005). Children's sex-stereotyped self-socialization through selective exposure to entertainment: Cross-cultural experiments in Germany, China, and the United States. *Journal of Communication, 55*(1), 122–138.

the boys. The authors conclude: "Undoubtedly, children choose media content in gender-stereotyped ways and thus clearly reinforce media socialization to this effect" (Knobloch et al., 2005, p. 135).

This third contemporary study by Knobloch and colleagues (2005) aligns with the previous two (Aubrey & Harrison, 2004; Calvert et al., 2003) in finding that boys express preference for media content that represents traditional gender roles for males (in this case, aggression) more than girls do for content that represents traditional gender roles for females (in this case, nurturing and peace). In this third study, however, it was the preschool-aged girls rather than the boys in two of the three countries examined (the United States and China) who were more likely to choose a same-sex protagonist, a difference from past research that could be attributed to cultural norms, the young age of the research participants, or the specific task to which they were assigned (choosing a videotape based on the cover). Nonetheless, each of the three recent studies firmly establishes the role of media selection and content preferences among children in subsequent gender-role socialization effects.

3. Gender Bias in Occupational Roles   A number of studies examine specifically the ability of television to contribute to views of career paths and options. Occupational roles are considered strong indicators of gender-related beliefs, as they tap into both desires (e.g., "What do you want to be when you grow up?") and global perceptions of skills (e.g., females are good nurses because they are compassionate; males should be scientists because they are decisive and stern).

a. Early Research   The earliest research traces back to the 1970s. Beuf (1974) found that three- to six-year-olds who were considered heavy television viewers were more likely than lighter viewers to espouse stereotypical views of occupational roles and opportunities. Stereotypes in the occupations performed by television characters have consistently been determined to be especially prominent in television content (Herrett-Skjellum & Allen, 1996; Levinson, 1975; Vande Berg & Streckfuss, 1992). Subsequent effects studies have found that such depictions have implications for children's beliefs about occupational roles (Kimball, 1986; O'Bryant & Corder-Bolz, 1978; Wrobleski & Huston, 1987). Wrobleski and Huston (1987), for example, studied questionnaire responses of 65 fifth and sixth graders and found that although the youngsters acknowledged television occupations as being more stereotyped by gender than real-life occupations, girls with greater exposure to gender-stereotyped television programming and less frequent exposure to counter-stereotypical programming were more likely to aspire to a female-stereotypical occupation.

Other early experiments documented that televised depictions of women in occupations traditionally dominated by men could destabilize children's ideas about gender-appropriateness (Atkin & Miller, 1975; Johnson & Ettema, 1982; O'Bryant & Corder-Bolz, 1978; Pingree, 1978). For example, O'Bryant and Corder-Bolz (1978) found that not only did girls' views of the appropriateness of particular occupations for males and females change, but the female subjects also became more likely to state a reverse-type career preference for themselves.

Johnston and Ettema (1982) conducted a large-scale evaluation involving hundreds of children across the country of a PBS television series called *Freestyle* that was designed to challenge stereotypical views of occupations among nine- to 12-year-old boys and girls. For example, the "Grease Monkey" episode depicted a young female becoming an auto mechanic, and "Helping Hands" portrayed a young male nurturing a non-English speaking peer. The data documented that watching the programs reduced stereotypes. However, there were two important qualifications. First, effects occurred primarily among those who engaged in extensive discussion of the programs as part of the school curriculum. Second, effects were largely confined to what the boys and girls thought were appropriate for others rather than themselves. These are common outcomes when the effectiveness of mass media is evaluated—reinforcement and clarification of the message facilitates attitude change, and change is usually greater for general principles than one's own behavior.

Eisenstock (1984) also used *Freestyle* as an experimental treatment and employed the Bem Sex Role Inventory to measure the preexisting gender ideologies of a sample of over 200 fourth through sixth graders. Those classified as having either androgynous or traditionally feminine personalities identified more strongly than those with more masculine personalities with the counter-stereotypical characters in *Freestyle*. Thus, the effectiveness of a counter-stereotypical portrayal may rest on the predispositions of those in the audience.

b. Recent Additions More recently, Thompson and Zerbinos (1997) conducted interviews with 89 children from four to nine years of age about their perceptions of cartoon characters and their occupational preferences. When asked to describe what "boy characters" and "girl characters" are like, the children responded with many gender-specific behaviors. Male characters used violence more often or engaged in silly or amusing behavior. Female characters were more often concerned with appearance or family-related issues. A significant correlation emerged between the mention of stereotypically masculine behaviors and the frequency with which the child listed stereotypically masculine occupations (e.g., police officer, athlete) as appropriate jobs for boys ($r = .50$, $p < .05$). Likewise, the mentioning of stereotypically feminine behaviors among cartoon characters was associated with a larger number of gender-stereotyped possible occupations for girls (e.g., nurse, teacher; $r = .63$, $p < .05$).

The potential for counter-stereotypical portrayals to broaden gender-role expectations was also evident. Noticing nonstereotypical activities exhibited by female characters was associated with a decreased frequency to list female-stereotyped occupations as possible for girls among both male and female respondents. The data indicate that children draw meaning from the behaviors in cartoons they see modeled by characters, and the salience of these observations is related to their views of appropriate gender roles for themselves and others.

c. Beyond Gender Signorielli (1993) performed a content analysis that determined that many jobs featured in primetime, network television programming are exciting, fast-paced, and glamorous, and are in high-paying fields such as medicine, law, and entertainment. She also analyzed the responses of over 3,000 high school seniors in the Monitoring the Future Survey, and found that amount of television viewing predicted their desire for future occupations that were lucrative, high-status, but also were perceived as easy to perform so that time could be spent on vacations or pursuing other interests in life. Television exposure predicted these views about work even after controlling for a number of demographic variables. Thus, in addition to shaping young people's perceptions of what occupations are best suited for themselves and others, television also may foster aspirations toward particular sorts of careers portrayed frequently and positively on the screen.

C. Media's Influence on Physical Presence

Television and other media have long had the ability to define what is "in" and what is "out" in clothing, accessories, footwear, hairstyles, weight and body shape, and other aspects of comportment and appearance. Because fitting in and appearing attractive are important objectives in adolescence, the media's role in defining what constitutes physical attractiveness has considerable importance.

Consumer socialization research (see Chapter V) has identified many cognitive developmental and environmental influences on the child, with the latter including the role of family, friends, and media (Ward, Wackman & Wartella, 1979). Young people learn preferences for products, their orientations toward shopping, and their responses to advertisements through modeling of important individuals in their interpersonal lives as well as media characters and advertising models (Carlson & Grossbart, 1990; Carlson, Grossbart & Walsh, 1991).

We focus now on clothing and appearance. We divide our treatment into two broad developmental stages, early and middle childhood and adolescence. Preoccupations, preferences, and behavior pertaining to fashion and appearance substantially differ across these two periods. We give particular attention to the confluence of events that occurs at adolescence that makes the outward presentation of the self so critically important as well as so emotionally charged.

1. The Importance of Appearance in Early and Middle Childhood

a. Clothing Children learn preferences for clothing and become psychologically involved in their purchase at a very early age. Haynes and colleagues (Haynes, Burts, Dukes & Cloud, 1993) surveyed parents and guardians of 336 three- to six-year-olds and found vast majorities of these very young children accompanied a parent (typically their mother) on shopping trips for clothing (69%) and expressed an interest in what to buy (73%). The older the child, the more likely the parent reported expressions of interest in particular clothing, and girls outscored boys in all clothing and shopping involvement measures. Brand names are not particularly salient at this age. Seventy percent of the adult respondents reported their child showed no interest in particular brands. Nevertheless, the presence of a favorite character on the dress, shirt, or other piece of clothing was a considerable temptation for children of this age. About 40 percent of parents said their child expresses a desire for clothing with a character on it at least half of the time and another 37 percent reported such desires conveyed at least some of the time. The preschoolers were more likely than the kindergartners and the boys more likely than the girls to prefer clothing bearing licensed characters (such as Barbie or the Teenage Mutant Ninja Turtles). Thus the underlying basis for brand preference, a reliance on symbols in making consumer choices, appears at an early age.

The importance of symbols—characters or other objects (such as vehicles, flowers, sporting accessories, insects, and butterflies)—in the clothing preferences of preschoolers points to an early awareness in childhood that what one wears says something about oneself (Derscheid, Kwon & Fang, 1996). Although the children in the Haynes and colleagues (1993) study appeared to be too young to have developed brand preferences, by the age of nine children recognize brands and slogans at the same rate as their parents (Dotson & Hyatt, 2000). Thus, beginning in early childhood children discriminate among appearance-related products on the basis of symbols. By middle childhood, knowledge of brands has developed sufficiently and concern about the impressions on others made by clothing and appearance is forceful enough that desires for specific brands become common.

b. Identification   One key process in socialization regarding matters of physical appearance is the wishful identification of young audience members with media characters, defined as the desire to be similar to the character (von Feilitzen & Linne, 1975). Identification promotes the acquisition of social expectations and norms through the close attention given to the behavior of the character (Hoffner, 1996; Maccoby & Wilson, 1957). The early work of Reeves and colleagues found that boys tended to experience wishful identification with characters based on their physical strength and activity level, whereas girls experienced wishful identification with characters based more strongly on their physical attractiveness (Reeves & Greenberg, 1977; Reeves & Lometti, 1979; Reeves & Miller, 1978). Physical attributes of media characters thus are important in determining wishful identification of both boys and girls. Indeed, one particular study that tested young people's responses to actors auditioning for the *Freestyle* program found "good looks" to be a critical predictor of identification for both girls and boys (Williams, LaRose & Frost, 1981).

Relatively recent research has further established the centrality of physical appearance in young people's desire to emulate media characters. When Hoffner (1996) interviewed seven- to 12-year-olds about their favorite media character, almost all the boys (91%) and about half the girls (53%) selected a same-sex character, pointing once again to the primacy of gender in media preferences. Girls were more likely to engage in wishful identification and parasocial interaction (the illusion of a friendship or intimate relation with the character; Horton & Wohl, 1956) with female characters compared to male characters. For all respondents, the attractiveness and intelligence of the character predicted parasocial interaction with that character, and for boys only, the character's strength was an additional significant predictor.

2. The Importance of Appearance in Adolescence

a. Fashion   Beginning in junior high and continuing throughout the high-school years, although with some diminished intensity, clothing, fashion, and outward appearance typically are accorded great importance. Number one among adolescent expenditures is on clothing, followed by entertainment and food (Gunter & Furnham, 1998; Stoneham, 1998).

Wearing particular styles and brands of clothing is a means for many early adolescents (sometimes called *tweens*) and teenagers to attempt to fit in (Daters, 1990; Forney & Forney, 1995; Frances, 1992; Storm, 1987). Clothing, in particular, may lead to acceptance or rejection by peers (Littrell & Eicher, 1973; Smucker & Creekmore, 1972) as well as to feelings of deprivation among those unable to wear the styles or labels that they desire (Francis, 1992). Clothing is also considered by adolescents as a way to match their outward appearance with their self-image (Zollo, 1995).

In a sample of nearly 300 junior high and high school students, Simpson, Douglas, and Schimmel (1998) found that, compared to older adolescents, a significantly larger percentage of tweens reported "usually" or "almost always" considering the brand of clothing in deciding what to purchase from a catalog. Sixty-six percent of the 12- to 14-year-old males and 60 percent of the 12- to 14-year-old females reported frequently considering brand name. Only 46 percent of females and 39 percent of males aged 15 to 18 reported doing so. Members of the younger age group were also more likely to consider whether the clothing was currently in style and whether it represented the latest in fashion. Thus, tweens place more emphasis on brand-name clothing and other products than do adolescents (Cuneo, 1989; Koester & May, 1985; McLaughlin, 1991).

Membership in a peer group can exacerbate the clothing deprivation experienced by youth. Francis and Liu (1990) found that valuing clothing for its social utility predicted feelings of clothing deprivation, suggesting that adolescents readily perceive the importance of clothing in communicating status. Peer groups are central. Francis and Browne (1992) compared groups of skateboarders and baseball players to a general group of same-age high school students. The skateboarders and baseball players were more likely to feel they lacked the proper clothing in comparison to their peers and expressed more resulting dissatisfaction, although in fact they were neither more nor less financially able to purchase clothing compared to the general group. Thus, teen subcultures appear to exert additional pressure regarding clothing styles and name brands. Adolescents' clothing decisions and feelings of satisfaction or dissatisfaction should be considered not as individual but rather as social processes.

We conclude substantial numbers of both preadolescents and adolescents express concern about clothing purchasing decisions that rest on prestige, social status, and how they are likely to be perceived and received by others. The importance of brand names and keeping up with the latest trends in fashion is most intensely experienced in junior high rather than high school, and can be especially acute in peer subgroups. This developmental shift reflects progress in self-confidence and individuality in later teenage years as well as, perhaps, the possibility of rebelling against convention. The role of peer subgroups nevertheless underscores the importance of social identity processes.

b. Motivations In adolescence, the influence of parents in consumer socialization that had previously been of primary importance subsides while the influence of peers becomes preeminent (Ward, 1974). As far back as the early 1960s, research identified recognition from others and conformity as key determinants of the clothing purchasing and donning behaviors of adolescents (Evans, 1964). It is, of course, in those product areas perceived by the young consumer as critical for peer acceptance and approval that the role of peers in shaping brand and product preferences is greatest (Keillor, Parker & Schaefer, 1996). As Chen-Yu and Seock (2002) observe, "clothing is one of the expressed symbols of peer identification" (p. 51), and wearing clothing articles that boast brand names is one way to communicate affinity with a peer group (Geen, 1995).

Keillor and colleagues (1996) conducted a cross-cultural study in the United States and Mexico of socialization influences on adolescents' responses to low- and high-involvement products. They collected data from a convenience sample of 360 middle school students about evenly divided between Americans and Mexicans. Same-aged individuals— that is, friends and peers—and siblings were the strongest sources of information impacting brand preferences for clothing and sneakers (see Table 7.1), two products adolescents consider central to identity. Friends and peers exerted a stronger influence for high-involvement, appearance-related products than for candy and soda (see Table 7.1). Cultural differences also emerged. Mexican adolescents reported they were more likely to consider the input of parents and advertisements compared to adolescents in the United States.

Chen-Yu and Seock (2002) surveyed about 140 ninth through twelfth graders and found that for both males and females, friends were the most important information source for clothing and price was the principal criterion for in-store purchase decisions. Clothes shopping was a fairly common activity. Sizable percentages of young women (41%) and young men (29%) indicated they went clothes shopping two to three times a month. Average monthly expenditures on clothing were approximately $100 for both males and females. Motivations differed somewhat by gender. Being attractive to the opposite sex and distinguishing themselves from others were the two top reasons cited by the young men for their clothing purchasing choices. Attractiveness to young men was the second most frequent reason cited by young women, outscoring all other choices except shopping for recreation and enjoyment. Conformity—fitting in with others by wearing similar

Table 7.1

The Importance of Interpersonal and Media Sources in U.S. Adolescents' Brand Preferences for Low- and High-Involvement Products *

| | Product | | | |
| | Low involvement | | High involvement | |
Information source	Candy	Soda	Clothing	Sneakers
Mother	2.49	2.60	2.24	2.57
Father	2.49	2.64	2.06	2.51
Brother(s)	3.75	3.67	3.55	3.55
Sister(s)	4.02	3.88	3.99	3.78
Friends	3.36	3.09	4.03	3.57
Peers	2.80	2.77	3.53	3.12
Advertisements	2.75	2.71	3.07	2.87
Sales people	2.16	2.09	2.65	2.65

*The adolescents were asked to rate the likelihood with which they would use each source when deciding which brand to choose for each of these four product types, ranging from 1 (definitely would not use) to 5 (definitely would use).

Adapted from Keillor, B.D., Parker, R.S. & Schaefer, A. (1996). Influences on adolescent brand preferences in the United States and Mexico. *Journal of Advertising Research*, 36(3), 47–56.

styles and pieces of clothing—was also a common self-reported motivation. Although the media—magazines, television, the Internet, and celebrities in general—were frequently chosen as sources of information, peers outscored the media in terms of importance. The authors conclude that "clothing is a product with a high social risk" (Chen-Yu & Seock, 2002, p. 72), and therefore peers encountered daily set the standards.

Clothing, footwear, and accessory purchases and preferences are important to many adolescents for their ability to express identity and alliance with social groups. Adolescents are at times guided by a desire to appear similar to friends and peers and at times motivated by a wish to be seen as different. Chen-Yu and Seock (2002) refer to these two contradictory motivations as conformity and recognition. In our view, the conflict between these two drives is the epitome of adolescence. Decisions about the presentation of outward appearance as well as constraints on ability to acquire the attendant preferences are sites of tension for adolescents.

This influence pattern is not universally experienced across countries and cultures. Peers are generally paramount but parents retain their influence in some cultures more than others (Keillor et al., 1996). Media affect young people's aspirations and purchases regarding what to wear, but are typically overshadowed by the role of peers and, occasionally, parents. For example, Sherry, Greenberg, and Tokinoya (1999) found similar and declining influence for peers, television advertising, and parents in a comparison of 12- and 16-year-olds in Japan and the United States, whereas Lachance, Beaudoin, and Robitaille (2003) also determined that peer influence and parental influence far outweighed television exposure in the apparel brand preferences of French Canadian adolescents.

Media, therefore, are sources of information and influence about clothing and fashion, but they pale in comparison to peers and friends. Clothing and outward appearance are obviously important forms of self expression for young people and are used to both conform to and stand apart from others, as well as to attract romantic interest. Brand preference develops in late childhood and is felt strongly in early adolescence and can be used to create a sense of affinity with peers.

c. Body Image   "Body image" pertains to evaluations of the physical self and feelings regarding the presentation of the physical self to others, and has most frequently been employed to study levels of satisfaction with one's physical appearance (Carlson Jones, 2001; Cash & Deagle, 1997). By providing the benchmark used to judge physical beauty— standards that emphasize thinness for girls and women and fitness and muscle tone for boys and men—television, fashion magazines, and advertisements contribute to individual adolescents' perceptions of their bodies, and those perceptions often lead adolescents to conclude that they are comparatively unattractive and overweight. Media again help to establish what is considered normal, acceptable, and even ideal.

Media operate in the context of additional socializing influences such as feedback on weight and appearance received from mothers, fathers, and friends. McCabe and Ricciardelli's (2003) analysis of survey results from 423 adolescent boys and 377 adolescent girls (see Table 7.2), shows numerous forces and factors shaping a number of body-related variables. Adolescent perceptions of pressures exerted by mothers, fathers, and close male and female friends were so highly intercorrelated that they could be considered together as "parent and friend pressure." Perceived pressures from parents and friends were typically stronger than those from media, but media influence was acknowledged. For example, pressures from the media to gain or to lose weight were correlated with strategies employed by the adolescents to try to change their bodies.

Female adolescents are believed to be most at risk for this type of an influence due to greater societal pressure to conform to thin ideal standards (Champion & Furnham, 1999), although studies have documented effects in adults and among males (Groesz, Levine & Murnen, 2002). In a meta-analysis summarizing 26 experimental studies in this area,

Table 7.2
Adolescents' Self-Reports of Select Media and Interpersonal Influences on Their Body-related Perceptions and Behaviors

Dependent variable	Predictor variable	Beta*
	Boys only	
Body dissatisfaction	Parent & friend pressure to decrease weight	.24
	Media pressure to increase muscles	.23
Body image importance	Parent & friend pressure to increase muscles	.25
Body change strategies to decrease weight	Parent & friend pressure to decrease weight	.42
	Parent & friend pressure to increase weight	−.17
	Parent & friend pressure to increase muscles	.15
	Media pressure to decrease weight	.34
	Media pressure to increase muscles	−.31
Body change strategies to increase weight	Parent & friend pressure to increase muscles	.30
	Media pressure to increase weight	.20
Body change strategies to increase muscle tone	Parent & friend pressure to increase muscles	.39
Consumption of food supplements/ diet pills	Parent & friend pressure to increase weight	.17
	Parent & friend pressure to increase muscles	.23
	Girls only	
Body satisfaction	Parent & friend pressure to decrease weight	.26
	Media pressure to decrease weight	.15
Body image importance	Media pressure to increase weight	−.14
Body change strategies to decrease weight	Parent & friend pressure to decrease weight	.20
	Parent & friend pressure to increase muscles	.14
	Media pressure to decrease weight	.19
Body change strategies to increase weight	Parent & friend pressure to decrease weight	.16
	Parent & friend pressure to increase muscles	.18
Body change strategies to increase muscles	Parent & friend pressure to increase weight	.12
	Parent & friend pressure to increase muscles	.27
Binge eating	Parent & friend pressure to increase weight	.20
Consumption of food supplements/ diet pills	Media pressure to increase weight	.14

*All Betas listed here are statistically significant.
Adapted from McCabe, M. P. & Ricciardelli, L. A. (2003). Sociocultural influences on body image and body changes among adolescent boys and girls. *The Journal of Social Psychology, 143*, 5–27.

Groesz and colleagues determined that the media had a small but consistent effect on female dissatisfaction with one's body, and such an effect was stronger for women below the age of 19 compared to college-aged or older women. Age importantly affects the salience of media portrayals of body image. Polce-Lynch and colleagues (Polce-Lynch, Myers, Kliewer & Kilmartin, 2001), for example, found eighth graders were more likely to believe the media have an influence on their body image compared to fifth and twelfth graders.

Past research then, has established that short-term exposure to television depicting thin-as-beautiful images (as measured in an experiment) leads to adolescent girls attaching greater importance to beauty (Tan, 1977), whereas overall television exposure (as measured in a survey) among female adolescents is associated with dissatisfaction with one's own body, a desire to be thinner, and symptoms of eating disorders such as anorexia or bulimia (Botta, 1999; Harrison, 2000; Harrison & Cantor, 1997). In a recent study, for example, Van den Bulck (2000), found the viewing of specific thinness-depicting programs (e.g., *Melrose Place, Friends*) among both male and female 17- and 18-year-olds predicted such discontent. Young women's definitions of their "ideal" weight were also lower among heavy viewers of this genre of programs. The total amount of weight women would like to lose correlated positively with their overall amount of television viewing. For the young men, amount of television viewing was related to unhappiness about their weight.

Carlson Jones, Vigfusdottir, and Lee (2004) analyzed the survey responses of 780 boys and girls in grades seven through 10. Among only the girls they found a direct relationship between exposure to appearance-oriented magazines and body dissatisfaction. Among both boys and girls, conversations with friends about appearance were associated with greater internalization of an ideal appearance which, in turn, was associated with heightened body dissatisfaction. Furthermore, among both boys and girls the young respondents' actual measurements on the Body Mass Index (which includes height and weight), criticism of their appearance from peers, and internalization of a body ideal each directly affected dissatisfaction. These data again identify an important role among girls for magazines (although we would not infer a causal influence from such correlational data), and they emphasize how a variety of factors—media, conversations, internalized standards—create a milieu favorable to dissatisfaction with one's body.

Hargreaves and Tiggeman (2003) experimentally exposed more than 300 13- to 15-year-olds to one of two conditions—20 television commercials that included a thin beauty ideal or 20 television commercials that contained no appearance-related images. The body dissatisfaction of the early adolescents was measured at three points: before exposure, immediately after, and 15 minutes after. Participants also completed a word-association task. Girls but not boys who had been exposed to the appearance-related commercials had higher body dissatisfaction immediately after exposure as well as 15 minutes later. Both boys and girls who had seen the commercials with thin and fit models listed more appearance-related words in the task. These data document short-term causation and demonstrate that media portrayals emphasizing ideal body types evoke the production of cognitive schema. Thus, they add cognitive to the affective processes involved in the favorable evaluation of body types (and the unfavorable evaluation of the self).

Media exposure among adolescents has also been recently associated with the use of protein powders, herbal supplements, steroids, diet pills and other products that claim to improve weight, muscularity, or shape (Field et al., 2005; McCabe & Ricciardelli, 2003). Field and colleagues (2005) analyzed data from thousands of girls and boys nationwide aged 12 to 18 and found boys who read three types of magazines (men's, fashion, and health and fitness-oriented magazines) and girls who reported attempting to look like women they had observed in the media were more likely than their counterparts to use these products. Overall amount of television viewing, on the other hand, had no statistical association with their use.

In our judgment, the data on body image show the media can and do contribute to adolescents' levels of satisfaction with their body shapes and sizes. In some cases, the dissatisfaction that typically occurs manifests itself in ostensibly corrective behavior like the consumption of diet pills or protein supplements. Particular television programs and magazines with a profound emphasis on beauty appear to be particular culprits but associations occur from overall television viewing, as well. The meta-analysis demonstrates that surveys and experiments largely concur in finding a link between media exposure and body image disturbances, especially for female adolescents.

In general, we conclude that the evidence is persuasive in documenting a role of media—particularly television programming, advertising, and magazines—in contributing to a range of thoughts, attitudes, and behaviors that pertain to adolescents' conceptualizations of their physical appearance. Experiments consistently demonstrate short-term influence. The survey data makes it clear that media use is associated with beliefs about the body. Media are by no means the sole influence but should be catalogued among the many forces that mold these conceptualizations. The media as well as peers, parents, and others act as socializing agents, informing the individual adolescent either directly or indirectly through modeling of the type of body that is acceptable and valued in society.

II. THEORETICAL EXPLANATIONS FOR HOW AND WHY MEDIA CONTRIBUTE TO SOCIALIZATION

We now briefly review key theories in psychology and communication that offer explanations for how and why media contribute to the socialization of individuals. We outline social comparison, social identity, social cognition, and cultivation theories, identifying their main propositions, and especially as they relate to mass communication and socialization. We then present for each theory a case study of the theory in action in regard to media.

A. *The Role of Social Comparison*

Social comparison is the label applied to the process of comparing oneself to others, and evaluating how one's own attributes and behavior measure up compared to those of others (Festinger, 1954). The theory holds that social comparisons are crucial to self-evaluations and are perceptual in nature, depending not on objective criteria but rather on subjective judgments on the part of the individual (Wood, 1989). Comparisons are considered both automatic (meaning people engage in these comparisons as a matter of course and often without conscious acknowledgement) and goal-oriented (in that there is a sought-after end state) (Festinger, 1954; Goethals, 1986). As communication scholar Renee Botta argues in her application of social comparison to adolescents' body image responses to media, individuals "who deem themselves as coming up short in their comparisons are more motivated to close the gap on that comparison" (Botta, 1999, pp. 26–27).

Comparisons often are made with others who are seen as being similar to the self on the attribute in question (Miller, Turnbull & McFarland, 1988). Festinger (1954) originally argued that people tend to compare themselves to those who are demographically similar because they would provide the most accurate benchmark. This assumes that accurate assessment is the goal. Other researchers (Ruble, 1983; Wood, 1989), however, have demonstrated that social comparisons are also employed to gain "information about highly valued attributes, social expectations, and norms" (Jones, 2001, p. 645). And still other scholars have suggested that since social comparison can be motivated by the desire to feel better about oneself (Taylor & Lobel, 1989; Wills, 1981, 1991), horizontal comparisons based on shared circumstances or status may be replaced or complemented by comparisons with those judged superior or inferior to the individual. Individuals engage in upward social comparisons (with those perceived as superior to the self on the issue in question) when looking for inspiration, motivation, or problem-solving strategies (Taylor & Lobel, 1989). Downward social comparisons (with those perceived as inferior to the self) can bolster self-esteem or improve feelings of well-being (Wood, Taylor & Lichtman, 1985). Thus, the population used for comparison depends on the motivation for the comparison.

There is considerable conceptual overlap between socialization and social comparison processes regardless of the direction of the comparison. Individuals make comparisons between themselves and others in order to learn about values and expectations in the culture and develop a perception of their legitimate place within the culture. Media characters as well as people encountered in real life can comprise the "others" with which individuals compare themselves. Consequences for self-evaluation and self-esteem ensue from how one fares in the comparison.

1. Case Study Social comparison theory has been applied to the effects of media portrayals of beauty and body on the body images of adolescents. Individuals, particularly adolescents who are feeling pressure to fit in, compare their physical attributes with those of others, with potential consequences both for feelings of discontent and for goal-oriented, "corrective" behavior. Dissatisfaction with one's body, experiencing a keen desire to be thinner or more attractive, and taking measures to lose weight or tone muscles (such as bingeing and purging, intensely exercising, or consuming supplements) often can be traced in part to a perceived contrast between individuals' conception of their own physical appearance and their impression of what others look like. The actual weight or body size of the adolescent matters less than her or his perception of not measuring up in comparison to others in day-to-day life or in the media.

Botta (1999) measured the overall amount of television exposure and exposure to particular television dramas that emphasize a thin beauty standard (such as *Melrose Place* and *Beverly Hills 90210*) of more than 200 high school-aged young women, as well as their estimates of the frequency with which they engage in the comparison of themselves and close others with characters that appear on television. The television exposure variables explained 33 percent of the variance for endorsement of the thin ideal (e.g., "Overweight women are unattractive." "The ideal woman should be slender and thin." p. 30), 17 percent for body dissatisfaction (including whether respondents think each of a number of body parts were too large), 15 percent for drive for thinness (measuring preoccupation and anxiety about gaining weight), and 16 percent for bulimic behaviors (covering such symptoms as bingeing on food and thinking about vomiting to purge food). Evidence pointed toward the critical role for social comparison. Frequency of comparing self or others to media characters was a significant predictor of all four dependent measures (thin ideal endorsement, body dissatisfaction, drive for thinness, and bulimic tendencies). The results support social comparison as an explanation for the ways in which young people process media content in a manner that contributes to negative self-esteem.

Carlson Jones (2001) asked seventh and tenth graders to report on the frequency with which they compared themselves to same-sex peers or to models and celebrities. When making social comparisons regarding physical attributes (that is, appearance), same-sex peers and models and celebrities were both frequently employed, a result that has since been replicated in additional data (Mc Cabe & Ricciardelli, 2003; see Tables 7.2 and 7.3). When making social comparisons regarding personal or social attributes (that is, skills and traits), same-sex peers were more commonly employed than models and celebrities (see Tables 7.2 and 7.3). Engaging in social comparison was related to feeling dissatisfied with one's body for nearly every physical attribute for both boys and girls. Media models and peers operated very similarly as means of comparison of physical attributes in their associations with dissatisfaction (see Table 7.3).

For both boys and girls, making weight-related social comparisons to either same-sex peers or models and celebrities was directly related to body dissatisfaction, even after controlling for additional variables (Carlson Jones, 2001). Also for boys only, facial comparisons, and for girls only, body shape comparisons, also predicted body dissatisfaction under multiple controls. Thus, the study supplies additional evidence that social comparisons shape the self-concept of young people, and that the ensuing evaluations of the self can negatively impact these body-image related outcomes. In general, the girls in the sample reported engaging in social comparisons with greater frequency than the boys.

These data underscore the importance of social comparison in the development of the self-concept of adolescents. Social comparisons

Table 7.3

Correlations between Body Dissatisfaction and Frequency of Particular Types of Social Comparisons to Models/Celebrities or Same-Sex Peers among Male and Female Adolescents

	Girls (N = 215)		Boys (N = 197)	
	Models/ celebrities	Same-sex peers	Models/ celebrities	Same-sex peers
Physical attributes				
Height	.06	.06	.18*	.27**
Weight	.54**	.66**	.39**	.38**
Shape/build	.54**	.56**	.25**	.30**
Face	.30**	.31**	.32**	.36**
Personal/social attributes				
Personality	−.04	.15	.19*	.21*
Intelligence	.08	.05	−.03	.06
Style	.04	.20*	.18*	.23**
Popularity	.18*	.32**	.28**	.28**

*p < .01, **p < .001.

Adapted from Carlson Jones, D. (2001). Social comparison and body image: Attractiveness comparisons to models and peers among adolescent girls and boys. *Sex Roles, 45*, 645–664.

with both media models and "real life" others are instrumental in the self-evaluative processes of adolescents. We cannot, of course, rule out the possibility that those with a well-developed sense of dissatisfaction engage more often in social comparison. We can, however, conclude with confidence that social comparison plays a role in the influence of the media in socialization, even were it restricted to confirming (rather than originating) dissatisfaction.

B. The Role of Social Identity

Conceptualizations of identity are dynamic and pressing in particular in adolescence. Teenagers are in the process of exploring their sense of self. They do so through their behavior and their interactions with peers, parents, romantic interests, and others. They have arrived upon a developmental stage in which they begin to look and feel different (Erikson, 1968). They become conscious of having left childhood behind. The developing ability to think abstractly assists adolescents in the active consideration of what others think of them. The importance of peers is represented by the care and concern given the feedback from others in the experimentations of adolescents with identity (Conger & Galambos, 1997; Erikson, 1968; Steinberg, 1993).

With social comparison theory, an abstract relationship is assumed between the individual and the group that serves the individual's needs in the comparison drawn. In social identity theory, we turn to relationships between individuals and groups that assist the individual in self-definition. Tajfel (1978) has defined social identity as "that part of an individual's self-concept which derives from ... knowledge of ... (and) membership of a social group (or groups) together with the value and emotional significance attached to that membership" (p. 63). Social identity theory posits that the self-concept is determined in part by membership in social groups and that the act of self-categorization into groups emphasizes perceived similarities between the self and some others while emphasizing perceived differences between the self and different others (Duck, Hogg & Terry, 1999). These social identities produce a motive to make "intergroup comparisons that favor the in-group" (Duck et al., 1999, p. 1882) in order to maintain or enhance self-esteem. Maass and colleagues succinctly put it: "People tend to create or maintain a positive self-image by enhancing the status of their own group with respect to relevant comparison groups" (Maass, Cadinu, Guarnieri & Grasselli, 2003, p. 854).

The media offer two primary ways in which young people can affirm their developing definition of themselves. One is through the use of media as symbols of alignment or disjunction. Another is through shared interests, in which media become the basis rather than the expression of interests and identity. In the first, the embrace or rejection of television programs, movies, celebrities, rock groups and rappers, and brands locate the individual in the nexus of group relations, and the media become a means of declaring membership in in-groups and demonstrating distance from out-groups. In the second, the media shift from being the expression of identity to being the basis of involvement with an in-group.

1. Case Study Any person with an Internet-connected computer and a fundamental set of skills can create web pages or other basic content potentially viewed by a large number of others. Self-expression is invited. Personal web pages on the Internet have been described as their creators' attempts to answer the question "Who am I?" through what they choose to include and emphasize in the content they have designed for others' viewing and consideration (Chandler & Roberts-Young, 1998). The relative anonymity of web pages creates a circumstance in which web page authors young and old can overcome inhibitions that may impede face-to-face interactions and experiment with their identities online, presenting changing representations of who they are or who they want to be (Turkle, 1995).

Stern (2004) used Yahoo's "Personal Home Pages" listing to examine the personal web pages of youth who explicitly identified their ages in their web page as being between 14 and 18. Of the over 200 personal web pages examined, 94 percent contained a "descriptive biography" in which the author wrote a narrative to describe herself or himself. This is a phenomenon not common in the personal web pages created by adults, which do not typically contain this type of information. Other expressions of identity were considerably less frequent than the biography, but included photos, poems or essays written by the author of the web page, and statements that included plans for the future (see Table 7.4). These young web page authors avoided, for the most part, extremely sensitive experiences such as diary entries. Thus, there is an attempt to elicit validation and feedback by making publicon the Internet topics considered "safe" while protecting private struggles from public scrutiny. Stern (2004) also discovered a number of gender differences. She notes that girls were three times more likely than boys to include original poetry, twice as likely to include quotes, and twice as likely to mention their appearance in their personal web pages. These gender disparities reflect ways in which girls and boys often differ in "offline" face-to-face interactions as well.

Stern (2004) examined the ways in which the interests of the web page authors were represented. Hobbies, media preferences, and references to school were among the most frequently discussed (see Table 7.4). Boys were more likely to list or link to sports-related topics and video games than girls. Girls were more likely than boys to mention religion or God, sex, and depression, although these very personal topics were much less frequent than self-description and other interests.

Finally, and most centrally to social identity theory, references to relationships were often found on the web pages. Friends and family were described (and in some cases, those additional web pages linked) by many young web page authors (see Table 7.4). An additional parallel to "off line" gender patterns was revealed here, with girls more likely than boys to discuss their families and their romantic relationships. Family and friends are important "in-groups" for adolescents, and the web pages reflect expressions of the social identity as well as the motivation to present the in-groups in a favorable manner in order to boost self-esteem. Stern (2004) concludes:

> Personal home pages on the Web comprise a quintessential place for identity exploration for adolescents. They constitute a comparatively safe space, where experimentation can take place within the privacy of one's bedroom or at a computer station. Yet simultaneously, they offer the unusual prospect of a large audience. Subsequently, authors can receive feedback from their home page visitors, helping them to fashion their identities in much the same way Erikson claimed social interaction facilitates identity construction offline. (p. 220)

We conclude that the ability of young people to create Internet content via their own personal web pages poses a unique opportunity for identity exploration and expression in the contemporary world. We concur with Stern (2004) that many of the means of identity expression engaged in by young people on the Internet reflect more general gender differences and developmental tendencies. In many ways, the web pages created by youth are not radically different from the ways they decorate their bedrooms or school lockers, including photos of friends and family, music lyrics or other cherished media content, and, especially for girls, poems or quotes that are meaningful to them. In the invitation of feedback, links to other sites, and inclusion of an e-mail address to facilitate subsequent communication, however, the opportunities provided by the Internet are novel and rich. Thus, the medium of the Internet provides a means of experimenting with self-identity, seeking affirmation from others, and demonstrating the connection of the self with others.

C. The Role of Social Cognition

Albert Bandura's (1986, 2002) social cognition posits the observation of others, whether in everyday life or in the media, as a major source of

Table 7.4
Elements of Personal Web Pages Created by 14- to 18-Year-Olds

Elements	% (N = 233)
Self-expression/description	
Descriptive biography	94.4%
Photos of author	44.6
References to appearance	27.9
Quotes	23.6
Discussion of future plans	22.7
Original essay	21.9
Original poetry	15.0
Likes/dislikes	6.9
Diaries/journals	5.6
Specific interests	
Links to hobbies	76.0%
References to media use	73.8
References to school	64.8
Links to music or music sites	39.1
Links to retail sites (products & services)	25.8
References to video games	24.9
Links to school sites	24.0
Links to film clips, trailers, or film sites	17.2
Links to sports	15.5
Links to social cause sites	10.3
Links to news sites	9.0
Links to magazine sites	5.6
References to relationships	
References to friends	69.8%
References to family	50.6
Links to friends' home pages	48.9
References to romantic relationships	20.6
References to participation in instant message/chat	17.2
Links to family members' homepages	14.6
References to intimate topics	
Religion/God	19.7%
Drugs/alcohol	12.0
Sex	8.2
Depression	6.9
Loneliness	3.0
Violence	2.1
Self-destructive behaviors	1.7

Adapted from S.R. Stern (2004). Expressions of identity online: Prominent features and gender differences in adolescents' World Wide Web home pages. *Journal of Broadcasting & Electronic Media, 48,* 218–243.

learning. This is in sharp contrast to a behavioralist conception of behavior, which restricts learning to direct experience. Social cognition dramatically widens the scope of sources of information from which to draw in learning about the social world to include vicarious experience. The key element determining whether an individual uses what has been observed to guide his or her behavior is the utility and properties ascribed to the behavior—which we have described elsewhere (Comstock & Scharrer, 1999) as efficacy (reward and goal attainment), normativeness (social approval and acceptance), and pertinence (relevance to the individual). Individuals observe the behavior of others and the consequences of their actions, learn what the consequences suggest for what is valued or deemed appropriate or inappropriate by society, and encode that information in the formation of attitudes and the enactment of behavior. The theory, therefore, reserves a central position for the socialization of the individual while also emphasizing the agency of the individual in making meaning from observations and regulating motivations and goals. A major element is the concept of symbolic enactment, by which individuals mentally construct a model to achieve a specific goal that includes considerable latitude for the varying circumstances of the individual. Thus, social cognition allows for creativity in the application of observation while also giving it priority—because of the wider range of circumstances it can encompass—over direct experience.

Importantly, the "others" who serve as behavioral models for individuals consist of both others in one's own environment and characters that appear in the media (Bandura & Huston, 1961; Bandura, Ross & Ross, 1963). However, direct contact with those in one's own environment is likely to be confined to largely the same set of people each day and especially so for children and adolescents. As a result, the media outweigh other sources in defining social reality because they not only broaden what individuals can observe but constitute experiences often perceived as more universal and less idiosyncratic (Bandura, 2002).

The theory also advances four subordinate processes on which observational learning depends (Bandura, 2002). Attentional processes include those factors that make the modeled event more or less likely to be attended to by the individual and that determine what the individual will construe from the event. These factors include the preconceptions of the individual and the attractiveness, functional value, and salience of the modeled event. Retention processes concern the resources of the individual employed in remembering the modeled event. Importantly, individuals have the capacity to transform the specific modeled event to "generative conceptions of style of behavior from modeled exemplars rather than merely scripts of behavioral routines" (Bandura, 2002, p. 127).

Thus, the type of media effect that social cognitive theory predicts is not limited to a mere "copycat," but rather allows for differentiation that takes into account varying circumstances and preferences of individuals and derives from "extracting the generic features from various social exemplars, and integrating the extracted information into composite rules" (Bandura, 2002, p. 131).

Production processes concern the ability of the individual to construct a cognitive representation of a behavior—concretely thinking about behavioral alternatives—and to use feedback and additional input to make repeated adjustments to behavior. Motivational processes govern whether the behavior actually will be enacted. Central to this is the consideration of costs and benefits that may accrue from the behavior and self-efficacy, or the individual's view of whether she or he can successfully achieve the benefits or avoid the costs. Behavior perceived as leading to reward is more likely to be enacted than behavior perceived as unrewarding or likely to be punished. Rewards and punishments, though social at root (because they derive from the behavioral and judgments of others), may be imposed by the self (i.e., disgust, embarrassment, shame) or by others (i.e., disapproval, condemnation, threat).

Those observed both in everyday life and in the media are transformed by mental operations into symbolic models. These display to the individual examples of what constitutes effective action. Individuals observe those models and take from them a central, generative lesson. Yet, that lesson is not singular, but rather is likely to be different for different audience members. It will be shaped by their preference for the medium in question, their conceptions of the attractiveness of those observed, and their own values and prior dispositions.

1. Case Study   Austin and Nelson (1993) use social cognition as a theoretical foundation for their study of the role of ethnic group membership and socialization to politics in the United States. They begin with the premise that adolescents from nondominant racial and ethnic groups must balance multiple environments, social norms, and layers of their identity. The authors argue that social cognition, with its emphasis on personal, environmental, and behavioral factors (Bandura, 1986), is a useful way to view these processes. They see television in particular as a means by which young people of color can experience the dominant culture.

In fact, for immigrants as well as members of a minority culture, television can take on particular relevance as a socialization tool, providing a means to determine larger cultural values and norms as well as to vicariously observe behaviors that are met with rewards in the larger culture (Chaffee, Nass & Yang, 1990; Chaffee & Yang, 1988).

The multiple layers of experience of young people of color (as members of the larger culture as well as members of specific ethnic or racial groups) can mean that television presents some norms that conflict with norms of their own ethnic or racial group (Tan, Tan & Tan, 1987). Thus, adolescents of color may have especially complex decisions to make about what television and other media suggest about social norms, expectations, and values.

Television entertainment as well as news and other media (and particularly news) can contribute to the political socialization of young people, their orientation toward political parties, candidates, political messages, and the electoral and governing systems. Parents and other interpersonal sources also have a key role to play in this type of socialization, sometimes dwarfing the contribution of media (Austin, Roberts & Nass, 1990; Dennis, 1986).

Austin and Nelson (1993) gathered data from a "multicultural" group of youth to examine both media and interpersonal communication in the formation of knowledge, efficacy, and values related to politics. Over 400 tenth through twelfth graders (225 of whom were Latino, 134 Anglo, and 42 Native American) responded to a survey measuring current events knowledge, political efficacy, whether they had spoken with a parent and/or a friend about candidates or about problems experienced by the country, communication styles of parents, and parental mediation of television viewing. Skepticism (as contrasted with cynicism) about politics on the part of parents predicted communication with others about candidates or social problems. Parental mediation of television and ethnic group membership each also predicted communication with others about candidates or social problems. Latino and Native American respondents reported being less likely to engage in political communication compared to the Anglo respondents. Attention to the news and political communication both predicted current events knowledge. Latino respondents scored lower on current events knowledge than the other two ethnic groups, and lower on political efficacy, as well. In general, the effects of family and parent communication styles and patterns overshadowed the effects of membership in an ethnic group in explaining political socialization in terms of effect size.

Austin and Nelson conclude, "The adolescent's socialization to politics appears to take place in a complex interaction of cultural background, family communication, and exposure to outside ideas through vehicles such as the mass media. Media effects, although striking, nevertheless take place in the context of the family and ethnic background, where adolescents first learn cultural values and problem-solving styles" (p. 430). Their results caution that ethnic group membership and family communication styles are far from perfectly correlated, as each functioned differently in the statistical analyses. Indeed, they explain that such styles "appeared to cross cultures as much as reflect them" (p. 429).

The Austin and Nelson (1993) data support the central axioms of social cognitive theory. Young people employ information and experiences from their actual lives as well as what they see in the media in the formation of knowledge about and orientations toward the political system. Adolescents appear to weigh cues about the dominant culture from media with conceptualizations derived from their own ethnic group and family environment. The universality of the primacy of parent communication styles in the development of adolescents' knowledge about and dispositions toward politics identifies the family as the foundation for other influences. In these data, young people constructed meaning from experiences and observations, regulated their behaviors in accord with personal motivations as well as in response to cues from the social world, and responded in ways they deemed likely to be effective and well received, all principles of social cognition (Bandura, 1986, 2001).

Social cognitive theory has also helped explain how adolescents receive and respond to messages about sexuality and sexual activity in the media. Prior analyses have found an association between exposure to sexual content on television and the initiation of sexual activity among young people, but have not advanced a theoretical explanation for the association (Brown & Newcomer, 1991; Collins et al., 2004; Peterson, Moore & Furstenberg, 1991). An additional study by Martino and colleagues (Martino, Collins, Elliott, Strachman, Kanouse & Berry, 2006) found a significant relationship between listening to music containing degrading sexual content at baseline and subsequent initiation of sexual intercourse and advancement to additional forms of sexual interaction among a national sample of adolescents. An article by Martino and colleagues (Martino, Collins, Kanouse, Elliott & Berry, 2005) provides convincing evidence that social cognitive processes lie at the heart of such associations.

The central notion is that young people observe models on television and in other media forms and make inferences about social norms and likely consequences attending particular actions. The concept of self-efficacy also plays an important role, in that "to the extent that adolescents acquire favorable beliefs about sex and confidence in their own sexual abilities as a result of viewing sexual content on TV, they become more likely to attempt the modeled behaviors" (Martino et al., 2005, pp. 914–915). Martino and colleagues (2005) test such a theoretical model on longitudinal data drawn from a diverse national sample of over 1,200 adolescents aged 12 to 17. First, the analysis revealed a direct effect of viewing television programs containing sexual content on whether the respondent had initiated sexual intercourse activity in the time period between the first and second survey (one year), regardless of the gender or race or ethnicity of the adolescent. Second, the structural equation model revealed a positive, significant relationship between exposure to televised sexual content and perceptions of "prosex norms" among peers (number of same-sex friends who have had intercourse) as well as a negative, significant relationship between such exposure and perception of negative outcome expectancies (including the likelihood of emotional, social, and health consequences of having sex). These two factors, derived from social cognitive theory, in turn, predicted the initiation of intercourse over the time period examined. Exposure to televised sexual content also predicted the third social cognitive theory-derived factor, safe-sex efficacy (ability to obtain or use condoms or to talk to a potential partner about sex), in African American and White adolescents but not in Latino adolescents. Safe-sex efficacy, in turn, predicted the initiation of intercourse, regardless of the race or ethnicity of the respondent.

D. The Role of Cultivation

The late George Gerbner and colleagues (Gerbner & Gross, 1976; Gerbner, Gross, Morgan & Signorielli, 1980b; Gerbner, Gross, Morgan, Signorielli & Shanahan, 2002) advanced cultivation theory to explain how exposure to the consistent themes that mark television content shapes audience members' views of reality. "Cultivation" is intended to connote the nurturing of beliefs and perceptions, with the emphasis on the subtlety and generally small size of the influence rather than the larger impact implied by the term "effects." A central assumption is that television is homogeneous enough in its presentations—as exemplified by such perennials as ubiquitous violence, preeminence in news, sports, and entertainment of the white male, and a strong focus on the middle and upper-middle classes—that amount of viewing is a reasonable index of exposure to the emphases of the medium, and therefore the cultivation effect will be a function of amount viewed. The proposition offered by cultivation theory that those who view more will be more likely to perceive the world as resembling what has been portrayed on television has found considerable support. Morgan (1989) catalogues a large number of such correlations; for example, heavier viewers perceive the world as racially and occupationally more like the demographics of television casts, or they come to view the world as a mean and dangerous place.

Cultivation theory is, fundamentally, a socialization or encultura-tion theory, with its chief focus on the ways that individuals learn about and engage with their social surroundings. The theory's origina-tor, Gerbner, in his introduction to Shanahan and Morgan (1999), *Television and Its Viewers: Cultivation Theory and Research*, makes this point, in the context of his rumination on the story-telling power of television.

> Stories socialize us into roles of gender, age, class, vocation and lifestyle, and offer models of conformity or targets for rebellion. They weave the seamless web of the cultural environment that cultivates most of what we think, what we do, and how we conduct our affairs. ... The stories that animate our cultural environment have three distinct but related functions. These functions are (1) to reveal how things work; (2) to describe what things are; and (3) to tell us what to do about them. (p. ix)

Television—and, by implication, other media when they meet the two criteria of regular and extensive use and homogeneous emphases and themes—interpret and disseminate the cultural environment. Viewers adapt television's depictions as guides for personal develop-ment, views of society, and social interaction. The greater the amount of exposure the more likely they are to do so. The central thrust of cultivation theory in regard to socialization is that growing up with television means drawing on its themes as a source of information about the world, and extending credibility to its subtle as well as overt messages about the people, places, and actions that populate the world.

1. Case Study Signorielli and Lears (1992) use cultivation theory as the basis for interpreting the relationships between children's television viewing and their dispositions toward gender roles. They investigated the views of housework and chore distribution as a means of illuminating beliefs regarding the suitability of particular tasks for males and females. With 530 fourth through sixth graders as respondents, Signorielli and Lears obtained data on average amount of television exposure and attitudes regarding whether just boys, just girls, or either boys or girls should perform certain domes-tic chores—such as doing the dishes, mowing the lawn, taking out the trash, or helping with the cleaning—as well as the actual chores performed.

Both boys and girls tend to engage in gender-specific chores in and around the home. The boys performed an average of two of the three stereotypically "masculine" chores compared to the girls' average of less than one. The girls performed an average of three of the four stereotypically "feminine" chores compared to the boys' average of two. On the attitude items, the boys were more likely than the girls to give a stereotyped response. However, attitudes and behaviors were correlated. Those children with stereotypical views of who should do what chore were more likely to perform chores that typically are assigned to their gender.

A significant, positive relationship emerged between television exposure and amount of gender stereotyping in attitudes about chores (see Table 7.5). The overall correlation was still statistically significant after controlling for a number of possible artefactual influences—gender, race, grade, reading level, parent occupation status, parent education, and actual chore behaviors, and held up in subgroups created by gender and race. Performance of chores, in contrast, was not directly related to television exposure in the sample as a whole. Although the bivariate correlation between the two initially was statistically significant for the performance of "feminine" chores among the entire sample (see Table 7.5), the relationship did not hold up under the multiple controls.

Among boys, a negative correlation that retained significance under multiple controls emerged between gender-stereotyped attitudes about chores and the tendency to report performing "feminine" chores (see Table 7.5) but amount of viewing was unrelated to the performance of such chores. Among girls, a parallel pattern emerged, and in this case became stronger with more television viewing (see Table 7.5). The greater the girls' gender stereotyping, the lower the frequency with which they reported engaging in chores typically assigned to boys. Television exposure thus did not directly shape chore-related behavior. However, exposure was associated with chore-related attitudes which, in turn, were associated with engaging in chores traditionally assigned by gender. And among girls, correlations between attitudes and behavior increased linearly from light to moderate to heavy television viewers.

The Signorielli and Lears (1992) data are consistent with a greater influence of media exposure on attitudes than behavior. This has been a frequent outcome, exemplified early by the *Freestyle* data on potential careers (although the survey methodology prohibits conclusions about causal direction). They also are suggestive of the cultivation by television (in the language of the theory) of the perceptions of young audience members regarding what is deemed appropriate for boys and girls in regard to household tasks. According to cultivation theory, continual and long-term exposure to the themes that pervade television would skew perceptions so that they align more closely with those themes (Gerbner & Gross, 1976; Gerbner et al., 1980b; Gerbner et al., 2002). In this case,

Table 7.5

Correlations and Partial Correlations among Television Viewing, Gender–Stereotyped Attitudes about Domestic Chores, and Actual Chore Performance, N = 524–528

	All	Boys	Girls	White Students	Students of color
TV viewing and attitudes	.25[c]	.25[c]	.22[c]	.22[c]	.29[c]
TV viewing and performing "masculine" chores	−.03	−.03	−.16[b]	−.03	.02
TV viewing and performing "feminine" chores	−.07[a]	−.09	.03	−.12[b]	−.08

	Television viewing					
	Light		Medium		Heavy	
	"Fem." chores	"Masc." chores	"Fem." chores	"Masc." chores	"Fem." chores	"Masc." chores
Attitudes and chore performance, boys only	−.45[c]	.03	−.28[c]	.15	−.45[c]	.00
Attitudes and chore performance, girls only	−.03	−.24[b]	−.18	−.43[c]	−.03	−.52[c]

Adapted from Signorielli, N. & Lears, M. (1992). Children, television, and conceptions about chores: Attitudes and behaviors. *Sex Roles, 27*, 157–170.

television would foster perceptions of limited and traditional domestic responsibilities for males and females among children.

Signorielli and Lears provide no evidence in the sample as a whole of a direct television effect on the performance of chores. However, significant relationships link attitudes and behavior in particular subgroups of children. Further, the relationship between the gender-role attitudes and gendered chore behavior among girls was stronger for those who watched more television. This suggests an indirect relationship between television viewing and behavior. Cultivation theory as employed by Signorielli and Lears encourages the view that television plays a role in the acquisition of cultural norms by the young.

VIII KNOWLEDGE FOR WHAT?

The social and behavioral sciences have often been the site of skirmishes by cantankerous observers. This particularly has been the case for those who would apply them to the solution of real and important problems. The proper methodology, the correct interpretation of data, the validity of inferences—these are persistently challenged, often by those with vested ideological or material interests. We have chosen a title used almost 70 years ago by Robert S. Lynd (1939), the pioneering sociologist who was coauthor (with his wife) of *Middletown* (1929) and *Middletown in Transition* (1937)—the quintessential studies that set the standards for describing American communities—to emphasize our enlistment in the long history of drawing on the social and behavioral sciences for practical guidance. His plea was that more should be made of what is known. We concur, and believe this is especially so for media and young people—although we are embarrassed this should remain the case after the passage of so much time.

I. USING THE SOCIAL AND BEHAVIORAL SCIENCES[1]

We are aware that a commitment to use the social and behavioral sciences is somewhat cyclical. The famous "golden fleece" award of Senator William Proxmire (D-Wisconsin) many years ago popularized

[1] Because sources are cited in each chapter, we have omitted citations from this concluding overview.

the belief in the useless—and seemingly often silly—research funded by federal agencies. (Many of the winning projects, of course, bask today in respect and honor as significant contributions to their fields.) The "experimenting society" was coined by Donald Campbell for use in the 1960s and early 1970s of the social and behavioral sciences to evaluate the effectiveness of major interventions (Head Start, *Sesame Street*, racial integration of public schools), a by-product of Lyndon Johnson's War on Poverty. The promotion of a "positive psychology" that relies on empirical findings (as opposed to ideology or philosophy) to enact better personal lives (Seligman, 2000) is a current example. The question then, is whether media and young people meet the criteria for applying social and behavioral science. We believe they do because of four circumstances:

- The research on many topics—for example, violent television and film entertainment, and time spent with media—has become extensive and much more informative and convincing than was the case not so long ago.
- A wide range of topics has now received some attention. This expansion of the research protocol is exemplified by the data documenting the very early years at which media use now begins.
- The development of theory allows us to extend the empirical evidence in useful ways because conclusions now can signal concerns beyond what was possible earlier. Examples include the application to prosocial behavior of the findings on media violence, and the role of the media in socialization.
- Research of the past decade has significantly extended knowledge. The new evidence includes a better understanding of the television viewing experience, and the use of media by young people.

From the perspective of a much earlier examination of priorities by the first author and colleagues (Comstock et al., 1978), the present landscape is quite different. Then, our emphasis was on abstract concepts and strategic maneuvers. We were trying to prescribe conditions for the maximum effectiveness of social and behavioral science in pursuit of practical application. We presented an analysis of the forces influencing television based on the sources of action (regulatory vs. nonregulatory) and the targets of action (industry structure vs. social effects). We advocated meticulous examination of the ways research might be used, including the identification of policy issues and the data that might affect their resolution. We preached on behalf of focused research, including the organizational features that would make such programs more influential. Our goal was a better knowledge machine. We did not specify much in the way of concrete concerns.

In retrospect, our emphases reflected the times. We were optimistically naïve about the malleability and promise of the scientific endeavor, and somewhat short—although hardly lacking—in identifying specific issues. We thought much could be resolved by the systematic design and implementation of research and policy strategies. We (mostly the first author, who does not want to burden unjustly his coauthors with his reasoning at the time) thought it possible to construct more efficient ways to make things better. We were concerned less with what had been learned and what it might mean than with how we could learn more and how we could ensure that what we learned had practical application.

In fact, things did not change at all in the directions we prescribed. Our arguments retain some validity, but they are not likely to see much in the way of implementation because none has occurred in the ensuing three decades. We thus embark on a quite different approach. We focus on specific areas of concern, and raise questions as well as deliver answers. We thus abandon the knowledge machine for an agenda of issues identified by social and behavioral science. This is more realistic in regard to the influence of research on policy and action (including those of parents in the home), where research seldom leads directly to a policy solution.

As we recently have written elsewhere (Comstock & Scharrer, 2006), we see social and behavioral science as importantly entering into the deliberations and negotiations that affect policy and action in regard to the media while rarely being determinative. Research raises questions and presents evidence that it is difficult for those engaged in these exchanges to ignore entirely. Two examples are television advertising and young viewers, and television and film violence and antisocial behavior. In both cases, research has influenced the fundamental framework of knowledge and shaped policy, whereas the immediate sources of policy have resided in social, political, and economic factors.

II. THE ACTORS THAT INFLUENCE THE ROLE OF MEDIA

There are primarily three parties that influence the role of media in the lives of young people in addition to the choices that young consumers themselves make. They are the federal regulatory apparatus, the media industries, and parents.

A. *The Role of Federal Regulation*

The Federal Communications Commission (FCC), Federal Trade Commission (FTC), and the Congress have important but in practice quite limited roles in regard to television and no role at all for other media. Our hope is that their actions would conform to pertinent research, but the past half century has not been encouraging. The emphasis, as expected with the license to broadcast the principle economic property of an outlet that otherwise would have no value, has been on structural issues—who is empowered to broadcast, how many signals the spectrum can handle in a market, the acceptable degree of concentration of ownership across outlets. The trend toward deregulation of the past few decades has left much unattended to—the program-length commercial (once banned, but now accepted as inevitable), host-selling outside the boundary of the home program (lowers ad recognition but easy to ban), the retreat imposed on the FTC by Congress in regard to advertising directed at children (a substitution of political force for evidence-based policy). In contrast, the FCC requirement, in accord with legislation passed by Congress that broadcasters allot three hours a week to educational and cultural programming for the young, has apparently been quite successful (as measured by the number of such programs available). However, the FCC's recent concern with indecency is ironic when faced with its comparative indifference to violent entertainment, since the research provides little reason (other than fastidiousness) for concern about the former and much cause for concern about the latter. Beyond broadcast television, other media, including cable, are not regulated. What can we expect from the federal regulatory apparatus is limited to one medium, and within that medium, very narrow in scope.

B. *The Role of Industries*

Those in the business of making and disseminating media products will be primarily motivated by economic interests, although in many cases a large role will be played by creative concerns. For the same economic reasons, we can expect them to be very sensitive to public concerns and expectations. The retreat of the television broadcasters in the face of the V-chip legislation is an example. The broadcasters vowed to fight the proposal to install devices in new television sets that would allow parents to scramble undesired signals based on codes that the industry would supply. They fled from the field of battle when polls produced about 80 percent of the public as dissatisfied with the amount of violence on television. The public relations cost was too high, and the threat of formal regulation, although in fact probably remote, too great. Research on the effects of violent entertainment played no visible part in the industry's decision, although it certainly influenced those who were calling for action. Whatever research might suggest, we cannot expect those engaged in profitable activities to suspend them because research will rarely be so compelling that all counter arguments can be vanquished. However, we can expect that an industry will respond to public concerns and these are in part set by research, and in particular in this case we can hope that descriptive codes and discretionary warnings offered as information to parents will be as accurate as possible.

C. The Role of Parents

The major responsibility in regard to media and young persons inevitably falls to parents and other caregivers. They determine the opportunities for very early use of television and the age at which other media become readily accessible, the household environment that figures so importantly in the use of all media, and the media stockpiling in bedrooms that makes isolated media use so frequent for so many young people. They also have the opportunity to discuss media with young persons, to emphasize the many positive features of media, to encourage constructive use of media, and to enhance the learning from the media by expanding on and reinforcing theses, portrayals, and accounts presented by the media. Parents, finally, establish the environment in the home that is more or less favorable for questionable media use—unfettered viewing of television and film that interferes with scholastic achievement, obsessive involvement in depictions of violence that encourage hostile thoughts and antisocial behavior, or exposure to pornography.

III. WHERE THE DATA POINT

We organize our concerns by the chapter in which the data on which we draw are primarily presented. This should make the link between evidence and conclusion clearer and more accessible. Our criterion for concern is that the data point to a problem or an unanswered question for some young people. We use the data as a warning; we do not require a compelling case, but we do require that the data identify a problematic circumstance.

A. Media Use

The data on media use raise four issues about the welfare of young persons. They concern very early media use, media use in isolation, media use apart from the family, and the preference for screen media and entertainment.

1. Early Media Use   The very recent Kaiser surveys make it clear that regular attention to a television screen now begins earlier than the age of two. We know, from the pioneering work of Meltzoff, that infants as young as six months can replicate—that is, imitate—physical actions they see on a screen. However, this does not mean that media effectively can substitute for interactions with humans. At this early age, when the infant is beginning to make sense of the world and perceive distinctions between his or her self and others, human interaction is crucial. The attentive care of parents is important for healthy development during infancy. Imitation of the parents becomes a means by which the infant establishes a sense of separateness and an understanding of human commonality. Language acquisition will be furthered by the flexible reinforcement of parents. Attention to television is not necessarily harmful, but it is no substitute for contact with parents.

2. Media Use in Isolation   Media use has increasingly become private and isolated. This trend began many years ago with the increase of multiset households. They are now ubiquitous. The trend was only slightly slowed early in the process by the tendency of parents to take the initial additional set for their own bedrooms. However, the increasing availability of a wide range of media, and particularly screen media, in the bedrooms of young people has been accompanied by extensive use of media alone. One consequence is that social exchanges with other members of the family, and particularly parents, become constrained. Another is that media use of which parents would disapprove becomes more likely—erotic, extreme violence, dangerous chat rooms.

3. Media Use Apart from Family   The trend among young people toward screen media use apart from the family—only young children and only during prime time do they spend a majority of their screen media time with parents—has an additional consequence. It places a severe limit on parental mediation. This results in a loss on three fronts: (a) parents cannot express their approval or disapproval of portrayed behavior, and thus cannot make their values clearer; (b) parents cannot guide the aesthetic and cultural choices of their children, and thus forego shaping tastes and preferences; and (c) parents cannot comment upon and discuss what has been said or portrayed, and thus surrender a means of increasing the educational impact of viewing certain screen media—because young people (and probably everybody) learns more from the screen when someone else reviews, reinforces, or comments upon the material presented.

4. Preference for Screen Media Despite all the attention to the Internet, surveys record that screen media, and primarily television, by far consume the great majority of time young people spend with media. The sole rival in terms of time use is audio media featuring music, and this occurs only among older teenagers and, in particular, teenage females. These data inevitably raise questions about the contribution of the large amounts of time that young people spend with media to their imaginative, creative, and intellectual growth while amply documenting that they have found an enjoyable way to spend time.

B. Data on Television Viewing

The data on the experience of viewing television leads to two very broad conclusions. On the one hand, attention is irregular, divided, partial, and certainly unlike that common to movie theaters. Remote controls and the increasing number of available channels make a surf-and-skip pattern likely much of the time. On the other hand, the primary motive for viewing is an escape from stress and unwelcome thoughts. The surf-and-skip pattern serves this end admirably, because it accommodates for content of maximal interest. The questions remain the same but the focus now is not on what is consumed but how it is consumed. Might not something more occasionally be expected from media use in the way of imaginative, creative, and intellectual development while recognizing that much of media use will be only passingly enjoyable?

C. Messages Disseminated by Media

There is much that is problematic about the messages that are disseminated by media, and particularly by television—after all, the most popular of media. Television offers much that is uninformative and quite wrong about the world. It also offers much in the way of bad advice. This bad advice extends from what young people consume to how they behave. It also fails to some extent in providing images and portrayals that confirm the viewer's self-worth. Our assumption is that television operates to some degree as a source of information and that the people it portrays function as models for emulation or the confirmation—when the viewer can identify with them—of oneself. This is not unreasonable as an assumption, because those presented on television usually are attractive, successful, or at least powerful, all of which encourage emulation and identification.

We draw attention to four areas where portrayals are problematic:

1. Stereotyping

Gender, race, and age are marked by depictions that distort the demographics of everyday life. Males, and particularly white males, are overrepresented. So, too, are young adults, and particularly white young adults. Children and old people are seldom seen. Typically, depictions of males emphasize muscularity, independence, authority, and power, whereas depictions of females typically emphasize slimness and physical attractiveness, dependence, and deference to males.

2. Exclusion

Some people seldom see those like themselves on the screen. This applies not only to the very young and the very old, but to gays, lesbians, and most minority ethnic groups other than blacks (who appear in proportions about equal to their proportion in the population).

3. Unhealthy choices

Much that is presented in the way of consumption on television is unhealthy. Advertisements promote alcohol and foods that are low in nutritional value. Programs frequently depict alcohol use. Tobacco use, although banned from commercials, appears often in programs, and particularly older shows in syndication and older movies. Both alcohol and tobacco use are frequently portrayed as the province of the glamorous, brave, or powerful. A diet based on foods advertised to the young would increase the risk of obesity.

4. Bad advice

The behavioral recommendations implied by much of television are often bad advice. Violence is frequently endorsed as a widespread, normative, and desirable way to behave that will gain respect and enjoy social approval. Sexual coupling is often depicted as common between the unmarried, and sexuality is seldom connected with health risks, responsibility, or safe options.

Just as frequent exposure to commercials for a product maintains a favorable position in an individual's hierarchy of options (and generally ensures an association between product category and brand), repeated exposure to stereotypes and bad advice will make such images more accessible when decisions are being made about how to act. In contrast, some viewers will find themselves excluded from the social acceptance implied by the portrayal of those resembling themselves.

D. Converting Young People to Customers

The data on advertising and young people raise a number of intriguing and sometimes puzzling questions. There is no doubt that children below the age of eight are exploited by advertising aimed at them, because before that age a majority do not comprehend the self-interested motives of advertisers. There is also no doubt that advertising directed at young people is often effective and that the language employed is often disingenuous. The fact that the giant food manufacturers sidestepped restraints on television commercials aimed at children by Congressional edict rather than the facts of the case is disturbing. So, too, is the extent to which the youth market—segmented by age and stage of cognitive development—has become a major target of marketers.

The fact that young people are not always easy prey to particular advertising campaigns does not translate into support for the often-heard industry claim that young people today are too smart or "savvy" to be manipulated. Converting young people to customers has become an ardently and artfully pursued goal of advertisers, and the calculated introduction of children to brands begins early. Concern has become great enough for the American Psychological Association to offer a task force report on the ethics of using social and behavioral science to market to young people. These issues—the exploitation of children, the use of science as a strategy in marketing to the young, the growing importance of the youth market—take on enhanced importance in the current communications context in which the Internet, computers, and other means of disseminating persuasive messages blur the border between advertising and sports, entertainment, or other media content. The protections made possible by the structured formality of television broadcasts and commercial inserts—the recognizability of the "pod"— is vanishing. The result is renewed significance for the research on advertising and marketing and young people, and a less certain environment in which to apply its results.

E. The Effect of Viewing on Academic Achievement

Amount of television viewing is negatively associated with scholastic achievement for all subjects, but the greatest concern is with the three basic skills of reading, writing, and arithmetic because they are fundamental to progress in most subjects throughout the academic career of a young person. The biggest news—although an old story to many teachers and parents—is the evidence that television socializes the aesthetic and leisure preferences of young people. Viewing is negatively correlated with an interest in and respect and liking for books, with the reading of challenging material, and reading outside of assignments, and positively correlated with a preference for television-like content—romance, and celebrity inside dope.

These factors that correlate negatively with television viewing, of course, correlate positively with achievement. Time use is at the center of our paradigm. Time spent with television may displace time acquiring or maintaining the skills of reading, writing, and arithmetic. The data support the proposition that the penalty for time displaced lies in the value of the displaced activity. It was no surprise that the greater the intellectual resources in the home—books, magazines, newspapers, encyclopedias—the more negative the association between viewing and achievement. In homes with fewer or no resources—often homes with high centrality of television to the virtual exclusion of other media—the negative association is less pronounced. Displacement effects become significant only among those who spend a great deal of time with television—above the eightieth percentile in average amount of viewing. The negative correlations between achievement and viewing are also in part attributable to greater viewing by those with attributes that predict lower achievement—lower socioeconomic status, stressful relationships with peers and parents, and lower mental ability. We are particularly concerned about a minority at risk, although the inhibition of serious reading may be somewhat more widespread.

F. Influence of Screen Media on Behavior

The several meta-analyses, the consistency of results for experimental designs and survey designs, and the parallel outcomes for violent and prosocial portrayals make a strong case for an influence of screen media on behavior. The meta-analytic coefficients are positive (and statistically significant) for a wide range of differing conceptualizations of the independent and dependent variables, which means the relationship between exposure to violent entertainment and aggressive and antisocial behavior is very robust. The well-documented positive correlation between everyday violence viewing and aggressive and antisocial behavior—not fully explainable by anything other than exposure to violent entertainment—suggests that the experimental proof of causation within that limited setting is generalizable to everyday settings. In scientific jargon, the surveys confirm the external validity of the experiments.

The parallel outcomes for violent and prosocial portrayals lead us to conclude that the principles developed in connection with violent portrayals apply widely to behavior. In our terminology, these principles hold that emulation of portrayed behavior is enhanced by depictions (or implications) of efficacy, normativeness, and pertinence, and by viewers susceptible to influence (which, in the context of violent portrayals, means a state of frustration, anger, or a motive to aggress).

There comes a time in the exploration of an area by social and behavioral science at which one chooses to continue to pursue questions within narrow parameters or to generalize on a wider basis. That time is at hand in regard to media and behavior. An important step was the development of the General Aggression Model (GAM), which synthesizes concepts from several different theories and research paradigms. Another step was the recognition that factors on which the effects of violent portrayals are contingent apply to a broad range of behavior. A good example is the health belief model, which has the same theoretical roots as much media violence research. In the case of the health belief model, however, the hypotheses concern the effects of media (and other interventions) on behavior related to health.

There are many parallels in the data on violent portrayals and the playing of violent video games. Video games nevertheless require further investigation because of their rapidly increasing degrees of reality, the greater physical and mental involvement, and variations across games in point of view of the player (or shooter). Age is also likely to matter. Television viewing returns to earlier, higher levels of viewing when education is completed, whereas video game use typically declines (or vanishes) after adolescence. There is also a major question regarding gender. Video game use so far has been much greater among males than females, but television viewing does not display such a disparity. The content of the games is one potential explanation, with many games emphasizing violence, action, and aggression, all of which tend to appeal more to boys and men than to girls and women.

The new evidence of media influence on sexual behavior is particularly impressive. The designs favor a causal interpretation indicting sexual depictions on television and in song lyrics, and the outcomes further support the kind of behavioral influence attested to by the data on violent television and film entertainment.

We emphasize that in the case of screen portrayals context is extremely important. The likelihood of influence varies with the properties of the portrayal and the state of the viewer. In addition, the social setting of the viewer matters. As the GAM posits, an environment filled with hostility or marked by the availability of a deserving target (from the point of view of a potential aggressor) enhances the likelihood of aggression and thus the likelihood of some influence by prior exposure to violent portrayals. Age enters because adolescents and young adults are more likely to be in social settings that encourage aggressive or antisocial behavior.

G. Socialization

Everything we have written about concerns socialization of one kind or another. Even the experience of viewing television deals with the circumstances in which socialization-relevant information is attended to. One of the keys to the influence of screen media is that they do not encourage a critical or thoughtful stance. They typically are consumed with enough attention to follow the narrative but do not engage much more in the way of cognitive scrutiny. This sort of processing opens the way to influence that a more guarded view might thwart. We root for the cop-killing bankrobber to get away because he is so charming. We're skeptical of the credibility of commercials but repetitive exposure enhances the salience—and implied goodness—of products. Then there is the justly famous research in which bigots saw Archie Bunker (*All in the Family*) as a spokesperson whereas the unprejudiced saw him as an object of satire.

We now extend our attention to socialization by turning to politics, gender, and physical presence. Media have assumed an increasingly important role in regard to politics as party loyalties have become less fixed and parents less frequently bestow on their children a rooted allegiance to one or the other of the major parties. Media have become newly important sources of information. Gender roles are particularly susceptible to media influence as options for females become wider. The overall emphasis of media is on conventional male and female roles, but the data on socialization also indicates that nonstereotypical portrayals can encourage a more liberal outlook. As the research on advertising and marketing suggests, the media are quite influential in regard to physical presence—fashion, brands, and body image—and particularly so for tweens and teenagers.

The typology developed by Roberts and Foehr reminds us that there is widespread variation among young people in media use. Use varies as a function of household availability, parental rules, and personal tastes, and these in turn can be traced in part to such factors as household socioeconomic status and ethnicity. The unavoidable conclusion is that media influence also will vary considerably across the segments that constitute the audience of children and teenagers, with influence greatest among those who use media the most or for some reason are particularly susceptible to media influence. This has two consequences. First, the journalistic commonplace of monolithic terminology ("children," "teenagers," "young adult women," "seniors," etc.) must be abandoned in favor of more varied segments. Second, our concern with effects of the media or other influences should focus on these narrower segments because they define vulnerability. The result is a two-step paradigm: use and consequence.

Four theories that help to explain socialization effects are social comparison, social identity, social cognition, and cultivation. Social comparison posits that individuals use media to evaluate themselves, shifting in perspective and behavior when comparisons are unfavorable. Social identity holds that media contribute to the sense of self and the use of in-groups and out-groups in establishing status and position in relating to the social environment. Social cognition emphasizes the use of internalized symbolic examples to further one's ability to emulate or model the behavior and attitudes of successful others. Cultivation argues that the emphases of the media become an important basis for the construction of reality. These formulations have a common thread—the media surpass their contribution of a set of entertaining and diverting images to become practical guides to growing up and getting on.

IV. THE THREE M'S—STRATEGIES TO ENCOURAGE A CRITICAL STANCE

When we are asked to speak to parent or teacher groups about young people and media, we are frequently asked what can be done to help negotiate the potential hurdles (violence, hypercommercialization, stereotypes, etc.) and encourage a critical stance toward media. In response, the second author has come up with a pithy list of three suggestions: moderation, mediation, and media literacy. Although we recognize the complexity of young people's orientations toward and responses to media, we offer these simple strategies as a place to begin. Each is firmly grounded in the research record.

Since many studies have identified heavy use of particular media forms with some types of influence, moderation in consumption is a potentially fruitful strategy. Such an approach allows for greater opportunity to compare media messages with other sources of information about the social world, encourages exposure to a more limited number of favorites rather than choices employed to simply pass the time, and is less likely to displace other activities important for personal and social development. Mediation, as we have explained, allows for the expression of one's own responses to media, thereby communicating what is deemed objectionable and why as well as what is preferred. In households in which mediation occurs, the development of a critical outlook is more likely (although far from guaranteed), modeled initially perhaps by parents and other adults but also adopted by children and teenagers themselves. Finally, media literacy is the inclusion in kindergarten through twelfth grade classrooms of lessons and units designed to develop knowledge about media industries, media practices, and audience responses; the ability to use and access media in its many forms; and the application of critical thinking skills to evaluate and analyze media. Research in this area shows promise that media literacy curricula can enhance learning about many of the media topics that we have covered in this book and may even make media effects less likely. Moderation, mediation, and media literacy are steps toward empowering young people to challenge media while still retaining the pleasures that media afford.

REFERENCES

ABC cancels gay sitcom "Ellen" after ratings fall. (1998, April 24). *Los Angeles Times*, A6.

Acuff, D. S. (1997). *What kids buy and why: The psychology of marketing to kids.* New York, NY: Free Press.

Adler, R. P., Lesser, G. S., Meringoff, L. K., Robertson, T. S., Rossiter, J. R. & Ward, S. (1980). *The effect of television advertising on children: Review and recommendations.* Lexington, MA: Lexington Books.

Aikat, D. (2004). Streaming violent genres online: Visual images in music videos on BET.com, Country.com, MTV.com, and VH1.com. *Popular Music and Society, 27,* 221–241.

Albarran, A. B. & Umphrey, D. (1983). An examination of television motivations and program preferences by Hispanics, blacks, and whites. *Journal of Broadcasting and Electronic Media, 37*(1), 95–103.

Alexander, A., Ryan, M. & Munoz, P. (1984). Creating a learning context: Investigations on the interactions of siblings during television viewing. *Critical Studies in Mass Communication, 1,* 345–364.

Allen, C. L. (1965). Photographing the TV audience. *Journal of Advertising Research, 5,* 2–8.

Allen, M., D'Alessio, D. & Brezgel, K. (1995). A meta-analysis summarizing the effects of pornography II: Aggression after exposure. *Human Communication Research, 22*(2), 258–283.

Anderson, B., Mead, N. & Sullivan, S. (1986). *Television: What do National Assessment results tell us?* Princeton, NJ: Educational Testing Service.

Anderson, C. (1997). Violence in television commercials during nonviolent programming: The 1996 Major League Baseball playoffs. *Journal of the American Medical Association, 278,* 1045–1046.

Anderson, C. & McGuire, T. (1978). The effect of TV viewing on the educational performance of thirteen elementary school children. *Alberta Journal of Educational Research, 24,* 156–163.

Anderson, C. A. (2004). An update on the effects of playing violent video games. *Journal of Adolescence, 27,* 113–122.

Anderson, C. A., Berkowitz, L., Donnerstein, E., Huesmann, L. R., Johnson, J. D., Linz, D., Malamuth, N. M. & Wartella, E. (2003). The influence of media violence on youth. *Psychological Science in the Public Interest,* 4(3), 81–110.

Anderson, C. A. & Bushman, B. J. (2001). Effects of violent video games on aggressive behavior, aggressive cognition, aggressive affect, physiological arousal, and prosocial behavior: A meta-analytic review of the scientific literature. *Psychological Science, 12,* 353–359.

Anderson, C. A., & Dill, K. E. (2000). Video games and aggressive thoughts, feelings, and behavior in the laboratory and in life. *Journal of Personality and Social Psychology, 4,* 772–790.

Anderson, C. A., Gentile, D. A. & Buckley, K. E. (2007). *Violent video game effects on children and adolescents: Theory, research and public policy.* New York: Oxford University Press.

Anderson, C. A. & Huesmann, L. R. (2003). Human aggression: A social-cognitive view. In M. A. Hogg & J. Cooper (Eds.), *Handbook of social psychology.* London: Sage.

Anderson, C. A. & Murphy, C. R. (2003). Violent video games and aggressive behavior in young women. *Aggressive Behavior, 29*(5), 423–429.

Anderson, D. R., Alwitt, L., Lorch, E. & Levin, S. (1979). Watching children watch television. In G. Hale & M. Lewis (Eds.), *Attention and cognitive development* (pp. 331–361). New York: Plenum.

Anderson, D. R., Bryant, J., Wilder, A., Santomero, A., Williams, M. & Crawley, A. M. (2000). Researching *Blue's Clues*: Viewing behavior and impact. *Media Psychology, 2,* 179–194.

Anderson, D. R., Choi, H. P. & Lorch, E. P. (1987). Attentional inertia reduces distractibility during young children's TV viewing. *Child Development, 58,* 798–806.

Anderson, D. R. & Collins, P. A. (1988). *The impact on children's education: Television's influence on cognitive development.* Washington, DC: U.S. Department of Education.

Anderson, D. R., Collins, P. A., Schmitt, K. L. & Jacobvitz, R. S. (1996). Stressful life events and television viewing. *Communication Research, 23*(3), 243–260.

Anderson, D. R., Huston, A. C., Schmitt, K. L., Linebarger, D. L. & Wright, J. C. (2001). Early childhood television viewing and adolescent behavior. *Monographs of the Society for Research in Child Development, 66* (1, Serial number 264).

Anderson, D. R., Huston, A. C., Wright, J. C. & Collins, P. A. (1998). *Sesame Street* and educational television for children. In R. G. Noll & M. E. Price (Eds.), *A communications cornucopia: Markle Foundation essays on information policy* (pp. 279–296). Washington, DC: Brookings Institute.

Anderson, D. R. & Levin, S. R. (1976). Young children's attention to *Sesame Street. Child Development, 47,* 806–811.

Anderson, D. R., Levin, S. & Lorch, E. (1977). The effects of TV program pacing on the behavior of preschool children. *AV Communication Review, 25*(2), 159–166.

Anderson, D. R. & Lorch, E. P. (1983). Looking at television: Action or reaction? In J. Bryant & D. R. Anderson (Eds.), *Children's understanding of TV: Research on attention and comprehension* (pp. 1–34). New York: Academic Press.

Anderson, D. R., Lorch, E. P., Field, D. E., Collins, P. A. & Nathan, J. G. (1986). Television viewing at home: Age trends in visual attention and time with TV. *Child Development, 57,* 1024–1033.

Anderson, D. R., Lorch, E. P., Field, D. E. & Sanders, J. (1981). The effects of TV program comprehensibility on preschool children's visual attention to television. *Child Development, 52,* 151–157.

Anderson, D. R. & Pempek, T. A. (2005). Television and very young children. *American Behavioral Scientist, 48,* 505–522.

Andison, F. S. (1977). TV violence and viewer aggression: A cumulation of study results. *Public Opinion Quarterly, 41*(3), 314–331.

Angier, N. (2001, December 9). In the movies, women age faster. *The New York Times*, 23.

Argenta, D. M., Stoneman, Z. & Brody, G. H. (1986). The effects of three different television programs on young children's peer interactions and toy play. *Journal of Applied Developmental Psychology, 7*, 355–371.

Armstrong, G. B. & Greenberg, B. S. (1990). Background television as an inhibitor of cognitive processing. *Human Communication Research, 16*(3), 355–386.

Atkin, C. (1975a). *Effects of television advertising on children—First year experimental evidence*. Report #1. East Lansing, MI: Department of Communication, Michigan State University.

Atkin, C. (1975b). *Effects of television advertising on children—Parent-child communication in supermarket breakfast selection*. Report #7. East Lansing, MI: Department of Communication, Michigan State University.

Atkin, C. (1975c). *Effects of television advertising on children—Survey of children's and mothers' responses to television commercials*. Report #8. East Lansing, MI: Department of Communication, Michigan State University.

Atkin, C. (1977). Effects of campaign advertising and newscasts on children. *Journalism Quarterly, 54*, 503–508.

Atkin, C. (1981). Communication and political socialization. In D. Nimmo & K. Sanders (Eds.), *Handbook of political communication* (pp. 299–328). Beverly Hills, CA: Sage.

Atkin, C., Hocking, J. & Block, M. (1984). Teenage drinking: Does advertising make a difference? *Journal of Communication, 34*(2), 157–167.

Atkin, C. & Miller, M. (1975). *The effects of television advertising on children: Experimental evidence*. Paper presented at the annual meeting of the International Communication Association, Chicago. As cited in Eisenstock, 1984.

Atkin, C. K. (1978a). Observations of parent-child interaction in supermarket decisionmaking. *Journal of Marketing, 42*, 41–45.

Atkin, C. K. (1978b). Effects of proprietary drug advertising on youth. *Journal of Communication, 28*, 71–78.

Atkin, C. K. (1983). Effects of realistic TV violence vs. fictional violence on aggression. *Journalism Quarterly, 60*, 615–621.

Atkin, C. K. (1988a). *A critical review of media effects on alcohol consumption patterns*. A report to the Alcoholic Beverage Medical Research Foundation, Baltimore, MD. East Lansing, MI: Department of Communication, Michigan State University.

Atkin, C. K. (1988b). Mass communication effects on drinking and driving. In *Surgeon General's Workshop on Drunk Driving* (pp.15–34). Washington, DC: U.S. Department of Health and Human Services.

Atkin, C. K. & Gantz, W. (1978). Television news and political socialization. *Public Opinion Quarterly, 42*, 183–198.

Atkin, C. K., Greenberg, B. S., Korzenny, F. & McDermott, S. (1979). Selective exposure to televised violence. *Journal of Broadcasting, 23*(1), 5–13.

Atkin, C. K., Nuendorf, K. & McDermott, S. (1983). The role of alcohol advertising in excessive and hazardous drinking. *Journal of Drug Education, 13*, 313–325.

Atkin, D. (1992). An analysis of television series with minority lead characters. *Critical Studies in Mass Communication, 9*, 337–349.

Aubrey, J. S. & Harrison, K. (2004). The gender-role content of children's favorite television programs and its links to their gender-related perceptions. *Media Psychology, 6*, 111–146.

Austin, E. W. & Pinkleton, B. E. (2001). The role of parental mediation in the political socialization process. *Journal of Broadcasting & Electronic Media, 45*, 221–240.

Austin, E. W., Roberts, D. F. & Nass, C.I. (1990). Influences of family communication on children's television interpretation processes. *Communication Research, 17*, 545–564.

Ball, S. & Bogatz, G. A. (1970). *The first year of "Sesame Street": An evaluation.* Princeton, NJ: Educational Testing Service.

Ballard, M. E., Lineberger, R. (1999). Video game violence and confederate gender: Effects on reward and punishment given by college males. *Sex Roles, 41*(7–8), 541–559.

Ballard-Campbell, M. (1983). *Children's understanding of television advertising: Behavioral assessment of three developmental skills.* Doctoral dissertation, University of California, Los Angeles.

Bandura, A. (1965). Influence of models' reinforcement contingencies on the acquisition of imitative responses. *Journal of Personality and Social Psychology, 1*, 589–595.

Bandura, A. (1973). *Aggression: A social learning analysis.* Englewood Cliffs, NJ: Prentice Hall.

Bandura, A. (1986). *Social foundations of thought and action: A social cognitive theory.* Upper Saddle River, NJ: Prentice-Hall.

Bandura, A. (2002). Social cognitive theory of mass communication. In J. Bryant & D. Zillmann (Eds.), *Media effects: Advances in theory and research, 2nd ed.* (pp. 61–90). Hillsdale, NJ: Erlbaum.

Bandura, A., Ross, D. & Ross, S. A. (1963a). Imitation of film-mediated aggressive models. *Journal of Abnormal and Social Psychology, 66*(1), 3–11.

Bandura, A., Ross, D. & Ross, S. A. (1963b). Vicarious reinforcement and imitative learning. *Journal of Abnormal and Social Psychology, 67*(6), 601–607.

Bankart, C. P. & Anderson, C. C. (1979). Short-term effects of prosocial television viewing on play of preschool boys and girls. *Psychological Reports, 44*, 935–941.

Barcus, F. E. (1983). *Images of life on children's television.* New York: Praeger.

Barner, M. B. (1999). Sex-role stereotyping in FCC-mandated children's educational television. *Journal of Broadcasting & Electronic Media, 43*, 551–564.

Barr, R., Chavez, M., Fujimoto, M., Garcia, A., Muentener, P. & Strait, C. (2003, April). *Television exposure during infancy: Patterns of viewing, attention, and interaction.* Paper presented at the biennial meeting of the Society for Research in Child Development. Tampa, FL.

Barr, R. & Hayne, H. (1999). Developmental changes in imitation from television during infancy. *Child Development, 70*, 1067–1081.

Bartholow, B. D., Anderson, C. A. (2001). Effects of violent video games on aggressive behavior: Potential sex differences. *Journal of Experimental Social Psychology, 38*(3), 283–290.

Bartholow, B. D., Sestir, M. A., Davis, E. B. (2005). Correlates and consequences of exposure to video game violence: Hostile personality, empathy, and aggressive behavior. *Personality and Social Psychology Bulletin, 31*(11), 1573–1586.

Bartsch, R. A., Burnett, T., Diller, T. R. & Rankin-Williams, E. (2000). Gender representation in television commercials: Updating an update. *Sex Roles, 43* (9/10), 735–743.

Barwise, T. P. (1986). Repeat-viewing of prime-time TV series. *Journal of Advertising Research*, 26, 9–14.

Barwise, T. P. & Ehrenberg, A. S. C. (1988). *Television and its audience*. Newbury Park, CA: Sage.

Barwise, T. P., Ehrenberg, A. S. C. & Goodhardt, G. J. (1982). Glued to the box?: Patterns of TV repeat viewing. *Journal of Communication*, 32(4), 22–29.

Baxter, R. L., De Reimer, C., Landini, A., Leslie, L. & Singletary, M. W. (1985). A content analysis of music videos. *Journal of Broadcasting & Electronic Media*, 29, 333–340.

Beal, C. R. (1994). *Boys and girls: The development of gender roles*. New York: McGraw Hill.

Beasley, B. & Collins Standley, T. (2002). Shirts vs. skins: Clothing as indicator of gender role stereotyping in video games. *Mass Communication & Society*, 5, 279–293.

Bechtel, R. B., Achelpohl, C. & Akers, R. (1972). Correlates between observed behavior and questionnaire responses on television viewing. In E.A. Rubinstein, G. A. Comstock & J. P. Murray (Eds.), *Television and social behavior. Television in day-to-day life: Patterns of use*. (Vol. 4). Washington, DC: U.S. Government Printing Office.

Becker, M. H. (Guest Ed.). (1974). The health belief model and personal health behavior. *Health Education Monographs*, 2(4).

Becker, M. H. & Maiman, L. A. (1975). Sociobehavioral determinants of compliance with health and medical care recommendations. *Medical Care*, 13, 10–24.

Beentjes, J. W. J. (1989). Salomon's model for learning from television and book: A Dutch replication study. *Educational Technology Research and Development*, 37(2), 47–58.

Beentjes, J. W. J. & van der Voort, T. H. A. (1989). Television and young people's reading behavior: A review of research. *European Journal of Communication*, 4, 51–77.

Bellotti, F. X. (1975, July). Petition before the FCC of the Attorneys General of Massachusetts, Alaska, Colorado, Delaware, Hawaii, Illinois, Maryland, Nebraska, New Hampshire, North Carolina, Maine, Pennsylvania, Rhode Island, and Wyoming to promulgate a rule restricting the advertising of over-the-counter drugs. Washington, DC: U.S. House of Representatives.

Belson, W. A. (1959). Effects of television on the interests and initiative of adult viewers in Greater London. *British Journal of Psychology*, 50, 145–158.

Belson, W. A. (1978). *Television violence and the adolescent boy*. Westmead, England: Saxon House, Teakfield.

Berg, C. (1990). Stereotyping in films in general and of the Hispanic in particular. *The Howard Journal of Communications*, 2, 286–300.

Berkowitz, L. (1984). Some effects of thoughts on anti- and prosocial influences of media events: A cognitive-neoassociationistic analysis. *Psychological Bulletin*, 95(3), 410–427.

Berkowitz, L. (1990). On the formation and regulation of anger and aggression: A cognitive-neoassociationist analysis. *American Psychologist*, 45(4), 494–503.

Berkowitz, L. & Alioto, J. T. (1973). The meaning of an observed event as a determinant of aggressive consequences. *Journal of Personality and Social Psychology* 28(2), 206–217.

Berkowitz, L. & Geen, R. G. (1966). Film violence and the cue properties of available targets. *Journal of Personality and Social Psychology* 3(5), 525–530.

Berkowitz, L. & Geen, R. G. (1967). Stimulus qualities of the target of aggression: A further study. *Journal of Personality and Social Psychology, 5*(3), 364–368.

Berkowitz, L. & Rawlings, E. (1963). Effects of film violence on inhibitions against subsequent aggression. *Journal of Abnormal and Social Psychology, 66*, 405–412.

Beuf, A. (1974). Doctor, lawyer, household drudge. *Journal of Communication, 25*, 142–145.

Bianchi, S. M. & Robinson, J. (1997). What did you do today? Children's use of time, family composition, and acquisition of social capital. *Journal of Marriage and the Family, 59*, 332–344.

Bickham, D. S., Vandewater, E. A., Huston, A. C., Lee, J. H., Caplovitz, A. G. & Wright, J. C. (2003). Predictors of children's electronic media use: An examination of three ethnic groups. *Media Psychology, 5*, 107–137.

Bickham, D. S., Wright, J. C. & Huston, A. C. (2001). Attention, comprehension, and the educational influences of television. In D. G. Singer & J. L. Singer (Eds.), *Handbook of children and the media* (pp. 101–119). Thousand Oaks, CA: Sage.

Bigler, R. S. & Liben, L. S. (1990). The role of attitudes and interventions in gender-schematic processing. *Child Development, 61*, 1440–1452.

Bigler, R. S. & Liben, L. S. (1992). Cognitive mechanisms in children's gender stereotyping: Theoretical and educational implications of a cognitive-based intervention. *Child Development, 63*, 1351–1363.

Bjorkqvist, K. (1994). Sex differences in physical, verbal and indirect aggression: A review of recent research. *Sex Roles, 30*(3/4), 177–188.

Blatt, J., Spencer, L. & Ward, S. (1972). A cognitive developmental study of children's reactions to television advertising. In E. A. Rubinstein, G. A. Comstock & J. P. Murray (Eds.), *Television and social behavior: Vol. 4. Television in day-to-day life: Patterns of use* (pp. 452–467). Washington, DC: U.S. Government Printing Office.

Blosser, B. J. & Roberts, D. F. (1985). Age differences in children's perceptions of message intent: Responses to TV news, commercials, educational spots, and public service announcements. *Communication Research, 12*(4), 455–484.

Bogatz, G. A. & Ball, S. (1971). *The second year of "Sesame Street": A continuing evaluation, Vols. 1 and 2*. Princeton, NJ: Educational Testing Service.

Bolton, R. N. (1983). Modeling the impact of TV food advertising on children's diets. *Current Issues and Research in Advertising, 6*(1), 173–199.

Botta, R. A. (1999). Television images and adolescent girls' body image disturbance. *Journal of Communication, 49*, 22–41.

Bower, R. T. (1985). *The changing television audience in America*. New York: Columbia University Press.

Brederode-Santos, M. E. (1993). *Learning with television: The secret of Rua Sesamo*. (English translation of Portuguese, M. E. Brederode-Santos, trans., 1991, *Coma Televiso o Segredo da Rua Sdsamo. Lisbon: TV Guia Editora*). Unpublished research report.

Breed, W. & DeFoe, J. R. (1981). The portrayal of the drinking process on prime-time television. *Journal of Communication, 31*(1), 58–67.

Brehm, J. & Rahn, W. (1997). Individual-level evidence for the causes and consequences of social capital. *American Journal of Political Science, 41*, 999–1023.

Brown, J. D., Campbell, K. & Fischer, L. (1986). American adolescents and music videos: Why do they watch? *Gazette, 37*, 19–32.

Brown, J. D., Childers, K., Bauman, K. & Koch, G. (1990). The influence of new media and family structure on young adolescents' television and radio use. *Communication Research, 17*, 65–82.

Brown, J. D. & Newcomer, S. F. (1991). Television viewing and adolescents' sexual behavior. *Journal of Homosexuality, 21*, 77–91.

Brown, L. (1977). *The New York Times encyclopedia of television*. New York: Times Books.

Browne, B. A. (1998). Gender stereotypes in advertising on children's television in the 1990s: A cross-national analysis. *Journal of Advertising, 27*, 83–97.

Bryant, J. (1989). Viewers' enjoyment of televised sports violence. In L. A. Wenner (Ed.), *Media, sports & society* (pp. 270–289). Newbury Park, CA: Sage.

Bryant, J., Comisky, P. & Zillman, D. (1981). The appeal of rough-and-tumble play in televised professional football. *Communication Quarterly, 29*, 256–262.

Bryant, J., Zillman, D. & Brown, D. (1983). Entertainment features in children's educational television: Effects on attention and information acquisition. In J. Bryant & D. R. Anderson (Eds.), *Children's understanding of television: Research on attention and comprehension* (pp. 221–240). New York: Academic Press.

Bushman, B. J. & Anderson, C. A. (2001). Media violence and the American public: Scientific facts versus media misinformation. *American Psychologist, 56*(6–7), 477–489.

Butler, E. J., Popovich, P. M., Stackhouse, R. H. & Garner, R. K. (1981). Discrimination of television programs and commercials by preschool children. *Journal of Advertising Research, 21*(2), 53–56.

Byrd-Bredbenner, C. & Grasso, D. (2000). What is television trying to make children swallow?: Content analysis of the nutrition information in prime-time advertisements. *Journal of Nutrition Education, 32*, 187–195.

Cairns, E., Hunter, D. & Herring, L. (1980). Young children's awareness of violence in Northern Ireland: The influence of Northern Irish television in Scotland and Northern Ireland. *British Journal of Social and Clinical Psychology, 19*(1), 3–6.

Calavita, M. (2004). Idealization, inspiration, irony. *Popular Communication, 2*, 129–151.

California Assessment Program. (1980). *Student achievement in California schools. 1979–80 annual report*. Sacramento: California State Department of Education.

California Assessment Program. (1982). *Survey of sixth grade school achievement and television viewing habits*. Sacramento: California State Department of Education.

California Assessment Program. (1986). *Annual report, 1985–86*. Sacramento: California State Department of Education.

Calvert, S. L. (2000). *Children's journeys through the information age*. Boston: McGraw Hill.

Calvert, S. L. & Huston, A. C. (1987). Television and children's gender schemata. In L. S. Liben & M. L. Signorella (Eds.), *Children's gender schemata* (pp. 75–88). San Francisco: Jossey-Bass.

Calvert, S. L., Kotler, J. A., Zehnder, S. M. & Shockey, E. M. (2003). Gender stereotyping in children's reports about educational and informational television programs. *Media Psychology, 5*, 139–162.

Calvert, S. L., Stolkin, A. & Lee, J. (1997, April). *Gender and ethnic portrayals in children's Saturday morning television programs*. Poster presented at the biennial meeting of the Society for Research in Child Development, Washington, D.C.

Canary, D. J. & Spitzberg, B. H. (1993). Loneliness and media gratification. *Communication Research, 20*(6), 800–821.

Cantor, J. (1998a). *"Mommy, I'm scared: How TV and movies frighten children and what we can do to protect them.* San Diego, CA: Harcourt Brace.

Cantor, J. (1998b). Ratings for program content: The role of research findings. In K. Jamieson (Ed.), *Annals of the American Academy of Political and Social Science, 557* (Special issue), 54–69.

Cantor, J. (2001). The media and children's fears, anxieties, and perceptions of danger. In D. G. Singer & J. L. Singer (Eds.), *Handbook of children and media* (pp. 207–222). Thousand Oaks, CA: Sage.

Cantor, J. & Hoffner, C. (1990). Children's fear reactions to a televised film as a function of perceived immediacy of depicted threat. *Journal of Broadcasting & Electronic Media, 34*(4), 421–442.

Cantor, J., Mares, M. L. & Oliver, M. B. (1993). Parents' and children's emotional reactions to televised coverage of the Gulf War. In B. Greenberg & W. Gantz (Eds.), *Desert storm and the mass media* (pp. 325–340). Cresskill, NJ: Hampton Press.

Cantor, J. & Nathanson, A. (1996). Children's fright reactions to television news. *Journal of Communication, 46*(4), 139–152.

Cantor, J. & Reilly, S. (1982). Adolescents' fright reactions to television and films. *Journal of Communication, 32*(1), 87–99.

Cantor, J., Wilson, B. J. & Hoffner, C. (1986). Emotional responses to a televised nuclear holocaust film. *Communication Research, 13*(2), 257–277.

Capella, J. N. & Jamieson, K. H. (1997). *Spiral of cynicism: The press and the public good.* New York: Oxford University Press.

Caprara, G. V., D'Imperio, G., Gentilomo, A., Mammucari, A., Ranzi, P., Travaglia, G. (1987). The intrusive commercial: Influence of aggressive TV commercials on aggression. *European Journal of Social Psychology, 17,* 23–31.

Carlson, L. & Grossbart, S. (1990). Mothers' communication-orientation and consumer-socialization tendencies. *Journal of Advertising, 19,* 27–39.

Carlson, L., Grossbart, S. & Walsh, A. (1991). Consumer socialization and frequency of shopping with children. *Journal of the Academy of Marketing Science, 19,* 155–164.

Carlson Jones, D. (2001). Social comparison and body image: Attractiveness comparisons to models and peers among adolescent girls and boys. *Sex Roles, 45,* 645–664.

Carlson Jones, D., Vigfusdottir, H.T. & Lee, Y. (2004). Body image and the appearance culture among adolescent girls and boys: An examination of friend conversations, peer criticism, appearance magazines, and the internalization of appearance ideals. *Journal of Adolescent Research, 19,* 323–339.

Cash, T. F. & Deagle, E. A. (1997). The nature and extent of body image disturbances in anorexia nervosa and bulimia nervosa: A meta-analysis. *International Journal of Eating Disorders, 22,* 107–125.

Celozzi, M. J., II, Kazelskis, R. & Gotsch, K. U. (1981). The relationship between viewing televised violence in ice hockey and subsequent levels of personal aggression. *Journal of Sport Behavior, 4*(4), 157–162.

Chaffee, S. H. (1972). Television and adolescent aggressiveness (overview). In G. A. Comstock & E. A. Rubinstein (Eds.), *Television and social behavior: Vol. 3. Television and adolescent aggressiveness* (pp. 1–34). Washington, DC: U. S. Government Printing Office.

Chaffee, S. H., Nass, C. I. & Yang, S. M. (1990). The bridging role of television in immigrant political socialization. *Human Communication Research, 17,* 266–288.

Chaffee, S. H., Ward, L. S. & Tipton, L. P. (1970). Mass communication and political socialization. *Journalism Quarterly, 47,* 647–659, 666.

Chaffee, S. H., Ward, L. S. & Tipton, L. P. (1973). Mass communication and political socialization", In J. Dennis (Ed.), *Socialization to Politics.* New York: Wiley.

Chaffee, S. H. & Yang, S. M. (1988). Communication and political socialization. In O. Ichilov (Ed.), *Political socialization for democracy* (pp. 137–157). New York: Columbia University, Teachers College Press.

Champion, H. & Furnham, A. (1999). The effect of the media on body dissatisfaction in adolescent girls. *European Eating Disorder Review, 7,* 213–228.

Chandler, D. & Roberts-Young, D. (1998). *The construction of identity in the personal homepages of adolescents.* Retrieved July 21, 1999 from http://www.aber.ac.uk/~dgc/strasbourg.html.

Chen-Yu, J. H. & Seock, Y. K. (2002). Adolescents' clothing purchase motivations, information sources, and store selection criteria: A comparison of male/female and impulse/nonimpulse shoppers. *Family and Consumer Sciences Research Journal, 31,* 50–77.

Children's Television Act of 1990. Pub. L., No. 101-437,104 Stat. 996-1000, codified at 47 USC Sections 303a, 303b, 394.

Childs, J. H. (1979). *Television viewing, achievement, IQ and creativity.* Doctoral Dissertation. Brigham Young University, Provo, UT.

Chirco, A. P. (1990). *An examination of stepwise regression models of adolescent alcohol and marijuana use with special attention to the television exposure— teen drinking issue.* Unpublished doctoral dissertation, Syracuse University, Syracuse, NY.

Cho, C. H. & Cheon, H. J. (2005). Children's exposure to negative Internet content: Effects of family context. *Journal of Broadcasting & Electronic Media, 49,* 488–509.

Christakis, D. A., Zimmerman, F. J., DiGiuseppe, D. L. & McCarty, C. A. (2004). Early television exposure and subsequent attention problems in children. *Pediatrics, 113*(4), 708–714.

Christenson, P. & Roberts, D. F. (1998). *It's not only rock n' roll: Popular music in the lives of adolescents.* Cresskill, NJ: Hampton Press.

Cline, V. B., Croft, R. G. & Courrier, S. (1973). Desensitization of children to television violence. *Journal of Personality and Social Psychology, 27*(3), 360–365.

Cobb, N. J., Stevens-Long, J. & Goldstein, S. (1982). The influence of televised models on toy preference in children. *Sex Roles, 8,* 1075–1080.

Cohen, E. E. (1988). *Children's television commercialization survey.* Washington, DC: National Association of Broadcasters.

Colder-Bolz, C. R. (1980). Mediation: The role of significant others. *Journal of Communication, 30,* 106–118.

Collins, W. A. (1981). Recent advances in research on cognitive processing television viewing. *Journal of Broadcasting, 25*(4), 327–334.

Collins, W. A. (1983). Interpretation and influence in children's television viewing. In J. Bryant & D. G. Anderson (Eds.), *Children's understanding of television: Research on attention and comprehension* (pp. 125–150). New York: Academic Press.

Collins, W. A., Sobol, B. L. & Westby, S. (1981). Effects of adult commentary on children's comprehension and inference from a televised dramatic narrative. *Child Development, 52,* 158–163.

Collins, R. L., Elliott, M. N., Berry, S. H., Kanouse, D. E., Kunkel, D., Hunter, S. B., Miu, A. (2004). Watching sex on television predicts adolescent initiation of sexual behavior. *Pediatrics 114*(3), 280–289.

Comstock, G. (1983). Media influences on aggression. In A. Goldstein (Ed.), *Prevention and control of aggression* (pp. 241–272).

Comstock, G. (1991). *Television and the American child.* San Diego, CA: Academic Press.

Comstock, G. (1993). The medium and the society: The role of television in American life. In G. Berry & J. Asamen (Eds.). *Children & television: Images in a changing sociocultural world.* Newbury Park, CA: Sage.

Comstock, G. (2004). Paths from television violence to aggression: Reinterpreting the evidence. In. L. J. Shrum (Ed.), *The Psychology of Entertainment Media: Blurring the Lines Between Entertainment and Persuasion* (pp. 193–212). Mahwah, NJ: Lawrence Erlbaum.

Comstock, G., Chaffee, S., Katzman, N., McCombs, M. & Roberts, D. (1978). *Television and human behavior.* New York: Columbia University Press.

Comstock, G. & Cobbey, R. (1979). Television and the children of ethnic minorities. *Journal of Communication, 29*(1), 104–115.

Comstock, G. & Scharrer, E. (1999). *Television: What's on, who's watching, and what it means.* San Diego, CA: Academic Press.

Comstock, G. & Scharrer, E. (2001). The use of television and other film-related media. In D. G. Singer, & J. L. Singer (Eds.), *Handbook of children and the media* (pp. 47–72). Thousand Oaks, CA: Sage.

Comstock, G. & Scharrer, E. (2003). Meta-analyzing the controversy over television violence and aggression. In D. A. Gentile (Ed.), *Media violence and children.* (pp. 205–226). Westport, CT: Praeger.

Comstock, G. & Scharrer, E. (1999). *Television: What's on, who's watching, and what it means.* San Diego, CA: Academic Press.

Comstock, G. & Scharrer, E. (2005). *The psychology of media and politics.* San Diego, CA: Elsevier.

Comstock, G. & Scharrer, E. (2006). *Media and Popular Culture.* In K. A. Renninger & I. Sigel (Vol. Eds.) *Child Psychology and Practice, Vol. IV;* W. Damon & R. Lerner (Eds.), *Handbook of Child Psychology,* New York: Wiley.

Conger, J. & Galambos, N. (1997). *Adolescence and youth: Psychological development in a changing world* (5th ed.). New York: Longman.

Cook, T. D., Appleton, H., Conner, R., Shaffer, A., Tamkin, G. & Weber, S. J. (1975). *"Sesame Street" revisited: A study in evaluation research.* New York: Russell Sage Foundation.

Cook, T. D. & Campbell, D. T. (1979). *Quasiexperimentation: Design and analysis issues for field settings.* Chicago: Houghton Mifflin.

Cook, T. D., Kendzierski, D. A. & Thomas, S. A. (1982). *Television research for science and policy: An alien perspective on the NIMH Report on Television and Behavior.* Unpublished manuscript prepared for the Committee on Research and Law Enforcement and the Administration of Justice of the National Research Council of the National Academy of Sciences, Northwestern University, Evanston, IL.

Cook, T. D., Kendzierski, D. A. & Thomas, S. A. (1983). The implicit assumptions of television research: An analysis of the 1982 NIMH report on *Television and Behavior: Public Opinion Quarterly, 47*(2), 161–201.

Cope, K. M. (1998). *Sexually-related talk and behavior in the shows most frequently viewed by adolescents.* Unpublished master's thesis, University of California, Santa Barbara.

Cotugna, N. (1988). TV ads on Saturday morning children's programming: What's new? *Journal of Nutrition Education, 20,* 125–127.

Craig, R. S. (1992). The effect of television daypart on gender portrayals in television commercials: A content analysis. *Sex Roles, 26,* 197–211.

Crawley, A. M., Anderson, D. R., Wilder, A., Williams, M. & Santomero, A. (1999). Effects of repeated exposures to a single episode of the television program *Blue's Clues* on the viewing behaviors and comprehension of preschool children. *Journal of Educational Psychology, 91,* 630–637.

Crawley, A. M., Anderson, D. R., Santomero, A., Wilder, A., Williams, M., Evans, M. K. & Bryant, J. (2002). Do children learn how to watch television? The impact of extensive experience with *Blue's Clues* on preschool children's television viewing behavior. *Journal of Communication, 52,* 264–280.

Csikszentmihalyi, M. (1990). *Flow: The psychology of optimal experience.* New York, NY: Harper.

Cumberbatch, G. & Negrine, R. (1992). *Images of disability on television.* London: Routledge.

Cuneo, A. (1989, March 10). Targeting teens: Madison Avenue's call of the child. *U.S. News & World Report, 106,* 84–85.

Dansky, J. L. (1980). Make-believe: A mediator in the relationship between play and associative fluency. *Child Development, 51,* 576–579.

Daters, C. (1990). Importance of clothing and self-esteem among adolescents. *Clothing and Textiles Research Journal, 8,* 45–50.

Dates, J. (1980). Race, racial attitudes, and adolescent perceptions of black television characters. *Journal of Broadcasting, 24*(4), 549–560.

Davidson, E. S., Yasuna, A. & Tower, A. (1979). The effects of television cartoons on sex-role stereotyping in young girls. *Child Development, 50,* 597–600.

Davis, D. M. (1990). Portrayals of women in prime time network television: Some demographic characteristics. *Sex Roles, 23,* 325–332.

Davis, S. N. (2003). Sex stereotyping in commercials targeted toward children: A content analysis. *Sociological Spectrum, 23,* 407–425.

DeBell, M. & Chapman, C. (2003). *Computer and Internet use by children and adolescents in the United States: 2001.* (NCES 2004-014). U.S. Department of Education. Washington, DC: National Center for Education Statistics.

DeFleur, M. L. & DeFleur, L. B. (1967). The relative contribution of television as a learning source for children's occupational knowledge. *American Sociological Review, 32,* 777–789.

Delli Carpini, M. X. (1986). *Stability and change in American politics: The coming of age of the generation of the 1960s.* New York: New York University Press.

Delli Carpini, M. X. & Keeter, S. (1996). *What Americans know about politics and why it matters.* New Haven, CT: Yale University Press.

Derscheid, L. E., Kwon, Y. H. & Fang, S. R. (1996). Preschoolers' socialization as consumers of clothing and recognition of symbolism. *Perceptual and Motor Skills, 82,* 1171–1181.

Desmond, R. J., Singer, J. L. & Singer, D. G. (1990). Gender differences, mediation, and disciplinary styles in children's responses to television. *Sex Roles, 16*(7/8), 375–389.

Desmond, R. J., Singer, J. L. & Singer, D. G., Calam, R. & Colimore, K. (1985). Family mediation patterns and television viewing: Young children's use and grasp of the medium. *Human Communication Research, 11*(1), 76–81.

Diaz-Guerrero, R. & Holtzman, W. H. (1974). Learning by televised *Plaza Sesamo* in Mexico. *Journal of Educational Psychology, 66,* 632–643.

Dietz, T. L. (1998). An examination of violence and gender role portrayals in video games: Implications for gender role socialization and aggressive behavior. *Sex Roles, 38,* 425–442.

Donnerstein, E. & Berkowitz, L. (1981). Victim reactions in aggressive erotic films as a factor in violence against women. *Journal of Personality and Social Psychology, 41,* 710–724.

Donnerstein, E., Linz, D. & Penrod, S. (1987). *The question of pornography: Research findings and policy implications.* New York: Free Press.

Donohue, T. R., Henke, L. L. & Donohue, W. A. (1980). Do kids know what TV commercials intend? *Journal of Advertising Research, 20,* 51–57.

Dornbusch, S. M., Ritter, P. L., Leiderman, P. H., Roberts, D. F. & Fraleigh, M. J. (1987). The relation of parenting style to adolescent school performance. *Child Development, 58,* 1244–1257.

Dotson, M. J. & Hyatt, E. M. (2000). A comparison of parents' and children's knowledge of brands and advertising slogans in the United States: Implications for consumer socialization. *Journal of Marketing Communications, 6,* 219–230.

Drabman, R. S. & Thomas, M. H. (1974). Does media violence increase children's tolerance of real-life aggression? *Developmental Psychology, 10*(3), 418–421.

Drabman, R. S., Robertson, S. J., Patterson, J. N., Jarvie, G. J., Hammer, D. & Cordua, G. (1981). Children's perception of media-portrayed sex roles. *Sex Roles, 7,* 379–389.

Drew, D. G. & Reese, S. D. (1984). Children's learning from a television newscast. *Journalism Quarterly, 61,* 83–88.

Drew, D. G. & Reeves, B. B. (1980). Children and television news. *Journalism Quarterly, 57,* 45–54.

Duck, J. M., Hogg, M. A. & Terry, D. J. (1999). Social identify and perceptions of media persuasion: Are we always less influenced than others? *Journal of Applied Social Psychology, 29,* 1879–1899.

DuRant, R. H., Rich, M., Emans, S. J., Rome, E. S., Allred, E. & Woods, E. R. (1997a). Violence and weapon carrying in music videos: A content analysis. *Archives of Pediatrics and Adolescent Medicine, 151.5,* 443–448.

DuRant, R. H., Rome, E. S., Rich, M., Allred, E., Emans, S. J. & Woods, E. R. (1997b). Tobacco and alcohol use behaviors portrayed in music videos: A content analysis. *American Journal of Public Health, 87,* 1131–1345.

Eagly, A. H. & Johnson, B. T. (1990). Gender and leadership style: A meta-analysis. *Psychological Bulletin, 108,* 233–256.

Eisenstock, B. (1984). Sex-role differences in children's identification with counter-stereotypical televised portrayals. *Sex Roles, 10,* 417–430.

Ekblad, S. (1986). Social determinants of aggression in a sample of Chinese primary school children. *Acta Psychiatrica Scandinavica, 73,* 515–523.

Ekman, P., Liebert, R. M., Friesen, W. V., Harrison, R., Zlatchin, C., Malstrom, E. J. & Baron, R. A. (1972). Facial expressions of emotion while watching televised violence as predictors of subsequent aggression. In G. A. Comstock, E. A. Rubinstein & J. P. Murray (Eds.), *Television and social behavior: Vol. 5. Television's effects: Further explorations* (pp. 22–58). Washington, DC: Government Printing Office.

Eriksen, E. (1968). *Identity: Youth and crisis.* New York: Norton.

Eron, L. D. & Huesmann, L. R. (1987). Television as a source of maltreatment of children. *School Psychology Review, 16*(2), 195–202.

Eron, L. D., Huesmann, L. R., Brice, P., Fischer, P. & Mermelstein, R. (1983). Age trends in the development of aggression, sex typing, and related television habits. *Developmental Psychology, 19*(1), 71–77.

Evans, M. L., Crawley, A. M. & Anderson, D. R. (2004). *Two-year-olds' object retrieval based on television: Testing a perceptual account.* Unpublished manuscript. University of Massachusetts–Amherst.

Evans, S. E. (1964). Motivations: Underlying clothing selection and wearing. *Journal of Home Economics, 56,* 739–743.

Eveland, W. P., Jr., McLeod, J. M. & Horowitz, E. M. (1998). Communication and age in childhood political socialization: An interactive model of political development. *Journalism & Mass Communication Quarterly, 75,* 699–718.

Everett, S. A., Schnuth, R. L. & Tribble, J. L. (1998). Tobacco and alcohol use in top-grossing American films. *Journal of Community Health, 23,* 317–324.

Faber, R. J., Meyer, T. P. & Miller, M. M. (1984). The effectiveness of health disclosures within children's television commercials. *Journal of Communication, 28,* 463–476.

Faber, R. J., Perloff, R. M. & Hawkins, R. P. (1982). Antecedents of children's comprehension of television advertising. *Journal of Broadcasting, 26*(2), 575–584.

Federal Communications Commission (1996). *Policies and rules concerning children's television programming: Revision of programming policies for television broadcast stations.* MM Docket No. 93-46.

Federal Trade Commission. (1978, April). Children's advertising: Proposed trade regulation rulemaking and public hearing. *Federal Register, 43*(82), 17967–17972.

Federal Trade Commission. (1981, March 31). *FTC final staff report and recommendation.* Washington, DC: Author.

Federal Trade Commission. (2000, Sept. 13). *Marketing violent entertainment to children: A review of self-regulation and industry practices in the motion picture, music recording, and electronic game industries.* Prepared statement before the Committee on Commerce, Science, and Transportation, United States Senate. Accessed 7/30/2002 at www.ftc.gov/os/2000/09/violencerpttest. htm.

Feshbach, S. (1961). The stimulating versus cathartic effects of a vicarious aggressive activity. *Journal of Abnormal and Social Psychology, 63,* 381–385.

Feshbach, S. (1972). Reality and fantasy in filmed violence. In J. P. Murray, E. A. Rubinstein & G. A. Comstock (Eds.), *Television and social behavior: Vol. 2. Television and social learning* (pp. 318–345). Washington, DC: Government Printing Office.

Feshbach, S. & Singer, R. D. (1971). *Television and aggression: An experimental field study.* San Francisco: Jossey-Bass.

Festinger, L. (1954). A theory of social comparison processes. *Human Relations, 7,* 117–140.

Fetler, M. (1984). Television viewing and school achievement. *Journal of Communication, 34,* 104–118.

Field, A. E., Austin, S. B., Camargo, Jr., C. A., Taylor, C. B., Striegel-Moore, R. H., Loud, K. J. & Colditz, G. A. (2005). Exposure to the mass media, body shape concerns, and use of supplements to improve weight and shape among male and female adolescents. *Pediatrics, 116,* 484–485.

Field, D. E. & Anderson, D. R. (1985). Instruction and modality effects on children's television attention and comprehension. *Child Development, 77,* 91–100.

Finkel, S. E. & Geer, J. G. (1998). Spot check: Casting doubt on the demobilizing effect of attack advertising. *American Journal of Political Science, 42,* 573–595.

Fisch, S. M. (2000). A capacity model of children's comprehension of educational content on television. *Media Psychology, 2,* 63–91.

Fisch, S. M., Goodman, I. F., McCann, S. K., Rylander, K. & Ross, S. (1995, April). *The impact of informal science education: Cro and children's understanding of technology.* Poster presented at the annual meeting of the Society for Research in Child Development. Indianapolis, IN.

Fisch, S. M., McCann Brown, S. K. & Cohen, D. I. (2001). Young children's comprehension of educational television: The role of visual information and intonation. *Media Psychology, 3,* 365–378.

Fisch, S. M., Truglio, R. T. & Cole, C. F. (1999). The impact of *Sesame Street* on preschool children: A review and synthesis of 30 years' research. *Media Psychology, 1,* 165–181.

Fisher, D. A., Hill, D. L., Grube, J. W. & Gruber, E. L. (2004). Sex on American television: An analysis across program genres and network types. *Journal of Broadcasting & Electronic Media, 48,* 529–553.

Fisher, E. P. (1992). The impact of play on development: A meta-analysis. *Play and Culture, 5,* 159–181.

Flanagan, C. & Gallay, L. S. (1995). Reframing the meaning of "political" in research with adolescents. *Perspectives on Political Science, 24,* 34–42.

Forney, J. & Forney, W. (1995). Gangs or fashion: Influence on junior high student dress. *Journal of Family and Consumer Sciences, 87,* 26–32.

Fouts, G. & Burggraf, K. (1999). Television situation comedies: Female body image and verbal reinforcements. *Sex Roles, 40,* 473–481.

Fraczek, A. (1986). Socio-cultural environment, television viewing, and the development of aggressioin among children in Poland. In L. R. Huesmann & L. D. Eron (Eds.), *Television and the aggressive child: A cross-national comparison* (pp. 119–159). Hillsdale, NJ: Erlbaum.

Frances, F. (1992). Effect of perceived clothing deprivation on high school students' social participation. *Clothing and Textiles Research Journal, 10,* 29–33.

Francis, S. K. & Bowne, B. (1992). Perceived clothing deprivation: Further evidence. *Perceptual and Motor Skills, 75,* 723–730.

Francis, S. K. & Liu, Q. (1990). Effect of clothing values on perceived clothing deprivation among adolescents. *Perceptual and Motor Skills, 71,* 1191–1201.

Frank, R. E. & Greenberg, M. G. (1980). *The public's use of television.* Newbury Park, CA: Sage.

Frankenfield, A. E., Richards, J. R., Lauricella, A. R., Pempek, T. A., Kirkorian, H. L. & Anderson, D. R. (2004, May). *Looking at and interacting with comprehensible and incomprehensible Teletubbies.* Poster presented at the Biennial International Conference for Infant Studies, Chicago.

Freedman, J. L. (1984). Effect of television violence on aggressiveness. *Psychological Bulletin, 96*(2), 227–246.

French, J. & Penna, S. (1991). Children's hero play of the 20th century: Changes resulting from television's influence. *Child Study Journal, 21*(2), 79–94.

Freuh, T. & McGhee, P. E. (1975). Traditional sex-role development and amount of time spent watching television. *Developmental Psychology, 11,* 109.

Friedrich, L. K. & Stein, A. H. (1973). Aggressive and prosocial television programs and the natural behavior of preschool children. *Monographs of the Society for Research in Child Development, 38*(4) Serial No. 151.

Friedrich, L. K. & Stein, A. H. (1975). Prosocial television and young children: The effects of verbal labeling and role playing on learning and behavior. *Child Development, 46*, 27–38.

Friedrich-Cofer, L. K., Huston-Stein, A., Kipnis, D. M., Susman, E. J. & Clewett, A. S. (1979). Environmental enhancement of prosocial television content: Effect on interpersonal behavior, imaginative play, and self-regulation in a natural setting. *Developmental Psychology, 15*, 637–646.

Funk, J. B. & Buchman, B. B. (1996). Children's perceptions of gender differences of social approval for playing electronic games. *Sex Roles, 35*, 219–232.

Gadberry, S. (1980). Effects of restricting first graders' TV viewing on leisure time use, IQ change, and cognitive style. *Journal of Applied Developmental Psychology, 1*(1), 161–176.

Gaddy, G. D. (1986). Television's impact on high school achievement. *Public Opinion Quarterly, 50*, 340–359.

Galst, J. P. (1980). Television food commercials and pronutritional public service announcements as determinants of young children's snack choices. *Child Development, 51*, 935–938.

Galst, J. P. & White, M. A. (1976). The unhealthy persuader: The reinforcing value of television and children's purchase influence attempts at the supermarket. *Child Development, 47*, 1089–1096.

Garramone, G. M. (1983). TV news and adolescent political socialization. In R. N. Bostrom (Ed.), *Communication Yearbook, 7* (pp. 651–669). Beverly Hills, CA: Sage.

Geen, R. G. (1968). Effects of frustration, attack, and prior training in aggressiveness upon aggressive behavior. *Journal of Personality and Social Psychology, 9*(4), 316–321.

Geen, R. G. (1995). *Human motivation: A social psychological approach.* Belmont, CA: Wadsworth.

Geen, R. G. & Berkowitz, L. (1967). Some conditions facilitating the occurrence of aggression after the observation of violence. *Journal of Personality, 35*, 666–676.

Geen, R. G. & Rakosky, J. (1973). Interpretations of observed violence and their effects on GSR. *Journal of Experimental Research in Personality, 6*(4), 289–292.

Geen, R. G. & Stonner, D. (1972). Context effects in observed violence. *Journal of Personality and Social Psychology, 25*(2), 145–150.

Geis, M. L. (1982). *The language of advertising.* New York: Academic Press.

Geist, E. & Gibson, M. (2000). The effect of network and public television programs on four and five year olds ability to attend to educational tasks. *Journal of Instructional Psychology, 27*, 250.

Gentile, D. A. & Anderson, C. A. (2003). Violent video games: The newest media violence hazard. In D. A. Gentile (Ed.), *Media violence and children: A complete guide for parents and professionals* (pp. 131–152). Westport, CT: Praeger.

Gentile, D. A., Lynch, P. J., Linder, J. R. & Walsh, D. A. (2004). The effects of video game habits on adolescent hostility, aggressive behaviors, and school performance. *Journal of Adolescence, 27*, 5–22.

Gentner, D. (1975). Evidence for the psychological reality of semantic components: The verbs of possession. In D. Norman & D. Rumelhart (Eds.), *Explorations in cognition* (pp. 211–246). San Francisco: Freeman.

Gerbner, G. (1999). What do we know? In J. shanahan & M. Morgan (Eds.) *Television and its viewers.* (pp. ix-xiii). Cambridge, UK: Cambridge University Press.

Gerbner, G. & Gross, L. (1976). Living with television: The violence profile. *Journal of Communication, 26*, 173–199.

Gerbner, G., Gross, L., Morgan, M. & Signorielli, N. (1980a). Aging on television: Images in television drama and conceptions of social reality. *Journal of Communication, 30*, 37–47.

Gerbner, G., Gross, L., Morgan, M. & Signorielli, N. (1980b). The "mainstreaming" of America. *Journal of Communication 30*(3), 10–29.

Gerbner, G., Gross, L., Morgan, M., Signorielli, N. & Shanahan, J. (2002). Growing up with television: Cultivation process. In J. Bryant & D. Zillmann (Eds.), *Media effects: Advances in Theory and Research, 2nd ed.* (pp. 43–67). Mahwah, NJ: Erlbaum.

Gerbner, G., Morgan, M. & Signorielli, N. (1994). *Television violence profile no. 16.* Unpublished manuscript, The Annenberg School of Communication, University of Pennsylvania, Philadelphia.

Gerbner, G. & Ozyegin, N. (1997, March 20). *Alcohol, tobacco, and illicit drugs in entertainment television, commercials, news, "reality shows," movies, and music channels (Robert Wood Johnson Foundation).* Princeton, NJ: Robert Wood Johnson Foundation.

Gerbner, G. & Signorielli, N. (1979). *Women and minorities in television drama, 1969–1978.* Philadelphia: Annenberg School of Communication, University of Pennsylvania.

Gilligan, C. (1982). *In a different voice: Psychological theory and women's development.* Cambridge, MA: Harvard University Press.

GLAAD. (2005). *GLAAD's 10th annual study examines diversity of the 2005–2006 primetime television season.* Accessed 8/29/05 at http://www.glaad.org/eye/ontv/overview.php.

Glass, G. V. (1976). Primary, secondary, and meta-analysis of research. *Educational Research, 5*, 3–8.

Goethals, G. R. (1986). Social comparison theory: Psychology from the lost and found. *Personality and Social Psychology Bulletin, 12*, 261–278.

Goldberg, M. E. & Gorn, G. J. (1978). Some unintended consequences of TV advertising to children. *Journal of Consumer Research, 5*, 22–29.

Golderg, M. E. & Gorn, G. J. (1979). Television's impact on preferences of non-white playmates: Canadian "Sesame Street" inserts. *Journal of Broadcasting, 23*, 27–32.

Goldberg, M. E., Gorn, G. J. & Gibson, W. (1978). TV messages for snacks and breakfast foods: Do they influence children's preferences? *Journal of Consumer Research, 5*, 73–81.

Goldstein, A. O., Sobel, R. A. & Newman, G. R. (1999). Tobacco and alcohol use in G-rated children's animated films. *Journal of the American Medical Association, 281*, 1131–1136.

Goldstein, J. H. (1994). Sex differences in toy play and use of video games. In J. H. Goldstein (Ed.), *Toys, play, and child development* (pp. 110–129). New York: Cambridge University Press.

Gorn, G. J. & Goldberg, M. E. (1982). Behavioral evidence of the effects of televised food messages on children. *Journal of Consumer Research, 9*, 200–205.

Gorn, G. J., Goldberg, M. E. & Kanungo, R. N. (1976). The role of educational television in changing the intergroup attitudes of children. *Child Development, 42*, 277–280.

Gortmaker, S. L., Salter, C. A., Walker, D. K. & Dietz, W. H. (1990). The impact of television viewing on mental aptitude and achievement: A longitudinal study. *Public Opinion Quarterly, 54*(4), 594–604.

Granger, C. W. (1969). Investigating causal relations by econometric models and cross-spectral methods. *Econometrica, 37*, 424–438.

Greenberg, B. S. (1974). Gratifications of television viewing and their correlates for British children. In J. G. Blumler & E. Katz (Eds.), *The uses of mass communication* (pp. 71–92). Newbury Park, CA: Sage.

Greenberg, B. S. (1994). Content trends in media sex. In D. Zillmann, J. Bryant & A. C. Huston (Eds.), *Media, children and the family*. Hillsdale, NJ: Erlbaum.

Greenberg, B. S. & Baptista-Fernandez, P. (1980). Hispanic Americans: The new minority on television. In B. S. Greenberg (Ed.), *Life on television* (pp. 3–12). Norwood, NJ: Ablex.

Greenberg, B. S. & Brand, J. (1993). Cultural diversity on Saturday morning television. In G. L. Berry & J. K. Asamen (Eds.), *Children and television: Images in a changing sociocultural world* (pp. 132–142). Newbury Park, CA: Sage.

Greenberg, B. S. & Brand, J. (1994). Minorities and the mass media: 1970s to 1990s. In J. Bryant & D. Zillmann (Eds.), *Media effects: Advances in theory and research* (pp. 273–314). Mahwah, NJ: Erlbaum.

Greenberg, B. S. & Busselle, R. W. (1996). Soap operas and sexual activity: A decade later. *Journal of Communication, 46*, 153–160.

Greenberg, B. S. & Collette, L. (1997). The changing faces on TV: A demographic analysis of network television's new seasons, 1966–1992. *Journal of Broadcasting & Electronic Media, 41*(1), 1–13.

Greenberg, B. S., Korzenny, F. & Atkin, C. (1980). Trends in the portrayal of the elderly. In B. S. Greenberg (Ed.), *Life on television* (pp. 23–34). Norwood, NJ: Ablex.

Greenfield, P. & Beagle-Roos, J. (1988). Television versus radio: The cognitive impact on different socio-economic and ethnic groups. *Journal of Communication, 38*(2), 71–92.

Greenfield, P., Farrar, D. & Beagle-Roos, J. (1986). Is the medium the message? An experimental comparison of the effects of radio and television on imagination. *Journal of Applied Developmental Psychology, 7*(3), 201–218.

Greenfield, P. M., Camaioni, L., Ercolani, P., Weiss, L., Lauber, B. A. & Perucchini, P. (1994). Cognitive socialization by computer games in two cultures: Inductive discovery or mastery of an iconic code? *Journal of Applied Developmental Psychology, 15*, 59–85.

Greer, D., Potts, R., Wright, J. & Huston, A. C. (1982). The effects of television commercial form and commercial placement on children's social behavior and attention. *Child Development, 53*(3), 611–619.

Grela, B., Lin, Y. & Krcmar, M. (2003, April). *Can television be used to teach vocabulary to toddlers?* Paper presented at the annual meeting of the American Speech Language Hearing Association, Chicago.

Groesz, L. M., Levine, M. P. & Murnen, S. K. (2002). The effect of experimental presentation of thin media images on body satisfaction: A meta-analytic review. *International Journal of Eating Disorders, 31*, 1–16.

Gross, L. & Jeffries-Fox, S. (1978). What do you want to be when you grow up, little girl? In G. Tuchman, A. K. Daniels & J. Benet (Eds.), *Hearth and home: Images of women in the mass media* (pp. 240–265). New York: Oxford University Press.

Grube, J. W. (1993). Alcohol portrayals and alcohol advertising on television: Content and effects on children and adolescents. *Alcohol Health & Research World, 17*, 61–66.

Grube, J. W. (1995). Television alcohol portrayals, alcohol advertising, and alcohol expectancies among children and adolescents. In S. E. Martin (Ed.), *The effects of the mass media on use and abuse of alcohol* (pp. 105–121). Bethesda, MD: National Institute on Alcohol Abuse and Alcoholism.

Gunter, B. & Furnham, A. (1998). *Children as consumers.* New York: Routledge.

Hamamoto, D. Y. (1993). They're so cute when they're young: The Asian-American child on television. In G. L. Berry & J. K. Asamen (Eds.), *Children and television: Images in a changing sociocultural world* (pp. 205–214). Newbury Park, CA: Sage.

Hamilton, J. T. (1998). *Channeling violence.* Princeton, NJ: Princeton University Press.

Hancox, R. J., Milne, B. J. & Poulton, R. (2004). Association between child and adolescent television viewing and adult health: A longitudinal birth cohort study. *The Lancet, 364.9430,* 257.

Hapkiewicz, W. G. & Stone, R. D. (1974). The effects of realistic versus imaginary aggressive models on children's interpersonal play. *Child Study Journal, 4*(2), 47–58.

Hargreaves, D. & Tiggeman, M. (2003). The effect of "thin ideal" television commercials on body dissatisfaction and schema activation during early adolescence. *Journal of Youth and Adolescence, 32,* 367–374.

Harrison, K. (2000). The body electric: Thin-ideal media and eating disorders in adolescents. *Journal of Communication, 50,* 119–143.

Harrison, K. & Cantor, J. (1999). Tales from the screen: Enduring fright reactions to scary media. *Media Psychology, 1*(2), 97–116.

Harrison, K. & Marske, A. L. (2005). *The American Journal of Public Health, 95,* 1568–1575.

Harrison, L. F. & Williams, T. M. (1986). Television and cognitive development. In T. M. Williams (Ed.), *The impact of television: A natural experiment in three communities* (pp. 87–142). Orlando, FL: Academic Press.

Hart, L. R. (1972). *Immediate effects of exposure to filmed cartoon aggression on boys.* Doctoral Dissertation, Emory University, Atlanta, GA.

Harwood, J. (1997). Viewing age: Lifespan identity and television viewing choices. *Journal of Broadcasting and Electronic Media, 41*(2), 203–213.

Hayne, H., Herbert, J. & Simcock, G. (2003). Imitation from television by 24- and 30-month-olds. *Developmental Science, 6,* 254–261.

Haynes, J., Burts, D. C., Dukes, A. & Cloud, R. (1993). Consumer socialization of preschoolers and kindergarteners as related to clothing consumption. *Psychology & Marketing, 10,* 151–166.

Hawkins, R. P. & Pingree, S. (1980). Some processes in the cultivation effect. *Communication Research, 7,* 193–226.

Hawkins, R. P. & Pingree, S. (1982). Television's influence on social reality. In D. Pearl, L. Bouthilet & J. Lazar (Eds.), *Television and behavior: Ten years of scientific progress and implications for the 80's. Vol. II, Technical reviews* (pp. 224–247). Rockville, MD: National Institute of Mental Health.

Hawkins, R. P., Pingree, S. & Adler, I. (1987). Searching for cognitive processes in the cultivation effect: Adult and adolescent samples in the United States and Australia. *Human Communication Research, 13*(4), 553–577.

Hawkins, R. P., Pingree, S. & Roberts D. F. (1975). Watergate and political socialization: The inescapable event. *American Politics Quarterly, 3*(October), 406–422.

Hazan, A. R. & Glantz, S. A. (1995). Current trends in tobacco use on prime-time fictional television. *American Journal of Public Health, 85,* 116–117.

Hazan, A. R., Lipton, H. L. & Glantz, S. A. (1994). Popular films do not reflect current tobacco use. *American Journal of Public Health, 84,* 998–1000.

Head, S. W. (1954). Content analysis of television drama programs. *Quarterly Journal of Film, Radio, and Television, 9*, 175–194.

Hearold, S. (1986). A synthesis of 1,043 effects of television on social behavior. In G. Comstock (Ed.), *Public communication and behavior* (Vol. 1, pp. 65–133). New York: Academic Press.

Hennigan, K. M., Heath, L., Wharton, J. D., Del Rosario, M. L., Cook, T. D. & Calder, B. J. (1982). Impact of the introduction of television on crime in the United States: Empirical findings and theoretical implications. *Journal of Personality and Social Psychology, 42*(3), 461–477.

Herrett-Skjellum, J. & Allen, M. (1996). Television programming and sex stereotyping: A meta-analysis. *Communication Yearbook, 19*, 157–185.

Hess, R. D. & Torney, J. V. (1967). *The development of political attitudes in children.* Chicago: Aldine.

Heyns, B. (1976). *Exposure and the effects of schooling.* Washington, DC: National Institute of Education.

Hill, J. M. & Radimer, K. L. (1997). A content analysis of food advertisements in television for Australian children. *Australian Journal of Nutrition and Dietetics, 54*, 174–181.

Himmelweit, H., Oppenheim, A. N. & Vince, P. (1958). *Television and the child.* London: Oxford University Press.

Hoffer, C. (1996). Children's wishful identification and parasocial interaction with favorite television characters. *Journal of Broadcasting & Electronic Media, 40*, 389–403.

Hoffner, C. & Cantor, J. (1985). Developmental differences in responses to a television character's appearance and behavior. *Developmental Psychology, 21*, 1065–1074.

Hogben, M. (1998). Factors moderating the effect of television aggression on viewer behavior. *Communication Research, 25*, 220–247.

Hollenbeck, A. & Slaby, R. (1979). Infant visual and vocal responses to television. *Child Development, 50*, 41–45.

Hopkins, N. M. & Mullis, A. K. (1985). Family perceptions of television viewing habits. *Family Relations, 34*(2), 177–181.

Horton, D. & Wohl, R. R. (1956). Mass communication and parasocial interaction. *Psychiatry, 19*, 215–229.

Hoy, M. G., Young, C. E. & Mowen, J. C. (1986). Animated host-selling advertisements: Their impact on young children's recognition, attitudes, and behavior. *Journal of Public Policy and Marketing, 5*, 171–184.

Hubert, S. J. (1999).What's wrong with this picture? The politics of Ellen's coming out party. *Journal of Popular Culture, 3*, 31–37.

Huesmann, L. R. (1982). Television violence and aggressive behavior. In D. Pearl, L. Bouthilet & J. Lazar (Eds.), *Television and behavior: Ten years of scientific inquiry and implications for the eighties: Vol. 2. Technical reviews* (pp. 126–137). Washington, DC: U.S. Government Printing Office.

Huesmann, L. R. & Eron, L. D. (Eds.). (1986). *Television and the aggressive child: A cross-national comparison.* Hillsdale, NJ: Erlbaum.

Huesmann, L. R., Eron, L. D., Lefkowitz, M. M. & Walder, L. O. (1984). The stability of aggression over time and generations. *Developmental Psychology, 20*(6), 1120–1134.

Huesmann, L. R., Lagerspetz, K. & Eron, L. D. (1984). Intervening variables in the TV violence-aggression relation: Evidence from two countries. *Developmental Psychology, 20*(5), 746–775.

Huesmann, L. R. & Miller, L. S. (1994). Long-term effects of repeated exposure to media violence in childhood. In L.R. Huesmann (Ed.), *Aggressive behavior: Current perspectives* (pp. 153–186). New York: Plenum.

Huesmann, L. R., Moise-Titus, J., Podolski, C. L. & Eron, L. D. (2003). Longitudinal relations between children's exposure to TV violence and their aggressive and violent behavior in young adulthood: 1977–1992. *Developmental Psychology, 39*(2), 201–222.

Hughes, M. (1980). The fruits of cultivation analysis: A reexamination of the effects of television watching on fear of victimization, alienation, and the approval of violence. *Public Opinion Quarterly, 44*(3), 287–302.

Hunt, M. (1997). *How science takes stock.* New York: Russell Sage.

Hunter, J. E. & Schmidt, F. L. (2004). *Methods of meta-analysis: Correcting error and bias in research findings (2nd ed.).* Thousand Oaks, CA: Sage.

Huston, A., Donnerstein, E., Fairchild, H., Feshbach, N. C., Katz, P. A., Murray, J. P., Rubinstein, E., Wilcox, B. L. & Zuckerman, D. (1992). *Big world, small screen: The role of television in American society.* Lincoln: University of Nebraska Press.

Huston, A. C. (1985). The development of sex typing: Themes from recent research. *Developmental Review, 5,* 1–167.

Huston, A. C. & Wright, J. C. (1983). Children's processing of television: The informative functions of formal features. In J. Bryant & D.R. Anderson (Eds.), *Children's understanding of television: Research on attention and comprehension* (pp. 35–68). New York: Academic Press.

Huston, A. C. & Wright, J. C. (1989). The forms of television and the child viewer. In G. Comstock (Ed.), *Public communication and behavior* (Vol. 2, pp. 103–158). New York: Academic Press.

Huston, A. C., Wright, J. C., Marquis, J. & Green, S. B. (1999). How young children spend their time: Television and other activities. *Developmental Psychology, 35,* 912–9325.

Huston, A. C., Wright, J. C., Rice, M. L., Kerkman, D. & St. Peters, M. (1990). The development of television viewing patterns in early childhood: A longitudinal investigation. *Developmental Psychology, 26,* 409–420.

Huston-Stein, A., Fox, S., Greer, D., Watkins, B. A. & Whitaker, J. (1981). The effects of TV action and violence on children's social behavior. *Journal of Genetic Psychology, 138,* 183–191.

Hyman, H. H. (1959). *Political socialization.* Glencoe, IL: Free Press.

Isler, L., Popper, E. T. & Ward, S. (1987). Children's purchase requests and parental responses: Results from a diary study. *Journal of Advertising Research, 27*(5), 28–39.

Jackson-Beeck., M. (1979). Interpersonal and mass communication in children's political socialization. *Journalism Quarterly, 56,* 48–53.

James, N. C. & McCain, T. A. (1982). Television games preschool children play: Patterns, themes, and uses. *Journal of Broadcasting, 26*(4), 783–800.

Jennings, M. K. & Niemi, R. G. (1974). *The political character of adolescence.* Princeton, NJ: Princeton University Press.

John, D. R. (1999). Consumer socialization of children: A retrospective look at twenty-five years of research. *Journal of Consumer Research, 26,*183–213.

Johnson, J. G., Cohen, P., Smailes, E. M., Kasen, S. & Brook, J. S. (2002). Television viewing and aggressive behavior during adolescence and adulthood. *Science, 295,* 2468–2471.

Johnston, J. & Ettema, J. S. (1982). *Positive images: Breaking stereotypes with children's television.* Beverly Hills, CA: Sage.

Jordan, A. (1996). *The state of children's television: An examination of quantity, quality and industry beliefs. Report no. 2.* Philadelphia: University of Pennsylvania, The Annenberg Public Policy Center.

Jordan, A. B. (2004). The three-hour rule and educational television for children. *Popular Communication, 2,* 103–118.

Josephson, W. L. (1987). Television violence and children's aggression: Testing the priming, social script, and disinhibition predictions. *Journal of Personality and Social Psychology, 53*(5), 882–890.

Justin, N. (1999, Nov. 7). Gays of our lives. *Minneapolis Star Tribune,* 1F.

Kahnemann, D. (1973). *Attention and effort.* Englewood Cliffs, NJ: Prentice-Hall.

Kang, N. (1990). *A critique and secondary analysis of the NBC study on television and aggression.* Unpublished doctoral dissertation, Syracuse University, Syracuse, NY.

Kathlene, L. (1995). Position power versus gender power: Who holds the floor? In G. Duerst-Lahti & R. M. Kelly (Eds.), *Gender, power, leadership, and government* (pp. 167–193). Ann Arbor: University of Michigan Press.

Katz, P. Q. & Boswell, S. (1986). Flexibility and traditionality in children's gender roles. *Genetic, Social, and General Psychology Monographs, 112,* 103–147.

Kaye, B. K. & Sapolsky, B. S. (2004). Watch your mouth! An analysis of profanity uttered by children on prime-time television. *Mass Communication & Society, 7,* 429–452.

Kaufman, G. (1999). The portrayal of men's family roles in television commercials. *Sex Roles, 41,* 439–458.

Keillor, B. D., Parker, R. S. & Schaefer, A. (1996). Influences on adolescent brand preferences in the United States and Mexico. *Journal of Advertising Research, 36*(3), 47–56.

Keith, T. Z., Reimers, T. M., Fehrmann, P. G., Pottebaum, S. M. & Aubey, L. W. (1986). Parental involvement, homework, and TV time: Direct and indirect effects on high school achievement. *Journal of Educational Psychology, 78*(5), 373–380.

Kerns, T. Y. (1981). Television: A bisensory bombardment that stifles children's creativity. *Phi Delta Kappan, 62,* 456–457.

Kimball, M. M. (1986). Television and sex-role attitudes. In T. M. Williams (Ed.), *The impact of television: A natural experiment in three communities* (pp. 265–301). Orlando, FL: Academic Press.

Kiousis, S., McDevitt, M. & Wu, X. (2005). The genesis of civic awareness: Agenda setting in political socialization. *Journal of Communication, 55,* 756–774.

Kirsh, S. J. (1998). Seeing the world through Mortal Kombat-colored glasses: Violent video games and the development of a short-term hostile attribution bias. *Childhood, 5*(2), 177–184.

Kirsh, S. J., Olczak, P. V. & Mounts, J. R. W. (2005). Violent video games induce an affect processing bias. *Media Psychology, 7*(3), 239–250.

Klapper, H. L. (1978). Childhood socialization and television. *Public Opinion Quarterly, 42,* 426–431.

Klapper, J. T. (1960). *The effects of mass communication.* New York: Free Press.

Knobloch, S., Callison, C., Chen, L., Fritzsche, A. & Zillmann, D. (2005). Children's sex-stereotyped self-socialization through selective exposure to entertainment: Cross-cultural experiments in Germany, China, and the United States. *Journal of Communication, 55,* 122–138.

Koblinsky, S. G., Cruse, D. F. & Sugaware, A. I. (1978). Sex role stereotypes and children's memory for story content. *Child Development, 49,* 452–458.

Koester, A. & May, J. (1985). Clothing purchase practices of adolescents. *Home Economics Research Journal, 13,* 227–236.

Kohlberg, L. (1966). A cognitive-developmental analysis of children's sex-role concepts and attitudes. In E. E. Maccoby (Ed.), *The development of sex differences.* Stanford, CA: Stanford University Press.

Kohlberg, L. (1981). *Essays on moral development: Vol. 1. The philosophy of moral development.* San Francisco: Harper and Row.

Kohlberg, L. (1984). *Essays on moral deveiopment: Vol. 2. The psychology of moral development.* San Francisco: Harper and Row.

Kohn, P. M. & Smart, R. G. (1984). The impact of television advertising on alcohol consumption: An experiment. *Journal of Studies on Alcohol, 45,* 295–301.

Kohn, P. M. & Smart, R. G. (1987). Wine, women, suspiciousness, and advertising. *Journal of Studies on Alcohol, 48,* 161–166.

Koolstra, C. M. & van der Voort, T. H. A. (1996). Longitudinal effects of television on children's leisure-time reading: A test of three explanatory models. *Human Communication Research, 23,* 4–35.

Koolstra, C. M., van der Voort, T. H. A. & van der Kamp, L. J. T. (1997). Television's impact on children's reading comprehension and decoding skills: A 3-year panel study. *Reading Research Quarterly, 32,* 128–152.

Kotch, J. B., Coulter, M. & Lipsitz, A. (1986). Does drinking influence children's attitudes toward alcohol? *Addictive Behaviors, 11*(1), 67–70.

Kotz, K. & Story, M. (1994). Food advertisements during children's Saturday morning television programming: Are they consistent with dietary recommendations? *Journal of the American Dietary Association, 94,* 1296–1300.

Krcmar, M. (2000). The effect of an educational/informational rating on children's attraction to and learning from an educational program. *Journal of Broadcasting & Electronic Media, 44,* 674–690.

Krugman, H. E. (1971). Brain wave measures of media involvement. *Journal of Advertising Research, 11,* 3–10.

Krull, R. (1983). Children learning to watch television. In J. Bryant & D. R. Anderson (Eds.), *Children's understanding of television: Research on attention and comprehension* (pp. 103–123). New York: Academic Press.

Kubey, R. & Csikszentmihalyi, M. (1990). *Television and the quality of life: How viewing shapes everyday experience.* Hillsdale, NJ: Erlbaum.

Kubey, R. & Larson, R. (1990). The use and experience of the new video media among children and young adolescents. *Communication Research, 17,* 107–130.

Kunkel, D. (1988a). Children and host-selling television commercials. *Communication Research, 15*(1), 71–92.

Kunkel, D. (1988b). From a raised eyebrow to a turned back: The FCC and children's product-related programming. *Journal of Communication, 38*(4), 90–108.

Kunkel, D. (2001). Children and television advertising. In D. Singer & J. Singer (Eds.), *Handbook of children and the media* (pp. 375–393). Thousand Oaks, CA: Sage.

Kunkel, D. & Canepa, J. (1994). Broadcasters' license renewal claims regarding children's educational programming. *Journal of Broadcasting & Electronic Media, 38,* 397–416.

Kunkel, D., Cope, K. M. & Colvin, C. (1996). *Sexual messages on family hour television: Content and context.* Menlo Park, CA: Kaiser Family Foundation.

Kunkel, D., Cope-Farrar, K. M., Biely, E., Farinola, W. J. M. & Donnerstein, E. (2001, May). *Sex on TV: Comparing trends from 1997–98 to 1999-2000.* Paper presented at the annual meeting of the International Communication Association, Washington, DC.

Kunkel, D. & Goette, U. (1996, May). *Broadcasters' response to the Children's Television Act.* Paper presented at the annual conference of the International Communication Association, Chicago.

Landau, S., Lorch, E. P. & Milich, R. (1992). Visual attention to and comprehension of television in attention-deficit hyperactivity disordered and normal boys. *Child Development, 63*, 928-938.

Larson, M. S. (2001). Interactions, activities, and gender in children's television commercials: A content analysis. *Journal of Broadcasting & Electronic Media, 45*, 41–56.

Larson, R. & Kubey, R. (1983). Television and music: Contrasting media in adolescent life. *Youth and Society, 15*, 13–31.

Lau, R. R. & Erber, R. (1985). Political sophistication: An information-processing perspective. In S. Kraus & R. M. Perloff (Eds.), *Mass media and political thought* (pp. 37–64). Beverly Hills, CA: Sage.

Lauzen, M. M. & Dozier, D. M. (1999). Making a difference in prime time: Women on screen and behind the scenes in the 1995–96 television season. *Journal of Broadcasting & Electronic Media, 43*(1), 1–19.

Lauzen, M. M. & Dozier, D. M. (2005). Recognition and respect revisited: Portrayals of age and gender in prime-time television. *Mass Communication & Society, 8*(3), 241–256.

Lefcourt, H. M., Barnes, K., Parke, R. & Schwartz, F. (1966). Anticipated social censure and aggression-conflict as mediators of response to aggression induction. *Journal of Social Psychology, 70*, 251–263.

Lefkowitz, M. M., Eron, L. D., Walder, L. O. & Huesmann, L. R. (1972). Television violence and child aggression: A followup study. In G. A. Comstock & E. A. Rubinstein (Eds.), *Television and social behavior: Vol. 3. Television and adolescent aggressiveness* (pp. 35–135). Washington, DC: Government Printing Office.

Lefkowitz, M. M., Eron, L. D., Walder, L. O. & Huesmann, L. R. (1977). *Growing up to be violent: A longitudinal study of the development of aggression.* Elmsford, NY: Pergamon.

Leifer, A. D. (1975, April). *How to encourage socially-valued behavior.* Paper presented at the biennial meeting of the Society for Research in Child Development. Denver, CO.

Lenhart, A., Rainie, L. & Lewis, O. (2001). *Teenage life online: The rise of the instant message generation and the Internet's impact on friendships and family relationships.* Washington, DC: Pew Foundation, June.

Levin, S. R., Petros, T. V. & Petrella, F. W. (1982). Preschoolers' awareness of television advertising. *Child Development, 53*, 933–937.

Levinson, R. (1975). From Olive Oyl to Sweet Polly Purebread: Sex role stereotypes and televised cartoons. *Journal of Popular Culture, 9*, 561–572.

Levy, M. R. (1978). The audience experience with television news. *Journalism Monographs, 55*, 1–29.

Lewis, M. K. & Hill, A. J. (1998). Food advertising on British children's television: A content analysis and experimental study with nine-year-olds. *International Journal of Obesity, 22*, 206–214.

Leyens, J. P. & Camino, L. (1974). The effects of repeated exposure to film violence on aggressiveness and social structure. In J. DeWit & W. P. Hartup (Eds.), *Determinants and origins of aggressive behavior.* The Hague, Netherlands: Mouton.

Leyens, J. P., Camino, L., Parke, R. D. & Berkowitz, L. (1975). Effects of movie violence on aggression in a field setting as a function of group dominance and cohesion. *Journal of Personality and Social Psychology, 32*(2), 346–360.

Lieberman Research. (1975). *Children's reactions to violent material on television* (Report to the American Broadcasting Company). New York: Author.

Liebert, D., Sprafkin, J., Liebert, R. & Rubinstein, E. (1977). Effects of television commercial disclaimers on the product expectations of children. *Journal of Communication, 27*(1), 118–124.

Linebarger, D. L. & Walker, D. (2005). Infants' and toddlers' television viewing and language outcomes. *American Behavioral Scientist, 48*, 624–645.

Linz, D., Donnerstein, E. & Adams, S. M. (1989). Physiological desensitization and judgments about female victims of violence. *Human Communication Research, 15*(4), 509–522.

Liss, M. B. (1981). Children's television selections: A study of indicators of same-race preferences. *Journal of Cross-Cultural Psychology, 12*(1), 103–110.

Littrell, M. & Eicher, J. (1973). Clothing opinions and social acceptance process among adolescents. *Adolescence, 8*, 197–212.

Livingstone, S. M. (2001). *Children and their changing media environment: A European comparative study.* Mahwah, NJ: Lawrence Erlbaum.

Li-Vollmer, M. (2002). Race representation in child-targeted television commercials. *Mass Communication & Society, 5*(2), 207–228.

LoSciuto, L. A. (1972). A national inventory of television viewing behavior. In E. A. Rubinstein, G. A. Comstock & J. P. Murray (Eds.), *Television and social behavior: Vol. 4. Television in day-to-day life: Patterns of use* (pp. 33–86). Washington, DC: Government Printing Office.

Lorch, E. P., Anderson, D. R. & Levin, S. R. (1979). The relationship of visual attention to children's comprehension of television. *Child Development, 50*, 722–727.

Loye, D., Gorney, R. & Steele, G. (1977). Effects of television: An experimental field study. *Journal of Communication, 27*(3), 206–216.

Lucas, K. & Sherry, J. L. (2004). Sex differences in video game play: A communication-based explanation. *Communication Research, 31*, 499–523.

Luecke-Aleksa, D., Anderson, D., Collins, P. & Schmitt, K. (1995). Gender constancy and television viewing. *Developmental Psychology, 31*, 773–780.

Lyle, J. & Hoffman, H. R. (1972a). Children's use of television and other media. In E. A. Rubinstein, G. A. Comstock & J. P. Murray (Eds.), *Television and social behavior, Vol. 4: Television in day-to-day life: Patterns of use* (pp. 129–256). Washington, DC: U.S. Government Printing Office.

Lyle, J. & Hoffman, H. R. (1972b). Explorations in patterns of television viewing by preschool-age children. In E. A. Rubinstein, G. A. Comstock & J. P. Murray (Eds.), *Television and social behavior: Vol. 4. Television in day-to-day life: Patterns of use* (pp. 257–273). Washington, DC: Government Printing Office.

Lynd, R. S. (1939). *Knowledge for what?* Princeton, NJ: Princeton University Press.

Maass, A., Cadinu, M., Guarnieri, G. & Grasselli, A. (2003). Sexual harassment under social identity threat: The computer harassment paradigm. *Journal of Personality and Social Psychology, 85*(5), 853–870.

Maccoby, E. E. (1951). Television: Its impact on school children. *Public Opinion Quarterly, 15*(3), 421–444.

Maccoby, E. E. (1954). Why do children watch television? *Public Opinion Quarterly, 18*(3), 239–244.

Maccoby, E. E. & Wilson, W. C. (1957). Identification and observational learning from films. *Journal of Abnormal and Social Psychology, 55*, 76–87.

Maccoby, E., Wilson, W. C. & Burton, R. V. (1958). Differential movie-viewing behavior of male and female viewers. *Journal of Personality, 26*, 259–267.

Macklin, M. & Kolbe, R. (1984). Gender role stereotyping in children's advertising: Current and past trends. *Journal of Advertising, 13*(2), 34–42.

Macklin, M. C. (1985). Do young children understand the selling intent of commercials? *The Journal of Consumer Affairs, 19*(2), 293–304.

Macklin, M. C. (1987). Preschoolers' understanding of the informational function of television advertising. *Journal of Consumer Research, 14*, 229–239.

Madden, P. A. & Grube, J. W. (1994). The frequency and nature of alcohol and tobacco advertising in televised sports, 1990 through 1992. *American Journal of Public Health, 84*, 297–299.

Maguire, B., Sandage, D. & Weatherby, G. (2000). Violence, morality, and television commercials. *Sociological Spectrum, 20*(1), 121–144.

Makas, E. (1981). *Guess who's coming to primetime.* Unpublished manuscript.

Makas, E. (1993). Changing channels: The portrayal of people with disabilities on television. In G. L. Berry & J. K. Asamen (Eds.), *Children and television: Images in a changing sociocultural world* (pp. 255–268). Newbury Park, CA: Sage.

Mares, M. L. (1998). Children's use of VCRs. *Annals of the American Academy of Political and Social Science, 557*, 120–132.

Mares, M. L. & Woodard, E. H. (2001). Prosocial effects on children's social interactions. In D. G. Singer & J. L. Singer (Eds.), *Handbook of children and the media* (pp. 183–205). Thousand Oaks, CA: Sage.

Mares, M. L. & Woodard, E. (2005). Positive effects of television on children's social interactions: A meta-analysis. *Media Psychology, 7*, 301–322.

Martino, S. C., Collins, R. L., Elliott, M. N., Strachman, A., Kanouse, D. E. & Berry, S. H. (2006). Exposure to degrading versus nondegrading music lyrics and sexual behavior among youth. *Pediatrics.* Downloaded from www.pediatrics.org on August 8, 2006.

Martino, S. C., Collins, R. L., Kanouse, D. E., Elliott, M. & Berry, S. H. (2005). Social cognitive processes mediating the relationship between exposure to television's sexual content and adolescents' sexual behavior. *Journal of Personality and Social Psychology, 89*, 914–924.

Mastro, D. E. & Behm-Morawitz, E. (2005). Latino representation on primetime television. *Journalism & Mass Communication Quarterly, 82*, 110–131.

Mastro, D. E. & Greenberg, B. S. (2000). The portrayal of racial minorities on prime time television. *Journal of Broadcasting & Electronic Media, 44*, 690–703.

Mayeux, L. & Naigles, L. (2000). *Linguistic and social influences on children's developing understanding of mental states.* Manuscript in preparation, University of Connecticut.

McArthur, L. Z. & Eisen, S. V. (1976). Television and sex-role stereotyping. *Journal of Applied Social Psychology, 6*, 329–351.

McCabe, M. P. & Ricciardelli, L. A. (2003). Sociocultural influences on body image and body changes among adolescent boys and girls. *The Journal of Social Psychology, 143*, 5–27.

McCarthy, E. D., Langner, T. S., Gersten, J. C., Eisenberg, J. G. & Orzeck, L. (1975). Violence and behavioral disorders. *Journal of Social Psychology, 97*, 209–220.

McCombs, M. E. & Shaw, D. L. (1972). The agenda-setting function of mass media. *Public Opinion Quarterly, 36*, 176–187.

McDevitt, M. & Chaffee, S. H. (2000). Closing gaps in political communication and knowledge: Effects of a school intervention. *Communication Research, 27*, 259–292.

McDevitt, M. & Chaffee, S. H. (2002). From top-down to trickle-up influence: Revisiting assumptions about the family in political socialization. *Political Communication, 19*, 281–301.

McGuire, W. J. (1986). The myth of massive media impact: Savagings and salvagings. In G. Comstock (Ed.), *Public communication and behavior* (Vol. 1, pp. 173–257). New York: Academic Press.

McIlwraith, R. D., Jacobvitz, R. S., Kubey, R. & Alexander, A. (1991). Television addiction: Theories and data behind the ubiquitous metaphor. *American Behavioral Scientist, 35*(2), 104–121.

McIlwraith, R. D. & Josephson, W. L. (1985). Movies, books, music, and adult fantasy life. *Journal of Communication, 35*(2), 167–179.

McIlwraith, R. D. & Schallow, J. (1982–83). Television viewing and styles of children's fantasy. *Imagination, Cognition and Personality, 2*(4), 323–331.

McIntyre, J. J. & Teevan, J. J., Jr. (1972). Television violence and deviant behavior. In G. A. Comstock & E. A. Rubinstein (Eds.), *Television and social behavior: Vol. 3. Television and adolescent aggressiveness* (pp. 383–435). Washington, DC: Government Printing Office.

McLaughlin, L. (1991, Oct. 14). Tweens blossom as consumer group. *Advertising Age, 62*, 33.

McLeod, J. M., Atkin, C. K. & Chaffee, S. H. (1972a). Adolescents, parents, and television use: Adolescent self-report measures from Maryland and Wisconsin samples. In G. A. Comsock & E. A. Rubinsein (Eds.), *Television and social behavior: Television and adolescent aggressiveness* (Vol. 3, pp. 173–238). Washington, DC: U.S. Government Printing Office.

McLeod, J. M., Atkin, C. K. & Chaffee, S. H. (1972b). Adolescents, parents, and television use: Self-report and other-report measures from the Wisconsin sample. In G. A. Comstock & E. A. Rubinstein (Eds.), *Television and social behavior: Television and adolescent aggressiveness* (Vol. 3, pp. 239–313). Washington, DC: U.S. Government Printing Office.

McLeod, J. M., Eveland, W. P., Jr. & Horowitz, E. M. (1998). Going beyond adults and voter turnout: Evaluating a socialization program involving schools, family, and media. In T. J. Johnson, C. E. Hays & S. P. Hays (Eds.), *Engaging the public: How government and the media can reinvigorate American democracy* (pp. 217–234). Lantham, MD: Rowman & Littlefield.

McNeal, J. (1987). *Children as consumers: Insights and implications.* Lexington, MA: Heath.

McNeal, J. (1992). *Kids as customers.* New York: Lexington Books.

McNeal, (1999). *The kids market: Myths and realities.* Ithaca, NY: Paramount.

Medrich, E. A., Roizen, J., Rubin, V. & Buckley, S. (1982). *The serious business of growing up: A study of children's lives outside school.* Los Angeles: University of California Press.

Meline, C. W. (1976). Does the medium matter? *Journal of Communication, 26*(3), 81–89.

Meltzoff, A. N. (1988). Imitation of televised models by infants. *Child Development, 59*, 1221–1229.

Meltzoff, A. N. (2005). Imitation and other minds: The "Like Me" hypothesis. In S. Hurley & N. Chater (Eds.), *Perspectives on imitation: From cognitive neuroscience to social science.* Cambridge, MA: MIT Press.

Menzies, E. S. (1971). *Preferences in television content among violent prisoners.* Unpublished master's thesis, Florida State University, Tallahassee, FL.

Menzies, E. S. (1973). *The effects of repeated exposure to televised violence on attitudes towards violence among youthful offenders.* Unpublished doctoral dissertation, Florida State University, Tallahassee, FL.

Meringoff, L. K. (1980a). The influence of the medium on children's story apprehension. *Journal of Educational Psychology, 72*, 240–249.

Meringoff, L. K. (1980b). The effects of children's television food advertising. In R. P. Adler, G. S. Lesser, L. K. Meringoff, T. S. Robertson, J. R. Rossiter & S. Ward, *The effects of television advertising on children: Review and recommendations* (pp. 123–152). Lexington, MA: Lexington Books.

Meyer, T. P. (1973). Children's perceptions of favorite television characters as behavioral models. *Educational Broadcasting Review, 7*(1), 25–33.

Milavsky, J. R., Kessler, R., Stipp, H. H. & Rubens, W. S. (1982a). Television and aggression: Results of a panel study. In D. Pearl, L. Bouthilet & J. Lazar (Eds.), *Television and social behavior: Ten years of scientific progress and implications for the eighties: Vol. 2. Technical reviews* (pp. 138–157). Washington, DC: Government Printing Office.

Milavsky, J. R., Kessler, R., Stipp, H. H. & Rubens, W. S. (1982b). *Television and aggression: A panel study.* New York: Academic Press.

Milavsky, J. R., Pekowsky, B. & Stipp, H. (1975–1976). TV drug advertising and proprietary and illicit drug use among teenage boys. *Public Opinion Quarterly, 39,* 457–481.

Milgram, S. & Shotland, R. L. (1973). *Television and antisocial behavior: A field experiment.* New York: Academic Press.

Miller, D. T., Turnbull, W. & McFarland, C. (1988). Particularistic and universalistic evaluation in the social comparison process. *Journal of Personality and Social Psychology, 55,* 908–817.

Miller, W. (1991). The puzzle transformed: Explaining declining turnout. *Political Behavior, 14,* 1–43.

Miron, D., Bryant, J. & Zillmann, D. (2001). Creating vigilance for better learning from television. In D. G. Singer & J. L. Singer (Eds.), *Handbook of children and the media* (pp. 153–181). Thousand Oaks, CA: Sage.

Mishkind, M. E., Rodin, J., Silberstein, L. R. & Striegel-Moore, R. H. (1986). The embodiment of masculinity. *American Behavioral Scientist, 29,* 545–562.

Moore, R. L. (1999). *Mass communication law and ethics. 2nd Ed.* Mahwah, NJ: Lawrence Erlbaum Associates.

Morgan, M. (1980). Television viewing and reading: Does more equal better? *Journal of Communication, 30*(1), 159–165.

Morgan, M. (1982). Television and adolescents' sex-role stereotypes: A longitudinal study. *Journal of Personality and Social Psychology, 43*(5), 947–955.

Morgan, M. (1989). Cultivation analysis. In E. Barnouw (Ed.), *International encyclopedia of communication: Vol. 3* (pp. 430–433). New York: Oxford University Press.

Morgan, M., Alexander, A., Shanahan, J. & Harris, C. (1990). Adolescents, VCRs, and the family environment. *Communication Research, 17*(1), 83–106.

Murray, J. P. & Kippax, S. (1977). Television diffusion and social behavior in three communities: A field experiment. *Australian Journal of Psychology, 29*(1), 31–43.

Murray, J. P. & Kippax, S. (1978). Children's social behavior in three towns with differing television experience. *Journal of Communication, 28*(4), 19–29.

Mutz, D. C., Roberts, D. F. & van Vuuren, D. P. (1993). Reconsidering the displacement hypothesis. Television's influence on children's time use. *Communication Research, 20*(1), 51–75.

Naigles, L. & Mayeux, L. (2001). Television as incidental language teacher. In D. G. Singer & J. L. Singer (Eds.), *Handbook of children and media* (pp. 135–152). Thousand Oaks, CA: Sage.

Naigles, L., Singer, D., Singer, J., Jean-Louis, B., Sells, D. & Rosen, C. (1995, June). *Watching "Barney" affects preschoolers' use of mental state verbs.* Paper presented at the annual meeting of the American Psychological Society, New York, NY.

Nathanson, A. I., Wilson, B. J., McGee, J. & Sebastian, M. (2002). Counteracting the effects of female stereotypes via active mediation. *Journal of Communication, 52*, 922–937.

National Television Violence Study (1998). *National Television Violence Study (Vol. III)*. Santa Barbara: Center for Communication and Social Policy, University of California.

Neuman, S. B. (1988). The displacement effect: Assessing the relation between television viewing and reading performance. *Reading Research Quarterly, 23*(4), 414–440.

Neuman, W. R. (1982). Television and American culture: The mass medium and the pluralistic audience. *Public Opinion Quarterly, 46*(4), 471–487.

Neuman, W. R.(1991). *The future of the mass audience*. Cambridge, UK: Cambridge University Press.

Newspaper Advertising Bureau (1978). *Children, mothers, and newspapers*. New York: Newspaper Advertising Bureau.

Nichols, S. L. (1999). Gay, lesbian, and bisexual youth: Understanding diversity and promoting tolerance in schools. *The Elementary School Journal, 99*, 505–524.

Niemi, R. & Hepburn, M. (1995). The rebirth of political socialization. *Perspectives on Political Science, 24*, 7–16.

Niemi, R. G. & Junn, J. (1998). *Civic education: What makes students learn?* New Haven, CT: Yale University Press.

Noble, G. (1970). Film-mediated aggressive and creative play. *British Journal of Social and Clinical Psychology, 9*(1), 1–7.

Noble, G. (1973). Effects of different forms of filmed aggression on children's constructive and destructive play. *Journal of Personality and Social Psychology, 26*(1), 54–59.

NPD. (2006). *Report from the NPD Group Shows Consumer Electronics Devices and Video Game Systems are Becoming More Entrenched in Kids' Lives.* Accessed 6/9/06 at http://www.npd.com/dynamic/releases/press_060524.html.

Obel C., Henriksen T. B., Dalsgaard S., Linnet K. M., Skajaa E., Thomsen P. H. & Olsen J. (2004). Does Childern's Watching of Television Cause Attention Problems? Retesting the Hypothesis in a Danish Cohort. *Pediatrics. 114*(5), 1372–373.

O'Bryant, S. & Corder-Bolz, C. (1978). The effects of television on children's stereotyping of women's work roles. *Journal of Vocational Behavior, 12*, 233–244.

Ogletree, S. M., Williams, S. W., Raffeld, R., Mason, B. & Fricke, K. (1990). Female attractiveness and eating disorders: Do children's television commercials play a role? *Sex Roles, 22*, 791–797.

Okagaki, L. & Frensch, P. A. (1994). Effects of video game playing on measures of spatial performance: Gender effects in late adolescence. *Journal of Applied Developmental Psychology, 15*, 33–58.

Oliver, M. B. & Kalyanaraman, S. (2002). Appropriate for all viewing audience? An examination of violent and sexual portrayals in movie previews featured on video rentals. *Journal of Broadcasting and Electronic Media, 46*(2), 283–300.

Owen, D. & Dennis, J. (1988). Gender differences in the politicization of American children. *Women and Politics, 8*(2), 23–43.

Paget, K. F., Kritt, D. & Bergemann, L. (1984). Understanding strategic interactions in television commercials: A developmental study. *Journal of Applied Developmental Psychology, 5*(2), 145–161.

Paik, H. (1991). *The effects of television violence on aggressive behavior: A meta-analysis*. Unpublished doctoral dissertation, Syracuse University, Syracuse, NY.

Paik, H. & Comstock, G. (1994). The effects of television violence on antisocial behavior: A meta-analysis. *Communication Research, 21*(4), 516–546.

Palmer, E. L. & McDowell, C. N. (1979). The program/commercial separators in children's television programming. *Journal of Communication, 29*(3), 197–201.

Palmer, E. L., Smith, K. T. & Stawser, K. S. (1993). Rubik's tube: Developing a child's television worldview. In G. L. Berry & J. K. Asamen (Eds.), *Children and television: Images in a changing sociocultural world* (pp. 143–154). Newbury Park, CA: Sage.

Pardun, C. J., L'Engle, K. L. & Brown, J. D. (2005). Linking exposure to outcomes: Early adolescents' consumption of sexual content in six media. *Mass Communication & Society, 8*, 75–92.

Parents Television Council. (2002). *TV bloodbath: Violence on prime time broadcast TV.* Accessed 4/15/04 at www.parentstv.org/PTC/publications/reports/stateindustryviolence/main.asp.

Pasek, J., Kenski, K., Romer, D. & Hall Jamieson, K. (2006). America's youth and community engagement: How use of mass media is related to civic activity and political awareness in 14- to 22-year olds. *Communication Research, 33*, 115–135.

Paulson, F. L. (1974). Teaching cooperation on television: An evaluation of *Sesame Street* social goals programs. *AV Communication Review, 22*, 229–246.

Pecora, N. O. (1998). *The business of children's entertainment.* New York: Guilford.

Peterson, C. C., Peterson, J. L. & Carroll, J. (1987). Television viewing and imaginative problem solving during preadolescence. *The Journal of Genetic Psychology, 147*(1), 61–67.

Peterson, J. L., Moore, K. A. & Furstenberg, F. F., Jr. (1991). Television viewing and early initiation of sexual intercourse: Is there a link? *Journal of Homosexuality, 21*, 93–118.

Peterson, P. E., Jeffrey, B. J., Bridgwater, C. A. & Dawson, B. (1984). How pronutritional television programming affects children's dietary habits. *Developmental Psychology, 20*(1), 55–63.

Pezdek, K. & Stevens, E. (1984). Children's memory for auditory and visual information on television. *Developmental Psychology, 20*, 212–218.

Pham, A. (July 21, 2005). Hidden sex scenes spark furor over video game. *Los Angeles Times.* Accessed 9/7/05 at http://www.latimes.com/business/la-fi-sexgame21jul21,0,5279713.story?coll=la-home-business.

Phillips, C. A., Rolls, S., Rouse, A. & Griffiths, M. D. (1995). Home videogame playing in schoolchildren: A study of incidence and patterns of play. *Journal of Adolescence, 18*, 687–691.

Piaget, J. (1971). The theory of stages in cognitive development. In D. R. Geen et al., (Eds.), *Measurement and Piaget* [Proceedings] (pp. 1–11). New York: McGraw Hill.

Piaget, J. & Inhelder, B. (1969). *The psychology of the child.* New York: Basic Books.

Pingree, S. (1978). The effects of non-sexist television commercials and perceptions of reality on children's attitudes about women. *Psychology of Women Quarterly, 2*, 262–276.

Pingree, S. & Hawkins, R. P. (1981). U.S. programs on Australian television: The cultivation effect. *Journal of Communication, 31*(1), 24–35.

Plomin, R., Corley, R., DeFries, J. C. & Fulker, D. W. (1990). Individual differences in television viewing in early childhood: Nature as well as nurture. *Psychological Science, 6*(1), 371–377.

Potter, W. J. (1987). Does television viewing hinder academic achievement among adolescents? *Human Communication Research, 14*(1), 27–46.

Potter, W. J. & Vaughan, M. (1997). Anti-social behavior in television entertainment: Trends and profiles. *Communication Research Reports, 14*, 116–124.

Potter, W. J. & Ware, W. (1987). Traits of perpetrators and receivers of antisocial and prosocial acts on TV. *Journalism Quarterly, 64*, 382–391.

Potts, R., Huston, A. C. & Wright, J. C. (1986). The effects of television form and violent content on boys' attention and social behavior. *Journal of Experimental Child Psychology, 41*, 1–17.

Potts, R. & Sanchez, D. (1994). Television viewing and depression: No news is good news. *Journal of Broadcasting and Electronic Media, 38*(1), 79–90.

Prescott, C. A., Johnson, R. C. & McArdle, J. J. (1991).Genetic contributions to television viewing. *Psychological Science, 2*(6), 430–431.

Putnam, R. D. (1995). Tuning in, tuning out: The strange disappearance of social capital in America. *PS: Political Science & Politics, 28*, 664–683.

Rahn, W. M. & Hirschorn, R. M. (1999). Political advertising and public mood: A study of children's political orientations. *Political Communication, 16*, 387–407.

Razel, M. (2001). The complex model of television viewing and educational achievement. *The Journal of Educational Research, 94*, 371–381.

Reeves, B. & Greenberg, B. S. (1977). Children's perceptions of television characters. *Human Communication Research, 3*, 113–127.

Reeves, B. & Lometti, G. (1979). The dimensional structure of children's perceptions of television characters: A replication. *Human Communication Research, 5*, 247–256.

Reeves, B. & Miller, M. M. (1978). A multidimensional measure of children's identification with television characters. *Journal of Broadcasting, 22*, 71–86.

Reichert, T. (1999). Cheesecake and beefcake: No matter how you slice it, sexual explicitness in advertising continues to increase. *Journalism and Mass Communication Quarterly, 76*, 7–20.

Reid, L. N. & Frazer, C. F. (1980). Children's use of television commercials to initiate social interaction in family viewing situations. *Journal of Broadcasting, 24*(2), 149–158.

Rice, M. L. (1990). Preschoolers QUIL: Quick incidental learning of words. In G. Conti-Ransden & C. Snow (Eds.), *Children's language* (Vol. 7). Hillsdale, NJ: Erlbaum.

Rice, M. L., Buhr, J. & Oetting, J. B. (1992). Specific language-impaired children's quick incidental learning of words: The effects of a pause. *Journal of Speech and Hearing Research, 36*, 1040–1048.

Rice, M. L., Huston, A. C., Truglio, R. & Wright, J. C. (1990). Words from Sesame Street: Learning vocabulary while viewing. *Developmental Psychology, 26*, 421–428.

Rice, M. L., Huston, A. C. & Wright, J. C. (1982). The forms and codes of television: Effects on children's attention, comprehension, and social behavior. In D. Pearl, L. Bouthilet & J. Lazar (Eds.), *Television and behavior: Ten years of scientific progress and implications for the eighties*. Washington, DC: U.S. Government Printing Office.

Rice, M. L., Oetting, J. B., Marquis, J., Bode, J. & Pae, S. (1994). Frequency of input effects on word comprehension of children with specific language impairment. *Journal of Speech and Hearing Research, 37*, 106–122.

Rich, M., Woods, E. R., Goodman, E., Emans, J. & DuRant, R. H. (1998). Aggressors or victims: Gender and race in music video violence. *Pediatrics, 101*, 669–674.

Rideout, V. & Hamel, E. (2006). *The media family: Electronic media in the lives of infants, toddlers, preschoolers and their parents*. Menlo Park, CA: Henry J. Kaiser Family Foundation.

Rideout, V. J., Foehr, U. G., Roberts, D. F. & Brodie, M. (1999). Kids & media at the new millennium. A Kaiser Family Foundation Report. Menlo Park, CA: Henry J. Kaiser Family Foundation. Accessed 6/30/05 at http://www.kff.org/entmedia/loader.cfm?url=/commonspot/security/getfile.cfm&PageID=13265.

Rideout, V. J., Vandewater, E. A. & Wartella, E. (2003). *Zero to six: Electronic media in the lives of infants, toddlers and preschoolers*. A Kaiser Family Foundation Study. Menlo Park, CA: Henry J. Kaiser Family Foundation.

Roberts, D. F. & Foehr, U. G. (2004). *Kids & media in America*. Cambridge, UK: Cambridge University Press.

Roberts, D. F., Foehr, U. G. & Rideout, V. (2005). *Generation M: Media in the lives of 8–18 year-olds. A Kaiser Family Foundation Study*. Menlo Park, CA: Henry J. Kaiser Family Foundation. Accessed 6/30/05 at http://www.kff.org/entmedia/7250.cfm.

Roberts, D. F., Henriksen, L. & Christenson, P. G. (1999). *Substance use in popular movies and music*. Washington, DC: Office of National Drug Control Policy.

Robertson, T. S. (1980a). The impact of proprietary medicine advertising on children. In R. P. Adler, G. S. Lesser, L. K. Meringoff, T. S. Robertson, J. R. Rossiter & S. Ward. *The effects of television advertising on children: Review and recommendations* (pp. 111–122). Lexington, MA: Lexington Books.

Robertson, T. S. (1980b). Television advertising and parent-child relations. In R. P. Adler, G. S. Lesser, L. K. Meringoff, T. S. Robertson, J. R. Rossiter & S. Ward. *The effects of television advertising on children* (pp. 195–212). Lexington, MA: Lexington Books.

Robertson, T. S., Rossiter, J. R. & Gleason, T. C. (1979). *Televised medicine advertising and children*. New York: Praeger.

Robinson, J., Keegan, C., Karth, M., Triplett, T. & Holland, J. (1985). *Arts participation in America*. College Park, MD: Survey Research Center, University of Maryland.

Robinson, J. D. & Skill, T. (1995). The invisible generation: Portrayals of the elderly on prime-time television. *Communication Reports, 8*, 111–119.

Robinson, J. P. (1972). Toward defining the functions of television. In E. A. Rubinstein, G. A. Comstock & J. P. Murray (Eds.), *Television and social behavior: Vol. 4. Television in day-to-day life: Patterns of use* (pp. 568–603). Washington, DC: Government Printing Office.

Robinson, J. P. (1972b).Television's impact on everyday life: Some cross-national evidence. In E. A. Rubinstein et al. (Eds.), *Television and social behavior. Television in everyday life: Patterns of use* (Vol. 4, pp. 410–431), Washington, DC: U.S. Government Printing Office.

Robinson, J. P. & Alvarez, A. S. (2005). The social impact of the Internet: A 2003 update. In W. H. Dutton, B. Kahin, R. O'Callaghan & A. W. Wyckoff (Eds.), *Transforming enterprise: The economic and social implications of information technology*. Cambridge, MA: The MIT Press.

Robinson, J. P. & Bachman, J. G. (1972). Television viewing habits and aggression. In G. A. Comstock & E. A. Rubinstein (Eds.), *Television and social behavior: Vol. 3. Television and adolescent aggressiveness* (pp. 372–382). Washington, DC: U.S. Government Printing Office.

Robinson, J. P. & Converse, P. E. (1972). The impact of television on mass media usages: A cross-national comparison. In A. Szalai (Ed.), *The use of time: Daily activities of urban and suburban populations in twelve countries* (pp. 197–212). The Hague, Netherlands: Mouton.

Robinson, J. P. & Godbey, G. (1997). *Time for life: The surprising ways Americans use their time.* University Park, PA: Pennsylvania State University Press.

Robinson, J. P., Neustadtl, A. & Kestnbaum, M. (2002). The online "diversity divide": Public opinion differences among Internet users and nonusers. *IT & Society, 1,* 284–302.

Roper Center. (1996, Aug.–Sept.). Men, women, and politics: All the data you've wanted (but could never find). *Public Perspective: A Roper Center Review of Public Opinion and Polling, 7,* 8–33.

Rosengren, K. E. & Windahl, S. (1989). *Media matter: TV use in childhood and adolescence.* Norwood, NJ: Ablex.

Rosekrans, M. A. (1967). Imitation in children as a function of perceived similarities to a social model of vicarious reinforcement. *Journal of Personality and Social Psychology, 7,* 305–317.

Rosekrans, M. A. & Hartup, W. W. (1967). Imitative influences of consistent and inconsistent response consequences to a model on aggressive behavior in children. *Journal of Personality and Social Psychology, 7,* 429–434.

Rosenthal, C. S. (1998). *When women lead.* New York: Oxford University Press.

Rosenthal, C. S., Rosenthal, J. A. & Jones, J. (2001). Preparing for elite political participation: Simulations and the political socialization of adolescents. *Social Science Quarterly, 82,* 633–648.

Ross, R. P., Campbell, T., Wright, J. C., Huston, A. C., Rice, M. L. & Turk, P. (1984). When celebrities talk, children listen: An experimental analysis of children's responses to TV ads with celebrity endorsement. *Journal of Applied Developmental Psychology, 5,* 185–202.

Rossiter, J. R. (1980a). Source effects and self-concept appeals in children's television advertising. In R. P. Adler, G. S. Lesser, L. K. Meringoff, T. S. Robertson, J. R. Rossiter & S. Ward, *The effects of television advertising on children: Review and recommendations* (pp. 61–94). Lexington, MA: Lexington Books.

Rossiter, J. R. (1980b). The effects of volume and repetition of television commercials. In R. P. Adler, G. S. Lesser, L. K. Meringoff, T. S. Robertson, J. R. Rossiter & S. Ward, *The effects of television advertising on children: Review and recommendations* (pp. 153–184). Lexington, MA: Lexington Books.Rossiter, J. R. & Robertson, T. S. (1974). Children's TV commercials: Testing the defenses. *Journal of Communication, 24*(4), 137–144.

Rossiter, J. R. & Robertson, T. S. (1980). Children's dispositions toward proprietary drugs and the role of television drug advertising. *Public Opinion Quarterly, 44*(3), 316–329.

Rothschild, N. (1984). Small group affiliation as a mediating factor in the cultivation process. In G. Melischek, K. E. Rosengren & J. Stappers (Eds.), *Cultural indicators: An international symposium.* Vienna, Austria: Osterrechischen Akademie per Wissenschaften.

Rothschild, N., Thorson, E., Reeves, B., Hirsch, J. E. & Goldstein, R. (1986). EEG activity and the processing of television commercials. *Communication Research, 13*(2), 182–220.

Rubenstein, D. J. (2000). Stimulating children's creativity and curiosity: Does content and medium matter? *Journal of Creative Behavior, 34,* 1–17.

Rubin, A. (1978). Child and adolescent television use and political socialization. *Journalism Quarterly, 55,* 125–129.

Rubin, A. M. (1983). Television uses and gratifications: The interactions of viewing patterns and motivations. *Journal of Broadcasting, 27*(1), 37–51.

Rubin, A. M. (1984). Ritualized and instrumental television viewing. *Journal of Communication, 34,* 67–77.

Rubin, R. S. (1972). *An exploratory investigation of children's responses to commercial content of television advertising in relation to their stages of cognitive development*. Doctoral dissertation, University of Massachusetts, Amherst.

Rubenstein, D. J. (2000). Stimulating children's creativity and curiosity: Does content and medium matter? *Journal of Creative Behavior, 34*, 1–17.

Ruble, D. & Martin, C. (1998). Gender development. In W. Damon & N. Eisenberg (Eds.), *Handbook of child psychology: Vol. 3. Social, emotional, and personality development, 5th ed.* (pp. 933–1016). New York: Wiley.

Ruble, D. N. (1983). The development of social comparison processes and their role in achievement-related self-socialization. In E. T. Higgins, D. N. Ruble & W. W. Hartup (Eds.), *Social cognition and social development: A sociocultural perspective* (pp. 134–157). London: Cambridge University Press.

Ruble, D. M., Balaban, T. & Cooper, J. (1981). Gender constancy and the effects of sex-typed televised toy commercials. *Child Development, 52*(2), 667–673.

Runco, M. & Pedzek, K. (1984). The effect of television and radio on children's creativity. *Human Communication Research, 11*, 109–120.

Ryan, J., Bales, L. & Hughes, M. (1988). Television and the cultivation of adolescent occupational expectations. *Free Inquriy in Creative Sociology, 16*, 103–108.

Ryan, E. L. & Hoerrner, K. L. (2004). Let your conscience be your guide: Smoking and drinking in Disney's animated classics. *Mass Communication & Society, 7*, 261–278.

Rychtarik, R. G., Fairbank, J. A., Allen, C. M., Foy, D. W. & Drabman, R. S. (1983). Alcohol use in television programming: Effects on children's behavior. *Addictive Behavior, 8*, 19–22.

Sachs, J., Bard, B. & Johnson, M. (1981). Language learning with restricted input: Case studies of two hearing children of deaf parents. *Applied Pscyholinguistics, 2*, 33–54.

Sahin, N. (1992, July). *Preschooler's learning from educational television.* Paper presented at the annual meeting of the 25th International Congress of Psychology. Brussels, Belgium.

Salomon, G. (1979). *Interaction of media, cognition and learning.* San Francisco: Jossey-Bass.

Salomon, G. (1981). Introducing AIME: The assessment of children's mental involvement with television. In H. Kelley & H. Gardner (Eds.), *Viewing children through television* (pp. 89–102). San Francisco: Jossey-Bass.

Salomon, G. (1983). Television watching and mental effort: A social psychological view. In J. Bryant & D. R. Anderson (Eds.), *Children's understanding of television: Research on attention and comprehension* (pp. 181–198). New York: Academic Press.

Salomon, G. (1984). Television is "easy" and print is "tough": The differential investment of mental effort as a function of perceptions and attributions. *Journal of Educational Psychology, 76*, 647–658.

Salomon, G. & Leigh, T. (1984). Predispositions about learning from television and print. *Journal of Communication, 34*, 119–135.

Sanchez, R. P., Lorch, E. P., Milich, R. & Welsh, R. (1999). Comprehension of televisied stories by preschool children with ADHD. *Journal of Children Child Psychology, 28*, 376–377.

Scharrer, E. (1998). *Men, muscles, and machismo: The relationship between exposure to television violence and antisocial outcomes in the presence of hypermasculinity.* Doctoral dissertation, Syracuse University, Syracuse, NY.

Scharrer, E. (2001). From wise to foolish: The portrayal of the sitcom father, 1950s–1990s. *Journal of Broadcasting & Electronic Media, 45*(1), 23–40.

Scharrer, E. (2004). Virtual violence: Gender and aggression in video game advertisements. *Mass Communication & Society, 7*, 393–412.

Scharrer, E., Bergstrom, A., Paradise, A. & Ren, Q. (2004, May). *Laughing to keep from crying: Humor and aggression in primetime television commercials.* Paper presented at the annual meeting of the International Communication Association, New York, NY.

Scharrer, E. & Comstock, G. (2003). Entertainment televisual media: Content patterns and themes. In E. Palmer & B. Young (Eds.), *The Faces of Televisual Media* (pp.161–194). Mahwah, NJ: Erlbaum.

Scharrer, E., Kim, D., Lin, K. M. & Liu, X. (2006). Working hard or hardly working? Gender, humor, and the performance of domestic chores in television commercials. *Mass Communication & Society, 9*, 215–238.

Schmitt, K. L. (2001). Infants, toddlers, and television: The ecology of the home. *Zero to Three, 22*, 17–23.

Schmitt, K. L. & Anderson, D. R. (2002). Television and reality: Toddlers' use of visual information from video to guide behavior. *Media Psychology, 4*, 51–76.

Schmitt, K. L., Anderson, D. R. & Collins, P. A. (1999). Form and content: Looking at visual features of television. *Developmental Psychology, 35*, 1156–1167.

Schmitt, K. L., Linebarger, D., Collins, P. A., Wright, J. C., Anderson, D. R., Huston, A. C. & McElroy, E. (1997, April). *Effects of preschool television viewing on adolescent creative thinking and behavior.* Poster presented at the biennial meeting of the Society for Research in Child Development. Washington, DC.

Schor, J. B. (2004). *Born to buy: The commercialized child and the new consumer culture.* [Location?]: Scribner.

Schramm, W., Lyle, J. & Parker, E. B. (1961). *Television in the lives of our children.* Stanford, CA: Stanford University Press.

Searls, D. T., Mead, N. A. & Ward, B. (1985). The relationship of students' reading skills to TV watching, leisure time reading, and homework. *Journal of Reading, 29*, 158–162.

Seidman, S. A. (1992). An investigation of sex-role stereotyping in music videos. *Journal of Broadcasting & Electronic Media, 36*, 209–216.

Seidman, S. A. (1999). Re-visiting sex-role stereotyping in MTV videos. *International Journal of Instructional Media, 26*, 11–13.

Seligman, M. E. P. (2002). *Authentic happiness: Using the new positive psychology to realize your potential for lasting fulfillment.* New York: Free Press.

Selnow, G. W. & Bettinghaus, E. (1982). Television exposure and language development. *Journal of Broadcasting, 26*, 469–479.

Sesame Street Research. (1988). *Pregnancy.* Unpublished research report.

Sesame Street Research. (1989). *Pregnancy (Part 4): The bottom line.* Unpublished research report.

Sesame Street Research. (1991). *Visiting Iesha.* Unpublished research report.

Shanahan, J. & Morgan, M. (1999). *Television and its viewers: Cultivation theory and research.* New York: Cambridge University Press.

Sheehan, P. W. (1987). Coping with exposure to aggression: The path from research to practice. *Australian Psychologist, 22*(3), 291–311.

Sheldon, J. P. (2004). Gender stereotypes in educational software for young children. *Sex Roles: A Journal of Research, 51*, 433–445.

Sherman, B. L. & Dominick, J. R. (1986). Violence and sex in music videos: TV and rock 'n' roll. *Journal of Communication, 36*, 79–93.

Sherry, J. L. (2001). The effects of violent video games on aggression: A meta-analysis. *Human Communication Research, 27*(3), 409–431.

Sherry, J., Greenberg, B. S. & Tokinoya, H. (1999). Orientations to TV advertising among adolescents and children in the U.S. and Japan. *International Journal of Advertising, 18,* 233–250.

Sherry, J. L. & Lucas, K. (2003, May). *Video game uses and gratifications as predictors of use and game preference.* Paper presented at the annual meeting of the International Communication Association, San Diego, CA.

Sheikh, A. A. & Moleski, M. L. (1977). Conflict in the family over commercials. *Journal of Communication, 27*(1), 152–157.

Shiffrin, R. M. & Schneider, W. (1977). Controlled and automatic human information processing: Perceptual learning, automatic attending, and a general theory. *Psychological Review, 84,* 127–190.

Shimp, T., Dyer, R. & Divita, S. (1976). An experimental test of the harmful effects of premium-oriented commercials on children. *Journal of Consumer Research, 3,* 1–11.

Shin, N. (2004). Exploring pathways from television viewing to academic achievement in school age children. *Journal of Genetic Psychology, 165,* 367–381.

Sidney, S., Sternfeld, B., Haskell, W. L., Jacobs, D. R., Chesney, M. A. & Hulley, S. B. (1998). Television viewing and cardiovascular risk factors in young adults: The CARDIA study. *Annals of Epidemiology, 6*(2), 154–159.

Siegel, D., Coffey, T. & Livingston, G. (2004). *The great tween buying machine: Capturing your share of the multi-billion-dollar tween market.* Paramount.

Sigel, R. S. (1995). New directions for political socialization research. *Perspectives on Political Science, 24,* 17–23.

Signorielli, N. (1984). The demography of the television world. In G. Melischek, E. Rosengren & J. Stappers (Eds.), *Cultural indicators: An international symposium* (pp. 137–157). Vienna, Austria: Osterreichischen der Wissenschaften.

Signorielli, N. (1985). *Role portrayal on television: An annotated bibliography of studies relating to women, minorities, aging, sexual behavior, health, and handicaps.* Westport, CT: Greenwood.

Signorielli, N. (1989). Television and conceptions about sex roles: Maintaining conventionality and the status quo. *Sex Roles, 21,* 341–360.

Signorielli, N. (1993). Television and adolescents' perceptions about work. *Youth and Society, 24,* 314–341.

Signorielli, N. (2001). Television's gender role images and contribution to stereotyping: Past, present, future. In D. G. Singer & J. L. Singer (Eds.), *Handbook of children and the media* (pp. 341–358). Thousand Oaks, CA: Sage. *Sex Roles, 40,* 527–544.

Signorielli, N. (2003). Prime-time violence 1993-2001: Has the picture really changed? *Journal of Broadcasting & Electronic Media, 47,* 36–58.

Signorielli, N. (2004). Aging on television: Messages relating to gender, race, and occupation in prime time. *Journal of Broadcasting & Electronic Media, 48,* 279–301.

Signorielli, N. & Bacue, A. (1999). Recognition and respect: A content analysis of prime-time television characters across three decades. *Sex Roles, 40,* 527–544.

Signorielli, N. & Lears, M. (1992). Children, television, and conceptions about chores: Attitudes and behaviors. *Sex Roles, 27,* 157–170.

Signorielli, N., McLeod, D. & Healy, E. (1994). Gender stereotypes in MTV commercials: The beat goes on. *Journal of Broadcasting & Electronic Media, 38,* 91–101.

Silverman, L. T. & Sprafkin, J. N. (1980). The effects of *Sesame Street*'s prosocial spots on cooperative play between young children. *Journal of Broadcasting, 24*, 135–147.

Silvern, S. B. & Williamson, P. A. (1987). The effects of video game play on young children's aggression, fantasy, and prosocial behavior. *Journal of Applied Developmental Psychology, 8*(4), 453–462.

Silverstein, B., Perdue, L., Peterson, B. & Kelly, L. (1986). The role of mass media in promoting a thin standard of bodily attractiveness for women. *Sex Roles, 14*, 519–532.

Simpson, L., Douglas, S. & Schimmel, J. (1998). Tween consumes: Catalog clothing purchase behavior. *Adolescence, 33*, 637–645.

Singer, D. G. & Singer, J. L. (1980). Television viewing and aggressive behavior in preschool children: A field study. *Annals of the New York Academy of Science, 347*, 289–303.

Singer, D. G. & Singer, J. L. (1990). *The house of make-believe: Play and the developing imagination.* Cambridge, MA: Harvard University Press.

Singer, D. G. & Singer, J. L. (2001). The popular media as educators and socializers of growing children. In D. G. Singer & J. L. Singer (Eds.), *Handbook of children and the media* (pp. 1–6). Thousand Oaks, CA: Sage.

Singer, J. L. (1980). The power and limits of television: A cognitive-affective analysis. In P. Tannenbaum (Ed.), *The entertainment function of television.* Hillsdale, NJ: Erlbaum.

Singer, J. L. & Singer, D. G. (1976). Can TV stimulate imaginative play? *Journal of Communication, 26*, 74–80.

Singer, J. L. & Singer, D. G. (1980). Television viewing, family type and aggressive behavior in preschool children. In M. Green (Ed.), *Violence and the family.* Boulder, CO: Westview Press.

Singer, J. L. & Singer, D. G. (1981). *Television, imagination, and aggression: A study of preschoolers.* Hillsdale, NJ: Erlbaum.

Singer, J. L. & Singer, D. G. (1987). Some hazards of growing up in a television environment: Children's aggression and restlessness. In S. Oskamp (Ed.), *Television as a social issue. Applied psychology annual* (Vol. 8, pp. 172–188). Newbury Park, CA: Sage.

Singer, J. L. & Singer, D. G. (1998). *Barney & Friends* as entertainment and education. In J. K. Asamen & G. Berry (Eds.), *Research paradigms, television, and social behavior* (pp. 305–367). Thousand Oaks, CA: Sage.

Singer, J. L., Singer, D. G., Desmond, R., Hirsch, B. & Nicol, A. (1988). Family mediation and children's cognition, aggression, and comprehension of television: A longitudinal study. *Journal of Applied Developmental Psychology, 9*, 329–347.

Singer, J. L., Singer, D. G. & Rapaczynski, W. S. (1984). Family patterns and television viewing as predictors of children's beliefs and aggression. *Journal of Communication, 34*(2), 73–89.

Slaby, R. G. & Frey, K. S. (1975). Development of gender constancy and selective attention to same-sex models. *Child Development,46*, 849–856.

Slife, B. D. & Rychiak, J. F. (1982). Role of affective assessment in modeling behavior. *Journal of Personality and Social Psychology, 43*, 861–868.

Smith, K. & Ferguson, D. A. (1990). Voter partisan orientations and the use of political television. *Journalism Quarterly, 67*, 864–874.

Smith, L. (1994). A content analysis of gender differences in children's advertising. *Journal of Broadcasting & Electronic Media, 38*(3), 323–337.

Smith, S. L. & Boyson, A. R. (2002). Violence in music videos: Examining the prevalence and context of physical aggression. *Journal of Communication, 52,* 61–83.

Smith, S. L., Lachlan, K. & Tamborini, R. (2003). Popular video games: Quantifying the presentation of violence and its context. *Journal of Broadcasting & Electronic Media, 47,* 58–76.

Smith, S. L., Wilson, B. J., Kunkel, D., Linz, D., Potter, W. J., Colvin, C. M. & Donnerstein, E. (1998). *National television violence study (Vol. III).* Santa Barbara, CA: Center for Communication and Social Policy, University of California.

Smith-Lovin, L. & Robinson, D. T. (1992). Gender and conversational dynamics. In C. L. Ridgeway (Ed.), *Gender, interaction, and inequality* (pp. 122–156). New York: Springer-Verlag.

Smucker, B. & Creekmore, A. M. (1972, Dec.). Adolescents' clothing conformity, awareness, and peer acceptance. *Home Economics Research Journal, 1*(2), 92–97.

Smythe, D. W. (1954). Reality as presented by television. *Public Opinion Quarterly, 18,* 143–156.

Sparks, G. G. (1986). Developmental differences in children's reports of fear induced by the mass media. *Child Study Journal, 16*(1), 55–66.

Sprafkin, J. N. & Liebert, R. M. (1978). Sex-typing and children's preferences. In G. Tuchman, A. K. Daniels & J. Benet (Eds.), *Hearth and home: Images of women in the mass media* (pp. 288–339). New York: Oxford University Press.

Steenland, S. (1990). *What's wrong with this picture: The status of women on screen and behind the scenes in entertainment TV.* Washington, DC: National Commission on Wider Opportunities for Women.

Steinberg, L. (1993). *Adolescence.* New York: McGraw Hill.

Stern, S. R. (2004). Expressions of identity online: Prominent features and gender differences in adolescents' World Wide Web home pages. *Journal of Broadcasting & Electronic Media, 48,* 218–243.

Steuer, F. B., Applefield, J. M. & Smith, R. (1971). Televised aggression and interpersonal aggression of preschool children. *Journal of Experimental Child Psychology, 11,* 442–447.

Stoneham, B. (1998, Jan.). Teen spending keeps climbing. *Forecast.* Retrieved from http://www.demographics.com.

Stoneman, Z. & Brody, G. H. (1981a). Peers as mediators of television food advertisements aimed at children. *Developmental Psychology, 17*(6), 853–858.

Stoneman, Z. & Brody, G. H. (1981b). The indirect impact of child-oriented advertisements on mother-child interactions. *Journal of Applied Developmental Psychology, 2,* 369–376.

Storm, P. (1987). *Functions of dress: Tools of culture and the individual.* Englewood Cliffs, NJ: Prentice Hall.

Story, M. & Faulkner, P. (1990). The prime time diet: A content analysis of eating behavior and food messages in television program content and commercials. *American Journal of Public Health, 80,* 738–740.

Strasburger, V. C. (1997). "Sex, drugs, and rock 'n' roll": Are the media responsible for adolescent behavior? *Adolescent Medicine: State of the Art Reviews, 8,* 403–414.

Strasburger, V. C. (2001). Children, adolescents, drugs, and the media. In D. G. Singer & J. L. Singer (Eds.), *Handbook of children and the media* (pp. 415–446). Thousand Oaks, CA: Sage.

Strickland, D. E. (1983). Advertising exposure, alcohol consumption and misuse of alcohol. In M. Grant, M. Plant & A. Williams (Eds.), *Economics and alcohol: Consumption and controls* (pp. 201–222). New York: Gardner Press.

Stutts, M. A. & Hunnicutt, G. G. (1987). Can young children understand disclaimers in television commercials? *Journal of Advertising, 16*(1), 41–46.

Stutts, M. A., Vance, D. & Hudleson, S. (1981). Program-commercial separators in children's television: Do they help a child tell the difference between *Bugs Bunny* and the *Quik Rabbit. Journal of Advertising, 10*, 16–25, 48.

Subervi-Velez, F. A. & Colsant, S. (1993). The television worlds of Latino children. In G. L. Berry & J. K. Asamen (Eds.), *Children and television: Images in a changing sociocultural world* (pp. 215–228). Newbury Park, CA: Sage.

Subrahmanyam, K. & Greenfield, P. (1994). Effect of video game practice on spatial skills in girls and boys. *Journal of Applied Developmental Psychology, 15*, 13–32.

Subrahmanyam, K., Kraut, R., Greenfield, P. & Gross, E. (2001). New forms of electronic media: The impact of interactive games and the Internet on cognition, socialization, and behavior. In D. G. Singer & J. L. Singer (Eds.), *Handbook of children and the media* (pp. 73–99). Thousand Oaks, CA: Sage.

Surlin, S. H. & Dominick, J. R. (1970). Television's function as a "third parent" for black and white teen-agers. *Journal of Broadcasting, 15*, 55–64.

Szalai, A. (Ed.) (1972). *The use of time: Daily activities of urban and suburban populations in twelve countries*. The Hague, Netherlands: Mouton.

Tajfel, H. (Ed.). (1978). *Differentiation between social groups: Studies in the social psychology of intergroup relations*. London: Academic Press.

Tan, A., Nelson, L., Dong, Q. & Tan, G. (1997). Value acceptance in adolescent socialization: A test of a cognitive-functional theory of television effects. *Communication Monographs, 64*, 82–97.

Tan, A. S. (1977). TV beauty ads and role expectations of adolescent female viewers. *Journalism Quarterly, 56*, 283–288.

Tan, A. S., Tan, G. K. & Tan, A. S. (1987). American TV in the Philippines: A test of cultural impact. *Journalism Quarterly, 64*, 65–72.

Tangney, J. P. (1988). Aspects of the family and children's television viewing content preferences. *Child Development, 59*, 1070–1079.

Tangney, J. P. & Feshbach, S. (1988). Children's television-viewing frequency: Individual differences and demographic correlates. *Personality and Social Psychology Bulletin, 14*(1), 145–158.

Taras, H. L. & Gage, M. (1995). Advertised foods on children's television. *Archives of Pediatric Adolescent Medicine, 149*(9), 649–652.

Taylor, S. E. & Lobel, M. (1989). Social comparison activity under threat: Downward evaluation and upward contacts. *Psychological Review, 96*, 569–575.

Tedin, K. L. (1974). The influence of parents on the political attitudes of adolescents. *American Political Science Review, 68*, 1579–1592.

Thomas, M. H. (1982). Physiological arousal, exposure to a relatively lengthy aggressive film, and aggressive behavior. *Journal of Research in Personality, 16*, 72–81.

Thomas, M. H., Horton, R. W., Lippencott, E. C. & Drabman, R. S. (1977). Desensitization to portrayals of real-life aggression as a function of exposure to television violence. *Journal of Personality and Social Psychology, 35*, 450–458.

Thompson, F. T. & Austin, W. P. (2003). Television viewing and academic achievement revisited. *Education, 124*, 94–203.

Thompson, K. M. & Haninger, K. (2001). Violence in E-rated video games. *Journal of the American Medical Association, 286*, 591–598, 920.

Thompson, K. M. & Yokota, F. (2001). Depictions of alcohol, tobacco, and other substances in G-rated animated films. *Pediatrics, 107*, 1369–1374.

Thompson, T. L. & Zerbinos, E. (1995). Gender roles in animated cartoons: Has the picture changed in 20 years? *Sex Roles: A Journal of Research, 32*, 651–674.

Thompson, T. L. & Zerbinos, E. (1997). Television cartoons: Do children notice it's a boy's world? *Sex Roles, 37*, 415–432.

Thornton, W. & Voight, L. (1984). Television and delinquency. *Youth and Society, 15*(4), 445–468.

Timmer, S. G., Eccles, J. & O'Brien, K. (1985). How children use time. In F. T. Juster & F. P. Stafford (Eds.), *Time, goods, and well-being* (pp. 353–382). Ann Arbor, MI: Survey Research Center, Institute for Social Research.

Todd, O. (2005). *Malraux: A Life*. New York: Knopf.

Tower, R. B., Singer, D. G., Singer, J. L. & Biggs, A. (1979). Differential effects of television programming on preschoolers' cognition, imagination, and social play. *American Journal of Orthopsychiatry, 49*, 265–281.

Trevor, M. C. (1999). Political socialization, party identification, and the gender gap. *Public Opinion Quarterly, 63*, 62–89.

Troseth, G. L. & DeLoache, J. (1998). The medium can obscure the message: Young children's understanding of video. *Child Development, 69*, 950–965.

Truglio, R. T., Huston, A. C. & Wright, J. C. (1986, March). *The relation of children's print and television use to early reading skills: A longitudinal study*. Paper presented at the Southwestern Society for Research in Human Development, San Antonio, TX.

Tucker, L. A. (1985). Television's role regarding alcohol use among teenagers. *Adolescence, 20*(79), 593–598.

Tucker, L. A. (1986). The relationship of television viewing to physical fitness and obesity. *Adolescence, 21*(84), 797–806.

Tucker, L. A. (1987). Television, teenagers, and health. *Journal of Youth and Adolescence, 16*(5), 415–425.

Tukey, J. W. (1977). *Exploratory data analysis*. Reading, MA: Addison-Wesley.

Turkle, S. (1995). *Life on the screen: Identity in the age of the Internet*. New York: Simon & Schuster.

Turner, C. W. & Berkowitz, L. (1972). Identification with film aggressor (covert role taking) and reactions to film violence. *Journal of Personality and Social Psychology, 21*, 256–264.

Turner, P., Gervai, J. & Hinde, R. A. (1993). Gender-typing in young children: Preferences, behavior, and cultural differences. *British Journal of Developmental Psychology, 11*, 323–342.

Turow, J. & Coe, L. (1985). Curing television's ills: The portrayal of health care. *Journal of Communication, 35*, 36–51.

Tyler, T. R. (1980). The impact of directly and indirectly experienced events. The origin of crime-related judgments and behaviors. *Journal of Personality and Social Psychology, 39*(1), 13–28.

Tyler, T. R. (1984). Assessing the risk of crime victimization: The integration of personal victimization experience and socially-transmitted information. *Journal of Social Issues, 40*(1), 27–38.

Ulitsa Sezam Department of Research and Content (1998, November). *Preliminary report of summative findings*. (Oral presentation to Children's Television Workshop). New York, NY: Author.

UNICEF. (1996). *Executive summary: Summary assessment of Plaza Sesamo IV-Mexico*. (English translation of Spanish). Mexico City, Mexico: Author.

U.S. Department of Education. (2005). *Rates of computer and Internet use by children in nursery school and students in kindergarten through twelfth grade: 2003*. Accessed 6/27/05 at http://nces.ed.gov/pubs2005/2005111.pdf.

U.S. Department of Health & Human Services, (2001). *Youth Violence: A Report of the Surgeon General*. Rockville, MD: U.S. Department of Health and Human

Services. Centers for Disease Control and Prevention, National Center for Injury Prevention and Control; Substance Abuse and Mental Health Services Administration, Center for Mental Health Services; and National Institutes of Health, National Institute of Mental Health.

Valkenburg, P. M. (2001). Television and the child's developing imagination. In D. G. Singer & J. L. Singer (Eds.), Handbook of children and media (pp. 121–134). Thousand Oaks, CA: Sage.

Valkenburg, P. M. & Beentjes, W. J. (1997). Children's creative imagination in response to radio and television stories. *Journal of Communication, 47*(2), 21–38.

Valkenburg, P. M. & van der Voort, T. H. A. (1994). Influence of television on daydreaming and creative imagination: A review of research. *Psychological Bulletin, 116*, 316–339.

Valkenburg, P. M. & van der Voort, T. H. A. (1995). The influence of television on children's daydreaming styles: A one-year panel study. *Communication Research, 22*(3), 267–287.

Valkenburg, P. M., Voojis, M. W., van der Voort, T. H. A. & Wiegman, O. (1992). The influence of television on children's fantasy styles: A secondary analysis. *Imagination, Cognition, and Personality, 12*, 55–67.

Valkenburg, P. M. & Vroone, M. (2004). Developmental changes in infants' and toddlers' attention to television entertainment. *Communication Research, 31*, 288–311.

Van den Bulck, J. (2000). Is television bad for your health? Behavior and body image of the adolescent "couch potato." *Journal of Youth and Adolescence, 29*, 273–288.

van der Molen, J. W. & van der Voort, T. (1997). Children's recall of television and print news: A media comparison study. *Journal of Educational Psychology, 89*, 82–91.

van der Molen, J. W. & van der Voort, T. (1998). Children's recall of the news: TV news stories compared with three print versions. *Educational Technology Research and Development, 46*, 39–52.

Van de Berg, L. R. & Streckfuss, D. (1992). Prime-time television's portrayal of women and the world of work: A demographic profile. *Journal of Broadcasting & Electronic Media, 36*(2), 195–208.

Van Evra, J. (1998). *Television and child development* (2nd ed.). Mahwah, NJ: Erlbaum.

Vernon, J. A., Williams, J. A., Phillips, T. & Wilson, J. (1991). Media stereotyping: A comparison of the way elderly women and men are portrayed on prime-time television. *Journal of Women & Aging, 2*, 55–68.

Vibbert, M. M. & Meringoff, L. K. (1981). *Children's production and application of story imagery: A cross-medium investigation.* Cambridge, MA: Harvard University Press.

Viemero, V. & Paajanen, S. (1993). The role of fantasies and dreams in the TV viewing-aggression relationship. *Aggressive Behavior, 18*(2), 109–116.

von Feilitzen, C. & Carlsson, U. (Eds.) (1999). *Children and media. Image education participation: Yearbook.* Goteborg: Nordicom.

von Feilitzen, C. & Linne, O. (1975). Identifying with television characters. *Journal of Communication, 25*, 52–55.

Walker-Andrews, A. & Grolnick, W. (1983). Discrimination of vocal expressions by young infants. *Infant Behavior and Development, 6*, 491–498.

Ward Gailey, C. (1993). Mediated messages: Gender, class, and cosmos in in-home video games. *Journal of Popular Culture, 27*, 81–97.

Ward, S. (1980). The effects of television advertising on consumer socialization. In R. P. Adler, G. S. Lesser, L. K. Meriingoff, T. S. Robertson, J. R. Rossiter & S. Ward, *The effects of television advertising on children: Review and recommendations* (pp. 185–194). Lexington, MA: Lexington Books.

Ward, S., Reale, G. & Levinson, D. (1972). Children's perceptions, explanations, and judgments of television advertising: A further exploration. In E. A. Rubinstein, G. Comstock & J. P. Murray (Eds.), *Television and social behavior: Vol. 4. Television in day-to-day life* (pp. 468–490). Washington, DC: U.S. Government Printing Office.

Ward, S. & Wackman, D. B. (1972). Children's purchase influence attempts and parental yielding. *Journal of Marketing Research, 9,* 316–319.

Ward., S. & Wackman, D. B. (1973). Children's information processing of television advertising. In P. Clarke (Ed.), *New models for mass communication research* (pp. 119–146). Newbury Park, CA: Sage.

Ward, S., Wackman, D. B. & Wartella, E. (1977). *How children learn to buy.* Beverly Hills, CA: Sage.

Watkins, B. (1988). Children's representations of television and real-life stories. *Communication Research, 15*(2), 159–184.

Watkins, B., Calvert, S., Huston-Stein, A. & Wright, J. C. (1980). Children's recall of television material: Effects of presentation mode and adult labeling. *Developmental Psychology, 16,* 672–674.

Webster, J. G. & Phalen, P. F. (1997). *The mass audience: Rediscovering the dominant model.* Mahwah, NJ: Erlbaum.

Wells, W. D. (1965). Communicating with children. *Journal of Advertising Research, 5,* 2–14.

Wells, W. D. (1973). *Television and aggression: Replication of an experimental field study.* Unpublished manuscript, Graduate School of Business, University of Chicago.

Wells, W. D. & LoSciuto, L. A. (1966). Direct observation of purchasing behavior. *Journal of Marketing Research, 3,* 227–233.

Williams, F., LaRose, R. & Frost, F. (1981). *Children, television, and sex-role stereotyping.* New York: Praeger.

Williams, M. E. & Condry, J. C. (1989, April). *Living color: Minority portrayals and cross-racial interactions on television.* Paper presented at the biennial meeting of the Society for Research in Child Development, Kansas City, MO.

Williams, P. A., Haertel, E. H., Walberg, H. J. & Haertel, G. D. (1982). The impact of leisure-time television on school learning: A research synthesis. *American Educational Research Journal, 19,* 19–50.

Williams, T. M. (Ed.) (1986). *The impact of television: A natural experiment in three communities.* New York: Praeger.

Wills, T. A. (1981). Downward comparison principles in social psychology. *Psychological Bulletin, 30,* 245–271.

Wills, T. A. (1991). Similarity and self-esteem to downward comparison. In B. Seidenberg & A. Snadowski (Eds.), *Social psychology: An introduction.* New York: Free Press.

Wilson, B. J., Kunkel, D., Potter, W. J., Donnerstein, E., Smith, S. L., Blumenthal, E. & Gray, T. E. (1996). *National television violence study: Executive summary, 1994–1995.* Studio City, CA: Mediascope.

Wilson, B. J., Kunkel, D., Potter, W. J., Donnerstein, E., Smith, S. L., Blumenthal, E. & Berry, M. (1997). *National television violence study (Vol. II).* Santa Barbara, CA: Center for Communication and Social Policy, University of California.

Wilson, B. J., Smith, S. L., Potter, W. J., Kunkel, D., Linz, D., Colvin, C. M. & Donnerstein, E. (2002). Violence in children's television programming: Assessing the risks. *Journal of Communication, 52,* 5–35.

Witt, S. D. (2000). The influence of peers on children's socialization to gender roles. *Early Child Development and Care, 162,* 1–7.

Wober, J. M. (1988). *The use and abuse of television: A social psychological analysis of the changing screen.* Hillsdale, NJ: Erlbaum.

Wolfe, K. M. & Fiske, M. (1954). Why they read comics. In W. Schramm (Ed.), *Process and effects of mass communication.* Urbana: University of Illinois Press.

Wood, J. V. (1989). Theory and research concerning social comparisons of personal attributes. *Psychological Bulletin, 106,* 231–248.

Wood, J. V., Taylor, S. E. & Lichtman, R. R. (1965). Social comparison in adjustment to breast cancer. *Journal of Personality and Social Psychology, 49,* 1169–1183.

Wood, W., Wong, F. & Chachere, J. (1991). Effects of media violence on viewers' aggression in unconstrained social interaction. *Psychological Bulletin, 109*(3), 371–383.

Woodard, E. H. (1999). *The 1999 State of Children's Television Report: Programming for children over broadcast and cable television.* Unpublished report. Annenberg Public Policy Center. University of Pennsylvania., Philadelphia. Accessed 8/29/05 at http://www.annenbergpublicpolicycenter.org/05_media_developing_child/childrensprogramming/rep28.pdf.

Worchel, S., Hardy, T. W. & Hurley, R. (1976). The effects of commercial interruption of violent and nonviolent films on viewers' subsequent aggressiveness. *Journal of Experimental Psychology, 2,* 220–232.

Wright, J. C. & Huston, A. C. (1995). *Effects of educational TV viewing of lower income preschoolers on academic skills, school readiness, and school adjustment one to three years later: A report to the Children's Television Workshop.* Lawrence, KS: Center for Research on the Influences of Television on Children, University of Kansas.

Wright, J. C., Huston, A. C., Murphy, K. C., St. Peters, M., Pinon, M., Scantlin, R. & Kotler, J. (2001). The relations of early television viewing to school readiness and vocabulary of children from low-income families: The early window project. *Child Development, 72,* 1347–1367.

Wrobleski, R. & Huston, A. C. (1987). Televised occupational stereotypes and their effects on early adolescents: Are they changing? *Journal of Early Adolescence, 7,* 283–297.

Yokota, F. & Thompson, K. M. (2000). Violence in G-rated animated films. *JAMA, 283,* 2716–2720.

Zielinska, I. E. & Chambers, B. (1995). Using group viewing of television to teach preschool children social skills. *Journal of Educational Television, 21,* 85–99.

Zill, N., Davies, E. & Daly, M. (1994). *Viewing of Sesame Street by preschool children and its relationship to school readiness: Report prepared for the Children's Television Workshop.* Rockville, MD: Westat, Inc.

Zillman, D. (1971). Excitation transfer in communication-mediated aggressive behavior. *Journal of Experimental Social Psychology, 7,* 419–434.

Zillman, D. (1982). Television viewing and arousal. In D. Pearl, L. Bouthilet & J. Lazar (Eds.), *Television and behavior: Ten years of scientific inquiry and implications for the eighties: Vol. 2. Technical reviews* (pp. 53–67). Washington, DC: U.S. Government Printing Office.

Zillman, D., Johnson, R. C. & Hanrahan, J. (1973). Pacifying effect of a happy ending of communications involving aggression. *Psychological Reports, 32,* 967–970.

Zola, I. K. (1985). Depictions of disability—Metaphor, message, and medium in the media: A research and political agenda. *Social Science Journal, 22,* 5–17.

Zollo, P. (1995, Nov.). Talking to teens. *American Demographics*. Retrieved from http://www.demographics.com.

Zuckerman, D. M., Singer, D. G. & Singer, J. L. (1980). Television viewing, children's reading, and related classroom behavior. *Journal of Communication, 30*(1), 166–174.

Zuckerman, P. & Gianinno, L. (1981). Measuring children's responses to television advertising. In J. Esserman (Ed.), *Television advertising and children: Issues, research and findings* (pp. 83–93). New York: Child Research Service.

AUTHOR INDEX

SUBJECT INDEX